FLOATING EXCHANGE RATES AT FIFTY

Douglas A. Irwin
and Maurice Obstfeld,
editors

FLOATING EXCHANGE RATES AT FIFTY

Douglas A. Irwin
and Maurice Obstfeld,
editors

Peterson Institute for International Economics
Washington, DC
April 2024

Douglas A. Irwin, nonresident senior fellow at the Peterson Institute for International Economics, is the John French Professor of Economics at Dartmouth College.

Maurice Obstfeld, C. Fred Bergsten Senior Fellow at the Peterson Institute for International Economics, is the Class of 1958 Professor of Economics emeritus at the University of California, Berkeley, and former economic counselor and director of the research department at the International Monetary Fund (2015–2018).

PETERSON INSTITUTE FOR INTERNATIONAL ECONOMICS

1750 Massachusetts Avenue, NW, Washington, DC 20036-1903
(202) 328-9000 www.piie.com

Adam S. Posen, President
Steven R. Weisman, Vice President for Publications

For reprints/permission to use please contact the APS customer service department at:

Copyright Clearance Center, Inc.,
222 Rosewood Drive, Danvers, MA 01923;
or email requests to: info@copyright.com

Library of Congress Cataloging-in-Publication

Paperback ISBN 9780881327496
Ebook ISBN 9780881327502

LC ebook record available at
https://lccn.loc.gov/2023047209

Cover Design: Peggy Archambault
Cover Art: Mycola/iStock

This publication has been subjected to a prepublication peer review intended to ensure analytical quality. The views expressed are those of the authors. This publication is part of the overall program of the Peterson Institute for International Economics, as endorsed by its Board of Directors, but it does not necessarily reflect the views of individual members of the Board or of the Institute's staff or management.

The Peterson Institute for International Economics is a private nonpartisan, nonprofit institution for rigorous, intellectually open, and indepth study and discussion of international economic policy. Its purpose is to identify and analyze important issues to make globalization beneficial and sustainable for the people of the United States and the world, and then to develop and communicate practical new approaches for dealing with them. Its work is funded by a highly diverse group of philanthropic foundations, private corporations, and interested individuals, as well as income on its capital fund. About 14 percent of the Institute's resources were provided by contributors from outside the United States. A list of all financial supporters is posted at https://piie.com/sites/default/files/supporters.pdf.

For Philippe Martin
1966–2023

Contents

Part II Politics, Institutions, and Ideas in International Monetary Evolution

Part III International Prices, International Adjustment, and Trade

Part IV Floating Exchange Rates and Emerging Markets

Preface

When the major industrial countries let their exchange rates float against the US dollar amid the foreign exchange market turbulence of March 1973, most observers viewed the move as a tactical retreat rather than the unintended dawn of a replacement for the international monetary system. A half century later, however, the dollar exchange rates of all advanced economies continue to float, their financial markets are if anything even more open to the world, and numerous emerging and developing economies have embraced some exchange rate flexibility and capital account openness.

While the post-1973 world has seen periods of exchange rate volatility and occasional financial crises, more than half of the world's economies show a robust preference for some degree of exchange rate flexibility—a free float, managed float, or crawling peg—and few show any appetite to revert to more rigid exchange rates. Moreover, international trade in goods, services, and financial assets has expanded enormously over the past fifty years. These developments would have surprised the architects of the postwar Bretton Woods system, who, in 1944, designed the International Monetary Fund and World Bank under the assumptions that a prosperous world economy would require fixed exchange rates and a dominant official role in managing international capital movements.

What explains the durability of what prominent economists like John Williamson and W. Max Corden characterized as an "international monetary nonsystem"? How has it performed relative to plausible alternative arrangements? How have major countries and regions adapted to floating rates in light of their domestic policy objectives? How have national and international institutions, formal and informal, evolved to take advantage of floating rate arrangements while containing their drawbacks? Has the maintenance of free capital flows between open markets been an unmitigated blessing, or has it caused problems as well?

To address these and other questions, the Peterson Institute of International Economics convened a conference on "Floating Exchange Rates at Fifty" on March 23 and 24, 2023. The conference brought together leading scholars and policymakers, some of whom participated in the debates about the future of the world monetary system as the Bretton Woods system came to an end. Their 29 contributions to this volume convey their varied views.

Despite a diversity of opinions among participants, several themes stand out. One is the critical importance of financial market shocks in determining exchange rates. Most economists in 1973 assumed that exchange rates would respond mostly to underlying shocks to trade flows, but empirical research has established a dominant role for financial factors in explaining both short- and medium-term exchange rate movements. This mechanism sharpens the tradeoffs policymakers confront between managing the macroeconomy and preserving financial stability.

A second theme is the importance of political economy. Flexible exchange rates have been durable in part because of the policy autonomy they give to governments, even if that autonomy still leaves the economy vulnerable to external shocks. Some governments, however, such as those of major oil exporters, continue to find exchange rate pegs feasible and preferable. Even such choices are influenced by geopolitical considerations as well as economic ones.

A third theme is US dollar dominance. The US dollar was central to the Bretton Woods system of fixed rates, but, contrary to many predictions of fifty years ago, it has remained the dominant international currency. This dominance continued despite US policies being the proximate cause of the demise of Bretton Woods and the dollar shows no sign of displacement by the main plausible alternatives, the euro and the renminbi. Moreover, the US Federal Reserve still exerts much more influence than other central banks over global financial conditions, especially for middle- and low-income countries.

A final, and related, theme is that more flexible exchange rates have not banished all of the classical problems of the Bretton Woods system—for example, the scarcity of international liquidity, the Triffin dilemma of inadequate outside reserve assets, global imbalances, misaligned real exchange rates, and the links between external payments imbalances and protectionist pressures. Although they sometimes look different in the global economy of today, these problems have persisted. During the Bretton Woods years, for example, rigid nominal exchange rates that became overvalued in real terms could inspire protectionist measures aimed at improving the balance of payments or raising employment. Under floating, however, real exchange rates have varied even more widely, likewise unleashing trade policy responses at times.

These conclusions are no surprise. The Peterson Institute has analyzed the challenges and successes of the flexible rate exchange rate system since the Institute was established in 1981 to provide a US-based center for intellectually rigorous thinking on international economic policy issues. In the first entry in the Institute's Policy Analyses in International Economics series, *The Lending Policies of the International Monetary Fund* (August 1982), John Williamson examined the IMF's role as a last-resort lender in the post-Bretton Woods world. In *The Exchange Rate System* (September 1983), Williamson argued that the floating exchange rate system had failed to prevent big long-lasting swings in current account imbalances and real exchange rates. Several influential studies and conferences by the Institute sought to evaluate the unwinding of the global imbalances of the 1980s—prominent among them *International Adjustment and Financing: The Lessons of 1985–1991* (January 1992), edited by C. Fred Bergsten. *The Euro at Ten: The Next Global Currency?* (July 2009), edited by Jean Pisani-Ferry and Adam S. Posen, surveyed Europe's project of a regional currency within the broader floating-rate environment shortly before the outbreak of the continent's debt crisis. In more recent years, PIIE scholars have continued to focus on foreign exchange intervention practices that have led to undervalued currencies and arguably contributed to US external deficits and protectionist pressures. A recent notable contribution is *Currency Conflict and Trade Policy: A New Strategy for the United States* (June 2017) by Joseph E. Gagnon and C. Fred Bergsten.

Discussion of the global exchange rate system has been muted in industrial countries in recent years as governments world-wide have simultaneously tightened monetary policies to counteract the shared global threat of inflation, and before that simultaneously aggressively loosened in response to the 2007–09 global financial crisis. A negotiated exchange rate peace among the G7 and China, restricting unilateral foreign exchange intervention, seems to have held for more than a decade. The benefits of competitive depreciation or persistent exchange rate undervaluation, and the significance of global imbalances, are more disputed than ever by analysts and policymakers, but their partisans remain.

Is the surprising longevity of the floating rate non-system a sign that the advanced economies have learned to live comfortably with floating rates, or even that the fears of the Bretton Woods architects were fundamentally misplaced? Or might severe economic and political tensions over exchange rates reemerge when growth and inflation prospects diverge again? For emerging-market and developing economies, the impacts of exchange rate fluctuations are potentially bigger, and divergences are already wide. Thus, debates over "currency wars" and monetary policy spillovers remain salient. Even in the United States, calls for a weaker dollar by the Trump administration and its obsession with bilateral trade imbalances rattled markets and could become relevant again.

We hope that the essays collected in this volume continue the Peterson Institute's tradition of deep and critical thinking about the exchange rate system's past and its performance, and give some ideas for shaping its possible future.

* * *

The Peterson Institute for International Economics is a private nonpartisan, nonprofit institution for rigorous, intellectually open, and indepth study and discussion of international economic policy. Its purpose is to identify and analyze important issues to making globalization beneficial and sustainable for the people of the United States and the world and then to develop and communicate practical new approaches for dealing with them.

The Institute's work is funded by a highly diverse group of philanthropic foundations, private corporations, and interested individuals, as well as income on its capital fund. About 35 percent of the Institute resources in our latest fiscal year were provided by contributors from outside the United States. A list of all our financial supporters for the preceding year is posted at https://piie.com/sites/default/files/supporters.pdf.

The Executive Committee of the Institute's Board of Directors bears overall Responsibility for the Institute's direction, gives general guidance and approval to its research program, and evaluates its performance in pursuit of its mission. The Institute's President is responsible for the identification of topics that are likely to become important over the medium term (one to three years) that should be addressed by Institute scholars. This rolling agenda is set in close consultation with the Institute's research staff, taking input from its distinguished Board of Directors and other stakeholders.

The President makes the final decision to publish any individual Institute study, following independent internal and external review of the work. Interested readers may access the data and computations underlying Institute publications for research and replication by searching titles at www.piie.com.

The Institute hopes that its research and other activities will contribute to building a stronger foundation for international economic policy around the world. We invite readers of these publications to let us know how they think we can best accomplish this objective.

ADAM S. POSEN
President
Peterson Institute for International Economics

Acknowledgments

We are grateful to PIIE President Adam S. Posen for supporting this project and to all the scholars and policymakers who contributed collaboratively to the content of this volume. Asher Rose provided invaluable assistance as project manager. Jessica Parada and Sarah Tew of PIIE's meetings department helped with conference logistics. Egor Gornostay and Julieta Contreras provided excellent assistance with checking the data and graphs presented in the chapters, and PIIE's publications team—Madona Devasahayam, Steven R. Weisman, Barbara Karni, and Susann Luetjen—assisted with producing the volume.

Introduction

DOUGLAS A. IRWIN AND MAURICE OBSTFELD

In March 1973, the advanced industrial countries gave up trying to peg their currencies to the US dollar, ending what had been a system of largely fixed exchange rates. In effect, these countries adopted—or acceded to—a regime of floating exchange rates, in which foreign exchange markets, rather than government authorities, set the price of one currency in terms of another.

This decision marked a major breakpoint in the world economy. In the years after the move to floating exchange rates, the world began to experience large exchange rate swings and large current account imbalances, increasing financial integration, and more frequent financial crises, all of which persist. The international economic environment became even more challenging for economic policymakers. Despite some predictions at the time that floating rates might insulate countries from foreign macroeconomic policy shifts or otherwise reduce interdependence, events in the world economy are now more central to national decision-making than ever before.

The March 1973 decision was the true end of the Bretton Woods system of "fixed but adjustable" exchange rates that emerged after World War II. The Bretton Woods system suffered from growing stress in the 1960s, as US inflation began to rise and capital outflows from the United States

Douglas A. Irwin, nonresident senior fellow at the Peterson Institute for International Economics, is the John French Professor of Economics at Dartmouth College. Maurice Obstfeld is C. Fred Bergsten Senior Fellow at the Peterson Institute for International Economics and the Class of 1958 Professor of Economics emeritus at the University of California, Berkeley.

increased (Bordo and Eichengreen 1993). This pressure culminated in the August 1971 decision by the Nixon administration to end the ability of foreign central banks to exchange their dollar reserves for US gold holdings at a fixed price of $35 per ounce (Garten 2021). For many, the decision severing the backing of the dollar by gold marked the end of Bretton Woods. But after some exchange rate adjustments negotiated in the December 1971 Smithsonian Agreement, the fixed-rate regime limped on. Eventually, that patchwork agreement, too, fell prey to market pressures, leading to the March 1973 decision.

The Peterson Institute for International Economics (PIIE) decided to mark the 50th anniversary of the historic move to floating exchange rates by convening an expert group of economists and former policymakers. The group was asked to reassess the consequences and challenges of the floating era in terms of the implications for inflation, the balance of payments, capital flows, macroeconomic management, trade relations, and more. Some participants also speculated about the future dominance of the dollar in the world economy and the rise of new electronic alternatives.

This conference volume begins with an overview by one of us (Maurice Obstfeld), which sets the stage for the chapters that follow by describing key developments in the last years of the Bretton Woods system preceding the March 1973 decision. Chapter 1 argues that those developments foreshadowed central global evolutions over the following half century.

Part I Historical Perspective on 1973 and Its Legacy

Part I of the book is devoted to reflections from economists who participated in debates over the international monetary and trading systems in the late 1960s and 1970s. Edwin Truman, who was at the Federal Reserve at the time, recalls the turbulent period leading up to the March 1973 retreat from fixed exchange rates. He argues in chapter 2 that although floating rates have not delivered on the promises of their most enthusiastic postwar advocates, the core Bretton Woods principles of monetary cooperation and the idea that exchange rate policies are a matter of mutual concern still undergird the international monetary system.

C. Fred Bergsten, who worked at the National Security Council in the Nixon administration, recalls expectations and uncertainties at the time of the transition to floating rates. In chapter 3, he judges the system as largely successful even under sometimes stressful conditions in terms of promoting current account adjustment (if sometimes belatedly), providing adequate international liquidity, and avoiding the periodic foreign exchange market dysfunction that brought Bretton Woods down.

The move to floating exchange rates is often associated with University of Chicago economists such as Milton Friedman, Harry G. Johnson, and George P. Shultz. But in chapter 4, Robert Aliber, who was also at Chicago at the time, laments the move to floating exchange rates. In his view, floating exchange rates have led to excessive capital mobility and financial crises, as well as pressures on US manufacturing industries from the large US current account deficits that emerged after the 1970s.

Anne Krueger, who occupied key posts at both of the central Bretton Woods international financial institutions around the midpoint of the floating rate era, focuses on developing economies, most of which did not abandon fixed rates in 1973 and have had a more gradual and uneven evolution to more limited exchange rate flexibility and financial openness. In chapter 5, she notes several prominent challenges regarding the interaction of emerging-market and low-income countries with private and official foreign lenders.

In chapter 6, Richard Portes, the founding president of the Europe-based Centre for Economic Policy Research, presents a broad overview of the development of international finance since 1973, identifying areas of continuity as well as change.

Part II Politics, Institutions, and Ideas in International Monetary Evolution

Part II situates the exchange rate regime within the broader context of underlying political forces and intellectual trends. In chapter 7, Jeffry Frieden argues that domestic politics play a leading role in limiting the scope for international cooperation to provide a stable and efficient world monetary system. He concludes that current political conditions around the world are likely to limit improvements in the functioning of the global financial order.

In the same spirit, Harold James quotes Chancellor Helmut Schmidt of Germany on "the primacy of politics"—presumably both US versus European and intra-European—in motivating the quest for European monetary integration. His discussion of the euro in chapter 8 makes clear, however, that the dividing line between economics and politics can be fluid, with the quest for efficient cross-country macroeconomic coordination sometimes constrained and sometimes facilitated by political developments. In James's view, political constraints on the euro have stood in the way of its becoming a global currency on a par with the dollar.

In chapter 9, Masazumi Wakatabe focuses on relations with the United States in forming Japanese macroeconomic regimes and outcomes under a floating yen. Starting around the time of the 1987 Louvre Accord (which

James discusses in the preceding chapter), US mercantile pressure for a Japanese "strong yen" policy (McKinnon and Ohno 1997), largely internalized by the Bank of Japan even after its statutory independence in 1998, created a strong domestic deflationary impulse. That impulse pushed Japan to the zero lower bound on interest rates and hampered growth until 2013, when the Bank of Japan, supported by the Abe government, adopted an inflation targeting regime with a clear definition of the price stability goal.

In chapter 10, Yanliang Miao and Zhou Fan document a drop in global investments (especially portfolio equity) in China, along with a rise in foreign claims on the United States, as US-China tensions intensified in recent years. They find no comparable shift in international trade patterns and therefore see a trade–finance disconnect, explained by the hypothesis that "since 2018 geopolitical alignment has become a more important determinant of equity holdings worldwide." Their analysis builds upon, and is consistent with, recent research by the International Monetary Fund (IMF 2023).

The history of international monetary regimes over the past century shows that intellectual trends not only influence but also reflect political developments. In chapter 11, Linda Tesar tracks how the evolving world exchange rate system since Bretton Woods, including the birth of the euro, manifests in the content of articles in the *Journal of International Economics*, the leading scholarly journal covering global macroeconomics, finance, and trade.

Part III International Prices, International Adjustment, and Trade

Key virtues once claimed for the international gold standard were that it ensured price stability and the efficient international adjustment of external imbalances. Few modern scholars believe that this was the case (Cooper 1982), which helps explain the gold standard's demise. How have floating exchange rates performed on these dimensions since 1973? How has the floating rate regime interacted with domestic resource allocation, employment, the gains countries achieve through international trade, and the distribution of those gains?

Part III focuses on the adjustment of international trade, trade imbalances, and prices in the floating exchange rate era. In chapter 12, Katheryn Russ studies how fluctuations in the dollar have affected the location of manufacturing employment in the United States. She argues that the effects of dollar fluctuations may matter more for employment patterns when they are driven by financial market developments and that local labor markets are most vulnerable where local industries are already in decline, manufacturing wages are relatively high, or education levels are low.

In chapter 13, Joseph Gagnon looks at the large trade imbalances that have emerged since the early 1970s and asks why US policymakers are not more worried about possible adverse effects of US deficits and the growing negative US net international investment position. He recommends that countries use foreign exchange intervention and capital flow measures to push trade imbalances to levels more consistent with demographic trends, development status, and cyclical positions.

Douglas Irwin assesses the impact of floating exchange rates on global trade and the trading system (chapter 14). There is little evidence, he reports, that fluctuating exchange rates have depressed the overall level of trade. There is more evidence that flexible exchange rates have facilitated unilateral tariff reduction and trade liberalization around the world.

In chapter 15, Catherine Mann surveys the extensive research on the pass-through of exchange rate changes to domestic prices. She suggests that an environment of higher exchange rate volatility, driven in part by financial shocks, could prove challenging for central banks' efforts to target inflation.

Kristin Forbes argues in chapter 16 that central banks in advanced economies have successfully replaced the nominal anchor that gold once provided with credible inflation targeting regimes. Progress in emerging-market and developing economies, although in many cases impressive, has been more uneven.

Part IV Floating Exchange Rates and Emerging Markets

Part IV focuses on the experience of emerging markets in the floating rate era. The United States, Western European countries, and Japan adopted flexible exchange rates in the early 1970s; developing economies attempted to maintain pegs for a longer period. Many of them eventually moved toward greater flexibility after 1990, often in concert with programs of deregulation and liberalization, including in trade and financial flows.

In chapter 17, Andrés Velasco argues that although flexible exchange rates are not a panacea for emerging markets that are exposed to global financial shocks, they provide some insulation from those shocks and a welcome degree of freedom for policy. In his view, a prerequisite for a successful policy regime is credibility not just with regard to price stability but also in the commitment to floating.

In chapter 18, José De Gregorio points to the relatively few emerging market crises during the 2000s compared with earlier, which he attributes to greater monetary policy credibility and more flexible exchange rates. He argues that flexible rates have played a key role in international adjustment.

Adnan Mazarei explains in chapter 19 why it makes sense for oil exporters in the Middle East and North Africa region to continue to peg their currencies to the dollar, a path not chosen by many other countries. For these economies, the risks of oil-price volatility and the effects of oil prices on fiscal constraints reduce the potential net benefits of more flexible exchange rates.

Muhamad Chatib Basri argues in chapter 20 that flexible exchange rates have acted as an important shock absorber, helping Indonesia—one of the biggest emerging-market economies—cope with three major financial shocks over the past 30 years.

Part V The Dollar and International Financial Markets

Part V focuses on the current role of the dollar in international financial markets. In chapter 21, Linda Goldberg observes that the dollar's central role in the global financial system implies that shortfalls in dollar liquidity, as occurred during the global financial crisis and the COVID-19 crisis, can severely damage global economic activity unless the Federal Reserve steps in as a global lender and market maker of last resort. She highlights the positive impacts of Federal Reserve swap facilities as well as the newer Foreign International and Monetary Authorities repurchase facility, both of which support the dollar's reserve currency role.

Complementing chapter 21 by Goldberg, in chapter 22 Hyun Song Shin documents the dollar's central global role by exploring the foreign exchange swaps market and the anatomy of dollar funding shortages.

The next two chapters focus on the dollar's importance for international financial spillovers and the role of flexible exchange rates in modifying or amplifying those spillovers. Şebnem Kalemli-Özcan (chapter 23) addresses the transmission of global risk sentiment shocks to emerging markets, where global "risk-off" episodes of market jitters tend to be associated with US dollar appreciation and a contractionary rise in the risk premia that domestic borrowers must pay for loans. She notes that a key insulating role of a floating exchange rate—perhaps more important than its role in shifting demand for exports and imports—is in moderating the volatility of the risk premia embedded in domestic interest rates.

Hélène Rey (chapter 24) judges that the dollar-based international system, in which the United States still plays a hegemonic role, may be superior to a hypothetical multipolar system. In light of the global financial cycle, driven in part by the dollar, however, the system needs to be supplemented by better macroprudential policies and possibly capital flow measures. Although a hegemonic system may be better able to cope with internationally shared challenges, Rey bemoans the failure of the US-led system to make swifter progress on the provision of key public goods (such as climate change mitigation) and the elimination of public bads (such as offshore tax havens and biodiversity loss).

Part VI The Futures of the Dollar, the Euro, and the Renminbi

Part VI concludes by addressing the future of the dollar and its role with respect to the euro and China's renminbi. In chapter 25, Jeffrey Frankel observes that the dollar's leading role in the international economy has withstood many blows over the past 50 years, often self-inflicted, such as domestic political strife over the US federal debt ceiling. He judges that the dollar's status as the leading international currency remains secure into the foreseeable future because of the lack of viable alternatives, given the serious weaknesses of the euro and the renminbi.

In chapter 26, Eswar Prasad asks whether other currencies, including new digital currencies, pose a threat to dollar dominance. He concludes that the dollar will likely continue as the main reserve currency but that new forms of money could lead to more centralization in international finance, perhaps even bolstering the dollar's role as a global payment medium.

Like Frankel, Philippe Martin, in chapter 27, stresses network externalities as a source of dollar dominance. He is pessimistic about an expanded global role for the euro. Although geopolitical tensions may argue for an expanded role for the renminbi, the extent to which the euro or renminbi can overcome market forces favoring continued dollar use remains unclear. He conjectures that further deglobalization could reduce the dollar's prominence while also reducing US gains from issuing the world's key currency.

In chapter 28, Philip Lane reviews the evolution of the euro since its inception in 1999. Although the euro, in his view, does not currently threaten the primacy of the dollar, euro area resilience would benefit from several reforms to its architecture, such as full banking union. Lane believes that the euro is "firmly established as the dominant currency for euro area trade" (both within the euro area and with the rest of the world) and for use in transactions involving European financial markets.

In chapter 29, Shang-Jin Wei addresses whether the renminbi will take on a greater role in the world economy. He reviews the renminbi's evolution since 1973, pointing out that China continues to manage the exchange rate and to control international payments to a degree more characteristic of developing than advanced economies. Its rapid growth and size, however, give China an important role in influencing global markets. Wei argues that

China's current account surpluses, which have been a significant source of international trade tensions, are rooted in structural factors affecting the saving–investment balance rather than its exchange rate policies. China's capital controls limit the renminbi's potential as an international currency, in Wei's view, although a digital renminbi might allow for better-targeted capital controls with lower efficiency costs.

The world economy has now been living with floating exchange rates for longer than it lived with fixed-rate arrangements under the Bretton Woods system (1947–73), which endured for just 26 years. Floating rates have also survived longer than the interwar gold standard, which lasted for just a short period after Britain's rejoining the gold standard in 1925 before falling apart in the early 1930s during the Great Depression. The resilience of the floating rate system owes much to the flexibility it gives policymakers and market participants to adapt to changing economic conditions. The chapters in this volume reflect some of what has been learned over the past 50 years and perhaps give some hints about where the world economy may go in the future.

***

Philippe Martin, who attended the March 2023 PIIE conference and whose writing appears in this volume, passed away at the age of 57 on December 17, 2023. The loss is enormous. Philippe's remarkable mix of intellect, administrative skill, and personal charm enabled important contributions to economic research, European economic policy, and academic institution building. He could have contributed much more if not for his premature death, and he will be sorely missed. We dedicate this volume to the memory of our friend Philippe Martin.

References

Bordo, Michael D., and Barry Eichengreen, eds. 1993. *A Retrospective on the Bretton Woods System: Lessons for International Monetary Reform*. Chicago: University of Chicago Press for the National Bureau of Economic Research.

Cooper, Richard N. 1982. The Gold Standard: Historical Facts and Future Prospects. *Brookings Papers on Economic Activity* 13, no. 1: 1–45.

Garten, Jeffrey E. 2021. *Three Days at Camp David: How a Secret Meeting in 1971 Transformed the Global Economy*. New York: HarperCollins.

IMF (International Monetary Fund). 2023. Geoeconomic Fragmentation and Foreign Direct Investment. Chapter 4 in *World Economic Outlook* (April). Washington: International Monetary Fund.

McKinnon, Ronald, and Kenichi Ohno. 1997. *Dollar and Yen: Resolving Economic Conflict between the United States and Japan*. Cambridge, MA: MIT Press.

1

From the Postwar World Economy to the Modern World Economy, 1973–2023

MAURICE OBSTFELD

The year 1973—the year the Bretton Woods system of pegged exchange rates conclusively expired—was a watershed for the international monetary system, although many did not realize it at the time. The year capped a brief period of tumult, which corresponded roughly to the first term of the US Nixon administration, in which the postwar world economy neared a close and the outlines of the modern world economy emerged. Indeed, the immediate origins of several key aspects of today's world economy are found in the years just before 1973. The changes set in train then went far beyond the international monetary system and have had momentous geopolitical and political as well as economic and financial implications.

It is within the context of a discontinuously evolving post-1973 world that the exchange rate regime has accommodated and influenced developments in trade, finance, and economic policy. Several novel threats to global prosperity—climate change, pandemics, cyber vulnerabilities—have gained salience over the past 50 years. But many of today's international tensions echo or even reincarnate those of a half century ago.

Maurice Obstfeld is the C. Fred Bergsten Senior Fellow at the Peterson Institute for International Economics. He thanks Serra Pelin and Asher Rose for excellent research assistance and Douglas Irwin for helpful suggestions.

Economic and Political Challenges Facing President Nixon in 1969

To illustrate how so many features of the modern world economy have proximate roots in 1973 and the handful of years leading up to it, consider the economic and political challenges Richard M. Nixon perceived as he was inaugurated as the 37th president of the United States on January 20, 1969.[1]

The World and the International Monetary System

At the end of the 1960s, an oversimplified but comprehensive description of the world placed countries into the three buckets of First, Second, and Third World—the rich democracies; the Communist world (principally the Soviet bloc and China); and the rest of the world (the developing economies of Latin America, Africa, and Asia, many of them former colonies of First World empires that had gained independence by the early 1960s). In the Third World, the First and Second Worlds vied for influence. Nowhere was this competition more evident and violent than in Vietnam. Over the late 1960s, an escalating US military effort had led to street protests in the United States, strains on US public finances and the balance of payments, and friction between the United States and its allies in Western Europe.

The key multilateral reference point for commercial and financial relationships in the non-Communist world was the Bretton Woods system, centered on the International Monetary Fund (IMF).[2] At Bretton Woods,

---

1. By framing initial conditions in 1969 with reference to Nixon's presumed perceptions, I do not mean to imply that the actions of individual policymakers, no matter how immediately consequential, are fully or even mostly determinative of the way history unfolds. Such actions can influence the timing and character of major transitional events and induce some degree of path dependence. But larger economic, social, and political forces, operating through institutions that themselves reflect historical factors, drive much of the action. They help explain which madmen gain authority and when. The Bretton Woods system would eventually have changed dramatically, as a result of underlying societal, geopolitical, and economic fundamentals, even if Hubert Humphrey had won the 1968 presidential election. It might have done so in a different way and on a different time scale, but I suspect that five decades later, the exchange rate system under the alternative history would have looked much as it does today.

2. Postwar planners in the United States and the United Kingdom initially hoped to include an International Trade Organization (ITO) as one of the bedrock multilateral economic institutions. However, the initial Bretton Woods conference took up in detail only monetary/exchange rate and growth/development issues (the latter the domain of the World Bank). Proposed rules for international trade were not included in the Bretton Woods architecture but were left instead to the Havana Charter, completed in March 1948. It never came into force, because the United States refused to ratify it. As a result, for nearly five decades, postwar trade negotiations were conducted under the aegis of the General Agreement on Tariffs and Trade (GATT), signed on October 30, 1947. It lacked a permanent institutional structure or membership and was originally intended as a

New Hampshire in 1944, the United States and 43 allies declared fixed (but infrequently adjustable) currency parities against gold or the US dollar and agreed to enforce those parities by buying or selling dollars in the foreign exchange market. On Inauguration Day 1969, for example, parities included 5 French francs per dollar, 4 Deutsche marks per dollar, 360 Japanese yen per dollar, and 2.40 dollars per pound sterling. But world foreign exchange markets were showing increasing signs of stress. Under the pressure of speculation, sterling had been devalued from 2.80 dollars per pound in November 1967; by the end of 1969, the French franc parity was 5.55 per dollar (an 11 percent devaluation) and that of the Deutsche mark was 3.7 per dollar (a 7.5 percent revaluation).

What was the United States' responsibility to the system? The US Gold Reserve Act of 1934 ratified President Franklin D. Roosevelt's Executive Order 6102 of 1933, which made it a criminal offence for US residents to hold or trade gold anywhere. The act gave the Executive Branch the authority to set the dollar price of gold at the level "most advantageous to the public interest." FDR set the price at $35 an ounce in 1934, raising it from the $20.67 level that had prevailed since the US Coinage Act of 1834. There the price remained when the IMF commenced operations, in 1947. The United States promised foreign economic authorities that it would redeem their dollar holdings at the US statutory price of $35 per ounce; until 1968, it made efforts (usually in concert with other central banks) to stabilize the gold price in the London market once it reopened in 1954. These commitments were extended in the global "public interest" of maintaining confidence in the dollar. The US government took the fixed dollar-gold parity very seriously, though; safeguarding it was viewed as a pillar of the US-led international monetary system centered on the IMF, which presupposed a fixed-dollar gold price by allowing countries to specify their currency's parities in terms of either gold or US dollars.[3]

This system gave the United States great power and responsibility—but at a cost. If there are N currencies in the world, there are only $N-1$ exchange rates. The United States was the Nth country, which effectively supplied the world's numeraire currency. It could not unilaterally "devalue" the dollar, however; its exchange rates were up to the $N-1$ other countries.

Until 1971, the United States felt responsible for maintaining foreign governments' confidence that it could and would redeem their dollar holdings at the promised $35 an ounce price, even as official foreign claims on the United States grew to exceed its gold holdings. This "confidence

provisional forum for tariff-reduction talks pending the establishment of an ITO. This state of affairs continued until the birth of the World Trade Organization in 1995.

3. See Hirsch (1969) and Yeager (1976).

problem" (or "Triffin dilemma") was to a large degree a US fiscal problem (Obstfeld 2014), but it was a real problem nonetheless.[4] As C. Fred Bergsten points out in chapter 3, during the 1960s much official energy was spent manipulating the London gold market, initiating reciprocal currency swap lines (in 1962), and using administrative measures to limit capital outflows from the United States, which exceeded the dwindling US current account surplus and therefore swelled the potential foreign official claims on US gold.

Because the United States alone had no obligation to intervene in foreign exchange markets, it alone had the "exorbitant privilege" of a fully independent monetary policy—provided foreign official holders of dollars exercised forbearance by not cashing their dollars in for gold. US monetary policy effectively provided the nominal anchor for the world economy, largely determining medium-term inflation rates everywhere. US inflation that was persistently higher than what trading partners were willing to accept would, however, set off an unstable doom loop in which specula-tors bought non-dollar currencies in anticipation of revaluation, foreign official reserves swelled even further beyond what the United States could feasibly redeem in gold at the $35 price, and foreign inflation rose to polit-ically unacceptable levels, increasing the temptation to convert official dollars into gold and revalue (Emminger 1977; De Groot 2019).[5]

Against this backdrop, the Soviet bloc and China were largely auton-omous economically. Third World countries tended to maintain heavily controlled economies, often with multiple exchange rate practices and extensive external payment controls. A majority had joined the IMF by the end of the 1960s, although most had not yet accepted the IMF's Article

---

4. For a discussion of the Triffin dilemma, see chapter 24 by Hélène Rey.

5. There is debate over the role of the Triffin dilemma in the collapse of the Bretton Woods system. Kindleberger (1965) famously argued that the United States functioned as a global financial intermediary, issuing a global currency that foreign countries willingly held in short-term maturities to enhance their liquidity. Like a bank, the United States might be "runnable" in principle under the gold commitment, but there was no inevitability that a run would occur, given the valuable financial services the United States provided through its balance sheet. Several subsequent authors—including Portes (2012), Matsui (2016), and Bordo and McCauley (2019)—have questioned Triffin's analysis. A more balanced view is that crises generally result from a confluence of multiple vulnerabilities. The Triffin dilemma alone need not have brought down the dollar's link to gold, but it became an additional destabilizing factor and an accelerant in the context of several more fundamental economic and political forces pushing the dollar decisively toward devaluation during the early 1970s. Kindleberger's views have regained prominence in light of recent research on the international roles of the dollar and the global liquidity of US Treasury liabilities.

VIII convertibility obligations.[6] Communist China and the USSR were not Fund members at the time, even though the USSR had been one of the initial parties to the Bretton Woods agreement.

Nixon's Challenges—and an Opportunity

In 1969, the incoming US president faced a number of domestic and international challenges and at least one big foreign policy opportunity. From the outset, a major priority was reelection in 1972.

In the US economy, the fiscal demands of the Vietnam War and the Great Society helped push the US (seasonally adjusted) unemployment rate down to 3.4 percent at the start of 1969. But inflation had been on the rise for several years, and in Nixon's first year in office it would reach 5.5 percent (figure 1.1, panel a).

The United States' international trade position was weakening, and there was growing concern that competition from European and Japanese imports could undermine the US manufacturing base and the wages of American workers, leading to political backlash (Alden 2016). US postwar reconstruction efforts (including the Bretton Woods project) had succeeded in their principal goal of reviving world trade—perhaps all too well. An influential study by Houthakker and Magee (1969, 122) suggested that the deterioration in the US trade balance was structural, that "the United States is gradually becoming a net importer of finished manufactures" and that only a substantial fall in the US terms of trade could offset those developments.[7] Foreign direct investment (FDI) outflows by US multinationals added to short-term balance of payments pressures; fueled growth in the offshore eurodollar market, where international banks freely borrowed and lent dollars; and supported initial forays into outsourcing American jobs.

In December 1969, a US recession began. Although mild, its conclusion in November 1970 left the unemployment rate at around 6 percent (it would not decline to below 5.5 percent before the 1972 presidential election). Any president would have found these economic circumstances daunting.

---

6. International Monetary Fund, *Article VIII Acceptance by IMF Members: Recent Trends and Implications for the Fund*, May 26, 2006, https://www.imf.org/external/np/pp/eng/2006/052606.pdf.

7. Subsequent research has tempered the conclusions about the US trade position that readers originally drew from the Houthakker-Magee study (Krugman 1989; Gagnon 2007). The shift should not obscure the fact that the study had a significant impact on the policy debate at the time. Houthakker, a professor at Harvard, won the American Economic Association's John Bates Clark Medal in 1963 and served as a member of President Nixon's Council of Economic Advisers from February 4, 1969, to July 15, 1971, leaving only a month before the announcement of Nixon's August 1971 economic package.

Figure 1.1
Inflation in major industrial economies, 1960–2022

a. United States

percent

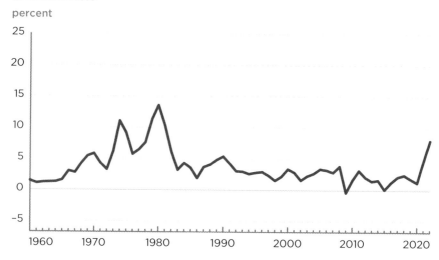

b. Germany, Japan, France, and the United Kingdom

percent

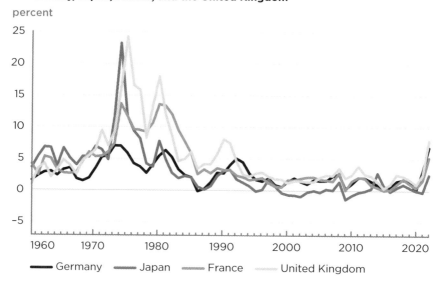

Source: Annual data from the World Bank's *World Development Indicators*, via Federal Reserve Bank of St. Louis, Federal Reserve Economic Data (FRED).

Accompanying the economic challenges was widespread domestic social unrest, amplified by the Vietnam War, and uneasy relations with US allies in Europe, exacerbated by unwelcome spillovers from the US economy. France had withdrawn from the NATO military command structure in 1966, part of its broader pushback against US "privilege." In West Germany, Willy Brandt (who became chancellor in October 1969) was seeking closer relations with Eastern Europe, and there was general unhappiness about US involvement in Vietnam. Western European countries were experiencing their own social unrest, accompanied by wage developments that were fueling inflation (Nordhaus 1972). Further price pressures emanating from US policies and propagated through the fixed exchange rate regime threatened to add to Europe's woes (see figure 1.1, panel b).

Not all prospects were ominous. Starting in the mid-1950s, doctrinal differences had opened a widening dispute between the USSR and Mao Zedong's China, exacerbated by commercial discontents and geopolitical disagreements over issues such as the USSR's support of India. Border tensions between the two countries eventually emerged, resulting in military clashes in the Manchurian and Xinjiang regions in 1969. As Nixon appreciated early on, the Chinese-Soviet rift offered a potential opening to drive a wedge between the two great Communist powers.

The Nixon Shock

Halfway into Nixon's first term, the United States faced dual problems of internal and external equilibrium. Nixon's surprise solution, announced August 15, 1971, accordingly contained domestic and international components.[8]

On the domestic front, the most striking aspect of the "Nixon shock" was a wage and price freeze, in total opposition to Republicans' traditional free market bent. The controls allowed Nixon to pressure the Federal Reserve, then headed by Arthur F. Burns, into a looser monetary policy, pumping the economy up before the 1972 election while measured inflation fell. Following the removal of controls, in 1973, inflation jumped to 11 percent in 1974 under the pressure of higher global oil prices. Also inconsistent with the sustainable moderation of wage and price increases, but consistent with the logic of political business cycles, was a package of tax cuts, announced even though the federal budget deficit had set a near postwar record in the fiscal year that had just ended.

The external measures Nixon unveiled were a lead-in to the events that motivated this conference. Economist Arthur Okun, chair of the Council

---

8. Garten (2021) provides detailed context around Nixon's policies.

of Economic Advisers in the Johnson administration, summarized Nixon's August television address by saying, "We just ended the Bretton Woods system forever."[9] The US Treasury announced that it would no longer convert foreign official dollars into gold, slamming shut the US "gold window." Nixon also imposed a 10 percent surcharge on all dutiable imports—the first general US tariff increase since the 1930 Smoot-Hawley tariff, as Irwin (2014) observes. The intent was to pressure US trade partners into revaluing their currencies.

In December 1971 at the Smithsonian Institution, Group of Ten (G10) economic officials agreed to a multilateral dollar devaluation.[10] According to Nixon's famous description, it was "the most significant monetary agreement in the history of the world." The import surcharge was rescinded. As part of the agreement, Nixon devalued the dollar against gold, raising the price to $38 an ounce. Markets reacted negatively, and the dollar was soon in crisis again, as Edwin M. Truman recounts in chapter 2. The last coordinated attempt to save fixed exchange rates came in February 1973, with a further negotiated 10 percent dollar devaluation, entailing a rise in the gold price to $42.22 an ounce. By the following month, under pressure of unrelenting speculation, exchange rates had been cut loose. That move, initially viewed as a temporary tactical retreat, has endured for a half century.

Gold had suddenly become irrelevant to the world monetary system. In 1974, President Gerald Ford signed legislation legalizing the holding of gold by US citizens. More than 50 years after the February 1973 change in the gold price, the US statutory price remains at $42.22 an ounce. The market price on November 30, 2023, was $2,046.28 an ounce.

The Economic Consequences of 1969–73

The events of 50 years ago seeded the ground for the modern world economy. Many recent events grew out of and in some respects echo events that took place then.

---

9. Edwin L. Dale, Jr., "Nixon Orders 90-Day Wage and Price Freeze, Asks Tax Cuts, New Jobs in Broad Plan; Severs Link between Dollar and Gold," *New York Times*, August 16, 1971, https://www.nytimes.com/1971/08/16/archives/severs-link-between-dollar-and-gold-a-world-effect-unilateral-us.html.

10. The G10 industrial countries include the current G7 (Canada, France, Germany, Italy, Japan, the United Kingdom, and the United States) along with Belgium, the Netherlands, and Sweden.

International Dollar Politics

The Nixon shock was hardly the first time in the postwar era that the United States had pursued its national interest with scant regard for allies' opinions. But it represented a new frontier in America's willingness to cut back on providing key international public goods when they became too costly in domestic economic or political terms. Allies had no warning of the new policy, despite their supposed partnership in operating the international monetary system and other joint endeavors. The new attitude was summarized in US Treasury Secretary John Connally's infamous quip to G10 finance ministers that "the dollar is our currency, but it's your problem." The episode did not end US participation in multilateral economic cooperation, which has continued through the IMF, the G7, and the G20, among other venues, but it set a precedent that the Trump administration embraced and future US administrations could revisit.

In particular, the external effects of US dollar fluctuations have been a recurring locus of disagreement. In the early 1980s, a combination of tight US monetary policy and loose fiscal policy drove the dollar to stratospheric heights (figure 1.2). This development complicated allies' own fights against inflation (because of upward pressure on dollar-invoiced import prices); it also set off a protectionist storm in the United States. The result was the Plaza Accord of September 1985, in which industrial countries, including the United States, intervened jointly to push the dollar down.

Exceptional dollar weakness has also been a source of contention at times. When the Federal Reserve's quantitative easing drove the dollar to unprecedented lows after the global financial crisis, some emerging-market policymakers accused the United States of engaging in currency wars. The Fed protested that it was merely following its mandate to stabilize the US economy and declined to recognize any serious conflict between its domestic mandate and the effects on trading partners. Dollar appreciation since 2021 has also raised concerns abroad, but the Fed has gotten better at at least acknowledging the global impact of the dollar.

OPEC's Influential Role

During the Arab-Israeli Yom Kippur War, in 1973, Arab members of the Organization of Petroleum Exporting Countries (OPEC) imposed an oil embargo on the United States and other countries supporting Israel. The price of oil nearly quadrupled, the largest part of the hike happening when OPEC boosted the oil price to $11.65 a barrel in January 1974 (it had been $2.90 before the war). The price hike called for supply reductions; supplies remained restricted even after the embargo ended, in March 1974,

Figure 1.2
US dollar real effective exchange rate, 1973–2023

index (March 1973 = 100)

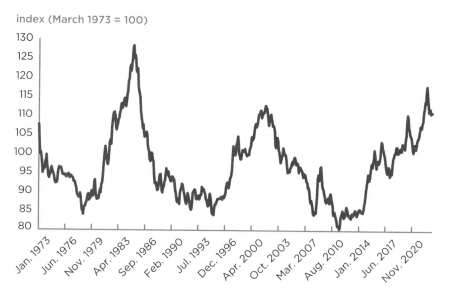

Note: The discontinued real broad dollar index (for goods only) was updated using the renormalized real broad dollar index starting in January 2006.
Source: Board of Governors of the Federal Reserve System via Federal Reserve Bank of St. Louis, Federal Reserve Economic Data (FRED).

so higher prices were maintained. The result in oil importers was lower growth coupled with higher inflation—stagflation (see figure 1.1).

OPEC had learned how to flex its muscles in 1973; it has remained a key actor in the global economy ever since, adding (and sometimes losing) members and at times seeking to coordinate its actions with non-OPEC members, such as Russia. The dollar's travails in the early 1970s were, however, one concern that encouraged OPEC to raise dollar oil prices. Just after the Smithsonian Agreement, in January 1972, OPEC raised the dollar price of its oil by roughly 8.5 percent to (nearly) match the dollar's devaluation in terms of gold. The action taken two years later was bolder but also motivated in part by the dollar's shrinking value in terms of gold, which in turn owed something to the oil shock (James 1996; Hammes and Wills 2005). Triffin (1978, 10) also tied the OPEC shock to the dollar's travails.

An interesting irony concerns one of the main arguments advanced by those who opposed raising the dollar gold price to defuse the Triffin problem (chapter 4 by Robert Aliber raises this alternative, which was widely discussed before the Nixon shock). The argument was that a rise in the gold price would benefit the USSR, which then supplied much of the world's newly mined gold. Both the rise in the gold price in the early 1970s and the related rise in the price of oil encouraged further development of Soviet deposits and a huge increase in oil exports by 1980. Russia's energy production and policies remain central to global economics and geopolitics.

Monetary Theory and Policy Frameworks

The burst of inflation that emerged under the Nixon administration was unprecedented since the early postwar period. It was much more prolonged than the earlier episodes (in 1946–47 and 1951). By the end of the 1970s, a second oil shock hit, and inflation moved into double digits again in the United States and several other industrial countries.

Macroeconomic theories based on the rational expectations paradigm showed how monetary authorities unable to commit themselves to low-inflation policies could enter high-inflation traps through their attempts to reduce inefficient unemployment or achieve other socially desirable goals (Kydland and Prescott 1977; Calvo 1978). In his Per Jacobsson lecture of September 1979, former Fed chair Arthur Burns, perhaps unknowingly channeling recent economic research, lamented that central banks in democratic societies necessarily find their price stability goals held hostage by political forces. "By and large," he said, speaking of the past decade, "[US] monetary policy came to be governed by the principle of undernourishing the inflationary process while still accommodating a good part of the pressures in the marketplace. The central banks of other industrial countries, functioning as they did in a basically similar political environment, appear to have behaved in much the same fashion" (Burns 1979, 16).

Returning from Burns's speech in Belgrade, Yugoslavia, then-Fed chair Paul Volcker decided to prove him wrong (Silber 2012). After a deep recession driven by exceptionally tight monetary policy, the United States entered a long period of moderate-to-low inflation that lasted until 2021. Inflation rates over this period moderated around the world; by the 2010s, they had fallen in many emerging-market and developing economies (EMDEs).

This striking development grew directly out of the inflationary turbulence of the 1970s. Volcker had demonstrated what a determined central banker, willing and able to stand up to political pressure, could do. But Burns had been fundamentally correct in his analysis of the obstacles that even well-intentioned monetary policymakers normally face. The problem was to create institutions and policy frameworks that could bolster the commitment capability of central banks. One was statutory central bank independence, which spread to many countries (albeit in several variants). A second was the policy framework of inflation targeting, with its emphasis on transparency in terms of goals and instruments, account-ability, and public communications (Bernanke et al. 2001). Many coun-tries, including many EMDEs, adopted this approach to monetary policy in at least some form; it was most effective where central banks were inde-pendent. Of course, inflation targeting also presupposed a reasonable degree of exchange rate flexibility, which by the 2000s many more EMDEs had embraced.

By the 2020s, the central banking landscape was radically different from what it had been in the early 1970s. The influential economist Harry G. Johnson had predicted in 1969 that in a world of floating exchange rates, central bankers would lose prominence, because their jet-setting role in propping up the fixed exchange rate system would disappear. He could not have been more wrong (Obstfeld 2020). One reason was the greater visibility of central banks attempting to communicate more transparently with the public. Another was the financial instability evidenced by the global finan-cial crisis and the euro crisis, which necessitated unprecedented market interventions by central bankers and brought home the fact that inflation targeting alone is not enough to guarantee overall macroeconomic stability.

The global reemergence of inflation in 2021 as economies relaxed COVID-19 lockdowns blindsided central bankers in the advanced econo-mies and illustrated that the issues raised by the 1970s were not ancient history. How do supply shocks influence inflation, especially when they come in an environment of demand pressures? Can central banks afford to "look through" supply shocks in these circumstances, assuming they are temporary and will not undermine inflation credibility much, even if there is no strong monetary response? Once inflationary momentum builds more broadly, how deep of a recession is needed to restore anchored price expectations? We are learning some of the answers in real time.

Global Financialization

The classic "trilemma" of international finance states that countries must choose two out of the following three: a pegged exchange rate, a monetary policy oriented toward domestic objectives, and open international finan-cial markets. The Bretton Woods system, at least as conceived in the orig-inal IMF Articles of Agreement, advanced a trilemma solution in which the freedom of private cross-border financial conditions would be limited. The move to more flexible exchange rates in 1973 freed the economies taking that path—at that time the advanced industrial economies—to liberalize international financial transactions consistent with more monetary policy autonomy. However, the trilemma alone does not explain why they chose to do so (Obstfeld and Taylor 2017).

As the dollar was under speculative attack in 1972, European countries floated proposals for developing more instruments to curtail private financial capital markets, including approaches coordinated among countries. The United States—channeling a free market ideology championed by officials such as Treasury Secretary George Shultz and Council of Economic Advisers Chair Herbert Stein, as well as outside advisers like Milton Friedman and Alan Greenspan—pushed back. As Helleiner (1994, 105) points out:

> Opposition by the US representatives to any type of cooperative controls, however, prevented the issuance of firmer recommendation. Indeed, the US representatives hoped to discourage other countries from controlling capital movements altogether. According to US representatives, a more fully liberal international financial order would permit international capital movements to encourage "the growth of international trade" and increase "the economic well-being of developed and developing countries." They also challenged the view that disequilibrating capital movements were necessarily undesirable, asserting that such movements prompted countries to take appropriate adjustment measures.

As part of its work in 1972–73, a working group of the Committee of 20 (which Truman discusses in chapter 2) considered European and Japanese proposals for cooperative regulatory measures among both capital-flow sender and recipient countries, as well as enhanced regulation of the offshore euro markets.[11] US negotiators rejected these ideas. Indeed, the United States had announced as early as February 1973, at the height of currency stresses, that its own capital controls would be lifted in December of the following year—and overdelivered by lifting them in January (Helleiner 1994).

Apart from ideology, officials in the Nixon administration had several practical, national interest motivations for rejecting international capital flow restrictions. Liberalized financial flows might weaken the dollar further, promoting desired employment and trade balance adjustment. A liberalized global financial system could also enhance the United States' position as a global financial hub.[12] That goal became even more important with the oil shock, after which huge oil surpluses suddenly needed to be banked and recycled. Throughout the 1970s, US money center banks pros-

---

11. The IMF board set up the Committee of 20 in 1972 to consider reforms of the international monetary system. The group contained one member from each of the 20 IMF constituencies.

12. The United Kingdom promoted the offshore London euro market with a similar motivation of regaining the City's past preeminence. Even though the market was providing finance for speculators, the UK government resisted proposals to rein it in (by, for example, imposing reserve requirements).

pered by recycling petrodollars to developing economies, notably in Latin America. But perils loomed. By 1981, just before the devastating developing-economy debt crisis emerged under the pressure of Volcker's tight monetary policies, the developing-economy loans of the eight largest US banks amounted to 264 percent of their capital (FDIC 1997). Official action saved the banks, but the developing-economy debtors suffered almost a decade of lost growth. The episode was a harbinger of crises to come. The frequency of financial crises, including severe ones, rose precipitously after 1973, and not just in the less prosperous countries (Reinhart and Rogoff 2009).

US domestic financial deregulation, pursued further under the Carter and Reagan administrations, cemented the United States' preeminent status in global finance, with an assist from the end of the Cold War. For various reasons, including competitive pressures and ideology, other countries followed the deregulatory trend. The result was an explosion of international financial transactions over the past five decades.

Figure 1.3 shows two possible measures of that growth: the sizes (relative to world GDP) of (a) current account deficits and surpluses and (b) total (gross) financial inflows and outflows. Five implications of the figures are noteworthy:

1. The absolute sizes of current account deficits and surpluses (global imbalances) have grown substantially over time. During the mid-2000s, about 3 percent of world GDP was intermediated to fund imbalances.

2. The financial inflows and outflows that finance global imbalances are far larger than the minimum that would be needed if each deficit country merely borrowed the excess of its imports over its exports and each surplus country lent out only its excess current foreign earnings. There is a good deal of two-way asset-for-asset trading in the global economy, some of it well-motivated (e.g., to seek portfolio diversification) but some of it of questionable or even negative social value (e.g., to avoid taxes, to finance asset bubbles).

3. Financial flows peaked massively just before the global financial crisis of 2007–09, a glaring sign of financial excess, as we now know. Their growth largely stabilized after around 2010.

4. Because the well-lubricated global financial system allows bigger and more persistent global imbalances, the medium-term link between exchange rate movements and trade imbalances has been weakened.

5. That link is weakened even further by the prevalence of financial transactions over "real" transactions involving goods and services in foreign exchange markets. There is now much more scope for purely financial disturbances to move exchange rates, in the light of which

Figure 1.3

Dispersion of global current account balances and financial flows as percent of world GDP, 1980–2022

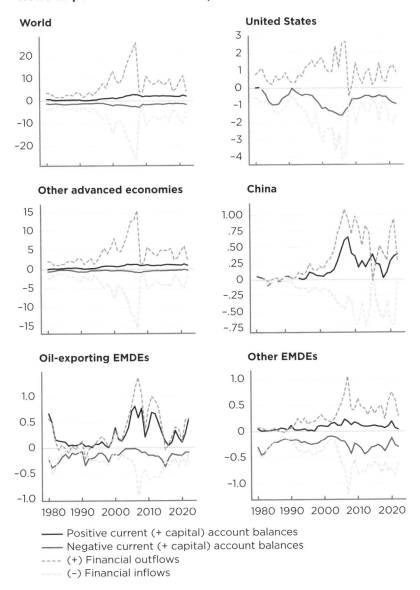

Positive current (+ capital) account balances
Negative current (+ capital) account balances
(+) Financial outflows
(–) Financial inflows

EMDE = emerging-market and developing economies

Source: Balance of payments data are from the IMF's *International Financial Statistics*; world GDP data are from the World Bank's *World Development Indicators*; country classifications are from the IMF's *World Economic Outlook*, April 2023.

their comparative stability among advanced economies in recent decades has been remarkable. However, all economies, but especially EMDEs, are buffeted by a global financial cycle in asset prices, leverage, and capital flows that drives an array of macro-relevant quantities and relative prices (Rey 2013).

Policymakers have not been blind to the financial risks of globalized capital markets. Regulatory initiatives have been pursued mostly at technical, nonpolitical levels, however (which is not to say that political and commercial considerations have been absent). Early instances of banking problems stemming from the new and relatively unfamiliar world of fluctuating exchange rates (Franklin National Bank, I.D. Herstatt Bank), as well as heightened perceived risks from petrodollar recycling through the eurodollar market moved international regulators to coordinate. A result was the Basel Committee on Banking Supervision, which met for the first time in February 1975 (see Goodhart 2011 for detailed background). Later came the Financial Stability Forum (which became the Financial Stability Board), established in 1999. The "soft law" promulgated in these forums, which participant countries largely adhere to without formal inter-governmental agreements, has no doubt helped avoid some financial risks, but it has also supported what some claim is excessive financialization of the world economy. Despite three waves of Basel reforms, with a fourth on the way, regulators continue to play catch up with evolving market innovations (such as digital finance), and wide supervisory gaps remain.

Global financial markets remain dominated by the US dollar, which 50 years after the death of Bretton Woods has emerged as a "currency among currencies"—essentially a global numeraire and medium of exchange (see chapters 24 to 27 in this volume). The persistence of the dollar's role as a global currency even after the end of the Bretton Woods regime that enshrined it—and despite the decline in the US share of world GDP—seems surprising from the standpoint of 1973, though it may well play a role in the relative resilience of international trade that Douglas Irwin describes in chapter 14.

Several factors explain the continued dominance of the dollar. They include Volcker's success in curbing US inflation; the depth and breadth of US financial markets; the comparative US laissez-faire attitude toward international transactions; and not least, US willingness to supply the world with ample safe assets in the form of US Treasuries, a process that began in earnest with the Reagan-era budget deficits. The dollar's de jure special status in the Bretton Woods system ended a half century ago, but US monetary and financial conditions still exert an outsized influence on the global macroeconomy.

Neoliberalism and Supply-Side Economics

The Nixon administration was heavily influenced by free market advocates, although Nixon departed from Chicago-style orthodoxy when he found it politically useful to do so. By the time Ronald Reagan took office, the neoliberal school of thought had become dominant in the US government. It had also migrated to the United Kingdom under Margaret Thatcher's premiership.[13]

A key talking point of conservative critics was that it was Keynesian economics that had given rise to the stagflation of the 1970s (see Clavin et al. 2023).[14] The solution, according to these voices, was to radically scale down the government's footprint in the economy by dismantling social safety nets and reducing or eliminating government regulations. To some degree, the case for a less interventionist state took hold in European countries beyond Britain as well as in many EMDEs, where more liberalization was sorely needed.

The impact of this philosophical shift on growth, inequality, market power, development, and democracy is too big a topic to pursue here. I note the shift as one outgrowth of the turbulent era after Bretton Woods came to an end and observe that in some respects the political pendulum is swinging back toward more *dirigisme* in several major countries and regions. The shift is most striking on the Right, where new skepticism ranges from pragmatic concerns about winning elections to cultural fears about "globalism" (which are eagerly amplified through social media to mobilize voters).

A key component of the conservative approach, in both the United States and the United Kingdom, has been the idea that tax cuts have powerful growth-enhancing effects beyond the effects identified by John Maynard Keynes under conditions of unemployment. The intellectual basis for this supply-side view comes in part from a May 1971 essay by Robert Mundell suggesting that the United States address its simultaneous internal and external imbalances through the joint use of fiscal and monetary policy. Contractionary monetary policy would exert downward pressure on inflation while drawing in foreign capital, thereby improving the US payments position. Targeted tax cuts would expand incomes, if not through Keynesian effects then through the supply-side effects of expanding labor supply and investment.

---

13. Reagan also heeded the voice of expedience when doing so was politically convenient, as in the case of some of his administration's trade policies.

14. Keynes was clear in his writings about the perils of inflation, in particular its regressive effects.

In the event, Nixon adopted tax cuts in August 1971 but opted to keep monetary policy loose while controlling prices administratively. This policy was not sustainable, and the world economy paid a price, which it seems hard to blame entirely on Keynes or even on Keynesians. Mundell's supply-side ideas found a home in the Reagan administration and continue to attract prominent US adherents five decades on.

Rise of China

In July 1971, US National Security Adviser Henry Kissinger traveled secretly to China to meet with Premier Zhou Enlai. As Nixon pondered his August 1971 announcement, he knew that he would soon be introducing a new China policy. Much of the urgency in unveiling the economic shock—apart from deteriorating economic fundamentals in the United States—was to avoid overshadowing press coverage of the upcoming foreign policy shock. On February 21, 1972, Nixon landed in China for the talks with Mao and Zhou that would eventually lead to China's entry into the world economy.

Deng Xiaoping gained power in December 1978. He quickly initiated a program of partial economic opening and market-based economic development that was enormously successful in propelling China into the ranks of upper-middle-income countries and creating an economy that is now the world's largest in purchasing power parity terms. Diplomatic relations with the United States were normalized in 1979, and Deng visited the White House that year. In April 1980, the People's Republic took over China's representation at the IMF from Taiwan.

Figure 1.4 illustrates China's steep economic ascent.[15] The impacts on the world's economies, financial system, domestic politics, and geopolitics have been dominating factors since China's entry into the World Trade Organization at the end of 2001. Events around China will reshape the global economy further in the years ahead.

Geopolitically, the US-China *rapprochement* ended an era of US foreign policy dominated by the imperative of containing Communism globally. The very open splintering of international Communist solidarity presaged the demise of the Soviet bloc and the Soviet Union in 1989–91, an event that has had immense repercussions, economic and otherwise.

---

15. For comparison, the IMF's *World Economic Outlook* database (October 2023) projected a US share of world output at PPP of around 15.4 percent for 2023.

Figure 1.4
China's economic growth, 1980–2022

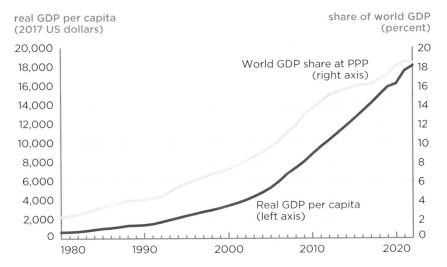

real GDP per capita
(2017 US dollars)

share of world GDP
(percent)

PPP = purchasing power parity
Source: International Monetary Fund, *World Economic Outlook*, April 2023.

The European Union and the Euro

With growing exchange rate instability in the late 1960s and early 1970s, member countries of the European Economic Community (EEC) sought ways to link their currencies more closely. (Chapter 8, by Harold James, discusses the European response to the dollar in detail; see also chapter 28, by Philip Lane.) The Werner Report of October 1970 set out a phased path to a single EEC currency within a decade, an idea the United States opposed at the time that became a reality in 1999.

The EEC's internal problems with variable exchange rates (see Giavazzi and Giovannini 1989) became more acute after the Nixon shock and the Smithsonian Agreement. In April 1972, EEC countries set up a "snake mechanism" to limit intra-European currency fluctuation margins to ±2.25 percent. The United Kingdom and Denmark, which did not become EEC members until 1973, joined the snake in May 1972, only to withdraw the next month (Denmark rejoined soon after; the United Kingdom did not). The snake eventually failed, succeeded in 1979 by the European Monetary System's Exchange Rate Mechanism (ERM), which eventually helped pave a path to the single currency (European Parliament 2015). Denmark was an early participant in the ERM. The United Kingdom did not join until October 1990, only to leave in September 1992 amid the

ERM crisis, when speculators attacked multiple ERM members' pegs to the Deutsche mark. To many in the United Kingdom, the ERM interlude indicated the folly of pegging sterling at the possible expense of internal balance and increased resentment of the European Union.

Both the United Kingdom and Denmark were able to negotiate opt-outs from the Maastricht Treaty requirements concerning accession to the single currency. Denmark has shadowed the euro closely within ERM II, the post-euro successor to the ERM, linking its monetary policy closely to that of the European Central Bank. In contrast, the United Kingdom followed its own monetary path and felt increasingly marginalized within the European Union, as economic decision centers linked to the euro (the Eurogroup of finance ministers, the Eurosystem of central banks) expanded. Britain's long-standing aversion to giving up its monetary autonomy, dating back to the debates over EEC accession in the early 1970s (see Obstfeld 2020), was one of several factors that led to Brexit in 2020.[16]

A Postmodern World Economy?

After the "America First" hostility of the Trump administration toward international cooperation and leadership, the COVID-19 pandemic, and the Russian invasion of Ukraine and its spillovers, the postwar world economy may be reverting in some ways to earlier forms. Trade tensions are rife, and the World Trade Organization is largely toothless. Governments are turning to industrial policies. Right-wing populism, often hostile to global economic integration, has gained ground in many democracies. The world seems to be sliding back into three blocs—the high-income economies, the China-Russia axis with a few associated countries, and the Global South—as nation groups take different stances with regard to economic sanctions and trade with Russia. Tensions have risen further with the war between Israel and Gaza. Disintegrative tendencies were certainly present to some degree before 2017, but they have intensified and accelerated.

A divided world is especially ill-suited to contend with the threats it now faces, which include but go beyond those apparent in the early 1970s. As the Bretton Woods system was buckling, April 1970 saw the first Earth Day, a milestone for the environmental movement. Its goals have not been realized. Instead, climate change has become an existential problem, as ocean levels rise, biodiversity plummets, humans interface increasingly with disease vectors, various forms of pollution proliferate, and events linked to extreme weather (including floods, droughts, and wildfires) occur with increasing

---

16. Chapter 8 by Harold James says more about British attitudes toward European currency projects.

frequency and severity. There are also other collective threats, old and new. Although the world has inevitably moved toward more national autonomy in economic policies, the interdependence that Richard Cooper famously highlighted in the late 1960s has deepened and broadened (Cooper 1968). Even more today than before, the world needs the cooperative spirit that inspired the founding of the Bretton Woods institutions.

References

Alden, Edward. 2016. *Failure to Adjust: How Americans Got Left Behind in the Global Economy*. Lanham, MD: Rowman & Littlefield.

Bernanke, Ben S., Thomas Laubach, Frederic S. Mishkin, and Adam S. Posen. 2001. *Inflation Targeting: Lessons from the International Experience*, rev. ed. Princeton, NJ: Princeton University Press.

Bordo, Michael D., and Robert N. McCauley. 2019. Triffin: Dilemma or Myth? *IMF Economic Review* 67 (December): 824–51.

Burns, Arthur F. 1979. *The Anguish of Central Banking*. The 1979 Per Jacobsson Lecture. Belgrade, Yugoslavia, September 30. Available at http://www.perjacobsson.org/lectures/1979.pdf.

Calvo, Guillermo A. 1978. On the Time Consistency of Optimal Policy in a Monetary Economy. *Econometrica* 46 (November): 1411–28.

Clavin, Patricia, Giancarlo Corsetti, Maurice Obstfeld, and Adam Tooze. 2023. Lessons of Keynes's *Economic Consequences* in a Turbulent Century. In *Keynes's* Economic Consequences of the Peace *after 100 Years: Polemics and Policy*, ed. Patricia Clavin, Giancarlo Corsetti, Maurice Obstfeld, and Adam Tooze, 1–56. Cambridge: Cambridge University Press.

Cooper, Richard N. 1968. *The Economics of Interdependence: Economic Policy in the Atlantic Community*. New York: Council on Foreign Relations.

De Groot, Michael. 2019. Western Europe and the Collapse of Bretton Woods. *International Journal* 74 (June): 282–300.

Emminger, Otmar. 1977. *The D-Mark in the Conflict between Internal and External Equilibrium, 1948–75*. Princeton Essays in International Finance 122 (June). Princeton, NJ: International Finance Section, Princeton University.

European Parliament. 2015. *A History of European Monetary Integration*. Briefing (March). Available at https://www.europarl.europa.eu/RegData/etudes/BRIE/2015/551325/EPRS_BRI%282015%29551325_EN.pdf.

FDIC (Federal Deposit Insurance Corporation). 1997. *History of the 80s: Lessons for the Future. Vol. I: An Examination of the Banking Crises of the 1980s and Early 1990s*. Washington.

Gagnon, Joseph E. 2007. Productive Capacity, Product Varieties, and the Elasticities Approach to the Trade Balance. *Review of International Economics* 15 (September): 639–59.

Garten, Jeffrey E. 2021. *Three Days at Camp David: How a Secret Meeting in 1971 Transformed the Global Economy*. New York: HarperCollins.

Giavazzi, Francesco, and Alberto Giovannini. 1989. *Limiting Exchange Rate Flexibility: The European Monetary System*. Cambridge, MA: MIT Press.

Goodhart, Charles. 2011. *The Basel Committee on Banking Supervision: A History of the Early Years 1974–1997*. Cambridge: Cambridge University Press.

Hammes, David, and Douglas Wills. 2005. Black Gold: The End of Bretton Woods and the Oil-Price Shocks of the 1970s. *Independent Review* 9 (Spring): 501–11.

Helleiner, Eric. 1994. *States and the Reemergence of Global Finance: From Bretton Woods to the 1990s*. Ithaca, NY: Cornell University Press.

Hirsch, Fred. 1969. *Money International: Economics and Politics of World Money*. Garden City, NY: Doubleday.

Houthakker, H.S., and Stephen P. Magee. 1969. Income and Price Elasticities in World Trade. *Review of Economics and Statistics* 51 (May): 111–25.

Irwin, Douglas A. 2014. The Nixon Shock after Forty Years: The Import Surcharge Revisited. *World Trade Review* 12 (January): 29–56.

James, Harold. 1996. *International Monetary Cooperation since Bretton Woods*. Oxford: Oxford University Press.

Kindleberger, Charles P. 1965. *Balance-of-Payments Deficits and the International Market for Liquidity*. Princeton Essays in International Finance 46 (May). Princeton, NJ: International Finance Section, Princeton University.

Kydland, Finn E., and Edward C. Prescott. 1977. Rules Rather than Discretion: The Inconsistency of Optimal Plans. *Journal of Political Economy* 85 (June): 473–92.

Krugman, Paul R. 1989. Differences in Income Elasticities and Trends in Real Exchange Rates. *European Economic Review* 33 (May): 1031–46.

Matsui, Hitoshi. 2016. International Money and Keynes: What Should We Learn from Him for a Sound Key Currency? *Journal of Tokyo International University: Economic Research* 1: 1–18.

Mundell, Robert A. 1971. *The Dollar and the Policy Mix: 1971*. Princeton Essays in International Finance 85 (May). Princeton, NJ: International Finance Section, Princeton University.

Nordhaus, William D. 1972. The Worldwide Wage Explosion. *Brookings Papers on Economic Activity* 3, no. 2: 431–66.

Obstfeld, Maurice. 2014. The International Monetary System: Living with Asymmetry. In *Globalization in an Age of Crisis: Multilateral Economic Cooperation in the Twenty-First Century*, ed. Robert C. Feenstra and Alan M. Taylor, 301–36. Chicago: University of Chicago Press.

Obstfeld, Maurice. 2020. Harry Johnson's "Case for Flexible Exchange Rates"—50 Years Later. *The Manchester School* 88 (September): 86–113.

Obstfeld, Maurice, and Alan M. Taylor. 2017. International Monetary Relations: Taking Finance Seriously. *Journal of Economic Perspectives* 31 (Summer): 3–28.

Portes, Richard. 2012. A Reassessment of the Triffin Dilemma. In *In Search of a New World Monetary Order: Proceedings of a Conference to Celebrate the 100th Anniversary of Robert Triffin*, ed. Jean-Claude Koeune and Alexandre Lamfalussy, 195–99. International Financial Relations no. 5. Brussels: Peter Lang.

Reinhart, Carmen M., and Kenneth S. Rogoff. 2009. *This Time Is Different: Eight Centuries of Financial Folly*. Princeton, NJ: Princeton University Press.

Rey, Hélène. 2013. Dilemma not Trilemma: The Global Financial Cycle and Monetary Policy Independence. In *Global Dimensions of Unconventional Monetary Policy*. Jackson Hole Symposium Proceedings. Kansas City, MO: Federal Reserve Bank of Kansas City.

Silber, William L. 2012. *Volcker: The Triumph of Persistence*. London: Bloomsbury Press.

Triffin, Robert. 1978. *Gold and the Dollar Crisis: Yesterday and Tomorrow*. Princeton Essays in International Finance 132 (December). Princeton, NJ: International Finance Section, Princeton University.

Yeager, Leland B. 1976. *International Monetary Relations: Theory, History, and Policy*, 2nd ed. New York: Harper & Row.

I

HISTORICAL PERSPECTIVE ON 1973 AND ITS LEGACY

2

From There to Here: 1973 Expectations and 2023 Reality

EDWIN M. TRUMAN

Fifty years ago, the authorities of the advanced economies met in Paris. They had run out of options for sustaining the Bretton Woods exchange rate regime and reluctantly agreed to allow their exchange rates to float against each other. They did not know what to expect from their decision.

An eclectic mixture of exchange rate regimes emerged. At least initially, no exchange rates were freely floating without intervention, and most were heavily managed. Even for currencies with regimes at the more flexible end of the spectrum, floating did not measure up to the promises of enthusiasts such as Milton Friedman (1953) and Harry Johnson (1969), who envisioned that floating rates would liberate a country's monetary and fiscal policies to focus on full employment and price stability. They postulated that associated expectations of stable economic and financial fundamentals would anchor exchange rates, produce stabilizing speculation, and eliminate external economic and financial crises.[1]

The Paris decisions marked the end of the exchange rate regime agreed to at Bretton Woods, New Hampshire, in July 1944. The meeting in Paris was

---

1. See Obstfeld (2020) for an analysis of Johnson's arguments.

Edwin M. Truman is research fellow at the Mossavar-Rahmani Center for Business and Government at the Harvard Kennedy School. He was senior fellow and nonresident senior fellow at the Peterson Institute for International Economics. He benefited from comments on earlier drafts, insights, and assistance from Bill Allen, Ralph Bryant, William Cline, Toni Gravelle, Christine Harper, Dale Henderson, George Henry, Douglas Irwin, Karen Johnson, John Murray, Maurice Obstfeld, Larry Promisel, Fred Ruckdeschel, Jeffrey Shafer, Ralph Smith, Aya Taketani, Ryland Thomas, and David Vines. See Truman (forthcoming) for an extended treatment of the evolution of the global exchange rate regime. He is solely responsible for the views expressed.

preceded by multiple efforts dating back to the early 1960s to preserve that regime. The final phase dates from President Richard M. Nixon's announcement on August 15, 1971, suspending purchases and sales of gold by the US Treasury at $35 an ounce with foreign officials. The announcement was followed by the December 1971 Smithsonian Agreement, which reset par values among the major currencies. The par-value regime crumbled in Paris on March 16, 1973.

Subsequently, increases in petroleum prices, inflation, recession, and expanding global payment imbalances buffeted the global economy and financial system, as the authorities debated how to reform the international monetary system. In 1978, floating exchange rates were permanently legalized, in an amendment to the Articles of Agreement of the International Monetary Fund (IMF). Some countries yearned for a return to fixed rates, and the amendment provided for the readoption of a "widespread system of stable but adjustable par values" by an 85 percent majority vote.

The Paris surrender did not deliver as promised by advocates of floating rates. Meanwhile, national exchange rate choices have evolved, along with the international monetary system of which they are an integral part.

Expectations in 1973

The US dollar and the international adjustment process were the principal joint focus of policymakers in 1973, as they had been for years. The dollar was front and center, because the Bretton Woods exchange rate system was built on currencies' par values with the dollar, whose par value was expressed in gold at the fixed price of $35 per ounce.

The focus on the international adjustment process reflected two features of that process and its operation. First, in the 1960s the United States recorded only small trade and current account surpluses. They were insufficient to offset net private capital outflows. The result was a buildup of foreign official claims on the United States and the US gold stock. The United States saw a substantially weaker dollar as the path to current account surpluses that would be large enough to offset the capital outflow. Depreciation of the dollar tends to shrink the US current account deficit, albeit with a lag, and vice versa. Figure 2.1 shows the link between the dollar's broad real value and the US current account position between 1971 and 2022.[2]

---

2. The broad real value of the dollar is the average value of the dollar's exchange rate with a broad set of other countries' currencies adjusted by changes in the price levels in those countries relative to the US price level.

Figure 2.1

US current account as percent of GDP and index of the broad real dollar, 1971–2022

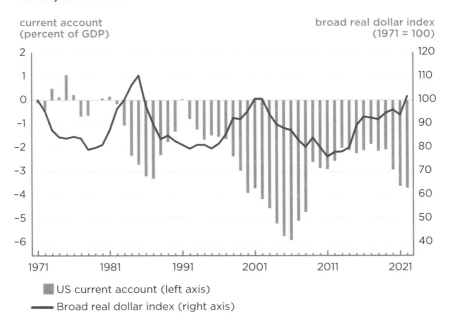

current account
(percent of GDP)

broad real dollar index
(1971 = 100)

██ US current account (left axis)
▬▬ Broad real dollar index (right axis)

Sources: Bureau of Economic Analysis, Federal Reserve Board.

Second, policymakers in the other advanced economies were reluctant to see their currencies appreciate, because increased imports and reduced exports meant lower economic growth unless other policies boosted domestic demand.

The Road to Paris

Within the widened margins of exchange rate fluctuation agreed to in the Smithsonian Agreement in December 1971, the Europeans established a "snake," with narrower margins. They were motivated in part by their participation in the European economic integration project and the vision of Economic and Monetary Union (EMU) that had been laid out in the 1970 Werner Report.[3] In June 1972, the United Kingdom withdrew from the arrangement and floated the pound, putting upward pressure on the snake relative to the dollar. To help calm markets, in July 1972 the Federal Reserve, with Treasury approval, reactivated its swap network with other

---

3. The move to floating exchange rates complicated the existing mechanisms of European economic integration and contributed to slow progress toward EMU.

central banks to obtain foreign currencies and resumed exchange market intervention operations in support of the dollar.

By early 1973, analysts at the Treasury and the Federal Reserve concluded that the Smithsonian Agreement exchange rates would not produce the improvement in the US current account position necessary to allow the United States to restore the dollar's gold convertibility. On the basis of these results, Charles Siegman and I wrote an exchange of memoranda to Ralph Bryant, director of the Division of International Finance at the Federal Reserve Board, on the merits of accepting a temporary float of the major currencies (Siegman) versus another realignment of currency values (Truman).

Meanwhile, Treasury Undersecretary Paul Volcker was sent around the world to prod other governments to adopt one of the two options. The United States wanted a significant further devaluation of the dollar and did not have a view about how other countries should accommodate the US objective. Volcker negotiated a second dollar devaluation of 10 percent against gold, with the implicit gold parities of the other major currencies unchanged. The Japanese yen, Swiss franc, Italian lira, British pound, and Canadian dollar continued to float.

The Paris Meetings of 1973

The calm restored to foreign exchange markets after the dollar's second devaluation was short-lived. European central banks found themselves buying truckloads of dollars to defend the new exchange rates. On March 1, 1973, European and Japanese exchange markets were closed to official operations. On March 9, the G10 ministers and governors met in Paris. Their communiqué stated that the crisis was caused by speculative movements of funds, that the existing parities and central rates met economic requirements, and that the authorities would meet again in a week (de Vries 1985).

A week later, confidence that a fixed exchange rate regime could be sustained at that time had evaporated. European ministers and governors concluded that floating was the least-bad option. On March 15, 1973, a subgroup of European countries announced that their currencies would float but they would float together. The Italian lira and pound continued to float separately.[4] The next day, the larger group

> agreed in principle that official intervention in exchange markets may be useful at appropriate times to facilitate the maintenance of orderly conditions, keeping in mind also the desirability of encouraging reflows of specula-

---

4. The Canadian dollar and Japanese yen also continued to float.

tive movements of funds. Each nation stated that it will be prepared to intervene at its initiative in its own market, when necessary and desirable, acting in a flexible manner in the light of market conditions and in close consultation with the authorities of the nation whose currency may be bought or sold.[5]

The statement did not celebrate the birth of a new exchange rate regime or a transformation of the international monetary system. It merely signaled a willingness to accept the reality that fixed rates could not be defended at that time. The statement also emphasized historical continuity and the crucial importance of cooperation.

Ministers and governors reaffirmed their attachment to the basic principles that had governed international economic relations since World War II: to facilitate the greatest possible freedom for international trade and investment and to avoid competitive depreciations of exchange rates. They stated their determination to continue to use the existing organizations of international economic cooperation to maintain these principles for the benefit of all their members.[6]

Eleven days later, the Committee on Reform of the International Monetary System and Related Issues, the Committee of Twenty (C20), met in Washington. Its communiqué contained a formulation for the reformed exchange rate regime that was drafted by Volcker. The formulation encapsulated the current reality and pointed to the future while preserving a link to the past:

> Members of the Committee recognized that exchange rates must be a matter for international concern and consultation and that in the reformed system the exchange rate regime should remain based on stable but adjustable par values. It was also recognized that floating rates could provide a useful technique in particular situations. There was also general agreement on the need for exchange market stability and the importance of Fund surveillance of exchange rate policies.[7]

What explains the difference between the Paris announcement and the language in the C20 communiqué? The C20 included representatives of developing economies. Floating rates among the currencies of the advanced economies would complicate their policymaking. A developing economy could no longer manage its own currency with confidence that a change in its peg to another currency, in almost all cases the dollar, would produce

---

5. Federal Reserve Board of Governors, Memorandum of Discussion, March 19–20, 1973.

6. Ibid.

7. See IMF (1974, 215).

an effective appreciation or depreciation. Their currencies were pegged to a currency that was floating and, consequently, were floating as well. The par value system was simpler (Cline 1976).

The C20 also agreed "on the need for exchange market stability and the importance of Fund surveillance of exchange rate policies." The principal concern was the potential reemergence of 1930s-style exchange rate unilateralism with large abrupt changes in exchange rates. Short of that outcome, exchange rate flexibility might be abused by countries seeking to strengthen their competitive positions. To guard against that outcome, the IMF promulgated a set of "guidelines for the management of floating exchange rates during the present period of widespread floating." They called for intervention to maintain orderly markets and discouraged aggressive intervention to accumulate reserves when a country's effective rate was rising or reduce reserves when the rate was falling (leaning with the wind). Despite these good intentions, countries generally did what they wanted to do.

Results of the Paris Agreements

The Paris agreements did not produce a regime of freely floating exchange rates; all exchange rates were managed to some degree. The G10 countries consulted daily on their foreign exchange operations. Transparency was not 100 percent, but there was no intervention at cross purposes (the United States selling dollars while Germany was buying them).

In March 1973, views on the future of the exchange rate regime were diverse. For decades, many academics and a few policymakers had advocated greater exchange rate flexibility. Advocates of floating argued that allowing the market to determine exchange rates would limit, if not eliminate, current account disequilibria and free monetary and fiscal policies to focus exclusively on the domestic economy.

A few of my Federal Reserve colleagues welcomed the move toward floating rates. But they also did not know what to expect from the Paris decisions other than an uncertain immediate future surrounded by more questions than answers. Would countries restore the par-value system? Could agreement be reached on a par-value system with greater flexibility of exchange rates, facilitating a less asymmetric external adjustment process, as the United States had proposed in September 1972? What did floating imply for countries' other policies? We at the Fed were floundering and confused.

The views of the officials gathered in Paris ranged from apprehension to grudging acceptance of floating at least temporarily. Many saw floating rates as a nonsystem. In their view, the Bretton Woods monetary system was grounded in the discipline of fixed or rarely adjusted par values. They feared a return to the undisciplined monetary chaos of the interwar period. They accepted the decisions of March 1973 because they saw no viable alternative, but they were skeptical that floating would improve the external adjustment process.

The nonsystem view is associated with the late John Williamson (1977) as well as with Max Corden (1983). But Williamson's use of the term *nonsystem* is misunderstood (Truman 2012). He wrote that the C20 reform negotiations had not produced a complete international monetary system in which competitive payments policies would be avoided, methods of payments adjustment would be orderly, and the provision of reserves would be controlled. On this basis, the Bretton Woods system was also a nonsystem, because it also lacked those elements. For Williamson and Corden, the then-prospective amendment of the IMF Articles had not reformed the system.

For some, the essence of the Bretton Woods system was the discipline that fixed, or rarely adjusted, par values exerted over economic policies. Those of us who had the privilege of working with Paul Volcker know that his views on almost all subjects were nuanced. He has been cited on both sides of the decision to adopt floating rates. For example, Jeffrey Garten (2021) reports Volcker's comment on the Camp David decision to close the gold window and to float the dollar that money needs an anchor; an exchange rate tied to gold served that purpose and imparted discipline on national policymakers. My impression is that in retrospect, Volcker considered the acceptance of his proposal to close the US gold window, thereby delinking the foreign exchange regime from gold, to have been his most memorable and impactful contribution to the international monetary system. In his autobiography (Volcker and Harper 2018, 71), he wrote the following about the Camp David meeting: "The day I had long anticipated, but also long feared, was about to be here. The structure of the international monetary system that I had spent years defending would be torn apart."

Five years after the Paris meeting, Volcker (1978, 9) balanced his regret over the abandonment of the par-value system and its disciplines with realism, writing, "I do not depart from the strong consensus that we have, on a worldwide scale, no other practical choice than to work within the broad framework of a floating rate system—and that system offers the most promising framework for 'managing integration' as far ahead as we now can see."

The exchange rate regime agreed to at Bretton Woods was motivated by the dominant official interpretation of the role of exchange rate flexibility in contributing to the severity of the Great Depression. But the Bretton

Woods exchange rate system never fully functioned as it was intended to. Moreover, two key elements of the international monetary system agreed to at Bretton Woods—a commitment to monetary cooperation and the recognition that countries' exchange rate policies are of mutual concern—were preserved in Paris and subsequently.

The 2023 Reality

The four major reserve currencies now float freely, with very infrequent market intervention.[8] The United States has not intervened to support or weaken the dollar since August 1995.[9] The exchange market operations of Germany, the principal European country in the Exchange Rate Mechanism (ERM), focused primarily on the mark-dollar rate and ended at the same point. The United Kingdom adopted a policy of only rare intervention after it left the ERM in 1992 and had covered its foreign exchange debts. Japan joined the group of de facto free floaters in 2004.[10]

In its classification of exchange rate regimes in 2021, the IMF (2022) identified 32 currencies that float freely.[11] With a few exceptions, they are currencies of advanced economies; managed floating remains the policy of most other countries. Movements of a major currency against the currencies of other countries may stir controversy. In 2010, for example, Brazil's finance minister, Guido Mantega, branded the Federal Reserve's policy of quantitative easing, which tended to weaken the dollar, as a "currency war" against other countries' currencies.

Mantega was right, up to a point. Exchange market intervention is only one factor affecting exchange rates; they may be affected by other policies as well. The distinction is between exchange rate movements as a by-product of other policies on the one hand and policies directed at moving the exchange rate on the other. In early 2013, in response to concerns about the exchange rate orientation of Japan's newly elected prime minister, Shinzo Abe, the G7 ministers and governors sought to constrain his government, declaring that "our fiscal and monetary policies have been and will remain

---

8. The share of the fourth currency, the pound sterling, in countries' foreign exchange reserves was 4.95 percent as of 2022Q4. The share of the fifth, China's renminbi, was a distant 2.69 percent, barely more than the Canadian dollar's 2.38 percent. See IMF's Currency Composition of Official Foreign Exchange Reserves (COFER) database, https://data.imf.org/?sk=E6A5F467-C14B-4AA8-9F6D-5A09EC4E62A4.

9. The three one-day intervention operations during the past 28 years were to support or weaken other currencies.

10. Canada, once a heavy intervener, adopted a nonintervention policy in 1998.

11. The IMF classification is only one product of the cottage industry of de facto and de jure classifications of countries' currency arrangements, but it is broadly representative.

oriented toward meeting our respective domestic objectives using domestic instruments, and that we will not target exchange rates." They added the usual boiler plate: "We will continue to consult closely on exchange markets and cooperate as appropriate."[12]

A few days later, the G20 ministers and governors stated that they would "refrain from competitive devaluation. We will not target our exchange rates for competitive purposes, we will resist all forms of protectionism and keep our markets open."[13] Talk is cheap, but this talk pointed toward a reinforced consensus on exchange rate policies.

Aggregate intervention in the form of purchases of foreign currencies appears to have tailed off in recent years. From the third quarter of 2018 to the fourth quarter of 2022, total foreign exchange holdings increased only 4.9 percent.[14] These data are distorted by the net appreciation of the US dollar over this period.[15] However, the increase in foreign exchange holdings has barely kept pace with the accumulation of interest on holdings.[16]

Exchange market intervention remains an important policy tool for many countries. Over the past 50 years, exchange rate crises were common and not confined to emerging market and developing economies. Some crises were linked to domestic banking, inflation, or external debt crises; some were exacerbated by movements in the exchange rates of the advanced economies. But it is difficult to argue that the global exchange rate regime—in contrast to a country's own exchange rate and other policies—was responsible for exchange rate crises, trade conflicts, unstable capital flows, or financial crises.

The quasi-floating exchange rate regime has not delivered the promises of some advocates that exchange rate crises would not be possible. Exchange rate movements are dominated by capital flows, which are affected by changing, and not always correct, expectations of the evolution

---

12. "Statement by G-7 Finance Ministers and Central Bank Governors," February 12, 2013, http://www.g7.utoronto.ca/finance/fm130212.htm.

13. "Communiqué of Meeting of G-20 Finance Ministers and Central Bank Governors," February 16, 2013, http://www.g20.utoronto.ca/2013/2013-0216-finance.html.

14. The IMF data (see footnote 8) before 2018Q3 are not comparable with data after that date because the holdings of the People's Bank of China were not fully integrated into the data before then.

15. Over the four-plus years, the dollar appreciated 8.3 percent against the currencies of other advanced economies, using the Federal Reserve Board staff's index. See Summary Measures of the Foreign Exchange Value of the Dollar, https://www.federalreserve.gov/releases/h10/summary/default.htm.

16. See footnote 8. Some analysts treat interest accumulation as intervention. Some regard foreign investment by sovereign wealth funds and government pension funds as intervention.

of economic fundamentals. Exchange rates are not anchored by prospects for trade balances, and trade balances adjust slowly to changes in exchange rates. Even under the assumption of rational expectations, exchange rates overshoot, as Rudi Dornbusch showed (Dornbusch 1976), and expectations are not always rational. Capital flows contributed importantly to the collapse of the Bretton Woods exchange rate system, and some see them as the Achilles heel of the global financial system today.

The relative calm for the major currencies over the past 25 years may not persist. The global adjustment process and the chronic US current account deficit dominated international policy concerns in Paris 50 years ago and for the following two decades. In recent years, concerns about global external imbalances have receded. I would not, however, exclude the possibility that they will reemerge.

Conclusion

The Paris surrender to floating rates did not mark the end of the Bretton Woods monetary system. It marked an inflection in the international monetary cooperation that lies at the core of the system constructed at the end of World War II. The fixed exchange rate regime agreed to at Bretton Woods was swept away, replaced primarily by managed floating. But the core Bretton Woods principles of monetary cooperation and the notion that exchange rate policies are a matter of mutual concern still undergird the international monetary system.

The economic context of the Paris meetings 50 years ago was persistent US current account deficits, an asymmetric global adjustment process, and unsustainable substantial external imbalances. Don't bet that those conditions will not return.

References

Cline, William R. 1976. *International Monetary Reform and the Developing Countries.* Washington: Brookings Institution.

Corden, W. Max. 1983. The Logic of the International Monetary Non-system. In *Reflection on a Troubled World Economy: Essays in Honor of Herbert Giersch,* ed. Fritz Machlup, Gerhard Fels, and Hubertus Müller-Groeling. London: Palgrave Macmillan for Trade Policy Research Centre.

de Vries, Margaret Garritsen. 1985. *The International Monetary Fund 1972–1978: Cooperation on Trial.* Washington: International Monetary Fund.

Dornbusch, Rudiger. 1976. Expectations and Exchange Rate Dynamics. *Journal of Political Economy* 84: 1161–76.

Friedman, Milton. 1953. The Case for Flexible Exchange Rates. In *Essays in Positive Economics.* Chicago: University of Chicago Press.

Garten, Jeffrey E. 2021. *Three Days at Camp David: How a Secret Meeting in 1971 Transformed the Global Economy*. New York: HarperCollins.

IMF (International Monetary Fund). 1974. *International Monetary Reform: Documents of the Committee of Twenty*. Washington.

IMF (International Monetary Fund). 2022. *Annual Report on Exchange Arrangements and Exchange Restrictions*. Washington.

Johnson, Harry G. 1969. The Case for Flexible Exchange Rates. *Review*, Federal Reserve Bank of St. Louis.

Obstfeld, Maurice. 2020. *Harry Johnson's "Case for Flexible Exchange Rates"—50 Years Later*. PIIE Working Paper 20-12. Washington: Peterson Institute for International Economics. Available at https://www.piie.com/publications/working-papers/harry-johnsons-case-flexible-exchange-rates-50-years-later.

Truman, Edwin M. 2012. The International Monetary System or "Nonsystem"? In *Global Economics in Extraordinary Times: Essays in Honor of John Williamson*, ed. C. Fred Bergsten and C. Randall Henning. Washington: Peterson Institute for International Economics. Available at https://www.piie.com/bookstore/global-economics-extraordinary-times-essays-honor-john-williamson.

Truman, Edwin M. Forthcoming. *International Economic Cooperation Will Survive: An American Perspective*.

Volcker, Paul A. 1978. The Political Economy of the Dollar. The Fred Hirsch Lecture, Warwick University, November 9. *FRBNY Quarterly Review* (Winter): 1–12.

Volcker, Paul A., and Christine Harper. 2018. *Keeping at It: The Quest for Sound Money and Good Government*. New York: PublicAffairs.

Williamson, John. 1977. *The Failure of World Monetary Reform, 1971-1974*. New York: New York University Press.

3

The Greatest of All International Monetary Reforms

C. FRED BERGSTEN

Expectations in 1973

In the summer of 1972, midway through the baseline period being considered in this volume, I attended the Summer Olympics in Munich, where Palestinian terrorists killed 11 Israeli athletes. When I arrived at the airport to book my rescheduled flight home, I learned that my ticketing period had expired and that I therefore owed an extra fee.

My dollars were not accepted; I had to find an alternative way to pay. The premier US airline of the day (Pan American) treated as inconvertible the world's dominant currency (the dollar) in the financial capital (Frankfurt) of the world's second key currency (the Deutsch mark). The international monetary system was obviously in bad shape.

Already a decade earlier, President John F. Kennedy had viewed threats to the dollar as second only to nuclear war on his worry list (Sorensen 1965). Sterling, gold, and dollar crises necessitated weekend rescue operations throughout that decade. The United States adopted a series of ever-tighter restraints on capital outflows, employed a "gold budget" to limit governmental offshore expenditures, seriously contemplated a tax on foreign travel by American tourists, and experienced its first serious bout of trade protectionism since World War II.

C. Fred Bergsten is nonresident senior fellow and director emeritus at the Peterson Institute for International Economics, of which he was founding director from its creation in 1981 through 2012. He was previously Assistant Secretary of the Treasury for International Affairs (1977–81) and Assistant for International Economic Affairs to the National Security Council (1969–71).

The minimum hope and expectation that surrounded the monetary upheavals of 1971–73 was a termination of this crisis-prone and rapidly eroding international economic order. Intellectual agreement had been reached on the three problems that needed to be remedied: a better adjustment process to prevent and correct payments imbalances, creation of adequate liquidity to finance a growing level of international transactions, and confidence that the ensuing system would be stable and sustainable over time.

There was no consensus, however, on what should replace the failing regime. Expectations for constructive reform were thus very low. This pessimism was greatly exacerbated when the reforms, rather than being negotiated as most observers had envisaged, were forced by the "Nixon shocks" of August 1971, which shattered the basic precepts of both the international monetary system (by ending dollar convertibility into gold for foreign monetary authorities) and the global trading regime (by imposing an across-the-board surcharge on most US imports) (Garten 2021).

Most officials at the time wanted, and probably expected, a return to fixed exchange rates (adjustable pegs) à la Bretton Woods; in fact, they negotiated two discrete realignments among the major currencies in late 1971 and early 1973. Most (though not all) academics wanted greater flexibility of exchange rates and a new international reserve asset; facing reality, they would have settled for limited flexibility via wider bands and/or crawling pegs. Governments could not agree on anything, however, and the Committee of Twenty, created at the International Monetary Fund (IMF) in an effort to construct a new system after the upheavals had occurred, was a total failure.[1]

The absence of clear expectations was epitomized by a six-hour meeting that I, along with three other outsiders, attended at the Treasury Department at the request of Secretary John Connally, the chief architect of the Nixon shocks, and his entire top Treasury team (including Undersecretary Paul Volcker) four days after their announcement. Connally, who ran the meeting throughout, began by saying: "You know what we have done. What do we do next?" It was a genuine question; they did not know, and they never did develop a strategy beyond negotiating two modest dollar devaluations (about 10 percent each) that helped ensure Nixon's reelection. Nixon and Connally soon became distracted by other developments (to put it mildly) and left the scene, and the international monetary system was left to evolve on its own. Volcker confirmed in retrospect that the officials

---

1. This assessment of expectations is drawn from two books I coedited or wrote at about that time (Bergsten et al. 1970 and Bergsten 1975).

(including himself), far from leading the reform process, eventually gave up and capitulated to the market pressure to let exchange rates float indefinitely (Volcker and Harper 2018).

The Successes

The upheavals and chaos of 50 years ago led to three major successes. First, the move to flexible exchange rates turned out to be the most sweeping and most important international monetary reform of all time. Floating rates have not been perfect. The dollar crashed in the late 1970s and required an international bailout. Large US current account imbalances recurred in the first half of the 1980s (requiring the Plaza Agreement) and hit record levels in the middle 2000s (with China running unprecedented surpluses). Markets periodically made major mistakes, as with the massive overvaluation of the "Reagan dollar." So did governments, as they did with China's intervention of almost $4 trillion to sharply limit appreciation of the renminbi.

But adjustment occurred, mainly via exchange rate changes (except within the eurozone). The successful correction of imbalances after the Plaza Agreement, with its 50 percent appreciations of the yen and Deutsche mark, represented "a textbook adjustment" (Krugman 1991). The Chinese surplus of 10 percent of GDP disappeared over a decade thanks to a 40 percent appreciation of the renminbi. These adjustments took time and imposed substantial costs in the meanwhile, and they often required governmental involvement to promote the needed currency movement. But they took place—and much greater economic costs would undoubtedly have ensued if the countries involved had tried to maintain fixed rates in the face of the huge shocks from their underlying policies (as China did for a while).

Second, international liquidity has been wholly adequate to finance even the explosion of trade and investment that has taken place during these decades of rapid globalization. A wide range of countries have amassed foreign exchange reserves of unprecedented magnitudes, led by China's $3 trillion–$4 trillion and including a number of other emerging-market economies, such as Brazil and India. The International Monetary Fund (IMF) has still stepped in with occasional programs (mainly for poorer countries), and the Federal Reserve has provided dollar liquidity to a few counterparts during crisis periods, but there have been no systemic financial shortages. These reserve buildups occurred during the decades of the Great Moderation, so there was no inflationary impact, as some had feared.

Third, confidence in the international monetary system was largely restored. There were no more episodes of inconvertibility like the one I experienced at the Frankfurt airport in 1972. Indeed, the foreign exchange markets have been islands of stability even during the most unsettled periods for the world economy, including the Asian financial crisis of 1997–98, the global financial crisis (centered on the United States and then Europe) in 2007–09, and the COVID crisis. The de facto reforms of the past half century have largely, if not totally, resolved the problems that caused the previous system to collapse.

The Surprises

At the same time, two major surprises took place. Most noteworthy is the continued supremacy of the dollar. Most observers (including me) thought that the dollar's international role would decline substantially as a result of the turmoil of that period, centered on the dollar itself. It is true that the dollar's market share has declined modestly, as discussed in several of the other chapters in this volume. There continues to be considerable grumbling about the exorbitant privilege that it supposedly provides for the United States, especially with its "weaponization" as a sanctions tool in recent years.

But the absolute level of dollar holdings has soared. The dollar still accounts for the bulk of global financial transactions on all relevant metrics. Its declines, on all metrics, have been very slow and very modest, even during the (frequent) periods of poor US economic performance and/or erratic policies.

There is still no viable alternative to the dollar. Most of its "decline" has been mirrored by increased roles for minor currencies, such as the Canadian dollar and the Australian dollar, which could never replace it to any significant degree. The dollar's role may still fall, but inertia is very powerful in global financial matters, and the case for a single asset that is widely used remains persuasive. The dollar is still going strong 50 years after the upheavals that many thought would dethrone it.

The second, related, surprise is the very limited progress toward establishing a truly international currency to rival or complement (take your choice!) the dollar. The Special Drawing Rights (SDRs) at the IMF were created for that purpose. They recently experienced a bit of a revival, but they have become neither a market participant nor a major component of international reserves. Indeed, the Federal Reserve, rather than the IMF via the SDR, remains the lender of last resort via the dollar in most crisis situations.

The euro is a supranational money and almost immediately succeeded its legacy components as the world's second leading currency. It has not evolved beyond that level, however, though completion of its economic and monetary union could alter that position. But the prospects for a truly global money still seem remote.

A Final Story

When Peter G. Peterson, the namesake of the Peterson Institute for International Economics, was considering President Richard M. Nixon's offer to come to the White House as assistant to the president for international economic policy—replacing me functionally, but with a much grander rank and title—he consulted Milton Friedman, his former professor at the University of Chicago. Milton's advice was typically crisp: "With flexible exchange rates, the job will be unnecessary. Without them, the job will be impossible. Do not take it."

Peterson of course took the job, and Friedman's enthusiasm for flexible rates was typically hyperbolic. But his counsel to move to flexible exchange rates was largely correct. Its realization is the lasting contribution of the events of 1973 to the world of 2023 and beyond.

References

Bergsten, C. Fred. 1975. *The Dilemmas of the Dollar: The Economics and Politics of United States International Monetary Policy*. New York: New York University Press.

Bergsten, C. Fred, George N. Halm, Fritz Machlup, and Robert V. Roosa. 1970. *Approaches to Greater Flexibility of Exchange Rates: The Burgenstock Papers*. Princeton, NJ: Princeton University Press.

Garten, Jeffrey E. 2021. *Three Days at Camp David: How a Secret Meeting in 1971 Transformed the World Economy*. New York: HarperCollins.

Krugman, Paul R. 1991. *Has the Adjustment Process Worked?* Washington: Institute for International Economics.

Sorensen, Theodore C. 1965. *Kennedy*. New York: Harper and Row.

Volcker, Paul A., and Christine Harper. 2018. *Keeping at It: The Quest for Sound Money and Good Government*. New York: PublicAffairs.

4

The Source of Monetary Instability, 1980–2020

ROBERT Z. ALIBER

Monetary instability between 1980 and 2020 was greater than in any previous comparable period. During this period, more than 70 countries experienced a banking crisis, and most of them experienced a currency crisis at the same time. Between 1980 and 1990, the United States morphed from the world's largest creditor country to the world's largest debtor, even though the US Treasury did not borrow in a foreign currency and few American firms borrowed in a foreign currency to get the money to finance payments in the United States. Purchases of US dollar securities by foreigners—central banks, sovereign wealth funds, insurance companies, mutual funds, households, and individuals—led to a secular increase in the price of the US dollar, an increasingly large US trade deficit, and an increase in the ratio of US net international indebtedness to US GDP to nearly 100 percent. The increase in foreign purchases of US dollar-denominated securities led to spikes in the prices of US real estate and US stocks. The global financial crisis of 2008 was triggered by the collapse of US real estate prices, which had more than doubled as a result of a surge in foreign purchases of US dollar-denominated securities. The increasingly large US trade deficit has eroded the United States' hegemonic position, compromising its initiatives to reduce barriers to international trade.

Robert Z. Aliber joined the faculty of the Graduate School of Business of the University of Chicago in 1965; he left the classroom in 2004. He has been a visiting faculty member at the Amos Tuck School of Business at Dartmouth College, Williams College, Brandeis University, and the London Graduate School of Business Studies.

This chapter examines the source of monetary instability and the costs of the US policy of benign neglect toward foreign purchases of US dollar-denominated securities on US economic welfare. Is US economic well-being enhanced more by a flexible exchange rate arrangement or by reliance on an adjustable parity arrangement like the one embedded in the Articles of Agreement of the International Monetary Fund? A flexible exchange rate arrangement has always been the default alternative; the price of a country's currency will be flexible unless its central bank intervenes to limit the changes in the price of its currency.

The move to flexible rates, in the early 1970s, was inevitable as a temporary arrangement because of the surge in the US inflation rate in the late 1960s and efforts by Germany and a few other countries to insulate their economies from increases in the US price level. The move to a flexible exchange rate as a permanent feature of the global economy was facilitated by a set of articles and books by Milton Friedman (1953), Gottfried Harbeler, Harry Johnson (1988 [1969]), and Egon Sohmen (1969), who presented a set of claims about the advantages of allowing market forces to set the price of each country's currency. A major claim was that changes in the price of each country's currency would track the difference between its inflation rate and rates in its trading partners. Another was that flexible exchange rates would help insulate countries from shocks in their trading partners (McCulloch 1985, MacDonald 1988).

There are now 50 years of data on cross-border investment flows and changes in both the price of the US dollar and the prices of the currencies of its trading partners. They provide no empirical support for any of the claims of proponents of flexible exchange rates. The difference between the changes in the market prices of currencies and the price level–adjusted prices have been very large: The price of the US dollar increased by 50 percent in the first half of the 1980s (Mussa 1986). There have been more than 70 banking crises, most of them associated with a currency crisis, and each has followed from the variability in cross-border investment inflows, which initially led to a spike in asset prices as an integral part of the balance of payments adjustment process. The single most important US monetary development in the last 80 years was the implosion of the US financial system in 2008, which followed a massive increase in foreign purchases of US dollar securities.

This chapter is organized as follows: The first section reviews the central issues in the debate between proponents and critics of flexible exchange rates. It involves the impact of the transactions of money market traders on the market price of a country's currency relative to the real price—the price consistent with the long-term equilibrium in the global goods market. One of the implicit assumptions in the case for flexible exchange rates is that the only participants in the market for currencies are goods market traders;

proponents of flexible rates did not accept the view that the transactions of money market traders would have a significant impact on the market price of a country's currency.

The second section develops the view that the case for flexible exchange rates is intellectually bankrupt because the focus of each central bank on its domestic employment and price level objectives means that the difference between domestic and foreign interest rates and the anticipated change in the price of each country's currency would be larger and more variable if currencies were not anchored to parities. Money market traders would increase their purchases of foreign securities in anticipation of profits from the increase in their price.

The third section reviews the balance of payments adjustment process in response to changes in money market traders' purchases of foreign securities. The argument is that increases in asset prices are induced as part of the balance of payments adjustment process. These prices decline when the inflows slow.

The fourth section evaluates the benefits and costs of the US policy of benign neglect toward foreign purchases of US dollar-denominated securities and the price of the US dollar. It examines (a) whether the flexible exchange rate arrangement would have led to an increase in US economic welfare if the price of the US dollar had been determined solely by market forces (that is, without the purchase of US dollar securities by foreign central banks) and (b) how foreign central banks' purchases of US dollar-denominated securities have affected the results of the cost-benefit comparison.

The Debate over Flexible Exchange Rates

Monetary systems evolve as importers and exporters and savers and borrowers search for efficiency and stability in payments, both within and between countries. The United States and most of its large trading partners severed the parities of their currencies in terms of gold at the onset of World War I. Inflation rates in the United States and other belligerent countries differed sharply during and after the war.

Ragnar Nurkse reviewed changes in cross-border investment flows and the prices of currencies in the 1920s and the 1930s in his 1944 monograph *The International Currency Experience*. In it, he concluded that cross-border investment flows had been "disequilibrating," that goods market traders had encountered greater uncertainty about the prices of currencies than when they were not attached to parities and goods market traders had encountered higher costs of hedging their foreign exchange exposures than when they were attached to parities (see also Nurkse 1945).

In the first half of the 1940s, the United States and the United Kingdom took the initiative to develop a treaty-based arrangement that would enhance economic openness and financial stability (Solomon 1983). One of the motives for the US initiative was to limit free-riding by smaller countries, which might reduce the prices of their currencies to gain a competitive advantage for their products in foreign markets.

The Articles of Agreement of the International Monetary Fund required that each member state declare a parity for its currency and limit changes in the price of its currency to a modest band around it. Member countries also committed to seek the approval of the Fund if they changed their parity by more than 10 percent.

The United States first developed what proved to be a persistent US payments deficit at the end of 1949, even though it had a trade surplus, which was smaller than its capital account deficit. Initiatives to reduce this deficit by exchange controls were not effective. Proponents of flexible exchange rates promised that the US payments deficit would disappear if the US dollar and other currencies were no longer anchored to parities.

One of the major normative objectives of the proponents of flexible exchange rates was central bank monetary independence. Once the commitment to a parity was discarded, each central bank would be able to follow the monetary policy it deemed most appropriate for its domestic price level and employment objectives. A central bank would no longer be constrained from following an expansive policy because of concern that its holdings of international reserve assets were too small or be deflected from managing the growth of its money supply because it was obliged to buy foreign currency to prevent the price of its currency from increasing.

Proponents of flexible exchange rates advanced several claims about the advantages of allowing market forces to determine the price of each country's currency. Each claim was a prediction about the behavior of markets, individual investors, or national governments. The principal claim was that changes in the price of each country's currency would track the difference between its inflation rate and those of its trading partners, so that deviations between the market price of the country's currency and the price level–adjusted (or real) price would be smaller than when currencies were attached to parities.

One implication of this view is that changes in the prices of currencies would be gradual, because they would be continuous. Proponents of flexible rates claimed that economic welfare would be enhanced if market forces determined the changes in the price of each country's currency. One of their metaphors was of the tail and the dog: If a change in the relationship between a country's price level and the price level in its trading partners was necessary to reduce a payments imbalance, it would be easier to allow the price of the country's currency to adjust to the national price levels than to have the price level adjust to the fixed price of the currency.

Another claim was that changes in the prices of currencies would buffer the response to shocks in the goods market. Each country, proponents argued, would be insulated from shocks in its trading partners because these shocks would lead to a change in the price of its currency rather than to a change in its trade balance.

A third major claim was that there would be fewer currency crises because changes in the prices of currencies would be continuous. Currency crises would be rarer.

Critics of flexible exchange rates (including Robert Roosa [1967], Robert M. Dunn, Jr. [1983], and myself [Aliber 1969, 1980]) responded that the data from the interwar period did not support any of the claims of the proponents. The thrust of their comments was that changes in the market prices of currencies were extraordinarily large relative to those predicted from the differences between each country's inflation rate and rates in its trading partners. In a debate with Friedman in 1967, Roosa cited a study that claimed that the data showed that speculation in several European currencies had been destabilizing in the 1920s. Several years later, in a debate with Sir Maurice Parsons (1970) and Charles Kindleberger (1970), Friedman remarked:

> Let me turn to what I regard as the single most important issue involved in the argument for and against flexible exchange rates. . . that there is less exchange risk under fixed rates. . . . In respect of this argument, I feel as if this is one of those continuous movies, and this is where I came in 20 years ago. In 1950, I took seriously the argument that there might be destabilizing specula- tion. . . . There has been an enormous amount of empirical work done on this issue. In a debate a couple of years ago with Bob Roosa, I challenged him—and now I challenge Professor Kindleberger and I challenge Sir Maurice Parsons— to provide not assertion, not fears but some empirical evidence that shows that such consequences do flow from flexible rates. Destabilizing speculation is a theoretical possibility, but I know of no empirical evidence that this has occurred even as a special case, let alone as a general rule (Federal Reserve Bank of Boston 1970, 114–15).

Nurkse focused on "disequilibrating" cross-border investment inflows, which automatically led to changes in employment and the inflation rate as part of the balance of payments adjustment process. Friedman's response about destabilizing speculation suggests that he misread Nurkse, as disequilibrating and destabilizing are orthogonal to each other. The overarching question posed by the discussion of disequilibrating cross- border investment flows and destabilizing speculation is whether the cross-border purchases of foreign securities by money market traders affect goods markets. Friedman's position appeared to be that he had seen no evidence that the purchases and sales of currencies by money market traders affected the goods markets and caused the market price of a country's currency to differ from the price projected from the differences in national inflation rates.

Central Bank Monetary Independence and Cross-Border Investment Flows

Proponents of flexible exchange rates have suggested that economic welfare would be enhanced if each central bank's monetary policy choices were not limited by its commitment to anchor its currency to a parity. They believe that the net impact of inward-looking monetary policies would be that changes in the price of each country's currency would reflect the difference between its inflation rate and those of its trading partners. The central question is whether changes in the market price of each country's currency would differ from the trajectory of prices projected from the difference between its inflation rate and those of its trading partners.

Carry-trade investors differ from momentum traders because they continually hedge the foreign exchange exposure when they buy a foreign security if the excess of foreign interest rates over domestic interest rates is larger than the anticipated decline in the price of the foreign currency (by selling the foreign currency in the forward market at the same time as they sell it in the spot market). Carry-trade investors are motivated by changes in the difference between the interest rate differential $(R_\$ - R_f)$ and the anticipated change in the price of the foreign currency $(\Delta F/\$)$ when they consider buying foreign securities.

The international money market is in equilibrium if the value of the currency term does not differ significantly from the value of the interest rate differential term. In this case, carry-trade investors would not have an incentive to change the currency composition of the securities in their portfolios. When currencies are attached to parities, the difference between the two terms is modest because each central bank is committed to suppressing changes in the price of its currency. When currencies are not anchored to parities, money market shocks and goods market shocks will lead to larger changes in the value of the interest rate differential term and the value of the anticipated change in the price of foreign currency term; changes in the difference between the two terms will be larger. The responses to both money market and goods market shocks are larger in each country's capital account surplus and in the price of its currency.

Money Market Shocks, Asset Prices, and Banking Crises

Sharp variability in the purchase of foreign securities by money market has led to the failure of banks in more than 70 countries since 1980. Nearly all of the banks in Japan failed in the 1990s. Many of the banks in Thailand, Indonesia, and South Korea collapsed during the 1997 Asian financial crisis (Fischer 2005). The massive failures of the US investment and commercial banks in 2006–10 were unprecedented. Iceland's banks were wiped out in the autumn of 2008, when stock prices plummeted, and banks in Ireland tanked. The generic explanation for these failures is that the price of real estate fell sharply, which led to dramatic declines in the prices of mortgages and mortgage-backed and asset-backed securities. Stock prices plunged when real estate prices tanked.

The prices of real estate and stocks in each of these countries had spiked in the years preceding the crises as part of the balance of payments adjustment process. Increases in household wealth led to consumption spending booms that involved larger purchases of both domestic and foreign goods. Each of these consumption booms developed in response to the increase in each country's capital account surplus to ensure that there was a counterpart increase in its current account deficit, without which the country's currency would not have cleared.

The relationship between cross-border investment inflows and economic growth within a country is symbiotic. An increase in employment, the price level of goods, or interest rates in a country may attract investment inflows; an increase in investment inflows leads to an increase in the price of a country's currency and securities. If a country experiences an increase in cross-border investment inflows (in balance of payments accounting terms, an increase in its capital account surplus), market forces will ensure that its spending on foreign goods increases by a comparable amount (in balance of payments accounting terms, an increase in its current account deficit).

Every change in the relationship between interest rates on US dollar-denominated securities and the interest rates on comparable securities denominated in the currency of one of the United States' trading partners and the anticipated change in the price of the US dollar in terms of each of these foreign currencies leads to a change in its capital account balance, which can occur only if there is a counterpart change in its current account balance. This increase in the US current account deficit occurs automatically, in part because of the increase in the price of the US dollar and in larger part because of the increase in the price of US stocks and real estate; the increase in the US current account deficit may be abetted by an increase in bank credit.

The increase in a country's current account deficit results from a sharp increase in consumption spending induced by a spike in asset prices and household wealth. The spike in asset prices develops to ensure that the country's current account deficit more or less continually corresponds with its capital account surplus; the smaller the increase in consumption spending in response to the increase in household wealth and the smaller the share of spending on imports as a share of consumption spending, the larger the spike in asset prices for a given increase in the country's capital account surplus.

The boom in consumption spending often facilitates a surge in bank loans. Households and firms are eager to borrow because of the economic boom, and banks are often eager to lend because their profits and capital have increased.

The spike in asset prices is a transient phenomenon and occurs only as long as the country's capital account surplus increases; when this surplus stops increasing, asset prices also stop increasing. Asset prices may fall sharply because the increase in the capital account surplus facilitates the rapid growth of domestic credit.

The boom produced in response to the increase in a country's capital account surplus almost always inspires a rapid increase in the growth of domestic credit; the actual and anticipated profits of banks often grow rapidly. Many countries have experienced a growth in bank loans that can be characterized as Ponzian because the increase in these loans is more rapid than the increase in interest payments on their indebtedness and some borrowers rely on money from new loans to pay the interest on their indebtedness. Any factor that limits the increase in bank loans may trigger a crisis because some of the indebted borrowers become distress sellers of stocks or real estate once they no longer have access to money from new loans for the debt service payments on their outstanding indebtedness.

The impact of the increase in Iceland's capital account surplus on the prices of its stocks and real estate was dramatic between 2000 and 2008; stock prices increased by a factor of nine to ensure that the increase in spending on foreign goods corresponded with the increase in foreign purchases of Icelandic securities. Iceland's capital account surplus increased by 20 percent a year; the counterpart increase in its current account deficit was facilitated by the rapid growth in bank loans, which reflected the fact that bank capital also climbed at a rapid rate.

Iceland became involved in Ponzi finance on its external indebtedness, which increased more rapidly than its interest payments on this indebtedness. Icelandic households were also involved in Ponzi finance, as the increase in their domestic indebtedness was several times larger than the interest payments on their indebtedness. When foreign demand for the IOUs of the Icelandic banks slowed, it was predictable that the price of the Icelandic krona would decline and that Icelandic banks would default on their indebtedness to foreign banks. It was also predictable that many Icelandic households and businesses would default on their indebtedness to the Icelandic banks, because they would no longer be able to rely on money from new loans to service the payments on their outstanding indebtedness. The market failure was that the international banks that bought the IOUs of the Icelandic banks did not foresee that household and business borrowers were on an unsustainable trajectory.

The spike in the prices of real estate and stocks in Japan in the second half of the 1980s was even more dramatic than the one in Iceland 15 years later. Japan experienced a massive increase in household wealth in the second half of the 1980s, as stock prices and real estate prices soared. (The now-traditional explanation for the increase is that the money supply increased rapidly. This explanation is incomplete because it does not explain why inflation hit asset prices rather than goods prices.) A surge in foreign purchases of Japanese stocks led to both an increase in the price of the yen and a sharp reduction in the country's capital account deficit, which could have occurred only if there was a counterpart decline in its current account surplus. The higher price of the yen led to a modest increase in spending on foreign goods. Japan needed a massive increase in household wealth to effect an increase in spending on foreign goods that was comparable to the increase in foreign purchases of Japanese stocks (Okina et al. 2001).

The United States has experienced four spikes in asset prices since 1980. Stock prices increased by a factor of five in the 1980s. They more than doubled in the last three years of the 1990s, peaking in March 2000. Real estate prices doubled between 2002 and 2006, peaking in the fourth quarter of 2006. US stock prices doubled during those four years.

Each of these spikes in US asset prices was part of the balance of payments adjustment process to ensure that the increase in the US current account deficit corresponded with the increase in the US capital account surplus. The shock that led to the increase in this surplus was that China and the oil-exporting countries experienced surges in their export earnings and used part of it to buy US dollar-denominated securities.

The spikes in the market values of stocks and real estate in the United States and Iceland were extraordinarily large relative to the increase in the value of each country's capital account surplus. Similarly, the spike in the market value of household assets in Japan was very large relative to the decline in its capital account deficit.

The increase in consumption spending had to be sufficiently large to ensure that the increase in spending on foreign goods corresponded to the change in a country's capital account balance. The smaller the increase in consumption spending as household wealth increases, the larger the increase in asset prices to ensure that the increase in the current account deficit corresponds to the increase in the capital account surplus. The smaller the increase in spending on imports as household wealth increased, the larger the needed increase in household wealth.

Proponents of flexible exchange rates did not recognize that changes in purchases of foreign securities would lead to a change in the country's capital account balance. Critics of flexible rates acknowledge that restoring the payments balance through changes in the price of a country's currency is less costly than doing so through changes in the price level. But the choice can be reformulated by asking whether the benefits of a flexible rate system in adjusting to a goods market shocks are larger or smaller than the costs of adjusting to money market shocks.

Benefits and Costs of the US Policy of Benign Neglect toward Foreign Purchases of US Dollar-Denominated Securities

The most important price in any country is that of its currency, because changes in this price affect the country's trade balance, the profit rate in manufacturing, the rate of economic growth, the distribution of income between labor and capital, corporate profits, and the bases for corporate and personal income taxes. Changes in a country's trade balance affect the government's fiscal balance: The lower the price of a country's currency, the larger its trade surplus and the larger its fiscal surplus.

Most US legislators would object if foreign residents or foreign central banks determined the US corporate tax rate or medical reimbursements under Medicare or the Social Security retirement fund. Yet none has objected to the fact that foreign central banks and foreign investors determine the price of the US dollar.

Former US Treasury Secretary John Connally is reported to have said at a conference with US trading partners, "The dollar is our currency but your problem." The price of the US dollar is determined by foreign purchases of US dollar securities; changes in the price of the dollar reflect changes in foreign purchases of US dollar-denominated securities. Connally's quip was cute, but it is one of the dumbest remarks ever made by a US Treasury secretary. Perhaps Connally believed that those remarkable invisible hands would have kept the price of the dollar at a level at which the international competitive position of US firms would not be handicapped. Another assumption is that foreign central banks would not buy US dollars to limit the increase in the price of their currencies.

The United States moved into this asymmetric position more than 100 years ago, at the beginning of World War I, when each of the European countries then at war temporarily suspended the convertibility of its currency into gold. The United States was the only country that maintained a fixed price relationship between its currency and gold, which it did, with a brief interruption, until August 1971.

Changes in both foreign purchases of US dollar-denominated securities and the price of the US dollar can be evaluated in relation to the major claims advanced by the proponents of flexible exchange rates. Both the increase in the price of the US dollar by 50 percent in the 1980s and its variability challenge their claim that changes in the price of a country's currency would reflect the difference between its inflation rate and those of its trading partners. Surges in the US capital account surplus have been major shocks to the US economy and have led to spikes in the prices of US assets (Wallich 1984).

Has US economic welfare been enhanced by unhindered foreign purchases of US dollar securities? The supply of goods available to Americans is larger as a result of these purchases. At some future date, some of these foreign owners of US dollar securities may repatriate part or all of their US investments, which will reduce the supply of US-produced goods available to Americans. Americans might still be better off, however, because US GDP is higher than in the counterfactual.

Americans are likely to be better off if the inflow of foreign funds enables the United States to finance a higher level of investment. But the data suggest that the inflows have led primarily to consumption booms and that foreign savings have displaced domestic saving. One of the purported advantages to the United States of abandoning currency parities is that the choice of US monetary policies is no longer constrained: If money market traders believe that US monetary policies are excessively expansive, or not sufficiently prudent, they sell dollars and the price of the dollar declines by a larger amount than justified by a higher inflation rate.

But the idea that eliminating fixed exchange rates means that there would no longer be an external constraint on the choice of US monetary policy is off base. Rather than eliminating the constraint, the move to flexible exchange rates simply changed its form.

Once the United States severed the gold anchor for the US dollar, other member countries of the International Monetary Fund no longer felt committed to maintain the parities for their currencies. One reason for introducing a commitment to parities was to reduce the likelihood that some US trading partners would follow exchange market intervention policies that might be deemed beggar-thy-neighbor policies. Supporters of flexible exchange rates claimed that the choice of US monetary policy would not be constrained by the commitment to a parity, which was more or less the case when the US dollar had a parity for gold.

The US Treasury needed to change the arrangement for transactions in gold, because the alternative to closing the gold window was to increase the US dollar price of gold, much as in 1934. Most other countries would have increased the price of gold in terms of their currencies by the same amount, retaining the adjustable parity arrangement. The objective in adopting a new and higher US dollar price of gold was to reduce the US payments deficit.

There are three aspects to the claim that floating exchange rates would eliminate the external constraint on the choice of US monetary policy. One is that closing the gold window did not eliminate the external constraint on the US monetary policy; instead, the form of the constraint changed from a formal treaty-based commitment to an informal market constraint. If the Fed were too expansive, the price of the US dollar would decline, much as it did in the late 1970s. Some analysts might rue the elimination of the treaty constraint that compelled foreign central banks to limit the range of changes in the prices of their currencies because they otherwise might depress the prices of their currencies to enhance net exports and wages, employment, and profits in the production of tradable goods.

The obsolescence of the parity arrangement meant that the external constraint on the monetary policies of the US trading partners was eliminated. The constraint on their choice of currency intervention policy was also eliminated.

Has the United States gained more from the elimination of the external constraint on the choice of US monetary policy than it has lost because of the elimination of the external constraint on the choices of monetary policy and currency intervention policy of its trading partners? The brilliance of the US initiatives that led to Article IV of the Articles of Agreement of the International Monetary Fund was that US trading partners accepted a treaty-based constraint of the management of their currency intervention policy, a major achievement on the part of the US negotiators.

US trading partners have underpriced their currencies, which has led the US international creditor position to morph into an increasingly large debtor position that now approaches 100 percent of US GDP. The US trade deficit has reached 4 percent of US GDP. Hundreds of towns and small manufacturing cities have been decimated, forcing their workers to rely on government transfer programs (such as disability insurance, etc.).

If the managed parity arrangement had been maintained, the United States would have either remained a creditor country or increased its international indebtedness at a far less rapid rate. The real price of the US dollar would have been lower.

Is the United States better off or worse off because of foreign purchases of US dollar-denominated securities? The supply of goods available to American residents is larger, so in that sense the United States is better off. At some future date, the foreign owners of US dollar securities may ask to have some of their money back, and at that time the United States will have to develop a trade surplus; Americans then will be worse off.

The flow of foreign funds to the United States has not enabled the United States to increase its investment spending. Instead, the United States has adjusted to the increase in foreign purchases of US dollar securities with a consumption boom. Asset prices have surged, bank lending has soared, and households have been on a consumption binge.

The flow of foreign funds to the United States has displaced American workers; the unemployment rate has increased. Workers have been shunted from manufacturing to the service sector, where they are less productive.

One explanation for the increase in foreign purchases of US dollar securities is that Americans save too little. The inflow of foreign savings displaced domestic saving, inducing consumption booms. In effect, there was a splurge in the supply of bank credit.

Virtually all of the increase in US international indebtedness reflects the fact that foreign savers or investors have purchase US dollar-denominated securities and US real assets; none of the American borrowers has believed it worthwhile to issue debt denominated in a foreign currency adjusted for the currency exposure as a way to reduce net borrowing costs. The implication is that if American borrowers do not find it financially attractive to issue debt denominated in a foreign currency, then the foreign investors or savers who buy US dollar-denominated securities are not motivated by the higher returns. Foreign central banks clearly do not acquire these securities because the anticipated returns are higher than on securities denominated in their own currency. Foreign central banks are not motivated by incremental investment income; they are the marginal buyers.

Conclusion

Proponents of flexible rates claim that it is less costly to allow market forces to determine the price of currencies than it is to rely on bureaucrats to set those prices. They believe that allowing market forces to adjust the price of the US dollar in response to developments in the US economy is preferable to compelling the economy to adjust in order to retain the established parity for the US dollar and the currencies of its trading partners. They also argue that changes in the price of the US dollar buffer the US economy from shocks in its trading partners. They believe that the only shocks that lead to changes in the prices of currencies are shocks to the goods market, such as changes in tastes or differences in inflation rates across countries.

Critics agree with proponents about the advantages of flexible exchange rates in the adjustment to shocks in the goods market. They differ from proponents with respect to the likelihood and severity of money market shocks in the form of increases in investor purchases of foreign securities, with proponents implicitly assuming that investor purchases of foreign securities are constant (Wallich 1983).

The data on cross-border investment inflows and changes in the market and real price of the US dollar challenge the model of the balance of payments adjustment advanced by the proponents of flexible exchange rates. The most significant claim of proponents is that if currencies are not attached to parities, the deviations between the market prices of currencies and the real or price level–adjusted prices would be smaller than when currencies were anchored to parities. In fact, the deviations have been much larger when currencies have not been attached to parities. There is also no empirical support for any of the other claims of the proponents.

Changes in the difference between the interest rates on US dollar-denominated securities and comparable securities denominated in other currencies and the anticipated change in the price of the US dollar in terms of the currencies of each of these foreign countries will be much larger and more variable than when currencies were attached to parities. Money market traders have much greater incentive to buy foreign securities to profit from the change in the interest rate differential relative to the anticipated change in the prices of foreign currencies. The case for flexible exchange rates is intellectually bankrupt, because proponents ignored capital account transactions (cross-border trade in securities). They failed to recognize the balance of payments adjustment process when a country experiences an autonomous increase in its capital account surplus.

Increases in money market traders' purchases of foreign securities led to four waves of banking crises between 1980 and 2020. Each of these crises was preceded by a boom caused by an increase in cross-border investment inflows. Domestic asset prices increased as part of the balance of payments adjustment process to ensure that the current account deficit increased as the capital account deficit increased. The inflows were too rapid to continue for more than a few years; when they slowed, asset prices declined.

Proponents of flexible exchange rates were naive about central bank behavior when central banks were not required to suppress changes in the price of their country's currency; many central banks purchased US dollar–denominated securities to reduce the price of their currencies and capture a larger share of the world market for manufactured goods. The overvaluation of the US dollar that resulted from foreign purchases of US dollar-denominated securities depressed the anticipated profit rate on the production of tradable goods and led to a lower level of investment in the production of those goods, reducing US economic growth. The US trade surplus of the 1950s and 1960s morphed into a trade deficit as US exports of securities displaced US exports of goods. US manufacturing employment declined as the US trade deficit increased; it is now 3 million jobs lower than it might have been had US exports and imports been in balance (Lawrence and Edwards 2013). The US fiscal deficit increased as US consumption spending was diverted to foreign sources of supply.

The primary knock on the case for flexible exchange rates as a guide for policy choices is that changes in investor purchases of foreign securities affect the exchange rate and yet those purchases are ignored and assumed to be constant. Proponents of flexible exchange rates failed to consider that investors would have a much greater incentive to buy foreign securities when currencies were not attached to parities because the changes in the relationship between the interest rates on US dollar-denominated securities and comparable securities denominated in the currency of one of its trading partners and the anticipated price of the US dollar would be larger and more frequent than when currencies were anchored to parities.

Proponents also ignored the balance of payments adjustment problem. If there were an autonomous increase in foreign purchases of US dollar-denominated securities, what market developments would ensure that there was a comparable increase in the US current account deficit?

Another question proponents ignored was the response of trading partners to a US decision to sever the link between the US dollar and gold. Would foreign central banks take a hands-off attitude toward the price of their currency or instead buy their currency to increase the price of the US dollar and enhance their share of the global market for manufactured and other tradable goods?

References

Ahamed, Liaquat. 2009. *Lords of Finance: The Bankers Who Broke the World*. New York: Penguin Press.

Aliber, Robert Z. 1969. *Choices for the Dollar: Costs and Benefits of Alternative Approaches to the Balance of Payments Problem*. Washington: National Planning Association.

Aliber, Robert Z. 1980. Floating Exchange Rates: The Twenties and the Seventies. In *Flexible Exchange Rates and the Balance of Payments; Essays in Memory of Egon Sohmen*, ed. John S. Chipman and Charles P. Kindleberger. Amsterdam: North Holland.

Argy, Victor. 1982. *Exchange Rate Management in Theory and Practice*. Princeton Studies in International Finance 50. Princeton, NJ: Princeton University Press.

Blinder, Alan S. 2022. *A Monetary and Fiscal History of the United States, 1961–2021.* Princeton, NJ: Princeton University Press.

Braude, Jacob, with Zvi Eckstein, Stanley Fischer, and Karnit Flug. 2013. *The Great Recession: Lessons for Central Bankers.* Cambridge, MA: MIT Press.

Cooper, Richard N. 1998. Exchange Rate Choices. In *Rethinking the International Monetary System*, ed. J.S. Little. Boston: Federal Reserve Bank of Boston.

Cooper, Richard N., with Peter B. Kenen, Jorge Braga de Macedo, and Jacques van Ypersele. 1982. *The International Monetary System under Flexible Exchange Rates: Global, Regional, and National.* Cambridge, MA: Ballinger Publishing Company.

Dalio, Ray. 2021. *Principles for Dealing with the Changing World Order: Why Nations Succeed and Fail.* New Yok: Simon and Schuster.

De Grauwe, Paul, Marc Janssens, and Hilde Lehaert. 1985. *Real Exchange Rate Variability from 1920 to 1926 and 1973 to 1982.* Princeton Studies in International Finance No. 56. Princeton, NJ: Princeton University Press.

Dornbusch, Rudiger. 2014. Expectations and Exchange Rate Dynamics. *Journal of Political Economy* 84, no. 6: 1161–76.

Dunn, Robert M., Jr. 1983. *The Many Disappointments of Flexible Exchange Rates.* Princeton Essays in International Finance 154. Princeton, NJ: International Finance Section, Princeton University.

Einzig, Paul. 1968. *Leads and Lags.* London: Macmillan.

Federal Reserve Bank of Boston. 1970. *The International Adjustment Mechanism.* Proceedings of a conference held in October 1969, New Hampshire. Conference Series No. 2. Boston.

Fischer, Stanley. 2005. Reforming the International Financial System. In *IMF Essays from a Time of Crisis.* Cambridge, MA: MIT Press.

Frenkel, Jacob A., Morris Goldstein, and Paul R. Masson. 1991. *Characteristics of a Successful Exchange Rate System.* Occasional Paper 82. Washington: International Monetary Fund.

Friedman, Milton. 1953. The Case for Flexible Exchange Rates. Reprinted in *Essays in Positive Economics.* Chicago: University of Chicago Press.

Friedman, Milton. 1967. *The Balance of Payments: Free versus Fixed Exchange Rates.* Washington: American Enterprise Institute for Public Policy Research.

Friedman, Milton. 1970. Discussion. In *The International Adjustment Mechanism.* Proceedings of a conference held in October 1969, New Hampshire. Conference Series No. 2. Boston: Federal Reserve Bank of Boston.

Gagnon, Joseph E., with Marc Hinterschweiger. 2011. *Flexible Exchange Rates for a Stable World Economy.* Washington: Peterson Institute for International Economics. Available at https://www.piie.com/bookstore/flexible-exchange-rates-stable-world-economy.

Geithner, Timothy. 2014. *Stress Test: Reflections on Financial Crises.* New York: Crown Publishers.

Gilbert, Milton. 1980. *Quest for World Monetary Order: The Gold Dollar System and Its Aftermath.* New York: John Wiley and Sons.

Greenspan, Alan. 2007. *Balance of Payments Imbalance*. Washington: Per Jacobsson Lecture.

Johnson, Harry G. 1988 (1969). The Case for Flexible Exchange Rates. Reprinted in *The Case for Flexible Exchange Rates: An Anthology*, ed. Leo Melamid. Fairfax, VA: George Mason University Press.

Kindleberger, Charles P. 1968 (1963). Flexible Exchange Rates. Reprinted in *Europe and the Dollar*. Cambridge, MA: MIT Press.

Kindleberger, Charles P. 1970. The Case for Fixed Exchange Rates, 1969. In *The International Adjustment Problem*. Proceedings of a conference held in October 1969, New Hampshire. Conference Series No. 2. Boston: Federal Reserve Bank of Boston.

Kohlhagen, Steven W. 1978. *The Behavior of Foreign Exchange Markets: A Critical Survey of the Empirical Literature*. Monograph 1978-3. New York: New York University.

Krueger, Anne O. 1983. *Exchange Rate Determination*. Cambridge: Cambridge University Press.

Lawrence, Robert Z., and Lawrence Edwards. 2013. *US Employment Deindustrialization: Insights from History and the International Experience*. PIIE Policy Brief 13-27. Washington: Peterson Institute for International Economics. Available at https://www.piie.com/publications/policy-briefs/us-employment-deindustrialization-insights-history-and-international.

MacDonald, Ronald. 1988. *Floating Exchange Rates: Theories and Evidence*. London: Unwin Hyman.

McKinnon, Ronald I., and Kenichi Ohno. 1995. *Dollar and Yen: Resolving Economic Conflict Between the United States and Japan*. Cambridge, MA: MIT Press.

McCulloch, Rachel. 1985. Unexpected Real Consequences of Floating Exchange Rates. In *The Reconstruction of International Monetary Arrangements*, ed. Robert Z. Aliber. London: Macmillan.

Melamed, Leo. 1988. Foreword to *The Merits of Flexible Exchange Rates, an Anthology*, ed. Leo Melamed. Fairfax, VA: George Mason University Press.

Minford, Patrick. 1978. *Substitution Effects, Speculation, and Exchange Rate Stability*. Amsterdam: North Holland.

Mussa, Michael, 1986. Nominal exchange rate regimes and the behavior of real exchange rates: Evidence and implications. *Carnegie-Rochester Conference Series on Public Policy* 25, no. 1 (January): 117–214.

Nurkse, Ragnar. 1944. *The International Currency Experience: Lessons of the Interwar Period*. Princeton, NJ: Princeton University Press for the League of Nations.

Nurkse, Ragnar. 1945. *Conditions of International Monetary Equilibrium*. Princeton Essays in International Finance 4. Princeton, NJ: International Finance Section, Princeton University.

Obstfeld, Maurice. 2020. Harry Johnson's "Case for Flexible Exchange Rates"—50 Years Later. *The Manchester School* 88, no. S1: 86–113. Available at https://onlinelibrary.wiley.com/doi/abs/10.1111/manc.12334.

Okina, Kunio, with Masaaki Shirakawa and Shigenori Shiratsuka. 2001. *The Asset Price Bubble and Monetary Policy: Japan's Experience in the Late 1980s and the Lessons*. Monetary and Economic Studies, Special Edition. Tokyo: Bank of Japan.

Parsons, Sir Maurice H. 1970. Stabilizing the Present International Payments System. In *The International Adjustment Mechanism*. Boston: Federal Reserve Bank of Boston.

Polak, J.J. 1957. *Monetary Analysis of Income Formation and Payments Problems*. Staff Paper. Washington: International Monetary Fund.

Roosa, Robert. 1967. *The Balance of Payments: Free vs. Fixed Exchange Rates*. Washington: American Enterprise Institute for Public Policy Research.

Simon, Matthew. 1979. *Cyclical Fluctuations and the International Capital Movements of the United States 1865–1897*. New York: Arno Press.

Sohmen, Egon. 1969. *Flexible Exchange Rates*, rev. ed. Chicago: University of Chicago Press.

Solomon, Robert. 1983. *The International Monetary System, 1945–1981*. New York: Harper & Row.

Taylor, Mark P. 1995. The Economics of Exchange Rates. *Journal of Economic Literature* 33, no. 1 (March): 13-47.

Wallich, Henry C. 1984. Capital Movements—the Tail that Wags the Dog. In *The International Monetary System*. Boston: Federal Reserve Bank of Boston.

Willett, Thomas D. 1977. *Floating Exchange Rates and International Monetary Reform*. Washington: American Enterprise Institute.

5

Reflections on Flexible Exchange Rates after 50 Years

ANNE O. KRUEGER

When the invitation came to participate in an analysis of what had changed in the 50 years since Bretton Woods, I cheerfully accepted, thinking that the answer would be simple and straightforward. But as I began thinking seriously about those 50 years, it became clear to me that much has changed and that it is worth assessing the evolution of the system.

Let me start at the beginning of the Bretton Woods years. A few years after the start of the Bretton Woods system, there was one balance of payments crisis after another. A balance of payments crisis occurs when a country's imports of goods and services exceed its exports and it does not have sufficient foreign exchange reserves or creditworthiness to continue covering the difference. As a result, foreign exporters no longer accept orders from the country, and the resulting "foreign exchange shortage" and lack of imports forces policy reform, including devaluation, usually with a fairly severe downturn in economic activity.

In 1946, only four countries (the United States, Mexico, Panama, and El Salvador) had entirely open capital accounts. Even on the current account, the Marshall Plan had been needed to pry open bilateral current account transactions in many recipient countries. As reconstruction proceeded and multilateral clearing replaced bilateral clearing, trade and growth accelerated. But crises still occurred.

Anne O. Krueger is a senior fellow at the School of Advanced International Studies, Johns Hopkins University, and the Herald L. and Caroline Ritch Emeritus Professor of Sciences and Humanities in the Economics Department at Stanford University. She was first deputy managing director of the International Monetary Fund from 2001 to 2006.

Belief in fixed-but-adjustable exchange rates was strong. Most governments stuck to unrealistic fixed exchange rates longer than they should have. In 1967, I was returning from Turkey (which had significant balance of payments problems) and agreed to stop in Washington to see the head of the powerful Exchange and Trade Relations Department of the International Monetary Fund (IMF), Ernest Sturc, who had been the Czech delegate to the Bretton Woods Conference. He had a PhD in economics from the University of Chicago. The day before I saw him, he had returned from London. The Brits were on the brink of disaster. He had led the Fund's team in negotiating with British and European officials with regard to the British foreign exchange crisis. The pound had finally been devalued, by 14 percent, to a new rate of $2.40 per pound. Sturc said that the continental Europeans had indicated that if the pound were devalued any further, they would follow, so 14 percent was all he could get. "I recall the final dinner at Bretton Woods, when Lord Keynes proposed a toast—'here is to no more competitive devaluations,'" he recalled. "Little did I dream that I would spend my life persuading countries to devalue."

That episode was one of many that took place in the fixed exchange rate era. Nominal exchange rates became unsustainable in the face of domestic inflation rates above those in the rest of the world or for other reasons. By the late 1950s, most advanced economies were able to abide by their Bretton Woods obligations. There were exceptions, such as Finland 1955 and France 1958, but it was the pressure on the dollar in the late 1960s and the early 1970s that led to the abandonment of the system.

For developing economies, the situation was different. They had fixed nominal exchange rates and initially held large sterling balances accumulated during World War II. Those that were already independent planned fiscal deficits. At first, the associated current account deficits could be covered by drawing down sterling balances. By the early 1960s, however, many more countries were independent, sterling balances had been exhausted, and government expenditures intended to spur development were rising. One consequence was accelerating inflation and the drawing down of reserves to fund current account deficits—a situation that could not and did not last long.

Using exceptions for developing economies in the General Agreement on Tariffs and Trade (GATT), most developing economies opted to use exchange controls and import licensing to ration foreign exchange among competing uses rather than tighten macro policies or alter their exchange rates. As shortages of foreign exchange worsened, however, these countries were cut off from access to even short-term financing, and import volumes shrank. At some point, the authorities acted, mostly after negotiating an

IMF program to change the exchange rate and get financing to enable resumption of the flow of imports and hence an upswing in economic activity.

Balance of payments crises were associated with "stop-go" cycles, as slowdowns were followed by resumptions of growth only to be followed by a repeat of the inflation, acceleration, shortage cycle. Devaluation from one fixed rate to another was the usual pattern.

Another feature of these earlier cycles was that private capital flows were relatively small and the capital that did go to poorer countries was mostly official. It was only in the 1990s that private capital flows across borders increased and became as large as official ones.

It was the advanced economies that abandoned the system of fixed exchange rates 50 years ago. Most developing economies persisted with exchange controls and overvalued exchange rates for some time after that. It was fortunate that the abandonment took place before the massive oil price increase in the fall of 1973: Oil-exporting countries placed their earnings in advanced-economy financial institutions, which could lend to developing economies, effectively recycling oil dollars.

Gradually, however, an increasing number of developing economies moved to more flexible exchange rates—or at least more willingness to adjust the exchange rate before the economic costs of fixed exchange rates rose to the proportions they had in earlier years (although Sri Lanka's large implosion in 2002–03 bears more resemblance to the earlier era).

As the fixed but adjustable exchange rate system was changing, however, a second change in the global payments system took place. Starting in the 1960s—and growing rapidly thereafter despite the Tequila Crisis of the early 1980s—private capital flows grew rapidly both among the advanced economies and between them and developing economies.

The result was that there were more "sudden stops," as Guillermo Calvo (1998) called them, especially for developing economies. Capital inflows to developing economies, which had been growing relatively rapidly when economic prospects looked reasonable, reversed quickly into capital outflows when doubts arose about policy sustainability, especially about the sustainability of debt obligations. Rather than evaluating the appropriateness of the real exchange rate on trade flows alone, investors, policymakers, and others had to assess the sustainability of capital flows. For some countries, policies and economic growth enabled large capital inflows that could readily be sustained. South Korea, for example, experienced annual (private) capital inflows of more than 10 percent of GDP in the 1960s. As its debt/GDP ratio was falling, there were no apparent concern about sustainability (Frank, Kim, and Westphal 1975). For many other developing economies, rising debt levels and the likelihood that there would be difficulties in sustaining them led to "sudden stops," which forced major policy adjustments.

For the advanced economies, the shift from fixed to floating exchange rates was fairly abrupt, although as Reinhart and Rogoff (2009) show, many governments chose to intervene in the foreign exchange markets on numerous occasions.

For most other countries, the move to greater flexibility has meant that the extent of distortion of exchange rates was usually corrected before the extreme difficulties of some earlier balance of payments crises were experienced. The average inflation rate in developing economies is far lower now than it was in the days when three-digit inflation rates were frequent and rates of four digits or more not unheard of.

Some advocates of fixed exchange rates (such as McKinnon 2012) argued for them because they thought that fixed rates imposed fiscal discipline and price stability. Under the Bretton Woods system, an exchange rate was fixed (despite inflation or other market pressures) for a sustained period and then abruptly and sharply altered. After the abandonment of Bretton Woods, exchange rates moved more frequently and more gradually. Most of the time the result was a smoother adjustment process.

Many countries have stuck with a fixed exchange regime for far too long, and some are even resorting to multiple exchange rates. Argentina's inflation rate crossed the 100 percent mark in 2023. Exports have understandably been sluggish, so the authorities are adopting multiple rates. First there was a "soy" dollar, at 200 pesos to the US dollar while the official rate is 150. The black market rate is reported in the local newspapers. In March 2023, the authorities announced there would be a Malbec dollar for wine exports, with more preferential rates to come.[1]

Turkey's inflation rate is well over 50 percent, but the government provides subsidies to local banks that borrow in foreign currency. As the country's president believes that high interest rates cause inflation, the current president of the Turkish central bank announced a cut of 50 basis points—to 8.5 percent—in the interest rate on February 23, 2023. Inflation was reported to be over 80 percent. So far, the money borrowed by Turkish banks and funds from friendly neighbor countries have covered Turkish needs. An important question is whether and for how long such borrowing will be able to continue.

---

1. Scott Squires, "A Guide to Argentina's Many Exchange Rates," Bloomberg, August 11, 2023, https://www.bloomberg.com/news/articles/2023-08-11/malbec-coldplay-qatar-a-guide-to-argentina-s-myriad-fx-rates.

Challenges Ahead

A major challenge for the world economy is how countries confronted with financial crises should be handled. The arrangements that worked in the past included IMF negotiations to lend when a country in crisis reluctantly undertook policy reform measures to start righting the ship. The IMF lent to enable normal financing of trade operations to resume. Official creditors met in the Paris Club to reschedule and restructure the country's debt when needed, and the IMF withheld its loan until private creditors had met and agreed on terms going forward, to help ensure debt-servicing sustainability.

China's emergence as a major official lender will induce major adjustments to this process. IMF lending to a country in which the terms on which its debt to private creditors is unsustainable and has not been rescheduled will surely mean that the IMF is lending to finance the debtor country's debt-servicing obligations to the holdout creditors—something that will be politically unacceptable to many in creditor countries.

Many low- and middle-income countries appear to have unsustainable debt burdens and be near or at the point at which they need to restructure and receive funds. Many observers have advocated debt forgiveness, because of the magnitude of the debt burden.

Forgiveness was extended to low-income countries 20 years ago, under the Heavily Indebted Poor Countries (HIPC) initiative. Many countries whose debts were erased then are now among the first in the queue for debt forgiveness again. At some point, ways need to be found to provide more incentives for political leaders to address their budgetary issues more effectively.

The international community does not have a coherent approach to sovereign debt restructuring. The issue has been around for a long time and has not been resolved. Long delays in agreement on debt restructuring mean a long period in which economic activity is depressed by uncertainty and lack of market access. But as private capital flows become larger and more important, it will be crucial to improve the framework.

A third issue that requires further thinking is how multilateral financial institutions are treated by their most important member countries. Of concern is the extent to which the official community is trying to use international financial institutions to address important social issues, including inequality and the environment. Although there are certainly policies that can simultaneously ameliorate economic and social difficulties, there is a risk that the international financial institutions' core missions will receive less attention and resources than they should as focus is diverted to new issues.

Governments exist to sort out conflicting claims and policy goals among different groups. The international community does not have a single government; multilateral institutions, especially international financial institutions, were created to serve global goals separately on different issues. New issues are important, but diverting the existing institutions' focus risks reducing their effectiveness in addressing the crucial problems they were created to address.

References

Calvo, Guillermo A. 1998. Capital Flows and Capital-Market Crises: The Simple Economics of Sudden Stops. *Journal of Applied Economics* (CEMA) 1 (November): 35–54.

Calvo, Guillermo A., and Carmen M. Reinhart. 2002. Fear of Floating. *Quarterly Journal of Economics* 117: 379–408.

Frank, Charles R., Kwang Suk Kim, and Larry Westphal. 1975. *Foreign Trade Regimes and Economic Development: South Korea*. New York: Columbia University Press.

McKinnon, Ronald I. 2012. *The Unloved Dollar Standard*. New York: Oxford University Press.

Reinhart, Carmen M., and Kenneth S. Rogoff. 2009. *This Time Is Different: Eight Centuries of Financial Folly*. Princeton, NJ: Princeton University Press.

6

International Finance in 1973 and 2023: What Changed in Half a Century?

RICHARD PORTES

Many academics and officials expected the collapse of the Bretton Woods exchange rate system to bring an era of international financial instability like that which followed the collapse of the gold standard in the early 1930s. Indeed, that instability was a primary motive behind the Bretton Woods accords ("never again"). But the return to floating rates did not herald a return to the prewar instability. There was a global financial crisis in 2007–09, but few would argue that floating exchange rates were a significant cause. Conversely, the exchange rate swings of the 1980s were extreme but did not bring a global financial crisis. What features of the pre-1973 system have persisted, and what has changed in the international financial system over the past half century?

What's the Same after 50 Years? An Asymmetric System

The United States resisted the breakdown of the Bretton Woods exchange rate system partly because it seemed an instrument of US hegemony. But this asymmetry offered advantages to other countries too. The United States was supplying a global public good: financial stability. A globally oriented Kindleberger (1973) argued that the absence of a hegemon was a factor behind the international financial instability of the interwar period. Keohane (1980) developed this proposition into what he called "hegemonic stability theory." Some observers (not only in the United States) feared that

Richard Portes, professor of economics at London Business School, is founder and honorary president of the Centre for Economic Policy Research (CEPR).

losing the world currency's link to gold would bring an era of worldwide unbridled fiat money issuance with inflationary consequences.

There was significant inflation in the 1970s, but not because of the move to flexible exchange rates. The oil shock and loose fiscal policies in several countries (the United Kingdom being a notable example) were the main culprits. Tight monetary policy (then inflation targeting) eventually brought inflation down.

The move to flexible rates did not significantly impair the United States's financial hegemony. The US dollar is still the world's dominant currency, the US financial system is still the center of the global financial system, and the United States is the world's banker. The dollar is still by far the most important vehicle currency (BIS 2022). The minor increases in invoicing in other currencies and declines in the US dollar's share in global reserves have not affected this dominance.

Nowhere is this clearer than during episodes of financial instability. In 2008–09 and March 2020, moves into cash were moves into US dollars. Swap agreements between the Federal Reserve and other key central banks, providing essential dollar liquidity abroad, were heavily utilized and played a key role in underpinning the return to financial market stability (Bahaj and Reis 2022). For the most part, central bank swap drawings were drawings of US dollars from the Federal Reserve.

Why has the euro not risen in prominence relative to the dollar? Its share in foreign exchange reserves rose until 2008, as did other measures of its role in financial markets (Papaioannou and Portes 2008). This trend ended during the global financial crisis and the reversal of financial integration in the eurozone, which was accentuated by the eurozone crisis of 2010–12 (see data in Lane 2023).

Shortly before the euro came into existence, Portes and Rey (1998) argued that the fundamentals underlying the international role of a currency are the breadth, depth, and sophistication of financial markets in that currency. Even its use as a means of payment depends on its capacity to act as a store of value in short-term financial markets. So the rise of the euro would depend on eurozone financial integration and the possible eventual accession of the United Kingdom, with the City's financial markets challenging those of New York. Neither happened.

The rise of China in the global economy has not brought a significant rise in the renminbi as an international currency for the same reasons. China has taken some steps in developing its financial markets, creating stock exchanges, markets for domestic government bonds, and the beginnings of derivatives markets; strengthening financial regulation; and more. It has pressured Chinese and foreign firms to invoice in renminbi, with some success. The renminbi has entered into the Special Drawing Rights (SDRs) of the International Monetary Fund. And China has developed swap agreements between the People's Bank of China and several foreign central banks.

But Chinese policymakers are deeply reluctant to risk losing their control over financial markets and the financial sector. The country's securities markets will therefore develop only slowly. Equally important is their unwillingness to give up capital controls. It is evidently impossible to have a major international currency that cannot be freely exchanged across national borders.

Why Is the System Still Asymmetric?

The characteristics of fiat money—in particular, network externalities and reliance on the credibility of the issuer—tend to lead to a dominant player. These attributes are in turn tied to the depth of the financial system and its integration with the global economy. So much is well understood and widely accepted.

We might, however, return to the hegemonic stability story, but in reverse, as the perceived need for stability drives the acceptance of a hegemon. Although there were financial disturbances in Europe in 2007, the initial shock of the global financial crisis came from the United States. Yet aside from academic discussion, the crisis did not lead to any major effort to reorder the system, to reduce the dominance of the dollar and move to greater symmetry via multipolarity. Neither market forces nor the many conferences discussing a "new Bretton Woods" have brought major change. The more developed are financial markets and instruments, the more complex the international financial system, the more the system may need a hegemon.

The United States may not be able to carry this responsibility indefinitely. There is much talk of deglobalization, although evidence of it is not yet clear in the data (Goldberg and Reed 2023). But the weight of the US economy in the global economy is falling. It has been asserted that a "New Triffin Dilemma" must eventually weaken the dollar's role in the international financial system (Farhi, Gourinchas, and Rey 2011). It has been well over a decade since that argument appeared; as yet, there is no evidence that multipolarity has arrived or is even just around the corner (see the criticism of the New Triffin Dilemma in Portes 2012). Might not deglobalization, dollar-based economic sanctions, a (relatively) diminished US economy, and the United States' limited fiscal capacity reduce the role of the dollar? If so, it may take a very long time. And if there is merit in hegemonic stability, asymmetry and unipolarity may be desirable.

The Macroeconomics: Not Much Change

Global imbalances still exist, and they are at least as consequential as those observed before 1973. They have appeared prominently in successive issues of the IMF's *World Economic Outlook* over the past two decades (see Pellegrino, Spolaore, and Wacziarg 2022 for a recent theoretical treatment and empirical evidence). The US current account imbalances have been the focus of periodic concern (e.g., Obstfeld and Rogoff 2007). They were an important factor in the global financial crisis (Portes 2009); similar imbalances in the eurozone were significant in the crisis of 2010–12 (Portes 2014).

The multicentury global downward trend in real interest rates has continued. Rates were low in 1973, declined sharply for a couple of years afterward, rose briefly in the early 1980s, and fell since then, with a recent blip upward (ESRB 2021; Rogoff, Rossi, and Schmelzing 2023).

The advent of the internet and the consequent rise in information transmission has apparently not significantly affected capital flows. Distance still plays a major role as a barrier to cross-border financial intermediation, for both portfolio flows and foreign direct investment (Portes and Rey 2005; Pellegrino, Spolaore, and Wacziarg 2022).

What Is New?

Financial crises go back many centuries. One could argue, however, that since 1973, the variety of crises has increased. The breakdown of the Bretton Woods exchange rate system was not a financial crisis, but it was followed by debt or financial crises in Latin America in 1982, Mexico in 1994–95, Asia in 1997, Russia in 1998, Argentina in 2001–02, the global financial crisis 2008–09, and the euro zone crisis of 2010–12. (Note that pre-1973 forced devaluations, as in the United Kingdom in 1967, did not lead to financial crises.) The exchange rate crises of the Bretton Woods years were mostly national liquidity crises, typically with macroeconomic roots.

Some elements of post-1973 crises are similar. Most exhibited interconnections between exchange rate crises, bank failures, and debt defaults—the nexus Eichengreen and Portes (1987) explore, in particular for the 1930s. What was the role of floating rates in the post-1973 crises? One could argue that fixed rates forced balance of payments adjustment—but many of these cases had pegged rates. The pegs simply broke down.

The succession and variety of crises inspired various theoretical models, focusing mainly on exchange rates and sovereign debt. The global financial crisis had a key new element: extreme counterparty risk.

Global Liquidity

Since 1973, there has been a major expansion of global financial assets and global liquidity relative to GDP. There is no identifiable shortage of investible assets.[1] But is the resulting system irreparably fragile? When necessary, major central banks can support global liquidity with currency swaps and can intervene as market makers of last resort (ESRB 2023c).

Is the expansion of global liquidity a consequence of floating exchange rates or low interest rates? Whatever the causal relationships, the search for yield and buildup of vulnerabilities have led to a focus on macroprudential policies. And since the global financial crisis, there has been a rise in non-bank financial intermediation relative to banks, in particular in cross-border finance (see ESRB 2023b). This increase has no obvious relation to floating exchange rates, but it calls for macroprudential measures.

Crypto Assets and "Decentralized Finance"

No one could have expected the advent of crypto-assets and decentralized finance (ESRB 2023a). Doubts about fiat money and exchange rate uncertainty undoubtedly contributed to crypto enthusiasm, although crypto has not been a good inflation hedge. Central bank digital currencies are likely to emerge. And one could argue that blanket deposit guarantees turn private bank money into central bank money and private banks into state banks. It is not clear why this evolution should reduce confidence in the store of value function of fiat money. Except among crypto enthusiasts and in some highly inflationary countries, that confidence is not in question.

Little of these recent developments is attributable to the breakdown of the Bretton Woods exchange rate system. Expectations in 1973 that the international financial system would undergo a major transformation did not materialize. Many of the basic issues that bedeviled the Bretton Woods system persist, in new forms.

References

Bahaj, S., and R. Reis. 2022. The Economics of Liquidity Lines between Central Banks. *Annual Review of Financial Economics* 14: 57–74.

BIS (Bank for International Settlements). 2022. *Bank for International Settlements Triennial Survey of Foreign Exchange*. Available at https://www.bis.org/statistics/rpfx22.htm.

---

1. Without entering into the "safe assets" discussion, we note that "safety" is a multidimensional continuum. For extended criticism of the "safe asset shortage," see Portes (2017).

Eichengreen, B., and R. Portes. 1987. The Anatomy of Financial Crises. In *Threats to International Financial Stability*, ed. R. Portes and A. Swoboda, 10-58. Cambridge: Cambridge University Press.

ESRB (European Systemic Risk Board). 2021. *Lower for Longer: Macroprudential Policy Issues Arising from the Low Interest Rate Environment*. Frankfurt.

ESRB (European Systemic Risk Board). 2023a. *Crypto-assets and Decentralised Finance*. Frankfurt.

ESRB (European Systemic Risk Board). 2023b. *EU Nonbank Financial Intermediation Risk Monitor 2023*. Frankfurt.

ESRB (European Systemic Risk Board). 2023c. *Stabilising Financial Markets: Lending and Market Making as a Last Resort*. Frankfurt.

Farhi, E., P.-O. Gourinchas, and H. Rey. 2011. *Reforming the International Monetary System*. CEPR eReport. Paris and London: CEPR Press.

Goldberg, P., and T. Reed. 2023. Is the Global Economy Deglobalizing? *Brookings Papers on Economic Activity* (Spring). Washington: Brookings Institution.

Keohane, R. 1980. *The Theory of Hegemonic Stability and Changes in International Economic Regimes, 1967–1977*. Center for International and Strategic Affairs, University of California, Berkeley.

Kindleberger, C. 1973. *The World in Depression, 1929–1939*. Berkeley: University of California Press.

Lane, P. 2023. *The Dynamics of the Financial System in the Euro Area*. Frankfurt: European Central Bank. Available at https://www.ecb.europa.eu/press/key/date/2023/html/ecb.sp230619~5a9b8b1e64.en.pdf?19ccc33eff678df93333eba59ce0b77d.

Obstfeld, M., and K. Rogoff. 2007. The Unsustainable US Current Account Position Revisited. In *G7 Current Account Imbalances: Sustainability and Adjustment*, ed. R. Clarida. University of Chicago Press for NBER.

Papaioannou, E., and R. Portes. 2008. *The International Role of the Euro: A Status Report*. Economic Papers 317. Brussels: European Commission. Available at https://ec.europa.eu/economy_finance/publications/pages/publication12409_en.pdf.

Pellegrino, B., E. Spolaore, and R. Wacziarg. 2022. *Barriers to Global Capital Allocation*. NBER Working Paper 28694 (June). Cambridge, MA: National Bureau of Economic Research.

Portes, R. 2009. Global Imbalances. In *Macroeconomic Stability and Financial Regulation: Key Issues for the G20*, ed. Mathias Dewatripont, Xavier Freixas, and Richard Portes, 19-26. Paris and London: CEPR Press.

Portes, R. 2012. The Triffin Dilemma and a Multipolar Reserve System. In *Rethinking Global Economic Governance in Light of the Crisis: New Perspectives on Economic Policy Foundations*, ed. R. Baldwin and D. Vines. London: Centre for Economic Policy Research.

Portes, R. 2014. Monetary Union and Financial Stability. Tommaso Padoa-Schioppa Professorship Inaugural Lecture. Fiesole, Italy: European University Institute.

Portes, R. 2017. Low Real Rates and the "Safe Asset Shortage." Slides for keynote lecture at Central Bank of Ireland conference, January 19, 2016. Revised version (2017) available from the author.

Portes, R., and H. Rey. 1998. The Emergence of the Euro as an International Currency. *Economic Policy* 26: 305–43.

Portes, R., and H. Rey. 2005. The Determinants of Cross-Border Equity Flows. *Journal of International Economics* 65: 269–96.

Rogoff, K., B. Rossi, and P. Schmelzing. 2023. *Long-Run Trends in Long-Maturity Real Rates 1311–2022*. Available at https://scholar.harvard.edu/sites/scholar.harvard.edu/files/rogoff/files/long_run_trends_in_long_maturity_rates_revised_version_july_2023.pdf.

II

POLITICS, INSTITUTIONS, AND IDEAS IN INTERNATIONAL MONETARY EVOLUTION

7

The Political Economy of International Monetary Arrangements

JEFFRY FRIEDEN

A well-functioning international monetary arrangement provides two bene-fits: monetary stability and a balance of payments adjustment mechanism. Both are economically important and politically controversial. Monetary stability among member states raises classic problems of public goods provision and the responsibilities of leadership. The balance of payments adjustment mechanism raises classic distributional issues. Both require domestic political support for the measures necessary to meet national governments' international commitments, which may be hard to secure.

An international monetary arrangement can be said to be successful to the extent that its operation and results are acceptable to all major member states. Such an arrangement could presumably be improved if a Pareto-superior redesign were both available and politically feasible. Both dimen-sions—success and improvability—depend on political relations among the principal participants. The willingness and ability of national governments to undertake the measures necessary to sustain and improve a mone-tary arrangement in turn depend on whether there is domestic political backing for them. If the policies necessary for the principal member states to sustain an international monetary arrangement are not supported by their domestic publics, the system will not be amenable to improvement, success, or survival.

Five decades after the demise of the Bretton Woods fixed exchange rates, the international monetary system continues to evolve under the

Jeffry Frieden is professor of Government at Harvard University.

pressure of new shocks from domestic politics, geopolitics, technology, climate, and public health, among other sources. The direction of change will depend on the interplay of these complex elements.

International Monetary Stability

International monetary stability is a global public good. As such, it is typically undersupplied. Very large actors may have strong enough incentives that they will attempt to supply the public good on their own, by providing a reliable anchor to which other currencies can link themselves, formally or informally, and more or less tightly. A stable anchor currency provides a focal point around which other monetary authorities can converge.

Stability reduces policy discretion. A monetary authority in a monetary arrangement with an explicit or implicit commitment to an anchor—whether the anchor is another currency or a commodity—loses some or all its policy autonomy and flexibility. The experience of the gold standard era convinced virtually everyone that a commodity currency was too inflexible for any reasonable purpose and that national currencies are the anchor of choice.

A national monetary authority that commits to a monetary arrangement with an anchor currency enters into an implicit (or explicit) bargain with the anchor currency's monetary authority. The anchor authority is expected to take account of the impact of its policies on other countries—to internalize the external effects of its policy choices. In return, the anchor country is rewarded with a series of benefits, including monetary autonomy, seigniorage, denomination rents, and other advantages to national banks and firms.

Commitments among nation states cannot be enforced by a third party; they rely on some level of mutual trust. Anchor-currency authorities trust other member states to cooperate to hold the system together; other member states trust anchor-currency authorities to be responsive to their concerns. International (including regional interstate) monetary arrangements break down when one or both dimension of trust erodes.

Trust among countries depends on expectations about the incentives policymakers face. International agreements provide some such incentives, but all national policymakers are first and foremost answerable to their domestic constituencies (electorates, elites, special interests); policymakers who do not act in accord with the preferences of their constituents will not be policymakers for very long.

History provides many examples of how politics among and within countries affects the course of international monetary affairs. In the Bretton Woods monetary order, member states were expected to treat dollars as "good as gold," as the foundation stone of the system. The United States was expected to pursue monetary policies that other member states regarded as responsible—that is, in line with their monetary policy preferences.

Over the course of the late 1960s and early 1970s, both expectations were violated. As inflation in the United States increased by substantially more than in its major economic partners, the sentiment spread that the world "cannot keep forever as our basic monetary yardstick a national currency that constantly loses value. . . . The rest of the world cannot be expected to regulate its life by a clock which is always slow" (French President Georges Pompidou, quoted in Frieden 2020, 345).

Toward the end of the Bretton Woods system, American domestic politics made it difficult for the US government to adopt the domestic macroeconomic measures necessary to bring inflation in line with the preferences of other member states. President Richard Nixon faced a potentially difficult shot at reelection in 1972. He believed—probably correctly—that his narrow loss in the 1960 presidential election had been caused in part by a restrictive Federal Reserve policy. As he remarked sardonically, "We cooled off the economy and cooled off 15 senators and 60 congressmen at the same time" (quoted in Gowa 1983, 68). Nixon resisted pressures from abroad, and from within his Cabinet, to endorse austerity measures. In the meantime, other member states were increasingly unwilling to hold (less valuable) dollars rather than (more valuable) gold. The political impasse was resolved in August 1971, when the Nixon administration closed the gold window, effectively bringing the Bretton Woods system to a close. From there, it was a short step to floating exchange rates for the major economies. The system had its inherent weaknesses; American domestic politics delivered the blow that ended it.

A similar dynamic bedeviled the European Monetary System (EMS) in the early 1990s. In practice, if not in design, it was a Deutsche mark-based monetary fixed exchange rate arrangement. In the aftermath of German unification and concern about the inflationary impact of unification-driven spending, the German monetary authorities pursued a highly restrictive policy, driving short-term interest rates from under 5 percent to nearly 10 percent. The economies of many of Germany's EMS partners were already growing slowly, and unemployment was already high. Germany's monetary policy—devised for entirely domestic reasons—therefore created serious political difficulties among many of the other member states. After a year and more of tension and recriminations, in the summer of 1992 the system was rent asunder as a series of EMS member states faced speculative attacks on their currencies and devalued heavily against the Deutsch mark. The EMS was effectively dead, although the 1992 crisis in many ways accelerated the movement toward European monetary unification with the euro, which, it was hoped, would banish speculation-prone fixed exchange rates within the European Union. In 1992, however, German politics demanded strong measures to avoid inflation; politics elsewhere demanded resistance to steeply rising unemployment (above 10 percent in France and Italy, above 15 percent in Ireland and Spain). Once more the contradictory necessities of domestic politics brought down an international (regional) monetary arrangement.

Neither Bretton Woods nor the EMS survived the anchor country's government breaking its implicit commitment to include the concerns of partner countries in its monetary policy formulation. In both cases, partner countries were unwilling to continue to participate with an anchor-country government on the same terms as before, and the anchor-country government was unwilling to bend its policies to meet the demands of its partners. This conflict highlights the fact that a successful monetary arrangement among national governments requires a level of trust on both sides—an implicit degree of monetary policy cooperation. The collapse of both systems was probably not caused by strategic opportunism (purposeful attempts to game the system) but rather by the exigencies of domestic politics, which required that national policymakers pursue policies that satisfied national constituencies whose interests were not aligned with those of foreigners.

The broader, crucial point is that international policy commitments can be very difficult to sustain domestically. American macroeconomic policies affect the rest of the world, but the rest of the world does not vote in American elections, which makes it hard for American administrations to take much account of the implications of its policies for the rest of the world. The exigencies of domestic politics require that the government and the Fed put America first, which may be the right thing to do democratically. There may be domestic support for more internationalist policies. However, even in the glory days of American internationalism, in the aftermath of World War II, support for America's role in the world, including in international monetary relations, did not garner domestic backing on the basis of its economic benefits to the United States but on the basis of its national security implications. It is difficult to convince people in the United States—or in any country—to make substantial sacrifices on behalf of a vague notion of international cooperation or global monetary stability. The same, for better or worse, is true of the distribution of the adjustment burden across countries.

The Adjustment Burden

Payment imbalances arise in any international monetary arrangement. Some are transitory. But given differences in saving rates, investment opportunities, and levels of financial and other development, some imbalances are long-lasting. Such imbalances may be sustainable for years, but at some horizon—and in some common circumstances—they need to be addressed and the imbalance redressed.

For a balance of payments adjustment mechanism to work there has to be adjustment. Along what margins adjustment takes place, and who does the adjusting, is another matter—and a topic open to political conflict (Frieden 2015). Although the rules of the game are rarely explicit, in principle both deficit and surplus countries make implicit commitments. Deficit countries commit to eventually address the causes of their deficits, so that debts do not become excessive. Surplus countries commit to finance reasonable deficits in expectation that they will eventually decline and to reduce their surpluses (Walter 2013).

The burden of adjustment is typically asymmetric. Deficit countries have no choice but to adjust if new credits are increasingly expensive or unavailable. Surplus countries are unlikely to find themselves under immediate pressure to reduce their surpluses. However, the continued accumulation of surpluses raises a series of potential problems. It may create incentives for borrowers to borrow excessively and for lenders to lend excessively. More generally, it can create conditions for global deflationary pressures and financial instability. Long-standing surpluses can also create protectionist pressures in deficit countries, causing tensions in trade relations (see chapter 14, by Douglas Irwin).

Over time, deficits become debts and surpluses become credits. With a few exceptions (discussed below), deficit countries cannot have negative net exports indefinitely. In some cases, borrowing is dependent on global conditions, and lender sentiment can turn around quickly, so that debtors, especially poorer countries, may face a sudden stop in financial inflows. In other cases, high levels of external debt may raise concerns about broader creditworthiness, leading to increased borrowing costs. Either way, the debtor-country government faces the need to adjust domestic policies to address the debt burden and reassure lenders that loans will be serviced.

The history of international finance is littered with bitter debtor-creditor conflicts driven by disagreements over how adjustment costs should be allocated between debtor countries (in the form of austerity) and creditors (in the form of haircuts). Lenders can threaten to charge difficult debtors higher interest rates or to reduce the amounts they are willing to lend; they may also have other retaliatory weapons (see, for example, Tomz

2007 and Tomz and Wright 2013). Debtors also have a powerful weapon: the threat of default (Ballard-Rosa 2020). Political conflict between international debtors and creditors has existed for as long as there has been international lending.

International financial stability is also a global public good, and a well-functioning balance of payments adjustment mechanism is part of such stability. The ways in which adjustments take place are not neutral. Indeed, they raise obvious distributional questions: Should the principal burden of adjustment be borne by deficit or surplus countries? Perhaps even more controversial have been the domestic distributional conflicts that debt—especially debt crises—bring to the surface.

The end of the Bretton Woods system can also be told as a story of disagreements about the way to adjust current account deficits (and surpluses). The American payments deficits of the late 1960s and early 1970s may seem trivial today—in 1970 the payments deficit was $3.8 billion, equal to less than 0.4 percent of GDP—but they were enough to erode confidence in the willingness and ability of the US government to restrain or reverse them. The Nixon administration rejected pressure from US financial partners to reduce the deficit through more restrictive macroeconomic policies; rather than undertake domestic adjustment via fiscal and monetary restraint, it chose to break up the existing international monetary order, devalue, close the gold window, and impose emergency tariffs and wage and price controls.

Substantial global macroeconomic imbalances developed in the early 2000s. The Organization of the Petroleum Exporting Countries (OPEC) and such other major exporting powerhouses as China, Germany, and Japan ran large surpluses while the United States, the United Kingdom, and peripheral members of the European Monetary Union ran large deficits. Despite warnings and some attempts to reduce the imbalances, neither surplus nor deficit countries were willing to adjust. These imbalances arguably contributed to the global financial crisis that began in 2007, especially the debt crisis, which hobbled the eurozone until at least 2015 (Frieden and Walter 2017). The pattern of surpluses and deficits within the European regional monetary arrangement seemed particularly unsustainable, yet none of the member states appeared willing to undertake the adjustment measures necessary. Indeed, the very architecture of the monetary union encouraged the imbalances—until the unsustainable, inevitably, came to an end (Hale and Obstfeld 2016; Frieden and Walter 2017).

The domestic politics of balance of payment adjustment are almost always controversial and conflictual. Inasmuch as a well-functioning international monetary and financial system requires that the balance of payments adjustment mechanism be operative at some level, the ultimate value and success of the monetary order will depend crucially upon the nature of domestic politics in the major member states. Foremost among these major member states is the central, reserve, or anchor currency country—today, the United States.

The Essential Country and Its Politics

The central player in any realistic monetary arrangement is the issuer of the anchor currency. The reserve-currency role of the dollar holds many advantages for the United States. Not least among them is the fact that it appears able to run more substantial payments deficits than would otherwise be the case—another potential asymmetry in the adjustment process. The size of these deficits is limited only by the confidence others hold in the anchor-country monetary authorities—and by the presence of realistic alternatives. Today, especially in the absence of realistic alternatives, the world's appetite for safe American assets does not seem to constrain the ability of the United States to run payments deficits and accumulate international debt.

However, interstate commitments depend on domestic political realities, especially in the United States, which appears to have a particularly fickle electorate when it comes to international economic relations.[1] The ability to shunt macroeconomic responsibilities onto others is part of the "exorbitant privilege" of being the world's supplier of a monetary anchor, reserve currency, and safe asset. But global patience with American political instability and unreliability almost certainly has its limits.

Concern that an international monetary order depends on an undependable foundation—American domestic politics—may lead some to hope for another, better order. A wide range of ways of running the global monetary system would be superior to the current one. The question is whether they would be politically acceptable to the major potential member states.

Is a Better International Monetary System Likely?

Is a Pareto improvement to the contemporary international monetary system available? A globally benevolent social planner could come up with many ways to improve upon the current order. But any such improvement would have to be politically acceptable to crucial publics within the major

---

1. The fickle nature of the American electorate when it comes to international economic policy may well reflect the relatively closed nature of the US economy, and the United States' geographical isolation from its principal trading and financial partners. See Frieden (1988).

players. A domestic political consensus willing and able to sacrifice something at the domestic level to encourage, maintain, sustain, and increase international macroeconomic collaboration would have to develop. There is abundant evidence of the lack of domestic political support for undertaking difficult economic measures solely because of their international implications. Indeed, attempts to get international commitments without domestic political support can backfire.

The weaknesses of the current system are largely political. The goal of global monetary stability is hindered by uncertainties about the degree to which American policymakers are willing and able to consider the impact of American policy on the rest of the world. Whether that stance will change depends on domestic US politics—currently hardly a stable foundation for improvement. The continued inability of the major players to agree on how to allocate the burdens of adjustment—something most major countries are unwilling even to discuss, primarily because of domestic political pressures and realities—makes it difficult for the balance of payments adjustment mechanism to function smoothly.

The domestic political economies of the world's major financial and monetary powers are the central constraints on the operation of the international monetary system. Domestic and international agreement is needed to sustain membership in or leadership of the system. Whether measures involve acceptance of the limitations imposed by the anchor country's policies or the responsibilities of the anchor country itself or agreement on the distribution of the adjustment burden or any other dimensions of relevance, they must be acceptable to domestic publics.

The classical gold standard eventually disintegrated because of the inability to secure that domestic political agreement. The Bretton Woods system collapsed because of the requirements of American domestic politics. The European monetary system, and later the euro itself, were nearly torn apart by conflicts between surplus and deficit countries over the appropriate, politically tolerable, responses to the macroeconomic conditions of the early 1990s and early 2010s.

This history suggests that one should be realistically pessimistic about the possibility of getting the world's major financial centers to agree to major reforms of the international monetary system. The one opening for such a development might come if there were very substantial pressures to do so, politically internalized by the major political players within domestic politics, such as a profound global economic (and/or political) crisis. Such a crisis is hardly something worth hoping for. More purposive attempts at international collaboration might help, by making domestic sacrifices more palatable and more appealing. But the sorry state of domestic political support for the difficult economic measures needed to sustain global economic cooperation does not create much room for optimism. In light of international and domestic political realities, the current international monetary system is likely to be with us for the foreseeable future.

References

Ballard-Rosa, Cameron. 2020. *Democracy, Dictatorship, and Default.* Cambridge: Cambridge University Press.

Frieden, Jeffry. 1988. Sectoral Conflict and US Foreign Economic Policy, 1914–1940. *International Organization* 42, no. 1: 59–90.

Frieden, Jeffry. 2015. The Political Economy of Adjustment and Rebalancing. *Journal of International Money and Finance* 52 (C): 4–14.

Frieden, Jeffry. 2020. *Global Capitalism: Its Fall and Rise in the Twentieth Century, and Its Stumbles in the Twenty First.* New York: W. W. Norton & Company.

Frieden, Jeffry, and Stefanie Walter. 2017. Understanding the Political Economy of the Eurozone Crisis. *Annual Review of Political Science* 20: 371–90.

Gowa, Joanne S. 1983. *Closing the Gold Window: Domestic Politics and the End of Bretton Woods.* Ithaca, NY: Cornell University Press.

Hale, Galina, and Maurice Obstfeld. 2016. The Euro and the Geography of International Debt Flows. *Journal of the European Economic Association* 14, no. 1: 115–44.

Tomz, Michael. 2007. *Reputation and International Cooperation: Sovereign Debt Across Three Centuries.* Princeton, NJ: Princeton University Press.

Tomz, Michael, and Mark Wright. 2013. Empirical Research on Sovereign Debt and Default. *Annual Review of Economics* 5, no. 1.

Walter, Stefanie. 2013. *Financial Crises and the Politics of Macroeconomic Adjustments.* Cambridge: Cambridge University Press.

8

The Euro: A Phoenix Rising from the Ashes of the Dollar?

HAROLD JAMES

The emergence of a shared fiat currency—a unique event in monetary history—was a direct response to the crisis of the US dollar and the breakup of the Bretton Woods system. In March 1973, in the final twist in the long saga of the collapse of the par value system and a shift to generalized floating, the search for a European policy response became more urgent. The events of 1973 put Europe on the road to currency union and the creation of the euro.

The response of European policymakers to dollar weakness in the early 1970s set a pattern in which the impact of subsequent episodes of dollar decline prompted new European initiatives and a belief that a European currency might at some time offer an alternative to the dollar. The European experience provides a template for the contemporary search for new key currencies and for a remaking of the international monetary order in responses to uncertainties about US monetary policy, political stability, and the management of fiscal debt and deficits, as well as the weaponization of the SWIFT payments systems.

The US dollar was always a "can do" currency, which could be used as an instrument of broader US strategic policy; the euro was constructed as an alternative that was tied down by rules, in particular on debt and fiscal deficits. These constraints, which made it look like a "can't do" monetary regime, made it harder to develop some of the mechanisms—notably a deep

Harold James, the Claude and Lore Kelly Professor in European Studies at Princeton University, is professor of history and international affairs at the Woodrow Wilson School and an associate at the Bendheim Center for Finance.

market for a common debt instrument—that might have made the euro a more realistic substitute for a world dominated by dollar-denominated financial instruments.

The Original Shock

The Smithsonian Group of Ten (G10) meeting of December 1971 produced a new exchange rate grid for the international monetary system. It settled little, however, largely because US monetary and fiscal policy continued to be highly expansive. On January 11, 1973, major movements out of the dollar started again, after US wage and price controls ended. The flow into Deutsch mark immediately hit the weaker European currencies, obliging the Bundesbank to intervene along the lines of an agreement it had concluded with other European central banks.

In early March, the storm on the currency markets was renewed, with the Bundesbank issuing DM8 billion on a single day (March 1), the equivalent of 16 percent of the value of currency in circulation. Of the total of around $10 billion of foreign exchange purchased, three-quarters was bought by Germany and an eighth by the Netherlands (BIS 1974). Bundesbank Vice President Otmar Emminger, a long-term proponent of greater exchange rate flexibility in the international system, concluded that the markets had sounded "the death knell of the Bretton Woods parity system."

On March 2, the Bundesbank announced that it would no longer intervene to support the dollar. On March 11–12, at the European Economic Community (EEC) Council of Ministers, France agreed to join a German float, with a 3 percent revaluation of the Deutsch mark relative to the franc and other currencies and a future fluctuation margin of 2.25 percent between the two currencies. France and the Benelux countries also retained a dual foreign exchange rate system. The United Kingdom, Ireland, and Italy remained outside this new system.

The March 1973 crisis lent itself to rather schizophrenic interpretations. On the one hand, the "snake" survived the currency chaos that seemed to have been produced primarily by the mismanagement of monetary policy in the United States.[1] On the other hand, the snake was not a complete monetary embodiment of the EEC. Some analysts therefore concluded that the snake "ceased to be a visible means of working towards economic and monetary union because it was no longer an instrument for promoting the integration of the Community" (Kruse 1980, 131–32).

---

1. The snake was the new European exchange rate system, agreed to in 1972 "as a first step towards the creation of [an EEC] monetary zone within the framework of the international system." It had a reduced fluctuation margin of ±2.25 percent, half the amount allowed under the terms of the Smithsonian Agreement.

Europe and the Global Framework

The late 20th century institutionalization of European monetary arrangements always occurred in a wider context of discussions of the global monetary system and its problems and of the weakness of the US dollar (figure 8.1). Debates about new institutional mechanisms (such as a basket currency) that took place at the global level were also replicated with respect to European affairs.

The first discussions of monetary union occurred in the late 1960s. They culminated with the 1969 Werner Plan, as a way of managing a European response to the crisis of the dollar and the breakdown of the fixed exchange (par value) system that had been devised in 1944 at Bretton Woods.

The next two surges of European monetary institutionalization followed acute crises in the international system. The creation of the European Monetary System (EMS) in 1979 was a response to the rapid decline of the dollar in 1977–78, the perceived crisis in American leadership under President Jimmy Carter, and the consequent international search for a new mechanism to replace the dollar standard. The core of the new approach was originally intended to be a basket currency—the European Currency Unit (ECU), which conveniently echoed the name of an ancient French coin—as a unit of account. A new European money would possibly replace the dollar, taking some of the strain out of the international monetary system. There were also parallels in thinking about how an international currency could operate between attempts to redesign or reform the International Monetary Fund's artificial currency (the Special Drawing Rights) on the one hand and ideas of making the ECU into a currency on the other.

In the mid-1980s, the dollar again caused worldwide chaos as its value soared until 1985, before then declining rapidly. Europeans felt especially vulnerable, because they did not control an international reserve currency that could stand up to the dollar. Responding to that international uncertainty produced a logic that led from the report of the Delors Committee in 1989, through the Treaty of Maastricht, to the legal realization of the euro in 1999. The establishment of the physical currency had its origins in an attempt to devise mechanisms in the mid-1980s that would generate a more stable global exchange rate regime. The critical policy innovators, in particular French Finance Minister Edouard Balladur, took an international answer and started to advocate for its realization on the European level.

By the 1960s, Germany had emerged as the strongest European economy, thanks to its powerful export performance. German current account surpluses—driven primarily by trade surpluses, which appeared briefly in the 1950s—were corrected after a currency revaluation in 1961. They reemerged again in surges in the late 1960s, the late 1970s, the late 1980s, and again in the 2000s (figure 8.2).

Figure 8.1

Exchange rate of US dollar against the Deutsch mark and its successor, 1960–2023

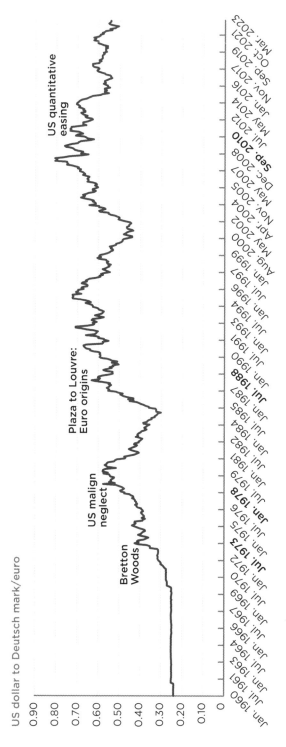

US dollar to Deutsch mark/euro

Note: The US dollar/Deutsch mark exchange rate is spliced in January 1999, with the dollar/euro exchange rate divided by 1.95583, the Deutsch mark/euro conversion rate at that time.

Source: IMF, *International Financial Statistics*.

Figure 8.2

European current account balances, 1960–2020

percent of GDP

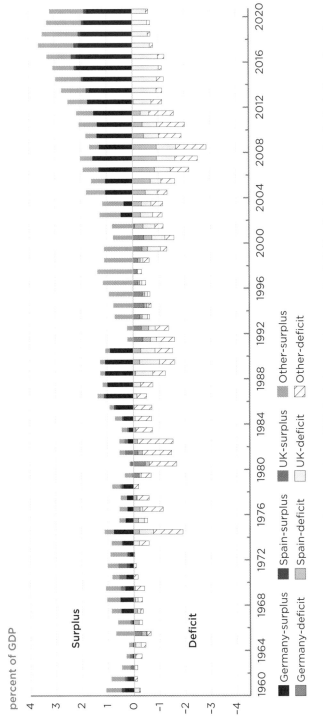

Notes: For Germany, forecasts are after 2017. From 1991 the balance-of-payments statistics for Germany also include the external transactions of the former German Democratic Republic. "Other" includes Belgium, Denmark, France, Greece, Ireland, Italy, Luxembourg, the Netherlands, and Portugal.

Source: James (2020).

The counterpart of the current account surplus was a high level of savings, which was in part channeled abroad to finance deficits that appeared elsewhere. Cooperation is more attractive, as it seems to provide more benefits for smaller countries, and it is the heavyweights that are likely to think that they can go it on their own. From the perspective of Germany's central bank, the Deutsche Bundesbank, central bank cooperation might involve the demand for some German support operations, which would exert pressure to adopt policies that might be costly or inflationary. Bundesbank President Karl Blessing consequently spoke out to German Chancellor Konrad Adenauer against any plan for a fund of EEC countries.[2]

German surpluses provided a focus of attention on both a global and a European scale. Could the imbalances be financed and sustained? If not, there was a need for adjustment. At each stage, the extent of the imbalance measured as a share of GDP increased, mostly because international capital markets became deeper and thus allowed larger imbalances to be financed for longer periods. Germany's partners, notably France, were faced with the prospect of austerity and deflation in order to correct deficits. This alternative was unattractive to the French political elite, because it constrained growth and guaranteed electoral unpopularity. The alternative was German expansion, which was unpopular with a German public worried about the legacy of inflation and was opposed by the powerful and independent Deutsche Bundesbank.

This version of the "German question" figured in analyses of both global and European economic challenges. All of the reform proposals that led to initiatives for European integration—in 1970, in 1978, and again after 1988—were conceived as ways to address imbalances within the European system. The most radical approach was monetary union, which had the intrinsic appeal of making current account imbalances apparently vanish as well as of providing a mechanism for non-Germans to constrain the Bundesbank. In the often held up example of the United States, there is no concern about imbalances between states, and the federal economy is seen as self-correcting (largely because of flows of labor and transfer payments in a federal fiscal system). It was thus a shock when the sustainability of current account imbalances reemerged as the major challenge to the eurozone after 2010.

---

2. Historical Archive of Deutsche Bundesbank, November 4, 1958, Zentralbankrat (Central Bank Council) and November 11, 1958, Zentralbankrat (Central Bank Council).

Developments over the Past 60 Years

The Prelude of the 1960s

In the 1960s, European statesmen—in particular, French policymakers—criticized the political benefits that the United States allegedly drew from the fixed exchange rate regime of the Bretton Woods order. Finance Minister Valéry Giscard d'Estaing termed this benefit the "exorbitant privilege" in 1965; President Charles de Gaulle explained to his confidant, the Information Minister Alain Peyrefitte, that "no domain escapes from American imperialism. It takes all forms. The most insidious is that of the dollar" (Peyrefitte 2002, 603).

De Gaulle's successor, Georges Pompidou, saw European monetary union as a card that Europeans could play in an international power game. President Giscard d'Estaing, together with German Chancellor Helmut Schmidt, saw politics as the major reason why Europeans needed to act in the monetary sphere.

The politicians who took this approach consistently believed that money was much too important to be left to technocrats and central bankers. At the highpoint of the debate in the late 1970s, Schmidt went to the Bundesbank to lecture the conservative bankers about the primacy of politics. If European power politics prevailed, the creation of a European order looked like a challenge to the US-based global system. As British Prime Minister James Callaghan, a veteran of many British struggles with the International Monetary Fund (IMF), put it, "I think there comes a clear question: Do we try to build a world monetary system or are we going to have a European one?" Replying to Callaghan, European Commission President Roy Jenkins stated, "I think we might move to a substantially more coordinated European monetary position, which could help to create a better world monetary position."[3]

The constant and inevitable clash between the two logics—the political one, which saw European money as an instrument of power politics, and the technocratic one, which saw European monetary integration as a more feasible version of desirable international cooperation—resulted in a peculiar European dynamic. To work effectively, the European monetary order had to be insulated from political pressures. The grand vision of the original creators looked less and less relevant to daily concerns. Trying to protect the monetary framework created substantial vulnerability, as national politicians would mobilize sentiment against the technocratic vision of a supranational European money. The often concealed underpin-

---

3. UK National Archives, PREM 16/1615, Couzens note for Wicks, March 31, 1978; PREM 16/1641, Prime Minister's conversation with Mr. Roy Jenkins on March 31, 1978.

nings of the struggle for a European money—above all, the idea that money was all about politics—then came to the surface at moments of trouble and distress. Such beliefs nourished all manner of paranoid interpretation. Europeans are still living with this history.

The Late 1970s

The fundamental problem for currency management lay not in European but in transatlantic incompatibilities and clashes. The major difficulties followed from the weakness of the dollar, the consequence of lax fiscal policy in the aftermath of the oil shock. But many Europeans felt that it reflected a deliberate US strategy that amounted to a competitive currency devaluation of the type that had been so disastrous in the 1930s. The Europeans believed that US Treasury Secretary Michael Blumenthal was "talking down the dollar." The German newspapers carried headlines such as "Crazy Blumenthal," and Helmut Schmidt called the Blumenthal strategy "suicidal."

For their part, US policymakers were pressing Germany to engage in more expansion and act as a "locomotive" for the world economy. Their German counterparts reacted allergically. In Paris, at the Organization for Economic Cooperation and Development (OECD), the leader of the German delegation, Hans Tietmeyer, explained that there would be no German stimulus measures and ridiculed the locomotive theory. At the political level, Chancellor Schmidt explained that "the United States has neither accepted nor even understood their leadership role in the economic field."[4] Dollar depreciation increased European coordination problems, because it strengthened the Deutsch mark, which was taking on a role as a reserve currency (see figure 8.1); the other European currencies correspondingly weakened. The phenomenon was later termed dollar/Deutsch mark polarization (Giavazzi and Giovannini 1989; see also Mourlon-Druol 2012).

The April 7–8, 1978, Copenhagen Summit meeting of the European Council changed the terms of the debate. The outcome reflected a highly personal initiative of President Giscard d'Estaing and Chancellor Schmidt. Schmidt in particular was skeptical about experts and central bankers and felt that economic diplomacy, whether on the world or the European level, needed to be personalized. In the lead-up to Copenhagen, he preferred to restrict discussion of his new initiative as much as possible. Schmidt's former press adviser and economic sherpa, Karl Otto Pöhl, who had been appointed vice president of the Bundesbank, had written to Schmidt to

---

4. Hans Roeper, "Der tolle Blumenthal, "*Frankfurter Allgemeine Zeitung*, July 22, 1977; see also Wiegrefe (2005).

inform him that the Bundesbank's directorate had discussed the question of a "European contribution to solve the problem of the dollar" but that "the views of my colleagues are known to you. They continue to be skeptical and critical of such an initiative."[5]

Schmidt did not really talk with the Bundesbank (later he did talk to or at the Bundesbank), but he did tip off the British prime minister on March 12 about what he quaintly called an "exotic idea" for European currency moves:

> The idea was to create another European snake, but of a different kind. [Schmidt] would not be going as far as [European Commission President] Roy Jenkins wished to in terms of European economic and monetary union (EMU), but what he would propose was that the FRG [Federal Republic of Germany] and certain other members of the Community should each put half of their reserves into a new currency pool, the currencies of which would be fixed against a European Unit of Account. . . . He would not want this pool to be tied to the dollar, because the US economy was too large and uncontrollable: The captain was not in charge, even though he was well meaning (Story 1988, 397).

The political urgency of a European stance against the dollar became much more evident over the following weeks. Schmidt became much angrier on April 4, when the *New York Times* announced that without even informing Schmidt, President Carter had abandoned the neutron bomb, leaving Schmidt—who had spent a great deal of political capital trying to persuade the Social Democratic Party of Germany (SPD) to accept the necessity of guaranteeing German security through a new American defense initiative—isolated in his party. His frustrations appeared when he told Giscard that "the Americans need to stop believing that if they whistle, we will obey" (Story 1988, 397).

During the course of the Copenhagen Summit, Schmidt proposed that a European Monetary Fund (EMF) be created, as a regional version of the IMF and a revival of some of the 1940s idealism that had driven the Bretton Woods conference. There was also to be a revival of some of the aspirations that had originally surrounded the Basel-based European Monetary Cooperation Fund, which had been established in 1973 to promote joint action by European Community (EC) member states working toward an EMU.

Details of his plan show the extent to which Schmidt was mesmerized by the Bretton Woods construction. Countries would pool 15–20 percent of their reserves, increasingly use EC currencies rather than dollars

---

5. Bundesbank Historical Archive, N2/264, Pöhl to Schmidt, March 21, 1978.

in foreign exchange intervention, and enhance use of the European Unit of Account (EUA), the precursor of the ECU (Ludlow 1982). In Schmidt's view, these proposals would move the world away from reliance on the dollar as the sole reserve currency; he even held out the prospect that OPEC members might invest a part of their surplus in the EUA and that the EMF might issue EUA-denominated Special Drawing Rights (SDRs). "To the extent that the EUA became an alternative reserve instrument," he wrote, "it would take the pressure off the dollar. . . . There is absolutely nothing anti-American in the scheme, although it might lead to the EC becoming a little bit more inward-looking than in the past."[6]

Despite Schmidt's assurances that there was nothing anti-American about the plan, British Prime Minister James Callaghan called President Carter 10 days after the meeting to denounce Schmidt's intentions:

> My understanding of his thoughts is that he believes the dollar is going to get into serious trouble, and we ought to try to insulate ourselves from it as much as possible. Now I don't know whether that thinking has got across to you, but with the strength of the German economy it could be extremely serious and I don't know, Jimmy, how to obviate it. . . . You see he knows about international finance, he understands it, he was a minister of finance himself, he cares about it and he believes American policy is all wrong. Now as long as that persists there's going to be trouble.[7]

Carter himself does not appear to have been very worried by the British indiscretions about Europe's money, but Assistant Treasury Secretary C. Fred Bergsten pushed his boss, Treasury Secretary Michael Blumenthal, into interpreting the European initiative as a threat to American interests.

The British government was much more worried than Washington, fearing marginalization. The UK Treasury suspected that the plan was a German exercise in power projection and sketched out a plausible interpretation of German motives:

> If other EEC [European Economic Community] countries stick with the mark more and with the dollar less, that helps intra–EEC German trade and also helps Germany in competition with its EEC partners in other markets. . . . The Germans have been much preoccupied with maintaining the competitiveness of their exchange rate and the German government has been under strong

---

6. UK National Archives, PREM 16/1615, Schmidt note on remarks at Copenhagen Summit.

7. Prime Minister's telephone conversation with President Carter, April 17, 1978, British Freedom of Information Release 248745.

pressure from industry on this, although that has not stopped the Germans from suggesting that any preoccupation by deficit countries with the competitiveness of their exchange rate was misguided inflationary Keynesianism.[8]

Indeed, later in the year, German Finance Minister Manfred Lahnstein allegedly told British Chancellor of the Exchequer Denis Healey that Germany expected to gain a competitive edge by limiting the scope for other currencies to depreciate (Stephens 1996, Healey 1989). Commentary of this kind, surfacing particularly during the 1978 negotiations, gave rise to the widely held concept that the EMS (as well as the later monetary union) were strategic political devices on the part of the German authorities to lock in competitive advantages for German exporters.

Aftermath of the Plaza: The Late 1980s

The next major impetus for an international reform initiative to build a new system of stable exchange rates came in the wake of a coordinate depreciation of the dollar at the G7 Finance Ministers' Plaza Meeting of September 1985. In February 1987, at a follow-up meeting at the Louvre, French Finance Minister Eduard Balladur proposed a system of target zones with a 5 percent range and a mechanism for triggering coordinated interventions as exchange rates moved to the boundaries of the zone. The proposals for specific figures ran into heavy criticism, above all from Germany and Japan. Looking back on 1987, Bundesbank's president concluded:

> Europe is not in a position to stabilize the dollar. Even large interventions do not work if the Federal Reserve does not participate and the US does not follow appropriate policies. What matters is to preserve the EMS intact, and the Bundesbank will do all that it can to realize that objective.[9]

European Commission President Jacques Delors spoke of "Europe's capacity to resist."[10] Balladur set in motion a new drama. He saw the January 1987 depreciation of the franc as a humiliation imposed on the French government by the market and the Germans. But in the opinion of the French Treasury, the EMS, as marginally augmented, was not capable of dealing with the issues that would arise from the creation of the integrated capital market. The French vision saw Germany as primarily responsible for the financial crisis of October 1987, which France claimed reflected

---

8. UK National Archives, PREM 16/1634, June 22, 1978, DWH: European Currency Arrangements.

9. ECB (European Central Bank) Archive, Committee of Central Bank Governors Meeting 219, November 10, 1987. See also James (2012, 227).

10. Ibid.

insufficient German economic stimulus, because of the Bundesbank's increase of interest rates at the "wrong moment" and German toleration of an excessive weakening of the dollar. A French Treasury memorandum of January 8, 1988, followed up by press articles and interviews, took up some of the themes of the 1970s, particularly the notion of "asymmetry" in the EMS. Balladur argued that all member states should be brought into its narrow bands; that asymmetries should be reduced (in other words, that Germany should undertake more adjustment); and that there should be a coordinated policy with respect to the dollar.

Historian Eric Bussière correctly sees Balladur's campaign as a "continuation of debates that had started in the era of Georges Pompidou" (Bussière 2007, 63). But the French report also spoke of the liberalization of capital markets and the logic of creating a zone with a single currency, managed by a common central bank and federal banks in all member countries (Dyson and Featherstone 1999). The new central bank would be given a "certain authority," but such a scheme would be likely to be realized only around 2000.[11]

When German foreign minister Hans-Dietrich Genscher appeared sympathetic, Delors asked Europe's central bankers to prepare a timetable and a plan for a currency union. The Delors Committee met between September 1988 and April 1989, at the Bank for International Settlements in Basel. It produced its report at a moment when no one in Western Europe seriously thought that a profound geopolitical transformation such as the collapse of the Soviet bloc and of communist ideology was at all likely (the crumbling of the Berlin Wall in November 1989 was a surprise to almost everyone, including European governments).

A comparison of the integration discussions of the 1970s and 1980s is instructive. The negotiations to create the EMS and its associated ERM were largely governmental. Although Roy Jenkins saw them as his initiative as Commission president, success actually depended on the high-level cooperation between Helmut Schmidt and Valéry Giscard d'Estaing. When Jenkins's successor, Jacques Delors, wanted to initiate a monetary discussion, he very deliberately started the process through an intense cultivation of the central bankers, largely through their regular meetings at the Committee of Central Bank Governors in Basel.

The positive outcome of the Delors Committee was a surprise, given that the most powerful central banker on the committee, Bundesbank President Karl Otto Pöhl, was generally believed to be opposed to any project for enhanced monetary cooperation and the Eurosceptic UK

---

11. Interview with Balladur, *Le Figaro*, January 14, 1988.

government tried to keep the British member of the committee working with Pöhl to frustrate such cooperation. As the report required unanimity in order to be convincing or effective, it thus seemed more or less certain at the outset that the project would not lead to the visionary result intended by Delors. Some of the success of the Delors Report—or at least its ability to formulate any final report—can be attributed to the character of Pöhl. Margaret Thatcher had consented to the constitution of the Delors Committee only because she believed that Pöhl's powerful presence would mean that the committee would not reach any dangerous conclusion on European monetary integration. But Pöhl was intellectually lazy and did not harness the resources of the Bundesbank to provide any support for his position. In contrast, his highly meticulous and well-prepared French colleague, Jacques de Larosière, and the enthusiastically pro-European rapporteur Tomaso Padoa-Schioppa, were ready to lay out a detailed and persuasive roadmap for monetary union.

The Delors Report clearly laid out the path to monetary union, defined as "a currency area in which policies are managed jointly with a view to attaining common macroeconomic objectives" (Delors 1989, 14). But the committee also added a rider:

> The adoption of a single currency, while not strictly necessary for the creation of a monetary union, might be seen for economic as well as psychological and political reasons as a natural and desirable further development of the monetary union. A single currency would clearly demonstrate the irreversibility of the move to monetary union, considerably facilitate the monetary management of the Community and avoid the transactions costs of converting currencies (Delors 1989, 15).

The report provided for a three-stage process. Stage one simply expanded existing cooperative arrangements, to which even the Eurosceptic government of Margaret Thatcher could have no objection. In stage two, a new European System of Central Banks (ESCB) would manage the transition from the combination of monetary policies of national central banks to a common monetary policy. In stage three, exchange rates would be finally and irrevocably locked. The ESCB would pool reserves and manage interventions with regard to third currencies. "With the establishment of the European System of Central Banks, the Community would also have created an institution through which it could participate in all aspects of international monetary coordination" (Section 38). Delors emphasized that monetary integration would need to be accompanied by a consolidation of the single market and competition policy, as well as by an evaluation and adaptation of regional policies (Section 56).

Finalization of the monetary union was also stimulated by a sharp episode of dollar weakness in April–August 1992, in which the dollar depreciated by almost 20 percent against the Deutsch mark (see figure 8.1). Despite this decline, the Federal Reserve cut interest rates on July 2. The cover of *The Economist* of August 29, 1992, depicted the falling dollar as the world's main problem. Dollar weakness then, as in the 1970s and 1980s produced the effect of "dollar polarization" in which the Deutsch mark strengthened relative to other European currencies.

A more efficient way of reducing the strains on the EMS might lie in intervening on a global level to stop the rise of the Deutsch mark against the dollar. The Europeans pressed the US Treasury to this effect. The Federal Reserve, which had been skeptical about this coordinated intervention, then pleaded to stop. One of the reasons the New York Fed officials later gave for opposing intervention was that the Bundesbank was opposed to it; the Frankfurt central bank viewed the crisis as an opportunity to fundamentally change the EMS.

The near collapse of the EMS in the currency crises of September 1992 and July 1993 made it clear that the choice was simple. It lay in what was termed at the time a "corner solution"—either floating or a completely, unalterably fixed exchange rate in the form of a monetary union. Anything else would be an easy target for currency speculation.

Postlude

In the long, drawn-out European debt crisis that followed the 2007–09 global financial crisis, the old concerns came to the fore once more: worry about the dollar, concern with German current account surpluses, and speculative flows (as markets took positions on a possible breakup of the currency union). The depreciation of the dollar as a consequence of a new monetary policy approach (quantitative easing) heightened fears of an uncompetitive European economy. In a notorious newspaper interview, former Fed Chair Alan Greenspan claimed that "America is also pursuing a policy of currency weakening."[12] The German finance minister promptly denounced US policy. But the move helped convince the European Bank, especially under its new president, Mario Draghi, that a more expansive monetary policy, including asset purchases, and a greater measure of fiscal integration were required. As in the past, response to the perception that the anchoring of the international monetary system around the dollar drove European crisis management and spurred institutional innovation.

---

12. Alan Beattie, "Greenspan Criticises China but Warns US over Weaker Dollar," *Financial Times*, November 11, 2010.

The new monetary policy became reality; the new fiscal policy did not. The euro remained a restricted, "can't do" currency. The lack of a common fiscal framework represents a long-standing limitation on ambitions for groups of countries to follow the logic of the debates at the end of the Bretton Woods system and seek a replacement for the US dollar.

References

BIS (Bank for International Settlements). 1974. *Théron Report No. 17*, January 2. Basel.

Bussière, Éric. 2007. Le ministère des Finances et les enjeux économiques européens à l'époque de la cohabitation 1986-1988. In *Milieux économiques et intégration européenne au XXe siècle*, ed. Eric Bussière, Michel Dumoulin, and Sylvain Schirmann, 147-63. Paris: Institut de la gestion publique et du développement économique.

Delors, Jacques. 1989. *Committee for the Study of Economic and Monetary Union: Report on Economic and Monetary Union in the European Community*. Brussels: European Commission.

Dyson, Kenneth, and Kevin Featherstone. 1999. *The Road to Maastricht: Negotiating Economic and Monetary Union*. New York: Oxford University Press.

Giavazzi, Francesco, and Alberto Giovannini. 1989. *Limiting Exchange Rate Flexibility: The European Monetary System*. Cambridge, MA: MIT Press.

Healey, Denis. 1989. *The Time of My Life*. London: M. Joseph.

James, Harold. 2012. *Making the European Monetary Union*. Cambridge, MA: Harvard University Press.

James, Harold. 2020. The BIS and the European Monetary Experiment. In *Promoting Global Monetary and Financial* Stability: The Bank for International Settlements after Bretton Woods, 1973–2020, ed. Claudio Borio, Stijn Claessens, Piet Clement, Robert McCauley, and Hyun Song Shin, 11–45. Cambridge: Cambridge University Press.

Kruse, Douglas C. 1980. *Monetary Integration in Western Europe: EMU, EMS and Beyond*. London: Butterworths.

Ludlow, Peter. 1982. *The Making of the European Monetary System: A Case Study of the Politics of the European Community*. London: Butterworths.

Mourlon-Druol, Emmanuel. 2012. *A Europe Made of Money: The Emergence of the European Monetary System*. Ithaca, NY: Cornell University Press.

Peyrefitte, Alain. 2002. *C'était de Gaulle*. Paris: Gallimard.

Stephens, Philip. 1996. *Politics and the Pound: The Conservatives' Struggle with Sterling*. London: Macmillan.

Story, Jonathan. 1988. The Launching of the EMS: An Analysis of Change in Foreign Economic Policy. *Political Studies* 36, no. 3 (September): 397–412.

Wiegrefe, Klaus. 2005. *Das Zerwürfnis: Helmut Schmidt, Jimmy Carter und die Krise der deutsch-amerikanische Beziehungen*. Berlin: Propyläen.

9

Has Japan Conquered the Fear of Freedom? Reflections on Exchange Rate Systems and Monetary Policy

MASAZUMI WAKATABE

I was deputy governor of the Bank of Japan until March 19, 2023, so as a freshly minted ex-policymaker, I suppose I am expected to offer both Japanese and policymaking perspectives. But I myself did not deal with any intrigues of yen-dollar diplomacy, so my observations are mainly on the relationship between exchange rate systems and monetary policy.

The question of my title captures the Japanese attitudes toward a floating exchange rate system. I borrowed it from Shinji Takagi's 2015 excellent overview of Japanese exchange rate policy up to the start of Abenomics, *Conquering the Fear of Freedom*. My answer to this question is "not really," but there have been important developments and improvements.

Exchange Rates and International Monetary Regimes at the Intersection of Politics and Economics

Exchange rates and international monetary regimes have been at the intersection of politics and economics, both domestic and international, and will remain so in the future. The choice of a regime is not only an economic but also a political decision (see chapter 7 by Jeffry Frieden). Economics and politics are intertwined, politics and public opinion matter a lot, and the issue of the exchange rate is easily likely to be politicized.

Institutionally, Japan's exchange rate policy is the sole responsibility of the Ministry of Finance, for which the Bank of Japan acts as agent. It is

Masazumi Wakatabe, former deputy governor of the Bank of Japan, is professor of economics in the Faculty of Political Science and Economics at Waseda University.

the Ministry of Finance that sets exchange rate policy. However, monetary policy has played an immensely important role in the movement of the exchange rate under the floating exchange rate system with free capital mobility. This institutional division of labor and macroeconomic logic have been a potential source of tensions.

There is also a question of central bank independence. The Bank of Japan did not have statutory independence before April 1998, but it made important policy decisions even without it.

Related to this issue is the adoption of inflation targeting. The Bank of Japan resisted adopting such a policy until 2013, hampering its fight against deflation, causing its monetary policy to drift unnecessarily, and exerting appreciating pressures on exchange rates. As Japan became a major external balance surplus country in the 1980s, trade tensions with the United States intensified and became highly politicized. Indeed, Japanese exchange rate and monetary policies have been under the strong influence of the fluctuating Japan-US relationship.[1] I return to these points later in this chapter.

Role of the Inflation Targeting Regime in Saving the Floating Exchange Rate System

The floating rate system has been resilient. The classical gold standard system lasted from around 1870 until 1914.[2] The interwar restoration period was short-lived, cut short by the Great Depression. The Bretton Woods system lasted from 1946 to 1973.

The current system has thus lived longer than any other international monetary system. One reason why is that floating exchange rates give countries more freedom and flexibility. Another reason is the evolution of a monetary policy framework. After some trial and error, including the Great Inflation of the 1970s to the early 1980s, central banks found a nominal anchor ("inflation targeting"). Since then, monetary policy framework has evolved into an inflation targeting regime, adopted by many countries. It is no coincidence that New Zealand adopted inflation targeting in 1990, after it had to abandon its exchange rate peg. One could thus think of the past

---

1. For one important aspect of Japan-US trade disputes (over semiconductors), see the excellent account by Miller (2022).

2. The classical international gold standard system started in 1873, when major countries and groups of countries, including the German Empire, the Latin Monetary Union, and the United States, adopted it. The Austro-Hungarian Empire adopted it only in 1882, and the Russian Empire did so only in 1897. Canada floated its currency from 1950 to 1962.

50 years as divided into two periods, the "adolescent" period (from 1973 to 1992 or the mid-1990s) and the more mature, coming-of-age period.[3]

A floating exchange rate system is more durable than other systems because (unlike Bretton Woods) it was not imposed from the top, and inflation targeting provided a much needed nominal anchor without too rigid constraints. Although inflation targeting has not yet outlasted the classical gold standard regime, it has outlasted the Bretton Woods regime. Table 9.1 compares international monetary regimes.

The subsequent evolution of the monetary policy regime enhanced the durability of the current exchange rate system by reducing exchange rate volatility. Figure 9.1 replicates (and extends to the end of 2022) the findings of Ilzetzki, Reinhart, and Rogoff (2020) on exchange rate volatility for the dollar-yen and dollar-euro exchange rates, both of which declined beginning around the late 1980s.

Testing the Principles of Japan's Exchange Rate and Monetary Policies

The Japanese experience shows that not only volatility but also the level of exchange rates matters a lot. The freedom of floating exchange rates has been testing the principles of Japanese policymakers on exchange rate and monetary policy. Given the freedom of the flexible exchange regime, policymakers are required to focus on domestic policy goals such as inflation or employment. Japan's experience shows that when policymakers deviate from the price stability goal in favor of exchange rate considerations, the economy suffers.

Figure 9.2 summarizes 60 years of Japanese economic history. It shows divergence between theoretical values and actual values of the dollar-yen exchange rate. It takes more than a grain of salt to take theoretical values based on purchasing power parity (PPP) using the producer price index at face value, but they provide one way to investigate data over time.[4]

---

3. Using this analogy, one is tempted to think about whether the current system is fit at 50 or having a midlife crisis, but I leave this question aside.

4. I calculated the theoretical PPP rate by dividing the producer price index in Japan by the producer price index in the United States. There have been discussions about which price indices one should use to calculate the PPP rate. Figure 9.2 should therefore be interpreted with caution (although an analysis based on the unit price of exports [Eichengreen 2006] results in similar conclusions).

Table 9.1

Features of the gold standard, the Bretton Woods, and the inflation targeting international monetary regimes

Feature	Gold standard	Bretton Woods	Inflation targeting
Regime durability	Low	Low	High
Exchange rate regime	Fixed	Fixed	Floating
Focus of monetary policy	International	International (at least in part)	Mostly domestic, while international for emerging targeters
Intermediate target	Exchange rate	Exchange rate	Inflation forecast
Capital mobility	Largely unrestricted	Controlled	Relatively unrestricted
Capacity for current account imbalances	Limited	Limited	High
System design	Unplanned	Planned	Unplanned

Role of the International Monetary Fund	n.a.	Key in principle	Small
Role of center country	Key in practice	Essential	Key in practice
Central banks	Dependent, unaccountable	Dependent, unaccountable	Independent, accountable
Alignment with academics	Low	Low	High

Source: Adapted from Rose (2007).

Figure 9.1

Exchange rates between the dollar and the yen, Deutsch mark, and euro, August 1971–December 2022

a. Dollar-yen exchange rate

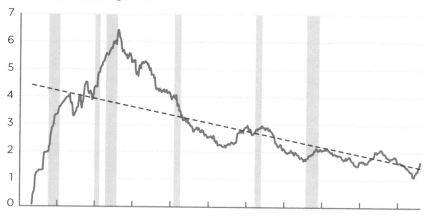

b. Dollar-euro exchange rate[a]

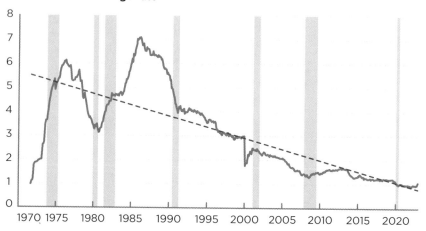

a. August 1971–December 1999, Deutsche mark per US dollar; from January 2000 onward, euro per US dollar.

Note: Figure shows five-year moving average of absolute values of month-on-month changes in the exchange rate. Vertical grey bars show US recessions.

Source: Author's calculations based on IMF, *International Financial Statistics*; and Ilzetzki, Reinhart, and Rogoff (2020).

Figure 9.2
Theoretical strengths and weaknesses in the dollar-yen market, January 1960–January 2023

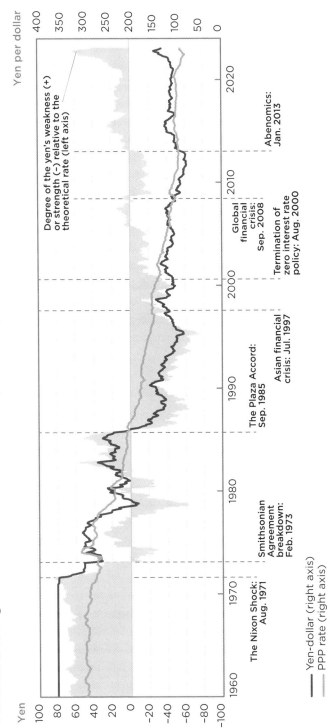

Notes: The purchasing power parity (PPP) rate is the theoretical dollar-yen rate based on the producer price indices in Japan and the United States. The base year for the producer price index is 2020. The base year for the United States is 1982, converted to 2020 by the author.

Source: Author's calculations based on data from Federal Reserve Bank of St. Louis, Federal Reserve Economic Data (FRED), and Bank of Japan.

The Bretton Woods system served Japan very well. Actual values were well under theoretical values, and the yen was consistently undervalued.[5] During this period, Japan became Asia's New Giant (Patrick and Rosovsky 1976), or "China before China," through rapid economic growth. Japan's inflation rate remained stable, at around 4–5 percent.

The breakup of the Bretton Woods system led to an appreciation of the yen, but there was no consistent pattern of appreciation from 1975 to 1985. During this period, Japan experienced the "Great Moderation before the Great Moderation." Its inflation rate declined rapidly, from a peak of 23.2 percent in 1974 to a comfortable 2.0 percent in 1985; its real growth rate was higher than that of other advanced economies; and it did not experience stagflation.

The period coincided with the Bank of Japan's taming of the Great Inflation and the adoption of quasi-monetary growth targeting. It is debatable whether the Bank of Japan ever followed a monetary growth–targeting rule, which monetarists advocated, but it did embrace a price stability mandate more forcefully and transparently than it had earlier.[6] Although the central bank did not have statutory independence before 1998, it showed that price stability was achievable when the government and the central bank cooperated closely, and the central bank had some sort of nominal anchor.

Things changed dramatically when the government and the Bank of Japan decided to target exchange rates instead of the inflation rate.[7] Japan's "lost decades" coincided almost exactly with the combination of deflation and appreciation of the yen; actual values of the yen were consistently well over theoretical values from 1985 to 2013.

The "ever-higher yen syndrome" started with the Plaza Accord of 1985.[8] The government and the Bank of Japan began targeting exchange rates to appreciate the yen in order to ease pressures from US government officials who were concerned with the increased trade deficits with Japan.[9]

---

5. Eichengreen (2006, 90) argues for the undervaluation of the yen, noting that "Japanese export prices fell by 29 percent relative to those of its industrial country competitors between 1951 and 1967. All this suggests growing undervaluation."

6. Cargill, Hutchison, and Ito (1997, 47–49) argue that the Bank of Japan did not adopt a monetary-targeting rule in a way that monetarists advocated.

7. On this critical episode in the history of Japanese exchange rate policy, see Obstfeld (2009).

8. I owe coinage of the phrase "ever-higher yen syndrome" to McKinnon and Ohno (1997). See Obstfeld (2009) for a macroeconomic policy explanation of the syndrome.

9. Wakatabe and Kataoka (2011) estimate the policy reaction function of the Bank of Japan in three periods: the Great Inflation (1967Q1 to 1974Q4), from stabilization to the

From 1985 until 2013, Japanese macroeconomic policy drifted and its performance deteriorated. This error in macroeconomic policy should be considered the starting point of Japan's "lost decades" (Wakatabe 2015).

What about central bank independence? The Bank of Japan was granted statutory independence in April 1998. It did not improve its performance, however, because the law did not clearly define the bank's price stability mandate.[10] As Japan's Great Moderation in the mid-1970s to mid-1980s showed, central bank independence is not necessary to achieve price stability, and without some clear inflation target, price stability is not ensured even if the central bank is independent.

From this perspective, one way to interpret Abenomics is that it ended the "ever-higher yen syndrome" by restoring the price stability target with the introduction of a 2 percent target. Since 2013 there has been no appreciating trend for the yen, and actual values have been above theoretical values.[11] In this sense, Abenomics could be considered as a regime shift in monetary policy to establish a full-fledged inflation targeting regime in Japan in a floating exchange rate system, with significant consequences for exchange rate movements.[12]

Plaza Accord (1975Q1 to 1985Q3), and from the Plaza Accord to the bubble economy (1985Q4 to 1989Q4). Our results, which are broadly consistent with the literature, show that (a) during the Great Inflation period, the coefficients on the inflation gap and interest rate smoothing were significant, suggesting that the weight of monetary policy was on the inflation gap; (b) during the period between stabilization and the Plaza Accord, the coefficients on the inflation gap, the GDP gap, and the interest rate smoothing were significant, suggesting that the weight was on both the inflation gap and the GDP gap; (c) during the period between the Plaza Accord and the bubble economy, the coefficients on the exchange rate gap were significant, suggesting that the weight was on the exchange rate; and (d) interest rate smoothing was significant throughout the entire period, but the degree of smoothing increased between the Great Inflation period and the stable growth period, before declining after the Plaza Accord period.

10. Orphanides (2018) emphasizes this point. It did not help that Masaru Hayami, the first governor under the new Bank of Japan Law, was a staunch believer in the "strong yen" and a Schumpeterian thesis that only innovation-induced structural reforms could help boost the economy during recessions (Wakatabe 2015).

11. For a brief period in 2004–05, the US authorities did not object to Japan's aggressive foreign exchange intervention, which they took as a measure for combating deflation. The period was too brief. For this episode, see an eyewitness account by Taylor (2007).

12. There is an intriguing and potentially significant question about whether undervaluation may be justified. One may argue that undervaluation represented a make-up strategy after a long period of overvaluation, a correction based on Japan's having experienced hysteresis.

Japan's economic performance improved considerably after 2013.[13] First, economic growth was restored. Reflecting the declining and aging population, as well as the downtrend in working hours, Japan's GDP growth rate is trending downward, but when excluding the decline caused by the pandemic, it has improved since 2013, as the unemployment rate declined and the number of employed persons increased. Real GDP growth per capita averaged 0.4 percent in the 2000s; it reached 1.3 percent in the 2010s, almost equivalent to the average growth rate of the 1990s.[14]

I have always believed that the negative impacts of a declining population on the economy have been exaggerated in general discussions. An international comparison of population growth rates and per capita GDP growth rates shows that there is no clear correlation between them. Although it is true that a declining population is a headwind for economic activity, economic growth is still possible even in such circumstances.

Second, despite the decline in the young population, employment increased. The increase was initially driven by a rise in nonregular employees, but the number of regular employees in Japan also increased after 2015.[15] Improvement in employment conditions led to an increase in the employment rate for new graduates and changed the situation drastically compared with the "employment ice age" (around 1993–2005). In addition, the labor force participation rates for seniors and women rose. Of course, providing support for people who struggled to find jobs during the employment ice age remains a crucial task. In this regard as well, large-scale monetary easing, which provides support for the economy, is playing an important role.

Third, tax revenues increased, reflecting economic growth. Before the pandemic, the debt-to-GDP ratio in both net and gross terms had been stabilizing. In this sense, monetary easing contributed to fiscal consolidation.

Fourth, Japan is no longer experiencing deflation, although it has not yet achieved the 2 percent price stability target in a sustainable and stable manner. The average year-on-year rate of change in the consumer price index (all items less fresh food) was –0.3 percent between fiscal 1998 and fiscal 2012; starting in fiscal 2013 to fiscal 2019, it averaged 0.5 percent.

---

13. The next five paragraphs draw on a speech I gave at a meeting with local leaders in Shizuoka, February 2, 2023 (https://www.boj.or.jp/en/about/press/koen_2023/ko230202a.htm), with some modifications. See also Haruhiko Kuroda, "Japan's Inflation Dynamics and the Role of Monetary Policy," speech at Columbia University, New York, April 22, 2022, https://www.boj.or.jp/en/about/press/koen_2022/ko220423a.htm.

14. See Kuroda, "Japan's Inflation Dynamics and the Role of Monetary Policy," figure 12.

15. See table 6-1 at https://www.stat.go.jp/data/roudou/sokuhou/nen/ft/pdf/index.pdf.

Fifth, wages rose. Base pay—which had barely risen for 15 years—began to increase in fiscal 2014, and nominal wages increased, albeit moderately.[16]

Conclusion

Has Japan conquered its fear of freedom? With the introduction of the Bank of Japan's 2 percent price stability target, it seems that Japan has finally achieved both freedom and stability within the floating exchange rate system.[17]

But the fear of freedom is not completely gone. Public opinion oscillates as exchange rates fluctuate (figure 9.3). When the yen appreciates, people worry about a "yen appreciation recession"; when the yen depreciates, people talk about "bad depreciation."[18]

The media began circulating stories about "bad yen depreciation" starting in September 2021, often citing the declining trend in the real effective exchange rate of the yen.[19] Combined with the perception that real wages in Japan had been stagnating, the depreciation of the yen became symbolic in the popular mind of Japan's declining "national strength." As depreciation accelerated starting in March 2022, when the Federal Reserve started to raise policy interest rates, the media intensified its criticism that Japanese monetary policy was responsible for the depreciation. At the same time, as the inflation rate in Japan finally rose to around 2 percent,[20] negative reactions in the media increased. This recent episode reminds us that the public has not yet conquered the fear of freedom.

16. There are serious issues concerning statistics in Japan for analyzing real wages, as I explain in a speech I gave at a meeting with local leaders in Hiroshima, September 1, 2021, https://www.boj.or.jp/en/about/press/koen_2021/ko210901a.htm. For prices to rise in a sustainable and stable manner, both wages and inflation expectations need to increase. I describe the link between prices and wages in a speech I gave at a meeting with local leaders in Okayama, June 1, 2022, https://www.boj.or.jp/en/about/press/koen_2022/ko220601a.htm.

17. A shift in US attention from Japan to China may have contributed to this more favorable environment in Japan.

18. This fluctuating public sentiment toward exchange rates is deeply rooted, as Hatase (2023) shows. In the period just before the return to the gold standard, in the 1920s, some groups of businesspeople whose interests should have been clearly opposed to the return to gold at the pre-World War I parity were in favor of the return, because they were more concerned with the volatility of exchange rates than with their level.

19. *Nihon Keizai Shimbun*, Japan's leading business newspaper, began using the phrase "bad yen depreciation" on September 29, 2021, when the exchange rate hit 111 yen per dollar. See Futoshi Oguri, "Lingering 'Bad Yen Depreciation' Would Damage the Economy," *Nihon Keizai Shimbun*, Morning Edition, September 29, 2021.

20. The Japanese government induced mobile phone carriers to lower their mobile phone charges starting in April 2021. This dampened the CPI inflation rate from April 2021 to March 2022, but the effects on the CPI disappeared a year later.

Figure 9.3

Public concern about yen appreciation and depreciation, as captured by Google Trends in Japan, 2004–23

popularity of term (100 = peak popularity)

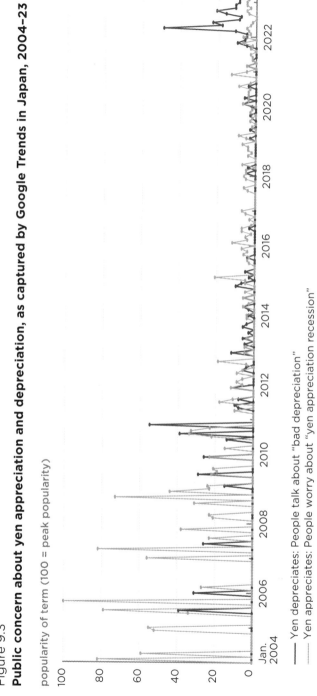

—— Yen depreciates: People talk about "bad depreciation"
---- Yen appreciates: People worry about "yen appreciation recession"

Note: Figure represents search interest relative to the highest point for the region and time. A value of 100 is the peak popularity for the term.

Source: Google Trends, https://www.google.com/trends.

References

Cargill, Thomas F., Michael M. Hutchinson, and Takatoshi Ito. 1997. *The Political Economy of Japanese Monetary Policy*. Cambridge, MA: MIT Press.

Eichengreen, Barry. 2006. *Global Imbalances and the Lessons of Bretton Woods*. Cambridge, MA: MIT Press.

Hatase, Mariko. 2023. *How Do People Form the Perception of the Linkage between Foreign Exchange Rates and Exports? An Experience of Modern Japan*. IMES Discussion Paper Series 2023-E-8. Institute for Monetary and Economic Studies, Bank of Japan.

Ilzetzki, E., C. M. Reinhart, and K.S. Rogoff. 2020. *Will the Secular Decline in Exchange Rate and Inflation Volatility Survive COVID-19?* NBER Working Paper 28108. Cambridge, MA: National Bureau of Economic Research.

McKinnon, Ronald, and Kenichi Ohno. 1997. *Dollar and Yen: Resolving Economic Conflict between the United States and Japan*. Cambridge, MA: MIT Press.

Miller, Chris. 2022. *Chip War: The Fight for the World's Most Critical Technology*. New York: Simon and Schuster.

Obstfeld, Maurice. 2009. *Time of Troubles: The Yen and Japan's Economy, 1985–2008*. NBER Working Paper 14816. Cambridge, MA: National Bureau of Economic Research.

Orphanides, Athanasios. 2018. The Boundaries of Central Bank Independence: Lessons from Unconventional Times. Keynote Speech by Athanasios Orphanides. *Monetary and Economic Studies* 36 (November): 35–56. Institute for Monetary and Economic Studies, Bank of Japan.

Patrick, Hugh, and Henry Rosovsky, eds. 1976. *Asia's New Giant: How the Japanese Economy Works*. Washington: Brookings Institution.

Rose, Andrew K. 2007. A Stable International Monetary System Emerges: Inflation Targeting Is Bretton Woods, Reversed. *Journal of International Money and Finance* 26: 663–81.

Takagi, Shinji. 2015. *Conquering the Fear of Freedom: Japanese Exchange Rate Policy since 1945*. Oxford: Oxford University Press.

Taylor, John B. 2007. *Global Financial Warriors: The Untold Story of International Finance in the Post-9/11 World*, New York: W. W. Norton & Company.

Wakatabe, Masazumi. 2015. *Japan's Great Stagnation and Abenomics: Lessons for the World*. New York: Palgrave/Macmillan.

Wakatabe, Masazumi, and Goushi Kataoka. 2011. *The Great Inflation in Japan: How Economic Thought Interacted with Economic Policy*. TCER Working Paper E-36. Tokyo: Tokyo Center for Economic Research. Available at https://www.tcer.or.jp/wp/pdf/e36.pdf.

10

The Trade-Finance Disconnect: Geopolitical Repricing and Its Consequences

YANLIANG MIAO AND ZHOU FAN

China's reintegration into the world economy can be said to have started with the historic meeting between President Richard M. Nixon and Chairman Mao Zedong in 1972, just as the Bretton Woods system was unraveling. Few would have predicted then that only 50 years later, China would be the world's second-largest economy—the largest on a purchasing power parity basis—and its renminbi a potential challenger to the US dollar's dominant-currency status.

Since the turn of the century, the dollar-based system has both supported and benefited from China's integration into world markets. China's accession to the World Trade Organization (WTO) in 2001 heralded its transformation into the world's largest trading country. Its manufacturing capabilities are a lynchpin for trade globalization, which in turn enhances the dollar's function as a medium of exchange.

A quieter but nonetheless significant landmark occurred in 2018, when China let the renminbi float, creating the conditions for independent

Yanliang Miao is Chief Strategist and Executive Head of the Research Department at China International Capital Corporation. Prior to his current position, he was Chief Economist at China's State Administration of Foreign Exchange. Zhou Fan holds a PhD in Economics from Cornell University, his research is focused on international capital markets and finance. The authors are very grateful to PIIE and conference organizers Douglas A. Irwin, Maurice Obstfeld, and Adam S. Posen. They are particularly grateful to the volume editor, Maurice Obstfeld, for his very helpful comments and suggestions. They also thank Shanwen Gao, Egor Gornostay, Beichen Huang, Yiping Huang, Hemin Li, Zhao Li, Kevin Liu, Richard Portes, Eswar Prasad, Hélène Rey, Dong Wei, and Shang-Jin Wei for helpful discussions. The views expressed in this chapter are solely those of the authors and do not necessarily represent those of their affiliated organizations.

monetary policy. China's independent monetary policy, economic cycle, and asset returns offer much needed diversification to a global economy highly sensitive to US shocks. Deepening risk-sharing between China and the world seemed a promising avenue for increasing the stability of the dollar-based system.

The past over five years have proved challenging for this dynamic. The China-US trade war, COVID-19, and the Russia-Ukraine war came on the heels of one another, driving sharp realignments from seeking efficiency to seeking geopolitical safety. With tensions between the world's two largest economies running high, global trade growth stagnated, and financial flows from advanced economies to emerging markets slowed. With a sea change in trade and financial flows at the aggregate level, a natural question to ask is whether the world is becoming bipolar, as some observers have warned.

How has the structure of trade and financial networks been reshaped in the past few years? Analysis of bilateral trade and financial claims data for 45 economies reveals a disconnect between trade and finance. Trade flows between China and advanced economies have remained highly resilient, but financial investments have exhibited geopolitical repricing. Financial investments from advanced economies to China have decreased while their investments in the United States have increased sharply. Equity investments—arguably the most effective means of risk-sharing—show the strongest signs of geopolitical repricing. Thus, both the aggregate amount and the composition of financial flows have become less supportive of global risk-sharing.

Is the trade-finance disconnect simply a natural phenomenon? The classical Heckscher-Ohlin-Mundell (Mundell 1957) trade framework states that trade and capital flows are substitutes, but most subsequent theories find that financial flows may complement trade flows through a wide range of mechanisms (Markusen 1983; Obstfeld and Rogoff 2000; Lane and Milesi-Feretti 2008; Portes and Rey 2005; Antras and Caballero 2009; Aviat and Coeurdacier 2007; Ding et al. 2019; Belke and Domnick 2021; Kalemli-Özcan, Nikolsko-Rzhevskyy, and Kwak 2020). Some scholars explain the complementary relationship between international trade and finance through bilateral relationships (Rose and Spiegel 2004; Taylor and Wilson 2006). Conventional theories cannot, however, explain the recent trade–finance disconnect.

Our hypothesis for the disconnect is that equity holdings are fickler and more sensitive to geopolitical tensions than trade flows are. We provide some preliminary analysis supporting this geopolitical repricing hypothesis. After 2018, geopolitical alignment has become a more important determinant of equity holdings worldwide. An alternative hypothesis that we cannot fully rule out is that advanced economies are shifting their investments simply because US equities provide better overall returns than do investments in China.

The ongoing disconnect between trade and finance suggests that the global economy and dollar-based system are at a crossroads that could lead to two possible futures. In the first, financial investments between advanced economies and China are eventually restored. Optimists could argue that the resilience of trade flows implies that financial investments have overreacted to geopolitical tensions. In this view, the current repricing is excessive and will eventually revert to normal.

In the second possible future, financial investments serve as a harbinger of the future segmentation of trade networks, indicating a fractured bipolar world ahead. A defining feature of this world would be two separate trade and financial networks, anchored by China and the United States, respectively. Fracturing would be detrimental to both efficiency and risk-sharing, because a globalized world offers the biggest market possible for realizing economies of scale and diversifying investments.

Whether we move back toward an integrated international world economy/financial system or edge toward the brink of a fractured bipolar world depends on actions taken. Constructive actions would provide support to the dollar-based system; destructive ones would cause instability. Enhancing the global safety net and encouraging financial flows between advanced economies and China would reduce the trade-finance disconnect.

A Gravity Model of the Trade-Finance Disconnect

To understand the changing landscape of global trade and finance, we use a workhorse gravity model common in the international trade and finance literature (Bergstrand 1985; Anderson and Van Wincoop 2004; Portes and Rey 2005; Lustig and Richmond 2020). This model allows us to control for natural predeterminants of trade and finance, such as size and distance between partners. We also include country-year fixed effects, to control for the overall intensity of trade/financial linkages that a country has with all other partners in a given year (see the online data appendix for details), so that we can control for year-specific common shocks, such as COVID-19, which may have affected all trade/financial investments.[1]

In the rest of this chapter, we examine excess trade/financial intensities to China and the United States, defined as the percentage of total trade (investment) that is not explained by the empirical gravity model inclusive of fixed effects. We believe that policymaker or investor choices to modify

---

1. The online data appendix is available in this volume's data replication package, available at https://www.piie.com/bookstore/2024/floating-exchange-rates-fifty.

economic and financial relationships with China or the United States affect excess intensities and their trends. The choices made may have been influenced by factors such as geopolitical tensions and domestic public opinion.

Trade Flows

Over the past 20 years, China became an increasingly important trading partner for advanced economies (figure 10.1).[2] From 1998 onward, (excess) trade intensities between China and advanced economies rose, and trade intensities between the United States and advanced economies remained relatively flat. These trends culminated in China surpassing the United States in terms of trade intensities for many countries (France, Germany, the United Kingdom, Italy, and Japan) around 2008.

Despite rising geopolitical tensions between allies of China and the United States, trade intensities between the world's manufacturing hub and advanced economies have remained remarkably resilient. Even since the China-US trade war in 2018, most countries have increased their trade intensities with China. China-US trade intensity dropped sharply in 2018 but rose from 2019 to 2021. Overall, these patterns reflect China's comprehensive manufacturing capacities. They also suggest that businesses in advanced economies have remained pragmatic, despite rising domestic populism and rhetoric.

China is also an increasingly dominant trade partner for emerging-market economies (figure 10.2). It has retained stronger trade intensities than the United States with a few countries (e.g., Chile) and gradually overtaken the United States in terms of trade intensities for many others (e.g., South Korea). The two outliers are India (which is geopolitically closer to the United States) and Mexico (which is a party to the North American Trade Agreement [NAFTA]/the United States-Mexico-Canada Agreement [USMCA]).

Portfolio Equity Holdings

For portfolio equity holdings, bond holdings, and foreign direct investment (FDI), we use bilateral directional holdings (country i's assets in country j). To obtain excess holdings and FDI, we adopt a gravity model similar to that of Aviat and Coeurdacier (2007). Holding measures are investment stocks; changes in them thus reflect both new investment flows and valuation adjustments to existing stock. Nonetheless, as inves-

---

2. For trade flows, we use the sum of imports and exports between countries i and j (see the online data appendix for details and data sources).

tors take past valuation adjustments into account when making allocation decisions each period, investment holdings serve as a valuable indicator in identifying financial decoupling.

Relative to trade flows, (excess) portfolio equity holdings have shown much stronger signs of geopolitical repricing. After the China-US trade war, portfolio equity holdings from advanced economies decreased in China and increased sharply in the United States (figure 10.3). The universal upward shift in advanced economies' holdings of US equities after 2018 is striking, far outpacing the earlier trend. Equally striking is the near-universal downward shift or stagnation in holdings of Chinese equities, especially by Germany, Italy, France, and Japan. The United States also significantly decreased its holdings of Chinese equities.

Most emerging-market economies also increased their holdings of US equities after 2018, though differences in the extent of the increase varied widely (figure 10.4). In contrast to holdings by advanced economies, emerging markets' increased holdings of US equities did not necessarily come at the expense of Chinese equities. Countries that increased their exposure to US equities and decreased their exposure to Chinese equities tend to be geopolitically aligned with the United States (e.g., India, South Korea).

Bond Holdings

(Excess) bond holdings paint a less stark picture of geopolitical repricing than do portfolio equity holdings. Increased holdings of US bonds are not universal, and for the countries that did increase their holdings, the pace was far more gradual than it was for equities.

One possible explanation is that with interest rates at the zero lower bound, "insurance" through investing in US bonds became more expensive (Gourinchas, Rey, and Truempler 2012; Gourinchas and Rey 2022). There is also limited evidence of advanced economies reducing their holdings of Chinese bonds, in part because of the steps China took to open its bond market (Clayton et al. 2023). The exception is the United States.

Many emerging-market economies decreased their holdings of US bonds after 2018 (figure 10.5); few countries significantly increased their exposure. One explanation for this trend is that the adoption of floating exchange rates in emerging markets may have reduced the need to hold US treasuries (Miao 2019b; Miao, Fei, and Li 2022). In other words, the insured became less willing to buy. There is some evidence that emerging markets (e.g., Greece, South Korea) decreased their investments in the Chinese bond market.

Figure 10.1

Excess trade flows of selected advanced economies, 1998–2021

percentage points of source country's GDP

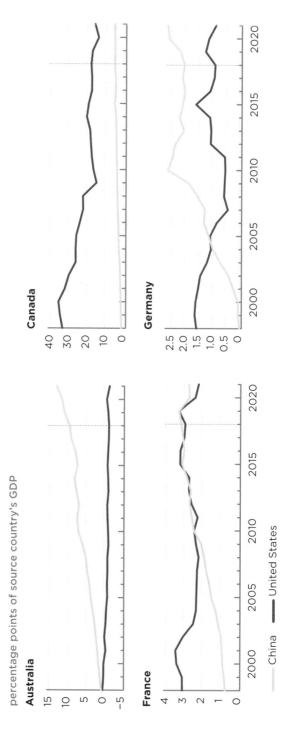

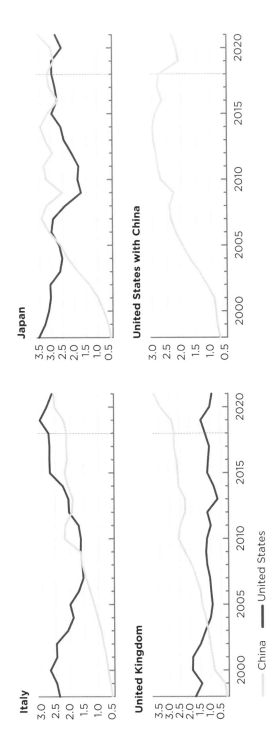

Italy

Japan

United Kingdom

United States with China

— China   — United States

Sources: Authors' calculations based on data from UN Comtrade database: World Bank, *World Development Indicators;* CIA World Factbook; La Porta, Lopez-de-Silanes, and Shleifer (2008); and Mayer and Zignago (2011).

Figure 10.2

Excess trade flows of selected emerging-market economies, 1998–2021

percentage points of source country's GDP

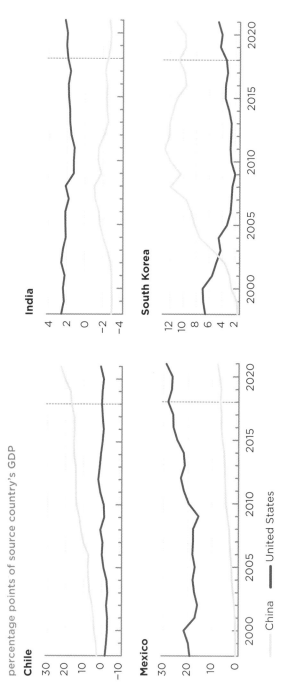

Sources: Authors' calculations based on data from UN Comtrade database; World Bank, *World Development Indicators*; CIA World Factbook; La Porta, Lopez-de-Silanes, and Shleifer (2008); and Mayer and Zignago (2011).

Foreign Direct Investment

There is some evidence (not shown here) of the fracturing of FDI as well, although it is much less significant than the fracturing of portfolio equity holdings. Traditional US allies such as Australia, Japan, and the United Kingdom increased their FDI in the United States, albeit by much less than their increases in US equities. FDI by advanced economies in China remained relatively stable, with some countries reducing their FDI slightly. US FDI in China plummeted between 2010 and 2017, rising for a year before again falling off (figure 10.6). In emerging markets, there was large cross-sectional variation in changes of FDI in China and the United States. There does not appear to be a systematic pattern of emerging markets increasing their FDI in China while decreasing it in the United States or vice versa.

Geopolitical Repricing

The trade-finance disconnect is most strikingly for portfolio equity holdings. Our hypothesis is that portfolio equity holdings, in contrast to trade flows, are fickler and more sensitive to geopolitical tensions than other types of investment, for several reasons. First, equity prices are the discounted value of future cash flows. Returns are therefore greatly affected by future uncertainty. Trade is currently far less affected by the future uncertainty of geopolitical conflicts. Second, it is easier to adjust equity portfolios in the secondary market; the adjustment cost of international trade is much higher. Adjustment costs are also important for greenfield FDI. For these reasons, in the short run the uncertainty of future international relationships affects portfolio equity flows but not trade.

To support our hypothesis, we examine the role of geopolitical alignment in shaping trade and financial linkages. Following Bailey, Strezhnev, and Voeten (2017), we measure bilateral geopolitical proximity by looking for similarities in voting patterns at the United Nations General Assembly. This "ideal point distance" tracks how closely countries' votes align. The main strength of this measure is its objectiveness and accessibility. To reduce the noisiness of the measure, we adopt a procedure similar to that used in the International Monetary Fund's April 2023 *World Economic Outlook*. We sort each country's partner countries into quartiles by ranking on geopolitical proximity. The resulting geopolitical alignment variable ranges from 1 to 4, with 1 indicating countries that are the least geopolitically aligned and 4 indicating countries that are the most aligned.

We then regress excess trade flows, portfolio equity holdings, bond holdings, and FDI on geopolitical alignment. For trade flows, we use the sum of bilateral exports and imports between countries i and j. For equity

Figure 10.3

Excess stock holdings of selected advanced economies, 2001–21

percentage points of source country's GDP

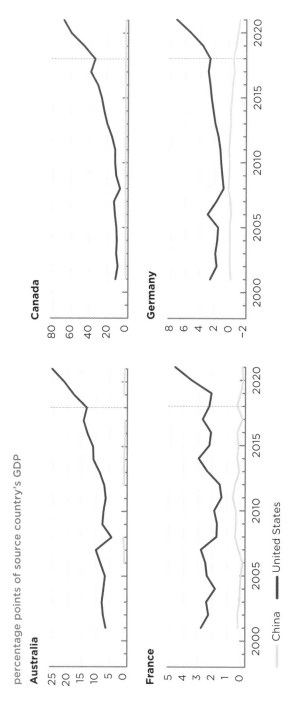

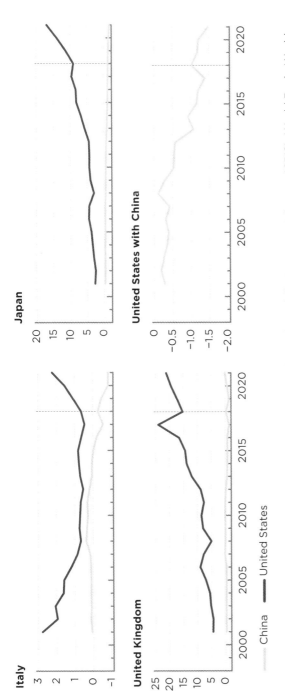

Italy

Japan

United Kingdom

United States with China

China ——— United States

Sources: Authors' calculations based on data from IMF, Coordinated Portfolio Investment Survey (CPIS); World Bank, *World Development Indicators*; CIA World Factbook; La Porta, Lopez-de-Silanes, and Shleifer (2008); and Mayer and Zignago (2011).

Figure 10.4

Excess bond holdings by selected advanced economies, 2001–21

percentage points of source country's GDP

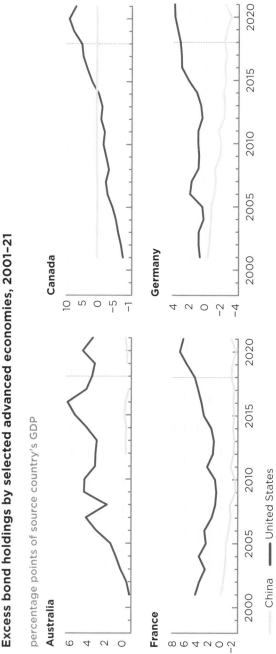

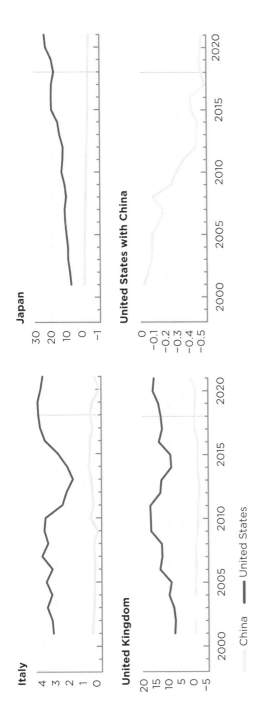

Italy

Japan

United Kingdom

United States with China

China ——— United States

Note: Advanced and emerging-market economies are defined per MSCI's classification, https://www.msci.com/our-solutions/indexes/developed-markets. Bilateral financial holdings for certain country pair-years are missing in the CPIS dataset, resulting in broken lines for certain figures.

Sources: Authors' calculations based on data from IMF, Coordinated Portfolio Investment Survey (CPIS); World Bank, *World Development Indicators;* CIA World Factbook; La Porta, Lopez-de-Silanes, and Shleifer (2008); and Mayer and Zignago (2011).

Figure 10.5

Excess bond holdings by selected emerging-market economies, 2001–21

percentage points of source country's GDP

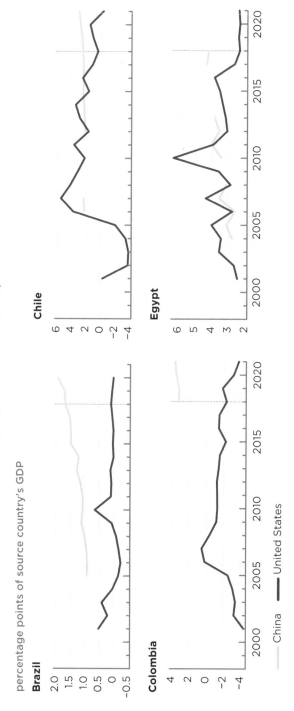

Brazil

Chile

Colombia

Egypt

China ——— United States

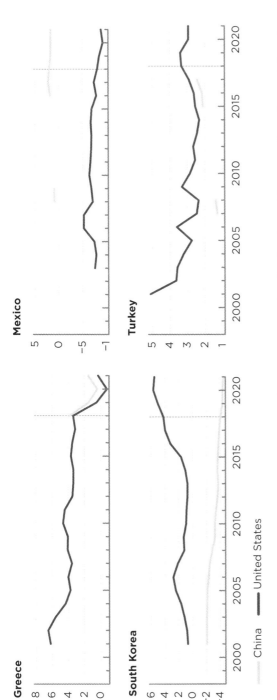

Greece

Mexico

South Korea

Turkey

China ── United States

Note: Advanced and emerging-market economies are defined per MSCI's classification, https://www.msci.com/our-solutions/indexes/developed-markets. Bilateral financial holdings for certain country pair-years are missing in the CPIS dataset, resulting in broken lines for certain figures.

Sources: Authors' calculations based on data from IMF, Coordinated Portfolio Investment Survey (CPIS); World Bank, *World Development Indicators*; CIA World Factbook; La Porta, Lopez-de-Silanes, and Shleifer (2008); and Mayer and Zignago (2011).

Figure 10.6
US excess foreign direct investment in China, 2009–21

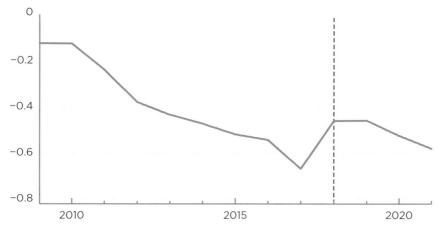

percentage points of source country's GDP

Sources: Authors' calculations based on data from IMF, Coordinated Direct Investment Survey (CDIS); World Bank, *World Development Indicators*; CIA World Factbook; La Porta, Lopez-de-Silanes, and Shleifer (2008); and Mayer and Zignago (2011).

and bond holdings and FDI, we use country i's investments in country j. We use excess flows or holdings because our goal is to understand whether geopolitical alignment explains trade and financial holding patterns, above and beyond normal gravity factors.[3]

Our main result of interest is whether the influence of geopolitical alignment in trade and financial linkages increased after 2018. For the entire sample period, we find no correlation between bilateral portfolio equity investment and geopolitical alignment (table 10.1). In contrast, after 2018, recipient countries received 0.086 percentage points more equity investments from source countries that are one quartile closer geopolitically (equivalent to moving from Canada–Qatar to Canada–Indonesia). The median value of bilateral portfolio equity holding intensities is 0.049 percent. Thus, an increase in geopolitical alignment from the first to the second quartile corresponds to an increase of over 170 percent in bilateral portfolio equity holding intensities for the median country pair. This finding is both economically and statistically significant.

---

3. This way of thinking about our approach is convenient, but singling out the effect of geopolitical alignment requires similarly adjusting the geopolitical alignment variable for the effects of the same gravity factors. In addition to source country-year fixed effects, recipient country-year fixed effects are included in the estimation.

Table 10.1

Geopolitical alignment and excess intensities

Item	Trade	Equity	Bond	FDI
Geopolitical alignment	−0.082*	0.013	0.097**	−0.041
	(−1.88)	(0.46)	(2.16)	(−1.19)
Geopolitical alignment x post−2018	−0.026	0.086***	−0.035	−0.023
	(−0.76)	(3.37)	(−1.37)	(−0.70)
R^2 (percent)	60.76	46.38	45.01	42.56
N	21,384	26,787	26,829	18,956

Note: Geopolitical alignment is lagged by one year. t-statistics are reported in parentheses. Standard errors are clustered at the source country level. The R^2 statistics are based on the fully specified model, including gravity factors as well as source country-year and recipient country-year fixed effects. See the online data appendix for details.

Sources: Authors' calculations based on data from UN Comtrade database; IMF, Coordinated Portfolio Investment Survey (CPIS) and Coordinated Direct Investment Survey (CDIS); World Bank, *World Development Indicators*; CIA World Factbook; Porta, Lopez-de Silanes, and Shleifer (2008); Mayer and Zignago (2011); Voeten (2013); and Bailey, Strezhnev, and Voeten (2017).

In stark contrast, bilateral trade intensities are slightly negatively correlated with geopolitical alignment, and there was no marked shift after 2018. A possible explanation for this finding is the influence of efficiency-seeking/economic interests over political tensions for trade during globalization. For bond holdings, over the entire sample period, countries one quartile closer geopolitically had 0.097 percentage points greater bond holding intensities, which is roughly 1.5 times the bond-holding intensity between the median country year pair (0.062 percent). The relationship is not significantly different after 2018.

The April 2023 *Global Financial Stability Report* of the International Monetary Fund (IMF) also shows that source countries tend to allocate a larger share of portfolio investment to recipient countries that are geopolitically closer. After 2015, however, the importance of geopolitical alignment increased for bond investments rather than equities. For FDI, the coefficient on geopolitical alignment and its interaction term are negative but not significant. The IMF's April 2023 *Global Financial Stability Report* and *World Economic Outlook* find positive correlations between FDI and geopolitical alignment. The qualitative difference in our results for cross-border portfolio holdings and FDI likely reflect different estimation methods (*Global Financial Stability Report*) and data sources (*World Economic Outlook*).

An alternative hypothesis that we cannot fully rule out is that advanced economies are shifting their investments purely out of economic self-interest (i.e., US equities simply provide better returns than Chinese equities). Our future work will try to quantify the risk premium induced by geopolitical tensions and other factors.

Policy Suggestions

The trade-finance disconnect since the onset of the China-US trade war reveals very different beliefs about future international relations. Whether we move back toward an integrated international world economy/financial system or continue to approach the brink of a fractured bipolar world depends on the actions taken.

What can be done? Enhancing the global safety net should be a top priority. The simplest, most straightforward, and most efficient solution is to have truly global currency swap line networks that include both the United States and China. Although creating such networks would be politically difficult, they would significantly increase risk-sharing.

Greater financial investments between advanced economies and China would also help reconnect trade and finance. As trade flows and financial investments are complements, linking them would help prevent the potential segmentation/fragmentation of trade networks.

Linkage is also important from a risk-sharing perspective. The current trend of advanced economies increasing their equity investments in the United States is a risky case of putting all of one's eggs in one basket. China's economic, monetary policy, and financial market returns are increasingly independent of the United States' (Miao 2019a), providing a deeply valuable source of diversification for foreigners. The correlation between Chinese and US stock market returns is lower than the correlation between returns in Europe and the United States (figure 10.7). And for both stocks and bonds, the correlation between market returns in China and the United States fell significantly in recent years, as geopolitical concerns deepened. More financial investments—particularly equity stock investments in China—would improve risk sharing. For its part, China should continue to improve its business environment and lift foreign shareholding caps after eliminating all quota limits for Qualified Foreign Institutional Investors (QFIIs) in 2019.[4]

---

4. The Qualified Foreign Institutional Investor program was introduced in 2002. It grants foreign institutional investors the right to buy and sell renminbi-denominated "A" shares of Chinese companies.

Figure 10.7

Correlations between asset returns in the United States and China and between the United States and Europe, 2009–2023

a. Bond returns

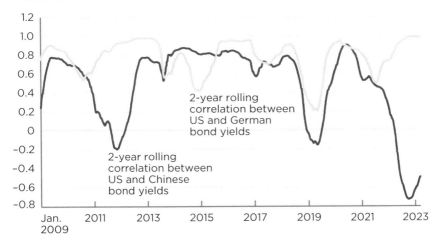

b. Equity returns

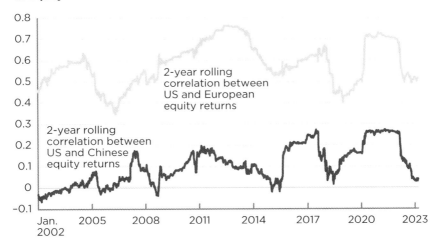

Note: Ten-year German government bond yields are used as a proxy for European bond yields.

Source: Authors' calculations based on data from Bloomberg. US, Chinese, and German 10-year government bond indexes are USGG10YR, GTCNY10YR, and GTDEM10YR, respectively. US, Chinese, and European equity indexes are SPX, SHCOMP, and SXXP, respectively.

References

Anderson, James E., and Eric Van Wincoop. 2004. Trade Costs. *Journal of Economic Literature* 42, no. 3: 691–751.

Antras, Pol, and Ricardo J. Caballero. 2009. Trade and Capital Flows: A Financial Frictions Perspective. *Journal of Political Economy* 117, no. 4: 701–44.

Aviat, Antonin, and Nicolas Coeurdacier. 2007. The Geography of Trade in Goods and Asset Holdings. *Journal of International Economics* 71, no. 1: 22–51.

Bailey, Michael A., Anton Strezhnev, and Erik Voeten. 2017. Estimating Dynamic State Preferences from United Nations Voting Data. *Journal of Conflict Resolution* 61, no. 2: 430–56.

Belke, Ansgar, and Clemens Domnick. 2021. Trade and Capital Flows: Substitutes or Complements? An Empirical Investigation. *Review of International Economics* 29, no. 3: 573–89.

Bergstrand, Jeffery H. 1985. The Gravity Equation in International Trade: Some Microeconomic Foundations and Empirical Evidence. *Review of Economics and Statistics* 67, no. 3: 474–81.

Clayton, Christopher, Amanda Dos Santos, Matteo Maggiori, and Jesse Schreger. 2023. *Internationalizing Like China.* NBER Working Paper 30336 (revised). Cambridge, MA: National Bureau of Economic Research.

Ding, Haoyuan, Yuying Jin, Ziyuan Liu, and Wenjing Xie. 2019. The Relationship Between International Trade and Capital Flow: A Network Perspective. *Journal of International Money and Finance* 91:1–11.

Gourinchas, Pierre-Olivier, and Hélène Rey. 2022. *Exorbitant Privilege and Exorbitant Duty.* CEPR Discussion Paper No. 16944. Paris and London: CEPR Press. Available at https://cepr.org/publications/dp16944.

Gourinchas, Pierre-Olivier, Hélène Rey, and Kai Truempler. 2012. The Financial Crisis and the Geography of Wealth Transfers. *Journal of International Economics* 88, no. 2: 266–83.

IMF (International Monetary Fund). 2023a. *Global Financial Stability Report: Safeguarding Financial Stability and High Inflation and Geopolitical Risks.* Washington.

IMF (International Monetary Fund). 2023b. *World Economic Outlook: A Rocky Recovery.* Washington.

Kalemli-Özcan, Şebnem, Alex Nikolsko-Rzhevskyy, and Jun Hee Kwak. 2020. Does Trade Cause Capital to Flow? Evidence from Historical Rainfall. *Journal of Development Economics* 147 (November), article 102537.

La Porta, Rafael, Florencio Lopez-de-Silanes, and Andrei Shleifer. 2008. The Economic Consequences of Legal Origins. *Journal of Economic Literature* 46, no. 2: 285–332.

Lane, Philip, and Gian Maria Milesi-Ferretti. 2008. International Investment Patterns. *The Review of Economics and Statistics* 90, no. 3 (August): 538–49.

Lustig, Hanno, and Robert J. Richmond. 2020. Gravity in the Exchange Rate Factor Structure. *Review of Financial Studies* 33, no. 8: 3492–540.

Markusen, James R. 1983. Factor Movements and Commodity Trade as Complements. *Journal of International Economics* 14, no. 3-4: 341–56.

Mayer, Thierry, and Soledad Zignago. 2011. *Notes on CEPII's Distances Measures: The GeoDist Database* (December 1). CEPII Working Paper No. 2011-25. Available at https://papers.ssrn.com/sol3/papers.cfm?abstract_id=1994531.

Miao, Yanliang. 2019a. *China's Quiet Central Bank Revolution*. Project Syndicate, May 6. Available at https://www.project-syndicate.org/commentary/china-central-bank-communication-exchange-rate-by-miao-yanliang-2019-03.

Miao, Yanliang. 2019b. *Towards a Clean Floating RMB*. Beijing: China Financial Publishing House.

Miao, Yanliang, Xuan Fei, and Xin Li. 2022. *The Dollar's Diminishing Privilege? The Evolution of Capital Flows and International Monetary System*. Working paper. Beijing.

Mundell, Robert A. 1957. International Trade and Factor Mobility. *American Economic Review* 47, no. 3: 321–35.

Obstfeld, Maurice, and Kenneth Rogoff. 2000. *The Six Major Puzzles in International Macroeconomics: Is There a Common Cause?* NBER Macroeconomics Annual. Cambridge, MA: National Bureau of Economic Research.

Portes, Richard, and Hélène Rey. 2005. The Determinants of Cross-Border Equity Flows. *Journal of International Economics* 65, no. 2: 269–96.

Rose, Andrew K., and Mark M. Spiegel. 2004. A Gravity Model of Sovereign Lending: Trade, Default, and Credit. *IMF Staff Papers* 51 (special issue): 50–63.

Taylor, Alan M., and Janine L.F. Wilson. 2006. *International Trade and Finance under the Two Hegemons: Complementarities in the United Kingdom 1870–1913 and the United States 1920–30*. NBER Working Paper 12543. Cambridge, MA: National Bureau of Economic Research.

Voeten, Erik. 2013. *Data and Analyses of Voting in the UN General Assembly*. Washington: Georgetown University. Available at http://ssrn.com/abstract=2111149.

11

Evolving Views on Exchange Rates and Currency Unions

LINDA TESAR

As a way of looking back, I thought it might be interesting to ask what academic economists wrote about exchange rates and the international monetary system in the post–Bretton Woods period. To tackle this question in a somewhat systematic way, I examined all articles published in the *Journal of International Economics* that included the word pairs (bigrams) *exchange rate* or *exchange rates* in the abstract. Research assistant Andrea Foschi and I recorded all bigrams that appeared in these abstracts and tabulated the frequency of each between 1981 and 2017.

Figure 11.1 shows the main bigrams associated with exchange rates that appeared in the 1980s. Given publication lags and the fact that academic work is influenced by what has happened in the recent past, it seems likely that the articles in this period focused on the major changes in global markets in the years following the collapse of the Bretton Woods system. The word cloud suggests that academics working on exchange rates focused on the current account balance, interest rates, and risk premia. The influence of the rational expectations revolution in macroeconomics is evident, as models of exchange rate determination based on portfolio balance and the current account gave way to forward-looking models based on interest rate parity and arbitrage. The fact that the terms

Linda Tesar is the Alan V. Deardorff Collegiate Professor of Economics in the Department of Economics at the University of Michigan and the senior faculty advisor to the dean on strategic budgetary affairs. She is the codirector of the International Finance and Macroeconomic Program at the National Bureau of Economic Research and vice president (2023) of the American Economic Association.

Figure 11.1

**Word pairs (bigrams) found in *Journal of International Economics*
articles on exchange rates, 1981–89**

money supply domestic price
foreign asset flexible exchange balance payment
rate return rate regime spot rate central bank
open economy
capital mobility interest rate purchase power
black market current account future price
relative price risk premium portfolio balance
power parity term trade rate change
nontraded good monetary policy price level
rational expectation forward exchange
wealth effect float exchange currency substitution

Note: Figure shows the top 30 bigrams (i.e., pairs of words); the size of each
bigram is proportional to its frequency. To construct the word cloud, we follow a
number of standard steps to prepare the text for textual analysis. First, we
collect all the abstracts into a single document, which we tokenize, i.e., we split it
into an array of words ("tokens") that computers can analyze. We then
lemmatize all the words, i.e., we remove affixes and reduce them to their root.
This includes, among other things, converting inflected verbs into their base form
(e.g., from "buys" to "buy," from "floating" to "float"), turning plurals into
singulars (e.g., from "expectations" to "expectation," from "data" to "datum"), and
reducing comparatives back to the plain adjective (e.g., from "larger" to "large").
Finally, numbers, punctuation, stop words (such as "the," "and," "in," etc.) and
words with fewer than 4 or more than 20 letters were removed. Also removed
were the following words, which would contaminate the word cloud because
they do not relate to the subject matter: *abstract, attempt, book, datum, develop,
DSGE, equation, equilibrium, evidence, examine, explain, fact, find, indicate, make,
measure, model, paper, parameter, permit, predictor, present, publication, result,
review, sample, section, show, strong, stylized, value.* The following bigrams were
also removed to avoid crowding out other top bigrams, since we are already
focusing on abstracts related to *exchange rates: exchange rate, foreign
exchange, change exchange, exchange market, and real exchange.*
Source: *Journal of International Economics* via ProQuest and author's calculations.

interest rate, monetary policy, and *money supply* were among the 10 most cited
words in the word cloud suggests that exchange rates were understood as
a monetary phenomenon.

Table 11.1 groups the bigrams into categories, in order to make
it easier to see trends over time. It shows the categories with the largest
number of mentions. The sample is restricted to bigrams with at least four
mentions in a decade. Categories are shown for four periods: the 1981–89,

Table 11.1
Most frequently cited categories of bigrams, by decade

Decade	Most frequently cited categories of bigrams
1981-89	Interest rate parity, forward rates, risk premia, exchange rate regime, monetary policy, purchasing power parity, trade, exports, balance of payments, current account, uncertainty, rational expectations, capital flow, foreign assets, interest rate, financial market, asset prices, fiscal policy
1990-99	Monetary policy, interest rate parity, forward rates, risk premia, uncertainty, exchange rate regime, target zones, purchasing power parity, balance of payments, current account, interest rates, speculative attacks and crises, capital controls, FDI, financial markets, asset prices, fiscal policy, exchange rate passthrough, European Monetary Union
2000-08	Uncertainty, monetary policy, exchange rate regime, interest rates, exchange rate passthrough, purchasing power parity, balance of payments, current account, exchange rate intervention, border, policy coordination, speculative attacks, capital flows, business cycles, financial markets, asset prices, fiscal policy, interest rate parity, forward rates, risk premia
2009-17	Trade, interest rates, uncertainty, monetary policy, exchange rate regime, balance of payments, current account, financial markets, asset prices, capital controls, speculative attacks and crises, purchasing power parity, business cycles, fiscal policy, interest rate parity, forward rates, risk premia

Note: Bigram categories are listed in decreasing order of frequency.
Source: Journal of International Economics via ProQuest and author's calculations.

1990–99, 2000–08, and 2009–17 (the last two decades are split at the year of the global financial crisis).

Monetary policy occupied the top spot in 1990–99, and *uncertainty* did so in 2000–08, revealing economists' understanding that exchange rates are a monetary phenomenon and floating exchange rates are volatile. *Exchange rate regimes* was among the top five most-cited phrases, indicating economists'—as well as policymakers'—struggle to understand the trade-offs associated with different policy mechanisms for managing exchange rates and inflation.

The table reveals interesting changes over time. The frequency of the term *capital controls* increased in the 1990s. It receded in frequency in the 2000s, when *capital flow* increased in frequency, perhaps a reflection of the impact of the Washington Consensus, which advocated greater openness of financial markets and less regulation. *Capital controls* reemerged in the last decade, reflecting a shift in views about the need for and efficacy of managing capital flows. The connection between business cycles and exchange rates emerged in the 2000s. Work citing interest rate parity and carry trade peaked in the 1990s and dropped to a lower berth after 2000.

Interest in the creation of and challenges associated with the euro evolved over the period studied.[1] In the 1980s, most euro-related articles focused on whether the euro area constituted an optimal currency area. Over time, the focus shifted to issues related to market integration, labor and capital mobility, and—coinciding with the European debt crisis—the importance of coordinated fiscal policy in a currency area. The central role of monetary policy figured prominently in all periods.

Figure 11.2 illustrates the evolving role of the euro. During the first decade after its introduction (2000–09), global use of the euro as a currency in international transactions soared, and support for the euro by EU citizens was strong, with well over half of the population supporting it. Writing about the prospects of the euro as a global currency, even a competitor to the dollar, Papaioannou, Portes, and Siourounis (2006, 4) noted that the "introduction of the euro, greater liquidity in other major currencies, and the rising. . . external debt of the United States have increased the pressure on central banks to diversify away from the US dollar." They concluded that the euro might already be "punching above its weight" and might "already enjoy an enhanced role as an international reserve currency."

The honeymoon for the euro as a major global currency ended with the global financial crisis of 2007–09 and the subsequent European debt crisis. Lack of fiscal policy coordination, lax and inconsistent financial regulations, and large macroeconomic asymmetries contributed to the accumulation of debt in member states on the periphery. The fiscal austerity policies imposed on debtor countries left deep and long-lasting macroeconomic scars (House, Proebsting, and Tesar 2020). In 2023, for example, real GDP in Greece was still only slightly above the level in the depths of the debt crisis, roughly equal to its real income in 2001 (OECD Statistics). In their assessment of the euro as a global currency, Maggiori, Neiman, and Schreger (2019) conclude that the fissures revealed by the global financial crisis caused a significant shift away from the euro to the dollar.

The importance of the euro as a global currency is uncertain. The magnitude and speed of responses by the European Union and the European Central Bank to the COVID-19 pandemic provide hopeful signs that coordinated, flexible Europe-wide policies are possible in the face of major macroeconomic shocks. At the same time, the underlying structure

---

1. The search for euro-related bigrams included the following terms: *currency area, currency union, monetary union, single currency, optimum currency, euro area*, and *European Union*.

Figure 11.2
The evolving role of the euro as a global currency, 2000–22

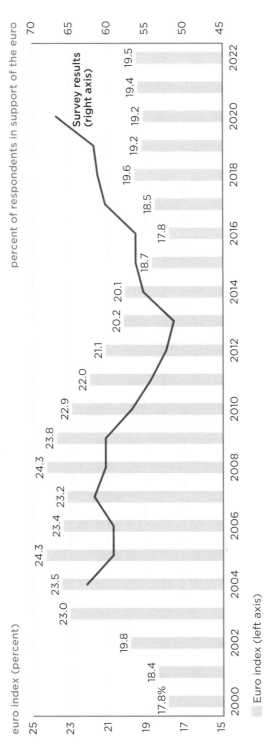

Note: The euro index is the annual average of the composite index of current exchange rates shown in figure 1 in "The International Role of the Euro," ECB press release, European Central Bank, 2023, (https://www.ecb.europa.eu/pub/ire/html/ecb.ire202306~d3340 07ede.en.html. The survey results are averages of two Public Opinion in the European Union surveys conducted by the European Commission in 2021.

Sources: European Commission, European Central Bank, author's calculations.

of the European economy remains far from what Robert Mundell might have envisioned as an optimal currency area (House, Proebsting, and Tesar 2023). For now, it seems clear that "we live in a dollar world: on the real side, where dollar invoicing is dominant; on the financial side, where dollar funding is essential to global banks and nonfinancial corporations; and on the policy side, where dollar anchoring and dollar reserves are prevalent" (Gourinchas 2021, 2).

References

Gourinchas, Pierre-Olivier. 2021. The Dollar Hegemon? Evidence and Implications for Policymakers. In *The Asian Monetary Policy Forum: Insights for Central Banking*, ed. S.J. Davis, E.S. Robinson, and B. Yeung, 264–300. Singapore: World Scientific Publishing.

House, C.L., C. Proebsting, and L.L. Tesar. 2020. Austerity in the Aftermath of the Great Recession. *Journal of Monetary Economics* 115: 37–63.

House, C.L., C. Proebsting, and L.L. Tesar. 2023. *The Benefits of Labor Mobility in a Currency Union*. Working paper. Ann Arbor: University of Michigan.

Maggiori, M., B. Neiman, and J. Schreger. 2019. The Rise of the Dollar and Fall of the Euro as International Currencies. *American Economic Association Papers and Proceedings* 109: 521–26.

Papaioannou, E., R. Portes, and G. Siourounis. 2006. *Optimal Currency Shares in International Reserves: The Impact of the Euro and the Prospects for the Dollar*. ECB Working Paper 694. Frankfurt: European Central Bank.

III

INTERNATIONAL PRICES, INTERNATIONAL ADJUSTMENT, AND TRADE

12

The Floating Dollar and the Geography of US Manufacturing

KATHERYN RUSS

Has the floating dollar been detrimental to US trade, particularly manufacturing industries that compete with foreign producers at home or in global markets? This question has provoked debate for decades. Twenty years ago, in a (Peterson) Institute for International Economics volume on the overvaluation of the dollar, Martin Neil Baily (2003) argued that swings in the dollar had no discernible negative impact on US manufacturing in the years following the advent of the floating dollar (1973–2000). In a contemporaneous piece for the Economic Policy Institute, Robert Blecker (2003) bemoaned the damage that a strengthening dollar inflicted on both the profitability of and employment by US manufacturers in the late 1990s.

The canonical economic theory at the time suggested that there should be no special harm from floating rates. In a Dornbusch-type (1976, 1987) setting, swings or misalignment in currencies can act as adverse shocks to domestic production. Obstfeld and Rogoff (1995) showed how with sticky prices, factors that generate an appreciation of the dollar may boost overseas demand in a way that offsets the expenditure-switching effect of a strong dollar. They conclude that "some of the intermediate policy targets emphasized in earlier Keynesian models of policy transmission (the terms of trade, the current account, and so on) turn out, on closer inspection, to be important individually but largely offsetting taken jointly" (p. 655). Fluctuations in the dollar need not present risks to US producers when

Katheryn Russ is Professor and Chair of Economics at University of California, Davis. She was nonresident senior fellow of the Peterson Institute for International Economics.

driven by factors that bring with them offsetting effects on foreign demand for US exports.

To see why this is the case, consider an example in which the US economy grows faster than China's or Europe's, the dollar appreciates, and the strong dollar makes foreign goods less expensive to US consumers. The resulting increase in US import demand for their goods ends up stimulating production in China or Europe. The flip side is that the strong dollar makes US goods expensive abroad, dampening US exports. But the opposite can also occur: When economic growth in the United States slows, the dollar weakens, stimulating foreign demand for US products. The result is a built-in cooling mechanism when the US economy grows faster compared to the rest of the world and a built-in stimulus when it grows more slowly.

What happens when the dollar is strong for other reasons, when the impacts of the strong dollar on orders may not be offset by strong overall demand either at home or abroad as in the canonical redux framework? In recent decades, economists have revisited swings and misalignments, analyzing distributional effects at the micro level. Closer attention to the geography of US manufacturing in future research might shed light on the impacts of the floating dollar on both industry and political economy.

Revisiting Currency Manipulation and the "Exorbitant Privilege" through the Lens of Geography

A large body of literature showing little systemic link between exchange rate volatility and trade flows has not deterred many from blaming the decline in US manufacturing on a key feature of the US–style float: the potential for currency manipulation and the implications of the United States' "exorbitant privilege."[1] Currency manipulation refers to misalignments that may arise when other countries fix their currency to the value of the dollar in a way that makes their own exports look cheap in comparison to US goods (Bergsten and Gagnon 2017). "Exorbitant privilege" refers to the special role of the dollar in global financial markets, which some argue may lead to structural overvaluation caused by demand for the dollar as a reserve currency (Nelson and Weiss 2022).

---

1. Tenreyro (2007), Wang and Barrett (2007), Hondroyiannis et al. (2008), Baum and Caglayan (2010), and Caglayan and Di (2010) find no consistent correlation between exchange rate volatility and trade flows. Lin, Shi, and Ye (2018) find that the relationship can be positive or negative. See earlier surveys by Ozturk (2006), Eicher and Henn (2011), Auboin and Ruta (2013), and Bahmanee-Oskooee and Arize (2020).

Figure 12.1

US dollar exchange rate and US manufacturing employment, 1973–2019

index (March 1973 = 100)

— Trade weighted US dollar index
— US manufacturing employment

Sources: US trade-weighted dollar series: Federal Reserve Board of Governors. Manufacturing employment: US Bureau of Labor Statistics (downloaded from Federal Reserve Bank of St. Louis FRED database series TWEXM_NBD19730301 and MANEMP_NBD19730301).

Figure 12.1 plots the US trade-weighted dollar exchange rate and US manufacturing employment between 1973 and 2019. It is not obvious that one drove the other or that there is a very tight relationship between them.

An historical perspective on the geography of trade-affected US industries also suggests exercising caution in drawing these connections. Eriksson, Russ, Shambaugh, and Xu (2021, hereafter ERSX) suggest that US manufacturing appears to have been driven by secular trends that started long before the fall of Bretton Woods in the early 1970s and later concerns about strategically undervalued pegs.

The most notable example of a country accused of currency manipulation that may have driven the decline in US manufacturing is China. ERSX look at where the industries affected by the China shock were located in 1910. To do so, they draw from Autor, Dorn, and Hanson's (2013, hereafter ADH) computation of China shock exposure, as measured by imports per worker by commuting zone. For each industry in which the United States experienced a surge in imports from China between 1991 and 2007, ADH divide the increase in imports by the number workers in that industry in the United States as a whole in 1990. They then take this national industry-level shock, weight it by the share of employment within a commuting zone concentrated in that industry in 1990, and sum across industries. The resulting figure provides a measure of the local (commuting-zone-level) exposure to the China shock in 1990 (the share of the workforce in 1990 that might be affected by the increase in competition from Chinese goods).

ERSX view local exposure to the China shock in historical perspective. They compute the same local shocks but weight them by local employment shares as they were in earlier years. Doing so allows them to ascertain which areas would have had the most exposure if the surge in imports in the same industries had happened before 1990. Figure 12.2 shows which commuting zones would have been most exposed had the surge in imports from China in 1991–2007 occurred in 1910 and 1974. The hardest hit areas are primarily in the Northeast and northern Midwest, an area known as the manufacturing belt.

ERSX find that "China shock" industries had begun moving away from innovative centers by 1960. Comparing maps a and b in figure 12.2, it is apparent that the most vulnerable industries had already been moving away from the centers of innovation where they originated before the China shock hit in 1990—that is, before most of the import surge from Japan and the "Asian Tigers." By 1974, just as Bretton Woods had fallen, these industries already had begun to age out and move to labor markets where wages were lower, workers had less education, and the number of patents per capita was lower.

ERSX suggest that the change is a manifestation of Vernon's product cycle, in which industries move toward low-wage areas within the United States and eventually to other countries. Vernon (1966) conjectured that industries need highly skilled labor and specialized inputs as they develop innovative new goods; as they standardize, firms move to places with lower wages and less skill abundance.

Vernon pointed to the movement of manufacturing in the United States away from the northern manufacturing belt toward the South(-east) as one example, but also to movement of manufacturing production to low-wage countries like China. Figure 12.2 suggests that although exchange rate pegs and misalignments may have contributed to the acceleration of this product cycle after 1975, they did not cause it. The process was already in motion and is a long-term phenomenon.

Figure 12.2
Employment shares in industries affected by the "China shock," by commuting zone, 1910 and 1974

a. Decile of exposure to China shock in 1910

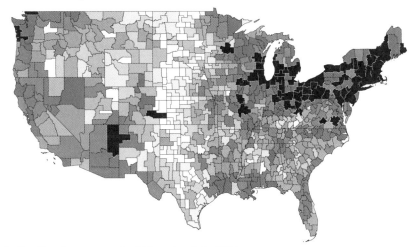

b. Decile of exposure to China shock in 1974

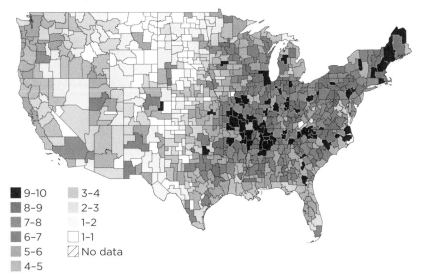

■ 9–10	▨ 3–4
■ 8–9	▨ 2–3
■ 7–8	▨ 1–2
■ 6–7	☐ 1–1
▨ 5–6	▨ No data
▨ 4–5	

Notes: These maps present simulated heatmaps of synthetic historical "China shock" exposure using contemporaneous historical employment shares and imports per worker during the "China shock" period 1991–2007. Areas in the top decile of exposure are designated black. White indicates areas in the lowest decile.

Source: Calculations based on Eriksson et al. (2021).

Risk-Off Events

Why, then, should one worry about the floating dollar at all in relation to trade? Beyond fundamentals-driven fluctuations in exchange rates, where expenditure switching is offset by demand effects, the exorbitant privilege can affect swings in the dollar, not just its long-term strength. The special role of the dollar and US Treasury bonds means that during periods in which investors become very uneasy about increases in perceived risks in financial markets, global investment floods into dollar-denominated assets. These events—known as *risk-off events*—can strengthen the dollar in a way that may have no offsetting effects on demand.

Although it is robust and growing, the body of literature on the firm-level impacts of risk-off events may have overlooked the geographic impacts of the exorbitant privilege. Dollar dominance means that global risk-off events strengthen the dollar. When investors dump foreign assets and flee into dollar-denominated assets, the dollar appreciates, putting intense pressure on import-competing industries in the United States and on US export industries. Caballero and Kamber (2019) estimate that these episodes can last up to nine months. Akinci, Kalemli-Özcan, and Queralto (2022) find that similar uncertainty shocks can lead to excess appreciation of the US dollar lasting up to a year. Research by Caballero and Kamber (2019) on the United States and by Kalemli-Özcan (2019) and Das, Gopinath, and Kalemli-Özcan (2022) on emerging markets finds that without accommodative monetary policy (or, in emerging markets, capital control measures), these episodes can have real adverse effects, as they are often accompanied by a credit crunch. Risk-off events are thus not a short or instantaneous phenomenon; they can cause businesses with already low profit margins to struggle.

The effects on individual firms and workers have been well studied; the effects on places have not. Work by Caballero and Kamber (2019) suggests what the field might learn by examining the geographic distribution of this kind of turbulence. They study China's Black Monday—the August 24, 2015, risk-off event, which was followed by a period of sustained relative strength in the US dollar. The dollar had been appreciating before Black Monday, thanks to fundamentals that generated normal expenditure switching. The analysis by Caballero and Kamber (2019) suggests that the episode may have been more prolonged or severe than would otherwise have been expected without the risk-off.

The period shown in figure 12.1 was marked by stalled growth in US manufacturing employment. At a time when US jobs reports were strong, there was a leveling-off of growth in US manufacturing jobs. Just as with the China shock, it is important for economists and policymakers to determine whether some places were hit harder than others. Silicon Valley was as exposed to the China shock as many other parts of the United States that were less resilient to it. The negative effects of the shock were highly localized. It is plausible that the same may be true of the fallout from dollar appreciation during these risk-off events. Local impacts may depend not only on trade exposure but also on the life cycle and general health of trade-exposed industries in the area or the level of education of the local workforce.

Studies of the distributional and geographic effects of large swings in exchange rates provide an example of what economists might find if they examine the impacts of risk-off events in the United States from a geographical perspective. Cravino and Levchenko (2018) show that low-income households in Mexico fared considerably worse in some geographic regions than others following the 1994 peso devaluation, as a result of both the spatial dispersion in price changes associated with the devaluation and the spatial dispersion of household consumption shares of affected goods. They also show that large currency swings can have very different effects on the real incomes of low-income and high-income households, with large devaluations exacerbating inequality.

Other studies find that large swings have real effects on firms and households. Fung and Liu (2009) find that a large appreciation of the Taiwan dollar following the Plaza Accord in 1985 was associated with the exit of many small firms and expansion of the survivors. Alessandria, Kaboski, and Midrigan (2010) show that firms may cope with large devaluations by suspending imports for a period and running down inventories, which they maintain at a higher level than otherwise as a precautionary measure to cushion against the threat of large swings. Large swings in the dollar may affect firms and the places where they are concentrated quite differently, with distributional consequences across both the income distribution and geographic areas.

Distributional impacts of the choice of currency regime may have both political and policy consequences. Frieden (2015) lays out a conceptual framework, applying it to the US experience in the 19th century and the emergence of the euro in the late 20th century. In chapter 7 of this volume, he draws on that framework to raise questions about the current situation in the United States.

New research suggests that these distributional impacts may be specific to place. Herreno, Morales, and Pedemonte (2023) find that the US counties most exposed to dollar appreciation as trading partners abandoned the gold standard punished the political party of the sitting (Republican) US president during elections in 1930 and 1932. They also show the converse case: The counties most exposed to the later dollar depreciation after the United States abandoned the gold standard (in 1933) increased support for the party of the sitting (Democratic) US president during elections in 1934 and 1936.

Analysis of more recent decades has not yet been conducted. Understanding which places suffer adverse effects from a sudden dollar appreciation driven by risk-off events is important from a policy point of view because it helps policymakers assess the strength of the social safety net and the potential need for place-based policies.

The geography of impacts from risk-off events may also be important from a political point of view. Looking at the dates of risk-off events studied by Caballero and Kamber (2019), many occur near a striking party change in Congress or the White House. For example, the risk-off event in autumn 2015 described above happened not long before the fall of the "Blue Wall" in November 2016.[2] The states that make up the Blue Wall encompass much of the manufacturing belt—places where ERSX show industries have been aging out and moving to lower-wage areas. It is plausible that these areas may be particularly sensitive to impacts from the sudden strengthening of the dollar during risk-off events, when there is no offsetting surge in domestic or foreign demand to cushion the blow to orders. The move to floating rates was less drastic a shift in the currency regime than going off the gold standard, but parallels in the responses of voters in areas with industries exposed to the dollar appreciation in 1930 and 1932 are hard to rule out.

This begs the question of whether mini-recessions in certain tradable goods sectors may generate political instability or other kinds of acute local impacts that both politicians and policymakers would do well to ponder, because right now political instability might be one of the biggest threats to the special role of the dollar.

References

Akinci, Ozge, Şebnem Kalemli-Özcan, and Albert Queralto. 2022. *Uncertainty Shocks, Capital Flows, and International Risk Spillovers*. NBER Working Paper 30026. Cambridge, MA: National Bureau of Economic Research. Available at https://www.nber.org/papers/w30026.

Alessandria, George, Joseph P. Kaboski, and Virgiliu Midrigan. 2010. Inventories, Lumpy Trade, and Large Devaluations. *American Economic Review* 100, no. 5: 2304–39.

---

2. Paul Steinhauser, "Holding Democratic "Blue Wall" Was Crucial for Obama Victory," CNN.com, November 13, 2012, https://www.cnn.com/2012/11/12/politics/blue-wall-democrats-election/index.html.

Auboin, Marc, and Michele Ruta. 2013. The Relationship between Exchange Rates and International Trade: A Literature Review. *World Trade Review* 12, no. 3: 577–605.

Autor, David H., David Dorn, and Gordon H. Hanson. 2013. The China Syndrome: Local Labor Market Effects of Import Competition in the United States. *American Economic Review* 103, no. 6: 2121–68.

Bahmani-Oskooee, Mohsen, and Augustine C. Arize. 2020. On the Asymmetric Effects of Exchange Rate Volatility on Trade Flows: Evidence from Africa. *Emerging Markets Finance & Trade* 56: 913–39.

Baily, Martin N. 2003. Persistent Dollar Swings and the US Economy. In *Dollar Overvaluation and the World Economy*, ed. Fred Bergsten and John Williamson, 81–134. Washington: Institute for International Economics. Available at https://www.piie.com/bookstore/dollar-overvaluation-and-world-economy.

Baum, Christopher F., and Mustafa Caglayan. 2010. On the Sensitivity of the Volume and Volatility of Bilateral Trade Flows to Exchange Rate Uncertainty. *Journal of International Money and Finance* 29, no. 1: 79–93. Available at DOI: 10.106/j/jimonfin.2008.12.003.

Bergsten, C. Fred, and Joseph E. Gagnon. 2017. *Currency Conflict and Trade Policy: A New Strategy for the United States*. Washington: Peterson Institute for International Economics. Available at https://www.piie.com/bookstore/currency-conflict-and-trade-policy-new-strategy-united-states.

Blecker, Robert A. 2003. *The Benefits of a Lower Dollar: How the High Dollar Has Hurt US Manufacturing and Why the Dollar Still Needs to Fall Further*. Briefing Paper 138. Washington: Economic Policy Institute. Available at https://www.epi.org/publication/briefingpapers_may03bp_lowerdollar/.

Caballero, Ricardo J., and Gunes Kamber. 2019. *On the Global Impact of Risk-Off Shocks and Policy-Put Frameworks*. NBER Working Paper 26031. Cambridge, MA: National Bureau of Economic Research. Available at https://www.nber.org/papers/w26031.

Caglayan, Mustafa, and Jing Di. 2010. Does Real Exchange Rate Volatility Affect Sectoral Trade Flows? *Southern Economic Journal* 77, no. 2: 313–35.

Cravino, Javier, and Andrei A. Levchenko. 2018. The Geographic Spread of a Large Devaluation. *American Economic Review AEA Papers and Proceedings* 108: 562–66. Available at DOI: 10.1257/pandp.20181072.

Das, Mitali, Gita Gopinath, and Şebnem Kalemli-Özcan. 2022. *Preemptive Policies and Risk-Off Shocks in Emerging Markets*. IMF Working Paper WP/22/3. Washington: International Monetary Fund.

Dornbusch, Rudiger. 1976. Expectations and Exchange Rate Dynamics. *Journal of Political Economy* 84, no. 6: 1161–76.

Dornbusch, Rudiger. 1987. Exchange Rate Economics. *Economic Journal* 97, no. 385: 1–18.

Eicher, Theo S., and Christian Henn. 2011. One Money, One Market: A Revised Benchmark. *Review of International Economics* 19, no. 3: 419–35.

Eriksson, Katherine, Katheryn Russ, Jay C. Shambaugh, and Minfei Xu. 2021. Trade Shocks and the Shifting Landscape of US Manufacturing. *Journal of International Money and Finance* 114: 102407. Available at DOI: 10.1016/j.jimonfin.2021.102407.

Frieden, Jeffry A. 2015. *Currency Politics: The Political Economy of Exchange Rate Policy*. Princeton, NJ: Princeton University Press.

Fung, Loretta, and Jin-Tan Liu. 2009. The impact of real exchange rate movements on firm performance: A case study of Taiwanese manufacturing firms. *Japan and the World Economy* 21, no. 1: 85–96.

Herreno, Juan, Matias Morales, and Mathieu Pedemonte. 2023. *The Effect of Local Economic Shocks on Local and National Elections.* Federal Reserve Bank of Cleveland Working Paper 23-08. Available at DOI: 10.26509/frbc-wp-202308.

Hondroyiannis, G., P. Swamy, G. Tavlas, and M. Ulan. 2008. Some Further Evidence on Exchange-Rate Volatility and Exports. *Review of World Economics* 144: 151–280.

Kalemli-Özcan, Şebnem. 2019. *US Monetary Policy and International Risk Spillovers.* NBER Working Paper 26297. Cambridge, MA: National Bureau of Economic Research. Available at https://www.nber.org/papers/w26297.

Lin, Shu, Kang Shi, and Haichun Ye. 2018. Exchange Rate Volatility and Trade: The Role of Credit Constraints. *Review of Economic Dynamics* 30: 203–22.

Nelson, Rebecca M., and Martin A. Weiss. 2022. *The US Dollar as the World's Dominant Reserve Currency.* CRS Report IF11707. Washington: Congressional Research Service.

Obstfeld, Maurice, and Kenneth Rogoff. 1995. Exchange Rate Dynamics Redux. *Journal of Political Economy* 103, no. 3: 624–60.

Ozturk, Ilhan. 2006. Exchange Rate Volatility and Trade: A Literature Survey. *International Journal of Applied Econometrics and Quantitative Studies* 3, no. 1: 85–102.

Tenreyro, Silvana. 2007. On the Trade Impact of Nominal Exchange Rate Volatility. *Journal of Development Economics* 82, no. 2: 485–508. Available at DOI: 10.1016/j.jdeveco.2006.03.007.

Vernon, Raymond. 1966. International Investment and International Trade in the Product Cycle. *Quarterly Journal of Economics* 80, no. 2: 190–207. Available at DOI: 10.2307/1880689.

Wang, Kai-Li, and Christopher B. Barrett. 2007. Estimating the Effects of Exchange Rate Volatility on Export Volumes. *Journal of Agricultural and Resource Economics* 32, no. 2: 225–55.

Xie, Yizhe Daniel, and Youngmin Baek. 2020. Impact of Exchange Rate and Firm Heterogeneity on Exports: Empirical Evidence from Four ASEAN Economies. *Journal of Southeast Asian Economics* 37, no. 2: 199–223.

13

Will Persistent Trade Imbalances Become a Problem?

JOSEPH E. GAGNON

A key goal of the architects of the International Monetary Fund (IMF), John Maynard Keynes and Harry Dexter White, was the avoidance of large trade imbalances and resulting international policy conflicts. Keynes closed the Bretton Woods conference with a toast to "the end of competitive devaluations," as Robert Aliber notes in chapter 4 of this volume.

The pegged exchange rate system agreed to at Bretton Woods was a hoped-for deterrent of competitive devaluations. After the advent of generalized floating in 1973, the IMF Articles of Agreement were revised to accommodate the new reality, but they still retained, as a central obligation for member countries, the avoidance of currency manipulation or other policies "to prevent effective balance of payments adjustment or to gain an unfair competitive advantage over other members." In 1973, many economists and policymakers hoped that automatic adjustment of floating exchange rates to market forces would push economies more quickly toward balanced trade, limiting any temptation toward competitive currency practices. However, experience over the last five decades has belied that hope.

Yet most participants at PIIE's Floating Exchange Rates at Fifty conference demonstrated remarkably little concern over the two conference days about the emergence of large and persistent trade surpluses under floating exchange rates in a number of countries and the corresponding large trade deficits located mainly in the United States.

Joseph E. Gagnon is senior fellow at the Peterson Institute for International Economics.

After decades of nearly continuous current account deficits,[1] the United States now has a net international investment position (NIIP) of –65 percent of US GDP and –17 percent of world GDP.[2] Never before has one country borrowed such a large share of world GDP; no other net debtor comes close. Its net debt will likely continue to grow as long as the United States continues to run massive trade deficits.

Reserve Accumulation, Sovereign Wealth Funds, and the US Trade Deficit

The current situation under dollar hegemony could not be more different than that under sterling hegemony prior to World War I, when the United Kingdom was the world's largest net *creditor*. In recent decades, the largest imbalances have been associated with cross-border investments of foreign governments, not those of the private sector, as is commonly assumed (Gagnon and Sarsenbayev 2021). For example, the Swiss National Bank purchased CHF 866 billion in foreign exchange reserves between 2008 and 2022, supporting a cumulative current account surplus of CHF 687 billion.[3]

The United States' NIIP largely reflects the impact of these foreign official transactions. Of nearly $12 trillion in global foreign exchange reserves, roughly $7 trillion are estimated to be in US dollars and likely held either directly in US assets or in deposits backed by US assets.[4] A rough estimate of the overall size of sovereign wealth funds (SWFs) is $10.5 trillion.[5] If half of SWF assets are held in the United States (a conservative but plau-

---

1. The current account is the broadest measure of the trade balance. It measures the difference between US income earned from foreigners (from exports, labor, and investments) and foreign income earned from US sources. In the absence of measurement error and asset price movements, the current account reflects the change in a country's net international investment position.

2. Data on the investment position (as of year-end 2022) and US GDP (for 2022) are from the Bureau of Economic Analysis. Data on world GDP are from the IMF *World Economic Outlook*, www.imf.org (retrieved on April 13, 2023). Because it is not a claim on foreign countries, the value of US monetary gold is excluded, as Lane and Milesi-Ferretti (2018) propose.

3. Data are from the Swiss National Bank, https://data.snb.ch/en.

4. Data on total reserves and dollar reserves are from the IMF's Currency Composition of Official Foreign Exchange Reserves for December 31, 2022, www.imf.org. The modest amount of reserves for which no currency was reported was assumed to have the same currency breakdown as the bulk of reserves which do report a currency breakdown.

5. Data are from the Sovereign Wealth Fund Institute, https://www.swfinstitute.org/fund-rankings/ (accessed on April 13, 2023).

sible estimate),[6] total foreign government holdings of US assets would be $12.3 trillion, or more than 70 percent of the US NIIP of –16.6 trillion. US government holdings of foreign assets are trivial in comparison, so the public sector accounts for the lion's share of the US net international debt.

For many countries, foreign exchange reserves provide self-insurance against financial turbulence. But for many of the largest accumulators of reserves and SWF assets, the motivation is clearly to support export industries and avoid currency appreciation that would shrink large trade surpluses. In the case of oil and gas exporters, a considerable amount of official asset accumulation is justified to spread the benefits of finite resource extraction across future generations. For Norway and possibly a few Persian Gulf exporters, the accumulation has been excessive, even judged solely by their own welfare maximization, without taking into account any negative spillovers onto their trading partners (see Gagnon 2018, 2022).

Reasons for Concern

US policymakers display little unease about the unprecedented and still growing US net debt. There are at least four reasons to be concerned:

- Large and growing trade deficits are often associated with rising protectionist pressures (Bergsten and Gagnon 2017; Delpeuch, Fize, and Martin 2021; chapter 14, by Douglas Irwin, in this volume). The tariff war started by former US president Donald J. Trump is only the latest example.

- The zero lower bound on interest rates constrained monetary policy in most advanced economies from 2009 through 2020. Economies may hit the zero bound again in coming years. Achieving growth through currency depreciation and rising net exports becomes particularly attractive in these circumstances. However, when most of the world also faces a binding lower bound on policy interest rates, foreign exchange intervention is a beggar-thy-neighbor policy that delivers higher domestic growth at the cost of lower foreign growth (Eggertsson, Mehrotra, and Summers 2016).

---

6. As of December 31, 2022, US bonds were 54 percent of Morgan Stanley's Global Fixed Income Opportunities Fund, https://www.morganstanley.com/im/en-us/individual-investor/product-and-performance/mutual-funds/taxable-fixed-income/global-fixed-income-opportunities-fund.shareClass.I.html. As of March 31, 2023, equities were 68 percent of iShares MSCI World ETF, https://www.ishares.com/us/literature/fact-sheet/urth-ishares-msci-world-etf-fund-fact-sheet-en-us.pdf.

- Market sentiment about the dollar may shift suddenly, and the magnitude of any shift likely increases with the size of the US NIIP relative to world GDP. The world may face a chaotic adjustment as the United States is no longer able to import more than it exports.
  - Because US external liabilities are overwhelmingly denominated in dollars, an unexpected dollar depreciation tends to reduce the magnitude of the negative US NIIP, which makes adjustment less painful for the United States than it would otherwise be.
- The US net international debt imposes a burden on future generations of Americans. Much has been made of the positive net investment income reported in the US national accounts, which suggests that there is no net burden. However, these data are massively distorted by profit-shifting to international tax havens. True net investment income flows are almost surely negative (Guvenen et al. 2017).
  - Low interest rates in the years after 2008 held down the burden of the net debt; interest expense rose sharply with the tightening of monetary policy that began in 2022. It is not clear whether and how far interest rates will decline in the years ahead.

Using Foreign Exchange Intervention and Capital Flow Measures to Reduce Trade Imbalances

Many economists and policymakers doubt that there are effective policy levers to address trade imbalances without sacrificing more important objectives. New research shows that this view is outdated.

It is increasingly clear that foreign exchange intervention has a significant effect on both exchange rates and trade balances (Adler, Lisack, and Mano 2015; Chinn 2017; Gagnon and Sarsenbayev 2021; and IMF 2022). Capital controls (or capital flow measures) also likely have significant effects on exchange rates and trade balances, although few studies have been conducted and the results are more ambiguous (Chamon 2016).

These results suggest that foreign exchange intervention and capital flow measures can be used to address large trade imbalances, without sacrificing the use of monetary and fiscal policy to achieve maximum employment and stable prices.

It would be a mistake, however, to try to use foreign exchange intervention or capital flow measures to target specific levels of exchange rates. History is littered with the detritus of failed attempts to target values of the exchange rate that proved to be inappropriate. It simply is not possible to know what level of the exchange rate will be needed to keep trade in balance—and the cost of targeting the wrong value is extreme.

Instead, policymakers should start with ranges for trade balances that are consistent with a country's demographic and development status in a global context and that allow for reasonable cyclical swings. When a country's trade balance threatens to diverge from a reasonable range, policymakers should use foreign exchange intervention and capital flow measures to push against this undesired trend. If the trade balance continues to diverge, they should progressively ramp up policy. But there should be no "line in the sand" for either the exchange rate or the trade balance.

Using foreign exchange intervention and capital flow measures to narrow excessive trade imbalances is fully consistent with countries' obligations to the IMF. Indeed, such policies are the exact opposite of manipulating exchange rates in order to prevent effective balance of payments adjustment, as they aim to enhance adjustment.[7]

References

Adler, Gustavo, Noemi Lisack, and Rui Mano. 2015. *Unveiling the Effects of Foreign Exchange Intervention: A Panel Approach.* IMF Working Paper 15/30. Washington: International Monetary Fund.

Bergsten, C. Fred, and Joseph Gagnon. 2017. *Currency Conflict and Trade Policy: A New Strategy for the United States.* Washington: Peterson Institute for International Economics. Available at https://www.piie.com/bookstore/currency-conflict-and-trade-policy-new-strategy-united-states.

Chamon, Marcos. 2016. Capital Controls in Brazil: Effective? *Journal of International Money and Finance* 61 (C): 163–87.

Chinn, Menzie. 2017. The Once and Future Global Imbalances? Interpreting the Post-Crisis Record. Paper presented at the Federal Reserve Bank of Kansas City's Jackson Hole Symposium, August.

Delpeuch, Samuel, Etienne Fize, and Philippe Martin. 2021. *Trade Imbalances and the Rise of Protectionism.* CEPR Discussion Paper 15742. Paris and London: CEPR Press.

Eggertsson, Gauti, Neil Mehrotra, and Lawrence Summers. 2016. Secular Stagnation in the Open Economy. *American Economic Review* 106, no. 5: 503–07.

Gagnon, Joseph. 2018. *Can a Country Save Too Much? The Case of Norway.* PIIE Policy Brief 18-7. Washington: Peterson Institute for International Economics. Available at https://www.piie.com/publications/policy-briefs/can-country-save-too-much-case-norway.

Gagnon, Joseph. 2020. *Taming the US Trade Deficit: A Dollar Policy for Balanced Growth.* PIIE Policy Brief 20-15. Washington: Peterson Institute for International Economics. Available at https://www.piie.com/publications/policy-briefs/taming-us-trade-deficit-dollar-policy-balanced-growth.

7. Gagnon (2020) explores how such policies might work in the case of the United States.

Gagnon, Joseph. 2022. *Oil Exporters Returned to Currency Manipulation in 2021.* PIIE Realtime Economics blog, June 8. Washington: Peterson Institute for International Economics. Available at https://www.piie.com/blogs/realtime-economic-issues-watch/oil-exporters-returned-currency-manipulation-2021.

Gagnon, Joseph, and Madi Sarsenbayev. 2021. *Fiscal and Exchange Rate Policies Drive Trade Imbalances: New Estimates.* PIIE Working Paper 21-4. Washington: Peterson Institute for International Economics. Available at https://www.piie.com/publications/working-papers/fiscal-and-exchange-rate-policies-drive-trade-imbalances-new-estimates.

Guvenen, Fatih, Raymond Mataloni, Dylan Rassier, and Kim Ruhl. 2017. *Offshore Profit Shifting and Aggregate Measurement: Balance of Payments, Foreign Investment, Productivity, and the Labor Share.* NBER Working Paper 23324. Cambridge, MA: National Bureau of Economic Research.

IMF (International Monetary Fund). 2022. Online Annex 1.1. EBA Methodology 2022 Refinements. *2022 IMF External Sector Report.* Washington.

Lane, Philip, and Gian-Maria Milesi-Ferretti. 2018. The External Wealth of Nations Revisited: International Financial Integration in the Aftermath of the Global Financial Crisis. *IMF Economic Review* 66: 189–222.

14

Floating Exchange Rates and Trade Policy

DOUGLAS A. IRWIN

The breakdown of the Bretton Woods system in the early 1970s—the closing of the gold window in 1971 and the adoption of flexible exchange rates in 1973—was a watershed moment for the world economy. This volume focuses primarily on how the shift to flexible exchange rates affected macroeconomic policy, including inflation, international capital flows, and the like. But the impact of flexible exchanges rates on world trade and trade policies, which were key concerns at the time, also deserves consideration.

The move to flexible exchange rates generated widespread apprehension because the world did not have much experience with such a regime. With respect to trade, there were two main concerns: Would exchange rate fluctuations inhibit world trade? Would flexible exchange rates affect trade policy? This chapter considers both questions.

Exchange Rate Volatility and Trade Flows

It has long been believed that exchange rate stability promotes international trade. Under the gold standard in the late 19th and early 20th centuries, world trade grew steadily, with the certainty that currencies would be exchangeable with each other at a fixed rate of exchange (López-Córdova and Meissner 2003). When the gold standard broke down, during the Great Depression of the 1930s, economists worried that constantly fluc-

Douglas A. Irwin, nonresident senior fellow at the Peterson Institute for International Economics, is the John French Professor of Economics at Dartmouth College. He is grateful to C. Fred Bergsten and Maurice Obstfeld for helpful comments on a draft of this chapter.

tuating exchange rates would at best disrupt and at worst reduce trade (Nurkse 1944). As a result, the Bretton Woods system of fixed but adjustable exchange rates was designed to give businesses engaged in trade some certainty about future exchange rates and to give countries the flexibility to adjust those rates when they faced a "fundamental disequilibrium" in their external accounts. The hope was that large exchange rate adjustments would be infrequent and not significantly disrupt the expansion of world trade.

Under the Bretton Woods system, Western European countries recovered from World War II, and world trade grew steadily. The shift to flexible exchange rates by the industrial countries in 1973 led to fears that this regime change might unleash exchange rate fluctuations that would set back this process of recovery and growth. In the event, despite oil shocks and a productivity slowdown, world trade continued to grow in the 1970s. Exchange rate movements did not seem to impair trade, perhaps because the growth of forward markets allowed firms to hedge against unexpected movements in exchange rates. The shift to floating rates may even have reinforced the dollar's dominance as an invoice currency, as multinational companies sought to mitigate the effects of exchange rate volatility.

Studies did not find that fluctuating exchange rates had a negative impact on world trade. Gagnon (1993) found that exchange rate variability had a trivial effect on the volume of trade. In a comprehensive review of research, the staff of the International Monetary Fund concluded: "If there is a negative impact of exchange rate volatility on trade, it is not likely to be quantitatively large and the effect is not robust. These findings suggest that, from the perspective of promoting world trade, exchange rate volatility is probably not a major policy concern" (Clark et al. 2004, 2). A survey of the literature by Bahmani-Oskooee and Hegerty (2007) also supported this conclusion. The dearth of more recent papers on the topic suggests that economists do not deem the issue important enough to merit additional research.

Of course, just because flexible exchange rates have not been found to reduce trade does not mean that fixed exchange rates do not encourage trade. The introduction of the euro led to a spate of research on the trade-promoting benefits of currency unions. Several studies, notably Frankel and Rose (2002), found that currency unions significantly increase trade. The magnitude of this effect remains controversial, however, particularly in the context of the euro (Baldwin and Taglioni 2007, Glick and Rose 2016). Furthermore, currency unions are different from simple fixed exchange rates in that they eliminate any exchange rate risk and facilitate trade more than fixed rates by using the same unit of account across countries.

Exchange Rates and Trade Policy

The relationship between the exchange rate regime and trade policy is more subtle than the relationship between exchange rates and trade flows. The deflation of the early 1930s led many countries on the gold standard to pursue more protectionist policies because they had to use monetary policy to maintain the exchange rate peg rather than help stabilize the domestic economy (Eichengreen and Irwin 2010). Countries that did not want to leave the gold standard or devalue their currency resorted to import tariffs, import quotas, and exchange controls to reduce spending on imports and capital outflow, all to prevent the loss of gold reserves.

By contrast, countries that abandoned the gold standard and let the exchange rate go could pursue expansionary monetary policies to address the economic downturn without resorting to trade or exchange controls or worrying about their gold reserves. These countries used monetary policy to stabilize the economy rather than fix the exchange rate. The relaxation of the monetary policy constraint even allowed some countries to start reducing trade barriers. The United States did so with passage of the Reciprocal Trade Agreements Act of 1934, which came on the heels of the US abandonment of the gold standard in 1933.

The beneficial effects of exchange rate adjustments were not fully appreciated at the time. Flexible exchange rates had such a bad reputation—for the disorder and chaos they seemed to introduce in the 1920s and the supposed failure to reduce external imbalances in the 1930s—that the 1944 Bretton Woods conference gave them little consideration (Irwin 2019). The few early supporters of flexible exchange rates—notably Milton Friedman and James Meade in the 1950s—did so because they put priority on using monetary policy rather than the exchange rate to stabilize domestic prices. But they also believed that flexible exchange rates would facilitate balance of payments adjustment and thereby hasten the reduction of trade barriers. A country reducing its tariff under fixed exchange rates would have an incipient balance of trade deficit, which would have to be rectified by foreign tariff reductions (reciprocity) or domestic deflation (reduction in domestic wages and prices), both of which presented difficulties. A country reducing its tariff under floating exchange rates would see its currency depreciate, thereby stimulating exports and restraining imports more or less automatically. The export response would also help reduce political opposition to the tariff reduction.[1]

---

1. Harry Johnson (1969, 18) shared this view, writing: "The removal of the balance-of-payments motive for restrictions on international trade and payments is an important positive contribution that the adoption of flexible exchange rates could make to the achievement of the liberal objective of an integrated international economy, which must be

For these reasons, Friedman (1953, 157) argued that "a system of flexible or floating exchange rates [is]. . . absolutely essential for the fulfillment of our basic economic objective: the achievement and maintenance of a free and prosperous world community engaging in unrestricted multilateral trade." Similarly, James Meade (1955, 6) concluded that "free trade and fixed exchange rates are incompatible in the modern world; and all modern free-traders should be in favor of variable exchange rates." Both Friedman and Meade wanted to use the exchange rate for external balance and monetary and fiscal policy for internal balance and allow trade policy to be freer.

Although some trade liberalization occurred in the 1950s and 1960s, many advanced economies also resorted to import surcharges to avoid—in reality, just postpone—a devaluation when their balance of payments was under pressure (Bergsten 1977). But the rigidity of exchange rates was a particular problem for the United States, especially as pressures built for the dollar to fall in value during the 1960s. As the world's reserve currency and the currency against which par values were defined, the dollar could not be devalued against other currencies. Other countries would have to revalue their currencies against the dollar, something they were reluctant to do. This reluctance was a major motivation for the Nixon Shock of 1971, when the president closed the gold window and imposed a 10 percent import surcharge to force the revaluation of the Japanese yen and other currencies (Irwin 2013).

The overvaluation of the dollar and the loss of US competitiveness—the shift from a merchandise trade surplus to a tiny (by today's standards) merchandise trade deficit in the late 1960s and early 1970s—was considered alarming at the time. It created negative spillovers for US trade policy, as key industries that had been in favor of freer trade shifted against it and Congress began considering a multitude of protectionist laws. Writing just before the United States closed the gold window, Bergsten (1971, 634) spoke of the "crisis" in US trade policy. He argued for more exchange rate flexibility to ease the growing protectionist pressures:

> Increased flexibility of exchange rates would ensure earlier correction of payments imbalances among national economies. They would thereby relieve the political pressure on marginal industries which can compete only if equilibrium exchange rates exist and avoid trade balance shifts which provide support for protectionist pleas. The United States has a particular interest

set against any additional barriers to international commerce and finance, in the form of increased uncertainty, that might follow from the adoption of flexible exchange rates."

in improving the exchange rate mechanism because the biases of the present system promote undervaluation of other currencies against the dollar.[2]

The move to flexible exchange rates in March 1973, and the subsequent depreciation of the dollar, alleviated some of these protectionist pressures, just as it had in 1933–34. It helped Congress pass the Trade Act of 1974, which authorized US participation in the Tokyo Round of the General Agreement on Tariffs and Trade (GATT) negotiations and clarified the US president's powers to set trade policy. The continued weakness of the dollar in the late 1970s facilitated the passage of the Tokyo Round agreement by Congress in 1979.

The situation changed completely with the Federal Reserve's tightening of US monetary policy under Chairman Paul Volcker starting in 1979. This policy shift, along with the liberalization of capital controls in other advanced economies (Obstfeld 2021), led to a dramatic rise in the foreign exchange value of the dollar. This appreciation put enormous pressure on US traded goods industries and demonstrated that flexible exchange rates could be associated with large swings in current account balances, with major consequences for trade and trade policy, when capital flows between countries are large. Flexible exchange rates were no longer simply a benign way of ensuring external balance.[3] In fact, Bergsten and Williamson (1982, 119–20) warned:

> The advent of flexible exchange rates has failed to assure the degree of equilibrium and currency relationships that is essential if liberal trade policies are to prevail; indeed, recent misalignments, particularly for the dollar and the yen, may be as great as existed in the final breakdown stages of the Bretton Woods system of fixed parities.

The relationship between the strong dollar and protectionist pressures was well understood at the time (Destler 1986). In 1985, Treasury Secretary James Baker helped engineer the Plaza Accord to bring down the foreign exchange value of the dollar and relieve the growing demands for trade protection in the United States (Bergsten and Green 2016). This effort proved successful. By the late 1980s, the current account deficit had

---

2. "Though not widely articulated at the time, trade policy concerns were an important motivation behind the US push for both the parity realignments of 1971 and 1973 and the systemic shift to flexible rates," write Bergsten and Williamson (1982, 110).

3. Bergsten and Williamson (1982, 99) warned that "the continued failure to link the trade and monetary aspects of international economic exchange is a major mistake." They felt that this linkage was ignored because of "the widespread assumption that the international monetary system will not permit the existence of substantial exchange rate misalignments for prolonged periods."

narrowed, and the George H. W. Bush administration was able to phase out many of the protectionist measures for automobiles, textiles and apparel, and steel that had been introduced earlier in the decade.

Since then, exchange rate misalignment has been an ongoing source of controversy, nowhere more so than in the case of China in the mid-2000s (Goldstein and Lardy 2008). By preventing the appreciation of the renminbi against the dollar, China saw its foreign exchange reserves soar from a few hundred million dollars to more than $4 trillion by 2010, as its current account surplus reached an astounding 10 percent of GDP in 2007. Even though China modified its policy in 2005 and allowed its currency to appreciate gradually, the renminbi remained undervalued for some time (Bergsten and Gagnon 2017).

Perhaps surprisingly, protectionist pressures were not as intense as they had been in the early 1980s, because American firms were sourcing from rather than facing direct head-to-head competition from Chinese firms. In retrospect, however, the bilateral currency misalignment intensified the China shock of this period and proved damaging to the domestic political consensus about US trade policy.

At the same time, flexible exchange rates have proven their value as a shock absorber. Bown and Crowley (2013) find that exchange rate movements played an important role in limiting new import protection during the Great Recession of 2009.

The advanced economies adopted flexible exchange rates in the early 1970s. Developing economies were much slower to move in this direction, with most accepting more flexible exchange rates only in the late 1980s and 1990s. Before then, many countries failed to adjust nominal exchange rates as rapidly as their domestic prices, resulting in overvalued currencies and their by-product, trade controls to help traded-goods producers and ease pressure on the balance of payments (Shatz and Tarr 2002). As part of the Washington Consensus type of reforms that proliferated in the late 1980s and early 1990s, exchange rate adjustments became more frequent, although the "fear of floating," remained, as Calvo and Reinhart (2002) note.

Greater exchange rate flexibility allowed countries to avoid having overvalued currencies, thus enabling them to dismantle trade controls and reduce high levels of protection. The result was a remarkable trade reform wave from 1985 to 1995, in which many developing economies moved toward much freer trade (Irwin 2022). Almost invariably, a maxi-devaluation was the initial step to opening up the economy, jumpstarting exports and giving momentum to the reform process (Freund and Pierola 2012).

Flexible exchange rates helped transition economies move toward more commercial openness (Drabek and Brada 1998). India's 1991 trade reforms began with a devaluation of the rupee and a move toward a more flexible exchange rate. China's 1994 devaluation of the renminbi boosted the country's exports and made possible significant tariff reductions. There was much more trade liberalization at the global level in the two and half decades after 1985 than in the two and a half decades before 1973. Flexible exchange rates facilitated trade liberalization, just as Friedman and Meade had argued.

The move from fixed to floating exchange rates a half century ago has not impeded trade liberalization, and it has often facilitated it. Of course, during periods of severe currency misalignment—as in the 1980s, with the strong dollar, and the 2000s, with the weak renminbi—exchange rates have been a source of trade friction, with consequences for trade policy. But avoiding such misalignments seems to be a better way of keeping the channels of world trade open than reverting to a less-flexible exchange rate regime, which gave rise to currency misalignments and even trade barriers to postpone currency adjustments.

References

Bahmani-Oskooee, Mohsen, and Scott W. Hegerty. 2007. Exchange Rate Volatility and Trade Flows: A Review Article. *Journal of Economic Studies* 34, no. 3: 211–55.

Baldwin, Richard, and Daria Taglioni. 2007. Trade Effects of the Euro. *Journal of Economic Integration* 22, no. 4: 780–818.

Bergsten, C. Fred. 1971. Crisis in US Trade Policy. *Foreign Affairs* 49, no. 4: 619–35.

Bergsten, C. Fred. 1977. Reforming the GATT: The Use of Trade Measures for Balance-of-Payments Purposes. *Journal of International Economics* 7, no. 1: 1–18.

Bergsten, C. Fred, and Joseph E. Gagnon. 2017. *Currency Conflict and Trade Policy: A New Strategy for the United States*. Washington: Peterson Institute for International Economics. Available at https://www.piie.com/bookstore/currency-conflict-and-trade-policy-new-strategy-united-states.

Bergsten, C. Fred, and Russell A. Green, ed. 2016. *International Monetary Cooperation: Lessons from the Plaza Accord after Thirty Years*. Washington: Peterson Institute for International Economics and Rice University's Baker Institute for Public Policy. Available at https://www.piie.com/bookstore/international-monetary-cooperation-lessons-plaza-accord-after-thirty-years.

Bergsten, C. Fred, and John Williamson. 1982. Exchange Rates and Trade Policy. In *Trade Policy in the 1980s*, ed. William R. Cline. Washington: Institute for International Economics.

Bown, Chad P., and Meredith A. Crowley. 2013. Import Protection, Business Cycles, and Exchange Rates: Evidence from the Great Recession. *Journal of International Economics* 90, no. 1: 50–64.

Calvo, Guillermo A., and Carmen M. Reinhart. 2002. Fear of Floating. *Quarterly Journal of Economics* 117, no. 2: 379–408.

Clark, Peter B., Natalia Tamirisa, and Shang-Jin Wei, with Azim Sadikov and Li Zeng. 2004. *A New Look at Exchange Rate: Volatility and Trade Flows.* Washington: International Monetary Fund.

Destler, I.M. 1986. *American Trade Politics.* Washington: Institute for International Economics. Available at https://www.piie.com/bookstore/american-trade-politics-4th-edition.

Drabek, Zedenek, and Josef Brada. 1998. Exchange Rate Regimes and the Stability of Trade Policy in Transitions Economies. *Journal of Comparative Economics* 26: 642–68.

Eichengreen, Barry, and Douglas A. Irwin. 2010. The Slide to Protectionism in the Great Depression: Who Succumbed and Why? *Journal of Economic History* 70, no. 4: 871–97.

Frankel, Jeffrey, and Andrew K. Rose. 2002. An Estimate of the Effect of Common Currencies on Trade and Income. *Quarterly Journal of Economics* 117: 437–66.

Freund, Caroline, and Martha Denisse Pierola. 2012. Export Surges. *Journal of Development Economics* 97, no. 2: 387–95.

Friedman, Milton. 1953. The Case for Flexible Exchange Rates. In *Essays on Positive Economics.* Chicago: University of Chicago Press.

Gagnon, Joseph. 1993. Exchange Rate Variability and the Level of International Trade. *Journal of International Economics* 34: 269–87.

Glick, Reuven, and Andrew K. Rose. 2016. Currency Unions and Trade: A Post-EMU Reassessment. *European Economic Review* 87: 78–91.

Goldstein, Morris, and Nicholas R. Lardy, eds. 2008. *Debating China's Exchange Rate Policy.* Washington: Peterson Institute for International Economics. Available at https://www.piie.com/bookstore/debating-chinas-exchange-rate-policy.

Irwin, Douglas A. 2013. The Nixon Shock after 40 Years: The Import Surcharge Revisited. *World Trade Review* 12: 29–66.

Irwin, Douglas A. 2019. The Missing Bretton Woods Debate over Flexible Exchange Rates. In *The Bretton Woods Agreement,* ed. Naomi Lamoreaux and Ian Shapiro. New Haven, CT: Yale University Press.

Irwin, Douglas A. 2022. The Trade Reform Wave of 1985-1995. NBER Working Paper 29973. Shorter version published in *AEA Papers and Proceedings* 112 (May): 244–51.

Johnson, Harry G. 1969. The Case for Flexible Exchange Rates. *Federal Reserve Bank of St. Louis Review* June: 12–24.

López-Córdova, J. Ernesto, and Christopher M. Meissner. 2003. Exchange-Rate Regimes and International Trade: Evidence from the Classical Gold Standard Era. *American Economic Review* 93, no. 1: 344–53.

Meade, James. 1955. The Case for Flexible Exchange Rates. *Three Banks Review* 27: 3–27.

Nurkse, Ragnar. 1944. *The International Currency Experience.* Geneva: League of Nations.

Obstfeld, Maurice. 2021. The Global Capital Market Reconsidered. *Oxford Review of Economic Policy* 37: 690–706.

Shatz, Howard J., and David G. Tarr. 2002. Exchange Rate Overvaluation and Trade Protection. In *Development, Trade, and the WTO: A Handbook,* ed. Bernard Hoekman, Aaditya Mattoo, and Philip English. Washington: World Bank.

15

Fifty Years of Exchange Rate Pass-Through from a Central Banker's Perspective

CATHERINE L. MANN

Fifty years have passed since the end of the fixed but adjustable exchange rate system under Bretton Woods. A key question, under both fixed and flexible exchange rates, has been how a change in the international exchange value of a domestic currency passes through to affect import and export prices and from there to affect trade quantities, domestic activity, and, particularly, domestic inflation.

Over the past 50 years, economic research on exchange rate pass-through (ERPT) has evolved, from aggregated data and a macro perspective to disaggregated data and micro-foundations, from rational homogeneous agents to behavioral and heterogeneous ones, and from a real-side focus to the incorporation of financial markets. In other words, ERPT research has mirrored the profession as a whole.

This agenda is far too large to cover in this short chapter. Given that I started my career at the Federal Reserve Board and my current position is at the Bank of England, I therefore focus on the ERPT to domestic inflation, taking the perspective of a central banker with an inflation objective.[1]

---

1. My remarks should not be interpreted as policy advice for either institution. They represent only my own views, not those of the Federal Reserve or of the Bank of England.

Catherine L. Mann is Professor of the Practice at Brandeis University, where she was the Rosenberg Professor of Global Finance (1996–2014). She is also an external member of the Monetary Policy Committee at the Bank of England. She was global chief economist at Citibank and before that chief economist, head of the economics department, and G20 finance deputy at the Organization for Economic Cooperation and Development (OECD) in Paris. The views expressed are her own and do not reflect the views of the Bank of England, the Monetary Policy Committee, or the staff of either.

I highlight some research from the past and offer some thoughts on where future research might be most insightful and policy relevant.

The Continued Importance of Exchange Rate Pass-Through

Even after 50 years of floating, economists do not fully understand how a change in the domestic currency affects domestic inflation. But there is a sense that ERPT doesn't matter as much as it used to. As Adam Posen noted in his introductory remarks at the conference on which this volume is based, "exchange rates" as a research category is not on the website of the Peterson Institute for International Economics!

One explanation is that dominant-currency invoicing limits ERPT at the first stage (from a change in the exchange rate to changes in the prices of traded products). Another view is that effective inflation targeting regimes of central banks short-circuit ERPT at the second stage (from trade prices to domestic prices). I suggest that understanding ERPT—to both the prices of goods and services and to financial markets—does matter for domestic inflation and therefore for inflation-targeting central banks.

The issue and estimation of ERPT was critical even before the floating rates of the post–Bretton Woods era, because the exchange rate was a distinct policy variable, albeit not one seen as a tool of the central bank. Under fixed exchange rates, the policy decision to devalue a currency was expected to improve a country's economic position through specific channels. By raising import prices and lowering export prices, a home-currency devaluation was supposed to change the quantities of trade (based on the price elasticity of demand and supply), with various positive implications. Given a balance of payments deficit, for example, a "successful" devaluation should increase exports and reduce imports, helping a country to avoid running out of foreign exchange or gold reserves. A "competitive"[2] devaluation should boost domestic economic activity by substituting domestic production for imports and promoting exports. The general equilibrium implications of these changes in external balance were known, but they did not take center stage.

Indeed, "elasticity pessimism" was a major concern of policymakers in the fixed-rate period. Would the devaluation of the home currency yield these beneficial outcomes? From the earliest models of the interwar period to early post-war analysis, the question of whether the Marshall-Lerner condition held was key. Econometric results did not give clear guidance.[3]

---

2. That is, a devaluation seen specifically to create a competitive advantage in the global marketplace for the domestic producers.

3. See, for example, Orcutt (1950) and Houthakker and Magee (1969).

In this early work, based on limited data, empirical estimation tended to confound changes in exchange rates and trade prices as well as changes in the elasticity of demand with respect to the elasticity of prices; it also did not incorporate other domestic prices and factors. These confoundings tended to bias the elasticities downward, strengthening the case for elasticity pessimism (a point that has reemerged today in the guise of dollar dominance in invoicing).

Because of these data issues, whether a change in a fixed exchange rate could be used to discipline domestic inflation was hard to evaluate statistically. Based on his case studies of Chile and Argentina, and the 1920s Germany hyperinflation, Dornbusch (1986, 1) concluded that "exchange rate policy can make an important contribution to stabilization but. . . it can also be misused and will then lead to persistent deviations from purchasing-power parity (PPP), with devastatingly adverse effects." In other words, adjusting a fixed exchange rate might work, but the adjustment must be complemented by other policy changes to achieve sustained inflation stabilization along with other objectives, a point that was relevant in the UK context in the fixed exchange rate period (Artus 1975).

As the floating rate period began, researchers started to disentangle these elements in order to understand how floating exchange rates worked.[4] Central bankers started to consider how varying exchange rates might pass through to affect the dynamics of prices and quantities, particularly prices. They now regularly estimate rules of thumb for how a given change in the home currency—usually some trade-weighted exchange rate—might affect their country's inflation rate through its effect on import prices.

Kristin Forbes (my predecessor as external member of the Monetary Policy Committee) outlined the Bank of England's rules of thumb in a 2015 speech, noting that they "traditionally estimated that the pass-through from exchange rate movements to UK import prices is roughly 60 percent to 90 percent, and the import intensity of the consumer price index (CPI) is about 30 percent."[5] These rules of thumb bear scrutiny, as discussed below.

In the context of central banking, I have been writing about ERPT for nearly all of the 50 years of floating exchange rates. My first job was in the International Finance Division at the Federal Reserve Board, headed by Edwin M. Truman. My first published article was in the *Federal Reserve*

---

4. For an historical assessment as Bretton Woods was breaking down, see Crockett and Goldstein (1976) and Obstfeld (1985).

5. Speech given at the Bank of England's 47th Money, Macro and Finance Research Group Annual Conference, Cardiff, September 11, 2015, https://www.bankofengland.co.uk/-/media/boe/files/speech/2015/much-ado-about-something-important-how-do-exchange-rate-movements-affect-inflation.pdf.

Bulletin, in 1986, based on one of the chapters in my 1984 MIT dissertation (Mann 1986). The introductory sentence emphasized the traditional macro link between central bank objectives and ERPT: "The decline in the exchange value of the dollar over the past year or so has had important implications for the outlook for the US current account balance and domestic inflation" (p. 366). But the title—"Prices, Profit Margins, and Exchange Rates"— emphasizes the second generation of ERPT analysis, which merged industrial organization theories and open economy macro, something that was just burgeoning at that time. The quote "recent changes in the pattern of US trade, the *unprecedented* appreciation of the dollar. . . and the *volatility* of bilateral exchange rates" (p. 366; emphasis added) was prescient about directions for research—directions I believe will be even more important going forward. As an external member of the Bank of England's Monetary Policy Committee, I have come full circle to central banking and ERPT!

Research on Exchange Rate Pass-Through

My 1986 article raised key questions about ERPT. How much do changing patterns of trade (including fragmentation, ownership relations, and associated currency invoicing) influence pass-through of a currency change to inflation? Are there asymmetries in how an appreciation or depreciation of the home currency passes through to domestic inflation? Are nonlinearities associated with a particularly large move in the currency? Does increased volatility in the exchange rate affect pass through into domestic inflation in any particular way? Does a financial driver of a currency move affect pass-through to domestic inflation differently from other shocks, possibly via overshooting? These are all questions on which much has been written.

Once industrial organization theories were combined with international trade and macro theories and disaggregated data became available, work on ERPT moved away from the perfect competition framework, suggesting many new margins on which exchange rates could operate and adjust before being passed through to inflation. Indeed, much has changed since 1986, when I used data disaggregated by two- and three-digit Standard Industrial Classification (SIC) categories hand-copied from microfiche. Data sets now cover individual transactions, and the research questions continue to evolve. But, both early work and now cutting edge focus on market structure and competition.

Another important area of research addresses how ERPT might be affected by global value chains versus sales of final products, ownership versus arm's-length relationships with suppliers, and the currency of invoicing and transfer pricing, all in various combinations, in the underlying theoretical specifications and empirical validations. An important conclusion of this new empirical work is that ERPT seems to have become both smaller and asymmetric, with dollar appreciation (home-currency devaluation) yielding less of a competitive improvement in export prices while being passed through as expected into import prices. Elasticity pessimism has reemerged in the guise of dominant currency pricing and via supply chain ownership and transfer pricing.

Two papers of two generations of researchers and data highlight this industrial organization–centric view of ERPT as applied to the United Kingdom. Both reveal a time-varying pass-through, at either stage one or stage two. In his 2003 article "The Effect of Exchange Rates on Prices, Wages, and Profits: A Case Study of the United Kingdom in the 1990s," Gagnon starts with the observation that over a four-year period (1992–96) the trade-weighted pound depreciated by 15 percent before appreciating by 20 percent, but consumer prices moved very little. He ascribes this phenomenon to offsetting changes in profit margins of manufacturers and distributors as a result of "the Bank of England's successful stabilization of consumer price inflation over this period. In order to keep overall prices stable in the face of changing tradables prices, prices of nontradable services, such as retailing, have to move in the opposite direction" (Gagnon 2003, 2). Pass-through at stage one was thus as expected; at stage two, the central bank dampened it. Gagnon implies a key endogeneity between central bank policy and ERPT, a point to which I will return.

A more recent study of the United Kingdom (Hjortsoe and Lewis 2020) investigates import prices for 55 sectors by constructing sector-specific trade-weighted exchange rates and examining whether invoicing was in dollars or euros. Its findings imply that large currency moves and dollar invoicing accentuate pass-through to import prices. For a central bank whose objective is price stability, a dollar-driven pound depreciation would put more upward pressure on import prices and on through to domestic prices than would be estimated by considering US-originated imports with a trade-weighted sterling exchange rate.

The next generation of research I would like to highlight is the shock dependency and time-varying nature of ERPT. The industrial organization approach focuses on the microeconomics of firm behavior and relationships. Shock dependency returns to the macro environment and the nature or source of shocks. Work by Forbes, Hjortsoe, and Nenova (2015) on this topic was precipitated by the puzzling fact that the depreciation of the pound after the global financial cycle of 2007–09 yielded a sharper rise in domestic prices than had been expected and the appreciation of 2013–15 less of a dampening effect. They concluded that the nature or source of the shock differed over these time periods, affecting ERPT.

Reviewing some of their findings for the United Kingdom makes it clear that the type of shock matters and that rules of thumb may therefore be misleading (Forbes, Hjortsoe, and Nenova 2015). The timing and extent of pass-through differ across types of shocks in both steps of ERPT. The authors normalize all shocks to a 1 percent appreciation of the pound. A domestic monetary policy shock has the highest pass-through to both import prices and to domestic prices, with a 1 percent appreciation associated with a 0.7 percent fall in import prices and a 0.20–0.25 percent fall in consumer prices. Tighter monetary policy (at least when undertaken independently of any other central bank) has the expected effect on inflation through both channels. A positive supply shock (such as a productivity gain) is associated with a rapid fall in import prices of about 0.7 percent, as importers fight to maintain competitiveness in the domestic market against domestic firms that now have lower costs. These cost improvements pass through to lower consumer prices—but not 1 for 1 and decreasingly so over time—to yield less than a 0.1 percent drop in consumer prices. From the microfoundation stories, this finding suggests that domestic firms may be enjoying larger profits. So far, so good, in terms of signs and approximate value of ERPT, with nuances taking a cue from the micro industrial-organization models.

For a domestic demand shock, however, the 1 percent appreciation is passed through less to import prices (only about 0.4 percent), and domestic prices actually rise by 0.2 percent. This example suggests that the positive demand shock limits how much the pound appreciation passes through to import prices and in fact offsets the appreciation effect on domestic prices. The microfoundations of ERPT explain the story. Given a strong demand environment (the positive demand shock), even with an appreciation, importers need not reduce their prices by as much to maintain their market position. Domestic firms face less competition from importers and enjoy strong demand, allowing them to raise their prices.

From the standpoint of monetary policy decision making, the source of the shock affects how exchange rates pass through to domestic inflation—and implicitly how the monetary policy authority should respond. In the case of a positive demand shock, and relying on a rule of thumb, the central bank may be expecting the appreciation to do more of the work to temper domestic inflation.

As the World Bank Group's 2019 *Global Economic Prospects* notes, "To design appropriate policies, it is important to quantify the ERPT to inflation associated with different domestic and global shocks and with different country characteristics. . . . Pass-through is significantly smaller when central banks pursue a credible inflation target, operate in a flexible exchange rate regime, and are independent from fiscal authorities. This highlights a self-reinforcing feedback loop between central bank credibility, exchange rate and price stability" (p. 69).

A multicountry analysis by Carrière-Swallow et al. (2016) tests the hypothesis that a credible central bank dampens ERPT, particularly on consumer prices. The argument is that firms perceive a credible central bank with an inflation target as leaning against trend inflation, which reduces the frequency and magnitude of price changes by firms, which in turn stabilizes aggregate inflation at a lower trend rate than would be the case without a credible central bank and inflation target.

The estimation in this chapter uses the disagreement among surveys of professional forecasters' inflation expectations as a proxy for how credible the central bank's inflation target is. It confirms that ERPT declined over time in advanced and, in particular, emerging markets after the global financial crisis. The estimated correlations for individual variables suggest that lower ERPT to domestic inflation is associated with lower and less volatile inflation, an appreciating home currency, and less disagreement about inflation forecasts. When all variables, as well as import shares, in trade are included in the estimation, only the disagreement variable is significant. These empirical results add to the evidence that ERPT is endogenous to the credibility of the central bank's reaction function.

If credible central bank inflation targets have tamed ERPT, is ERPT no longer worth analyzing as a factor affecting central bank decision making? Not at all. Paying attention to ERPT in the context of monetary policy decision making remains important, particularly because the exchange rate is not just the relative price of goods and services at home and abroad but also the relative price of two financial assets that yield returns at home and abroad. A vast body of literature exists on the relationship between exchange rates, financial market variables, inflation, and monetary policy. Where do ERPT and monetary policy fit into this financial view?

Another branch of the microfoundations of ERPT research introduces financial flows by considering different measures of the exchange rate, including a financial flow–weighted measure. This vein of research harkens back to Dornbusch's (1976) open economy macro model with both goods and asset markets. In that model—in which asset prices adjust more quickly than goods prices—the exchange rate must overshoot to equilibrate goods markets in the face of a shock.[6] As the exchange rate is not only the relative

---

6. For a review of Dornbusch's model, see Ken Rogoff, "Dornbusch's Overshooting Model after Twenty-Five Years," Mundell-Fleming Lecture, November 30, 2001 (revised in 2002) (https://www.imf.org/en/News/Articles/2015/09/28/04/53/sp112901). I took Dornbusch's open economy macro class a year or so after Ken Rogoff did (probably 1981).

price of goods and services but also the relative price of financial assets, the role for overshooting of one exchange rate versus the other and how that overshooting might affect pass-through to inflation in goods and services and central bank policy bears further consideration.

In a speech on global spillovers I gave in June 2022, I examined these two types of ERPT (the real channel and the financial channel) given a global shock and considered alternative central bank policy paths to achieve domestic price stability.[7] The context for this exercise was to consider my own monetary policy decision as other central banks around the world were tightening monetary policy to address inflation surges.

Although my neighboring central banks were raising their policy rates, work by Miranda-Agrippino and Rey (2022) showed the dominance of the Federal Reserve policy decisions in the global financial cycle. In my speech, I examined the spillover effect on UK inflation of a 1 percentage point increase in the policy rate by the Federal Reserve. A priori, the sign of the spillover is not clear, as the trade channel and the financial channel work in opposite directions. In the face of monetary tightening from abroad, the global demand channel should induce the same signs in output and inflation at home and abroad (slowing activity and disinflation), whereas the global financial channel should induce the opposite sign in the foreign economy (increasing activity and inflation). Which way the activity and inflation break in the non–US economy depends critically on the reaction function of monetary policy in that economy.

Based on historical UK data and the embodied central bank reaction function, I found that a Federal Reserve tightening is associated with a slowdown in the UK economy coming from the 'imported' Fed tightening, but also a jump in the UK price level of about 0.5 percentage point that persists and a depreciation of the pound of about 4½ percent by year two. UK policy rates rise initially but are then cut to mitigate output loss. The interest rate differentials between the United States and the United Kingdom remain in favor of the United States throughout. This differential is the deciding factor for the financial channel, which is why the bilateral exchange rate traces out a persistent depreciation of the pound as a result of the shock and why the jump in the price level lingers.

Is there an alternative central bank reaction function that can avoid a persistent jump in the price level? A central banker could take a more activist stance and raise the policy rate immediately to meet the US mone-

---

7. Catherine Mann, "UK Monetary Policy in the Context of Global Spillovers," speech given at a Market New International Connect event, June 20, 2022, https://www.bankofengland. co.uk/speech/2022/june/catherine-l-mann-speech-at-a-market-news-international-connect-event.

tary policy shock. Or it could be more gradualist and move in steps. What happens to the pound and the price level determine what happens under these hypothetical central bank strategies via a pass-through of the shock to the exchange rate and then to domestic inflation. An activist approach avoids the price-level jump and better stabilizes the price level: In the simulations, less price level volatility is achieved through more volatility in the policy rate and the exchange rate.

The Great Moderation was associated with reduced volatility in output, inflation, and exchange rates. Going forward, volatility in the exchange rate, other asset prices, and inflation is more likely to be higher than lower. Considering traditional ERPT and its theoretical underpinnings, higher volatility creates space for firms to increase the amount or frequency of price changes, yielding higher aggregate inflation. Considering financial ERPT, there is much opportunity for a more complete integration of the work of Kalemli-Özcan and Rey (chapters 23 and 24 in this volume) on how financial flows and asset valuation risks can be incorporated into ERPT to domestic inflation dynamics. We have much more data to analyze, particularly linking the whole distribution of firms' prices, financial exposures, and expectations, to understand ERPT.

A new era is likely dawning for research on ERPT. Higher volatility may well test the hypothesis that central bank independence and inflation targeting have been the key factors underlying the Great Moderation of inflation.

References

Artus, Jacques R. 1975. *The 1967 Devaluation of the Pound Sterling*. IMF Staff Papers 22, no. 3. Washington: International Monetary Fund.

Carrière-Swallow, Yan, Bertrand Gruss, Nicolas E. Magud, and Fabian Valencia. 2016. *Monetary Policy Credibility and Exchange Rate Pass-Through*. WP 16/240. Washington: International Monetary Fund. (Published in 2021 in the *International Journal of Central Banking* 17, no. 3: 61–95.)

Crockett, Andrew, and Morris Goldstein. 1976. *Inflation under Fixed and Flexible Exchange Rates*. IMF eLibrary. Washington: International Monetary Fund. Available at https://www.elibrary.imf.org/view/journals/024/1976/003/article-A001-en.xml.

Dornbusch, Rudiger. 1976. Expectations and Exchange Rate Dynamics. *Journal of Political Economy* 84: 1161–76.

Dornbusch, Rudiger. 1986. *Inflation, Exchange Rates, and Stabilization*. Princeton Essays in International Finance 165. Princeton, NJ: International Finance Section, Princeton University.

Forbes, Kristin, Ida Hjortsoe, and Tsvetelina Nenova. 2015. *The Shocks Matter: Improving Our Estimates of Exchange Rate Pass-Through*. External MPC Unit Discussion Paper 43. London: Bank of England. Available at https://www.bankofengland.co.uk/external-mpc-discussion-paper/2015/the-shocks-matter-improving-our-estimates-of-exchange-rate-pass-through.

Gagnon, Joseph. 2003 (updated 2004). *The Effect of Exchange Rates on Prices, Wages, and Profits: A Case Study of the United Kingdon in the 1990s*. Washington: Federal Reserve Board. Available at https://www.federalreserve.gov/pubs/ifdp/2003/772/ifdp772r.pdf.

Hjortsoe, Ida, and John Lewis. 2020 (updated 2022). *Non-linearities, Asymmetries and Dollar Currency Pricing in Exchange Rate Pass-Through: Evidence from the Sectoral Level*. Staff Working Paper 868. London: Bank of England. Available at https://www.bankofengland.co.uk/-/media/boe/files/working-paper/2020/non-linearities-asymmetries-and-dollar-currency-pricing-in-exchange-rate-pass-through.pdf.

Houthakker, H.S., and Stephen P. Magee. 1969. Income and Price Elasticities in World Trade. *Review of Economics and Statistics* 51, no. 2: 111–25.

Mann, Catherine L. 1986. Prices, Profit Margins, and Exchange Rates. *Federal Reserve Bulletin* June: 366–79. Available at https://fraser.stlouisfed.org/files/docs/publications/FRB/pages/1985-1989/31910_1985-1989.pdf.

Miranda-Agrippino, Silvia, and Hélène Rey. 2022. The Global Financial Cycle. In *Handbook of International Economics*, vol. 6, ed. Gita Gopinath, Elhanan Helpman, and Kenneth Rogoff, 1–43. Amsterdam: Elsevier.

Obstfeld, Maurice. 1985. Floating Exchange Rates Experience and Prospects. *Brookings Papers on Economic Activity*: 369–464. Washington: Brookings Institution.

Orcutt, Guy H. 1950. Measurement of Price Elasticities in International Trade. *Review of Economics and Statistics* 32, no. 2: 117–32.

World Bank Group. 2019. Special Focus 1.2: Currency Depreciations, Inflation, and Central Bank Independence. In *Global Economic Prospects: Heightened Tensions, Subdued Investment*. Washington.

16

Replacing the Golden Anchor for Price Stability

KRISTIN FORBES

When policymakers discussed alternatives to the Bretton Woods exchange rate system in the late 1960s, a frequent concern was the loss of an anchor for price stability. Paul Volcker (then an undersecretary at the US Treasury Department) highlighted these concerns in discussions leading up to the 1971 meeting at Camp David on changes to the international monetary system. He believed that "money needed an anchor, some price that was a fixed point, and that an exchange rate tied to gold served that purpose. . . . He was convinced that fixed currencies imparted a necessary discipline on national policy makers, who otherwise would too easily resort to lax fiscal and monetary policies that would lead to inflation" (Garten 2021, 84).[1]

Initially, concerns about prices "unanchoring" focused on risks from easy monetary and fiscal policies. In the last 25 years, another risk to price

---

1. Fixed rates could also entail less price stability, because the price level rather than the exchange rate must adjust to real shocks under a peg (an argument John Maynard Keynes made). This view presupposes that the central bank can and will engage in price stabilization, anchoring inflation credibly through some means, such as an inflation target, without pegging a nominal price. If credibility is lacking, it will be difficult to fix the exchange rate absent some external political context, such as Bretton Woods or the euro. These concerns were also part of Volcker's hesitation over abrogating the Bretton Woods arrangement. By 1979, however, he believed that the Federal Reserve could stabilize prices without a fixed nominal anchor.

Kristin Forbes is the Jerome and Dorothy Lemelson Professor of Management and Global Economics at MIT's Sloan School of Management. She thanks Maurice Obstfeld and participants at the PIIE conference for helpful comments and suggestions and Chris Collins for research assistance and helpful input.

stability has emerged: increased globalization. As the global economy became more integrated in the 1990s and 2000s, through trade, capital flows, and supply chains, inflation became more sensitive to global factors (Forbes 2019). When global shocks more frequently push consumer price index (CPI) inflation far from central bank targets (as seen recently during the COVID-19 pandemic), it may be even more important than it used to be to have some type of anchor to achieve price stability.

Have economies been able to achieve price stability in the face of large global shocks without some type of anchor for price stability? Over the last 25 years, many advanced economies allowed their exchange rates to float (albeit with different degrees of "dirty" intervention). Others replaced the "golden" anchor with a new disciplining structure, such as pegging to the euro, adopting the euro, or establishing a currency board.

To understand the importance of maintaining some type of exchange rate anchor during the recent era of heightened globalization, this chapter focuses on advanced economies and compares those with flexible exchange rates with those that adopted more rigid arrangements. It evaluates the performance of each group along three metrics: inflation rates, inflation sensitivity to a common global factor, and inflation sensitivity to specific global shocks. The results suggest that over the last 25 years, inflation in advanced economies with floating exchange rates was no less stable or more vulnerable to global shocks than it was in advanced economies that had some type of anchor. Advanced economies appear to have been able to replace the "anchor of gold" with inflation targeting central banks combined with a variety of exchange rate arrangements.

Review of the Literature on Inflation, Globalization, and Exchange Rate Regimes

An extensive body of literature examines the advantages and disadvantages of flexible versus fixed exchange rates (see Rogoff et al. 2004 for a summary). Much of this work focuses on the correlation between the exchange rate regime and subsequent growth, investment, interest rates, trade, and the likelihood of experiencing a crisis. A subset of these papers discusses the advantage of pegged exchange rates as a disciplining device for fiscal and monetary policies that stabilizes inflation (Giavazzi and Giovannini 1989). The experience of countries in Latin America in the 1980s and 1990s suggested that exchange rate pegs helped economies prevent high inflation (Edwards 2001).

Empirical studies examining a broader set of economies and periods also generally find that fixed exchange rates correspond to lower inflation, even after controlling for other determinants of inflation (Ghosh, Gulde, and Wolf 2003). Results, however, can be sensitive to how exchange rate regimes are defined and what other variables are controlled for (Rogoff et al. 2004). The relationship between the exchange rate regime and price stability is also more consistently significant for emerging-market and developing economies (EMDEs) than for advanced economies. This sensitivity of results to sample selection highlights a key issue in all of these analyses: selection bias. Countries that chose to peg their exchange rates in the post–Bretton Woods era tend to be different in many ways from economies with flexible exchange rates.

A more recent branch of literature focuses on how globalization has affected the inflation process. Over the 50 years since the breakdown of the Bretton Woods system, most economies became more tightly integrated with the global economy, through a range of channels. Several papers explore how this increased global integration, especially the period of hyperglobalization in the 1990s and 2000s, could have reduced inflation, including through the greater availability of low-cost imports and the greater ease of shifting production to low-cost economies.

Recently, attention has shifted not only to how globalization has affected the level of inflation but also to its sensitivity to global shocks. Forbes (2019) shows that the sensitivity of CPI inflation to factors such as oil prices, nonoil commodity prices, global slack, and supply chains increased. As these global shocks drive larger movements in CPI inflation, it has become more difficult for economies with all types of exchange rate arrangements to achieve price stability in any given year.

Is it easier to achieve price stability in the face of these large global shocks without some type of anchor for the exchange rate? To help answer this question, the rest of this chapter compares advanced economies with flexible exchange rates with advanced economies with some type of exchange rate anchor (primarily through some type of link to the euro) in terms of inflation rates, the sensitivity of inflation to a common global factor, and the sensitivity of inflation to specific global shocks.

What Happened to Inflation after 1999?

As a preliminary look at whether some type of exchange rate anchor is important to achieve price stability in the post–Bretton Woods era, I begin with a simple comparison of inflation rates for advanced economies with different exchange rate regimes. Figure 16.1 shows average annual CPI inflation from 1999 through 2023 (with estimates starting in 2022) for a sample of 35 advanced economies, including economies with "rigid" and "flexible" exchange rate regimes.[2]

---

2. Inflation data are from the IMF's *World Economic Outlook* database (October 2022). Inflation data for 2022 are estimates as of that date. The sample consists only of advanced

Figure 16.1

Average CPI inflation rate in advanced economies, by exchange rate regime

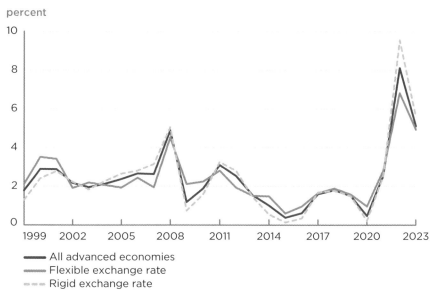

percent

All advanced economies
Flexible exchange rate
Rigid exchange rate

Notes: A rigid exchange rate is defined as a conventional peg, currency board, or no separate legal tender. A flexible exchange rate is defined as any form of a float (independent float, free float, or managed float with no predetermined path). The sample is the 35 advanced economies listed in appendix 16A at the end of this chapter. Inflation is the annual consumer price index (CPI) inflation rate, averaged across countries in the group.

Sources: Exchange rate definitions are based on the IMF's *Annual Report on Exchange Arrangements and Exchange Restrictions* (IMF 2020). Inflation data are from the IMF's *World Economic Outlook* (October 2022), with forecasts starting in 2022.

Exchange rate regimes are defined based on the IMF's *Annual Report on Exchange Arrangements and Exchange Restrictions* (IMF 2020). An exchange rate is defined as flexible if it is any form of a float (independent float, free float, or managed float with no predetermined path); it is defined as rigid if it is a conventional peg (including a crawling peg), a currency board,

economies, based on IMF definitions, excluding small islands (appendix table 16A.1 lists the economies). Economies that are not classified as having a fixed or flexible exchange rate are included in statistics for the full sample (e.g., for advanced economies) but not the subgroups of fixed exchange rate or flexible exchange rate economies.

or no separate legal tender.[3] Almost all the advanced economics defined as having a rigid exchange rate used the euro or linked their currency to it during this period, so the analysis largely compares economies that were part of this European arrangement with economies that were not. Although most of these "rigid" economies had adopted the euro by 2023, many started the sample period with different types of anchors to the euro, including various types of pegged arrangements and currency boards.[4] The only economy in the sample of "rigid" exchange rates that did not have some type of link to the euro is Hong Kong, which maintains a currency board to the US dollar.

Figure 16.1 shows that the average inflation performance of advanced economies with very different exchange rate regimes was almost identical: 2.41 percent for economies with flexible exchange rates and 2.40 percent for economies with rigid exchange rates. Of course, average inflation rates can conceal large deviations of inflation from target. Countries that lacked an anchor through the exchange rate, however, did not appear to have less stable inflation than economies with an anchor. If anything, economies with a more rigid exchange regime appear to have had somewhat more volatile inflation, with inflation farther above 2 percent in 2006–08 and 2021–22 and farther below 2 percent in 2013–16 and 2020. The average deviation of inflation from 2 percent was 0.86 percent for economies with a flexible exchange rate and 1.28 percent for economies with a rigid exchange rate.

These simple comparisons provide no evidence that economies that relinquished any type of exchange rate anchor in the post–Bretton Woods era had higher or more volatile CPI inflation than economies that did not.

How Sensitive Is Inflation to Global Factors?

This section shifts from comparing the average rate and volatility of inflation for countries with and without an exchange rate anchor to assessing the sensitivity of inflation to shared global factors in today's more integrated global economy.

---

3. In 2019, 21 economies had a rigid exchange rate regime, 13 countries had a flexible regime, and 1 (Singapore) had a regime that did not fall in either category.

4. Denmark's currency is pegged to the euro, and Greece joined the euro in 2001. In 1999, the currencies of Cyprus, Estonia, Latvia, Lithuania, Malta, the Slovak Republic, and Slovenia were linked to the euro through various arrangements; these countries eventually adopted the euro (Cyprus in 2008, Estonia in 2011, Latvia in 2014, Lithuania in 2015, Malta in 2008, Slovak Republic in 2009, and Slovenia in 2007). See appendix table 16A.1 for the full list of economies.

Sensitivity to a Shared Global Factor

Forbes (2019) examines how globalization may be affecting the inflation process through increased trade flows, the greater heft of EMDEs and their impact on commodity prices, the greater ease of using supply chains to shift parts of production to cheaper locations, and a corresponding reduction in local worker bargaining power. That paper shows that the shared global component of CPI inflation in advanced economies more than doubled between 1990–94 and 2015–17, rising from 27 percent to almost 57 percent. It breaks this shared global component down into specific factors, such as energy prices, nonenergy commodity prices, global slack, exchange rate movements, and supply chains. The analysis does not test whether this shared global component in inflation varies across economies with different exchange rate regimes.

Does the fact that common global shocks are increasingly driving inflation increase the importance of having some type of anchor for prices? If large global shocks are more likely to cause inflation to deviate substantially from the inflation target, is it more important to have some mechanism to ensure that such an inflation shock does not become embedded in price and wage setting? If so, has an anchor through the exchange rate become more important to achieve price stability in the face of these larger global shocks?

To test whether having an anchor affects the sensitivity of economies to this shared global component of inflation, I updated and improved on the analysis in Forbes (2019). I calculated the first principal component of CPI inflation for sets of economies over the same sample but calculated four-year rolling averages (rather than averaging over fixed windows).[5]

The results show that the proportion of the variance explained by the shared global component of CPI inflation increased over the last 25 years—for the full sample, for economies with rigid exchange rate regimes, and for economies with flexible regimes (figure 16.2). These findings are even stronger than the results in Forbes (2019). The shared global component of inflation for the full sample of advanced economies increased from about 45–60 percent of CPI inflation in the mid-2000s to 94 percent in 2019–22. This increased comovement in inflation rates in advanced economies at the end of the sample period reflects the impact of the large, common global shocks experienced during the COVID-19 pandemic. The findings provide no evidence that economies lacking some type of anchor were more vulnerable to this shared global factor than economies that had an anchor. In fact,

---

5. The data point for 2003 is the principal component for inflation over the previous four years (1999, 2000, 2001, and 2002); the data point for 2023 reflects the principal component for inflation between 2019 and 2022.

Figure 16.2

First principal component of CPI inflation in advanced economies, by exchange rate regime

proportion of variance explained

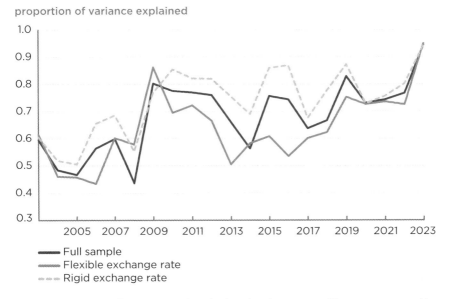

- ▬▬ Full sample
- ▬▬ Flexible exchange rate
- ▬ ▬ Rigid exchange rate

Notes: First principal component is calculated as four-year rolling averages, so the statistic for 2003 is the principal component from 1999 through that start of 2003 (i.e., end-2002). A rigid exchange rate is defined as a conventional peg, currency board, or no separate legal tender. A flexible exchange rate is defined as any form of a float (independent float, free float, or managed float with no predetermined path). The sample is the 35 advanced economies listed in appendix table 16A.1. Inflation is the annual connsumer price index (CPI) inflation rate.

Sources: Exchange rate definitions are based on the IMF's *Annual Report on Exchange Arrangements and Exchange Restrictions* (IMF 2020). Inflation data is from the IMF's *World Economic Outlook* (October 2022), with forecasts starting in 2022.

inflation in economies with flexible exchange rates appears to have been less tightly linked to this shared global factor in inflation. The first principal component for economies with more rigid exchange rate arrangements was consistently higher than that for economies with more flexible rates, especially in 2010–22. It explains 74 percent of inflation variation for rigid regimes over the full period on average and 64 percent for economies with flexible rates; since 2010, the shared component is 80 percent for economies with rigid exchange rates and 67 percent for economies with flexible rates. This greater comovement for economies with more rigid regimes partly reflects the fact that most of the economies in this sample are European (countries that are either in the euro area or have some type of peg to the euro), and therefore likely to share other common characteristics and be more tightly linked through trade and capital flows as part of a common market.[6]

This analysis does not provide information on what is driving different patterns across time and exchange rate regimes. Factors that could explain a larger principal component, or an increase over time, include larger global shocks (e.g., greater commodity price volatility), greater sensitivity to global shocks (e.g., through global supply chains), stronger direct linkages between economies (e.g., from greater trade or financial integration), or more similarity in other country characteristics (e.g., in their economic structures or policy reaction functions).

Sensitivity to Specific Global Shocks

To further explore what is driving this increased global comovement in inflation rates and any differences linked to the exchange rate regime, I directly estimate the impact of specific global shocks on CPI and core inflation. I use a version of the New Keynesian Phillips curve developed in Forbes, Gagnon, and Collins (2022) to analyze inflation in a cross-section of economies. This model builds on the standard, hybrid version of the Phillips curve developed in Galí and Gertler (1999) and Galí and Lopez-Salido (2005), which includes controls for domestic slack, inflation expectations, and lagged inflation. It then adds controls for a series of more disaggregated global variables and allows for different forms of nonlinearity in the relationship between slack (i.e., the amount of spare capacity or underutilized resources in an economy) and inflation.[7]

In the analysis below, I focus on specifications that include four of these global variables: oil price inflation, nonoil commodity price inflation, world slack, and the growth in global value chains (as originally discussed in Forbes 2019). I also examine a nonlinear specification called the low-inflation bend model, in which the Phillips curve is normally steep but becomes flat when slack is high and inflation low (as originally discussed in Gagnon and Collins 2019).

---

6. The only "rigid" economy that is not linked to the euro is Hong Kong. As Hong Kong's currency is tied to the US dollar through its currency board arrangement, and the US dollar is highly correlated with the global financial cycle, it is not surprising that Hong Kong is also highly correlated with the shared global factor.

7. The estimates use the same data and model as Forbes, Gagnon, and Collins (2022), with two changes: The sample includes only advanced economies (to be consistent with the preceding analysis), and the model does not include a control for the real exchange rate (to better test for the role of exchange rate regimes).

The resulting regressions take the following form:

$$\pi_{it} = \alpha_i + \beta_1 SLACK_{it}^D + \beta_2 SLACK_{it}^D \times NL\_DUMMY_{it} + \beta_3 \pi_{it}^e + \beta_4 \pi_{it}^4 - 1$$
$$+ \gamma_1 SLACK_t^W + \gamma_2 POIL_{it}^W + \gamma_3 PCOMM_{it-1}^W + \gamma_4 GVC_{t-1}^W + \varepsilon_{it}. \quad (16.1)$$

Variables are defined as follows:

- π_{it} is quarterly CPI inflation or core inflation (CPI excluding food and energy) at a seasonally adjusted annual rate.[8]
- π_{it}^e is medium-run inflation expectations, measured by the five-year-ahead forecast for CPI inflation from the IMF's *World Economic Outlook.*
- π_{it-1}^4 is a four-quarter average of CPI or core inflation, lagged one quarter.
- $SLACK_{it}^D$ is domestic economic slack (the negative of the output gap), measured as the principal component of seven variables.[9]
- NL_DUMMY_{it} is a dummy that captures nonlinearities; it equals 1 when slack is positive and inflation is low and 0 otherwise (to generate the "low-inflation bend model").[10]
- $SLACK_t^W$ is world economic slack, measured as a weighted average of the estimated output gap in advanced economies and China.
- $POIL_{it}^W$ is the quarterly annualized change in world oil prices (from Datastream) relative to country i's CPI inflation.
- $PCOMM_{it}^W$ is the quarterly annualized change in world nonfuel commodity prices (from Datastream) relative to country i's CPI inflation.

---

8. Adjustments are also made for large value-added tax increases in Australia in 2000Q3, Japan in 1997Q2 and 2014Q2, New Zealand in 2010Q4, and the United Kingdom in 2010Q1 and 2011Q1.

9. This calculation builds on Albuquerque and Baumann (2017) and Hong et al. (2018), which show the importance of measuring different dimensions of slack. The principal component is calculated following Forbes (2019), which uses three "gaps" (for output, unemployment, and participation) based on OECD data and four "gaps" (for hours worked per person employed, the share of involuntary part-time workers, the share of temporary workers, and the share of self-employed workers) as percent deviations from the "normal" level calculated using data from Hong et al. (2018).

10. I define inflation as low when it is less than 3 percent, but Forbes, Gagnon, and Collins (2022) show that the results are robust to using thresholds ranging from 2 to 4 percent.

- GVC^W_t is the principal component of four variables capturing the growth in global value chains.[11]
- α_i refers to the coefficients on a full set of country fixed effects.

The regression sample includes a cross-section of 27 advanced economies from 1996Q1 through 2017Q4 (using 1995 data for initial lagged inflation).[12]

Table 16.1 reports the results for equation (16.1). Column (1) shows results for the standard New Keynesian model (without controls for global variables and without any nonlinearity in the relationship with slack). Column (2) adds the four global variables. Column (3) adds the dummy variable, to allow the relationship with slack to change for economies with positive slack (i.e., an output gap) and low inflation. In all of these specifications, coefficients have the expected sign and are usually significant. Countries have significantly higher inflation if they have less slack, higher lagged inflation, or higher inflation expectations. The relationship with slack is nonlinear and close to zero when there is positive slack and low inflation; otherwise the Phillips curve is steep. Inflation is also significantly higher when there is higher inflation in oil prices and nonoil commodity prices; it is significantly lower when there is more world slack and faster growth in global value chains.

Columns (4) and (5) test whether a country's exchange rate regime affects its sensitivity to the four global variables. These specifications include an interaction term for each of the global variables with a dummy equal to one if the country has a flexible exchange rate (column 4) or a rigid exchange rate (column 5).[13] The new estimates at the bottom of table 16.1 (in bold) are striking in that almost all are insignificant, suggesting that economies with a flexible exchange rate were not significantly more affected by the global shocks that affect inflation than the full set of economies.

---

11. The four variables in the principal component are (a) the growth of merchandise trade volumes as a share of global GDP; (b) traded intermediate goods as a share of global GDP; (c) the share of these traded intermediate goods that are "complex," defined as crossing country borders at least twice; and (d) the dispersion in producer price indices (PPI). The first three components are from Li, Meng, and Wang (2019) and the fourth is based on OECD data.

12. The sample is the same as in the previous section less Cyprus, Estonia, Hong Kong, Lithuania, Malta, Singapore, Slovenia, and South Korea, for which data were not available.

13. Exchange rate regimes are based on the "fine" classifications in Ilzetzki, Reinhart, and Rogoff (2019), with flexible exchange rates defined as classifications 10–13 and rigid exchange rates as classifications 1–4. The analysis in earlier sections of this chapter used the IMF's *Annual Report on Exchange Arrangements and Exchange Restrictions* to classify exchange rate regimes, in order to use more updated classifications than were available in Ilzetzki, Reinhart, and Rogoff (2019).

Economies with more rigid exchange rate regimes were also not affected in a significantly different way. The only variable that is occasionally significant is the one capturing the interaction of global value chains with the flexible exchange rate dummy. This positive coefficient is equal in value, but of opposite sign, to the coefficient on global value chains for the full sample, suggesting that global value chains had no significant impact on inflation in economies with flexible exchange rates but lowered inflation in economies with rigid rates. These results suggest that CPI inflation is not more sensitive to global shocks in economies lacking some type of an exchange rate anchor. Does this finding apply to core inflation (excluding food and energy prices) as well? Movements in core inflation tend to be more persistent than movements in CPI inflation, and central banks are more concerned if a global shock becomes embedded in core inflation than in the more volatile CPI inflation.

Table 16.2 replicates the analysis from table 16.1 for core inflation.[14] The results in columns (1) to (3) without controls for the exchange rate regime are consistent with those in Forbes, Gagnon, and Collins (2022): Countries have higher core inflation if they have higher inflation expectations, higher lagged inflation, and less slack, with the effect of slack nonlinear and close to zero for economies with positive slack and low inflation. The results in columns (4) and (5) are very similar to the results for CPI inflation; countries with a flexible (or rigid) exchange rate regime do not have a significantly different sensitivity of inflation to global shocks, except for sensitivity to changes in global value chains (to which economies with more rigid regimes are more sensitive).

This series of results suggests that inflation in economies with flexible exchange rates is not more sensitive to changes in oil prices, nonoil commodity prices, world slack, or global value chains than it is in economies with rigid exchange rates. The exchange rate regime could interact with global shocks in various ways, with the direction of the effect unclear. If, for example, economies do not have some type of anchor to stabilize prices, sharp movements in inflation from global shocks could be more likely to become engrained in price and wage setting, leading to larger deviations of inflation from targets. Or, working in the other direction, economies with more flexible exchange rates could experience currency movements that partially counteract the impact of global shocks on inflation, leading to smaller deviations of inflation from targets.

---

14. The specification follows Forbes (2019) and Forbes, Gagnon, and Collins (2022) by combining commodity prices into one variable instead of breaking out the individual effects of oil and nonoil prices.

Table 16.1

Phillips curve regressions of headline CPI inflation

	(1) Standard	(2) + Global variables	(3) + Nonlinear PC term	(4) + Flexible ER interactions	(5) + Rigid ER interactions
Domestic Slack	-0.22*** (0.04)	-0.17*** (0.05)	-0.33*** (0.08)	-0.33*** (0.07)	-0.33*** (0.07)
Nonlinear PC Term			0.39*** (0.11)	0.41*** (0.10)	0.41*** (0.11)
Inflation Expectations	0.81*** (0.13)	0.71*** (0.14)	0.74*** (0.13)	0.76*** (0.15)	0.74*** (0.14)
Lagged Inflation	0.40*** (0.06)	0.45*** (0.05)	0.48*** (0.05)	0.47*** (0.05)	0.47*** (0.05)
World Slack		-0.10** (0.05)	-0.11* (0.05)	-0.15** (0.06)	-0.08 (0.06)
World Oil Prices		0.03*** (0.00)	0.04*** (0.00)	0.04*** (0.00)	0.04*** (0.01)
Nonfuel Commodity Prices		0.05*** (0.01)	0.05*** (0.01)	0.05*** (0.01)	0.04*** (0.01)
Global Value Chains		-0.08** (0.04)	-0.11*** (0.04)	-0.20*** (0.06)	-0.05 (0.04)
Intercept	-0.41* (0.23)	-0.36 (0.23)	-0.78*** (0.23)	-0.81*** (0.22)	-0.52 (0.38)

	(1)	(2)	(3)	(4)	(5)
World Slack * ER Dummy				0.08 (0.07)	-0.04 (0.06)
World Oil Prices * ER Dummy				-0.00 (0.01)	0.00 (0.01)
Nonfuel Commodity Prices * ER Dummy				-0.00 (0.02)	0.00 (0.02)
Global Value Chains * ER Dummy				0.20** (0.08)	-0.11 (0.06)
ER Dummy				0.01 (0.21)	-0.43 (0.36)
R-squared	*0.269*	*0.351*	*0.366*	*0.370*	*0.368*
Observations	*2,342*	*2,342*	*2,342*	*2,342*	*2,342*
Countries	*27*	*27*	*27*	*27*	*27*

PC = Phillips curve; ER = exchange rate; CPI = consumer price index

Notes: Regressions of CPI inflation (quarterly, seasonally adjusted) from 1996Q1–2017Q4. Sample is 27 advanced economies. ER Dummy is equal to 1 if country has a flexible exchange rate in column (4) or rigid exchange rate in column (5). The "Nonlinear PC term" is a dummy equal to 1 if domestic slack is positive and CPI inflation is less than 3 percent. A country is defined as having a flexible exchange rate if it is classified in regimes 10–13, or having a rigid exchange rate if it is classified in regimes 1–4, all according to the fine classifications in Ilzetzki, Reinhart, and Rogoff (2019). See text for other variable definitions. All estimates have robust standard errors in parentheses, with * p < 0.10, ** p < 0.05, *** p < 0.01.

Table 16.2
Phillips curve regressions of core CPI inflation

	(1) Standard	(2) + Global variables	(3) + Nonlinear PC term	(4) + Flexible ER interactions	(5) + Rigid ER interactions
Domestic Slack	-0.18*** (0.03)	-0.17*** (0.04)	-0.26*** (0.04)	-0.26*** (0.04)	-0.26*** (0.04)
Nonlinear PC Term			0.25*** (0.04)	0.27*** (0.04)	0.27*** (0.04)
Inflation Expectations	0.78*** (0.17)	0.77*** (0.17)	0.76*** (0.15)	0.77*** (0.16)	0.76*** (0.15)
Lagged Inflation	0.49*** (0.04)	0.50*** (0.04)	0.53*** (0.04)	0.52*** (0.03)	0.52*** (0.03)
World Slack		-0.03 (0.04)	-0.03 (0.04)	-0.08 (0.05)	-0.00 (0.05)
World Commodity Prices		0.01** (0.01)	0.01* (0.01)	0.01* (0.01)	0.01 (0.01)
Global Value Chains		-0.00 (0.03)	-0.02 (0.03)	-0.10* (0.05)	0.04 (0.03)
Intercept	-0.64** (0.30)	-0.63** (0.28)	-0.86*** (0.28)	-0.88*** (0.29)	-0.70** (0.33)

				World Slack * ER Dummy

	(1)	(2)	(3)	(4)	(5)
World Slack * ER Dummy				0.09 (0.06)	-0.06 (0.07)
World Commodity Prices * ER Dummy				-0.01 (0.01)	0.01 (0.01)
Global Value Chains * ER Dummy				0.18** (0.06)	-0.12** (0.06)
ER Dummy				-0.02 (0.18)	-0.30 (0.33)
R-squared	0.371	0.374	0.382	0.386	0.384
Observations	2,342	2,342	2,342	2,342	2,342
Countries	27	27	27	27	27

PC = Phillips curve; ER = exchange rate; CPI = consumer price index

Notes: Regressions of core CPI inflation (quarterly, seasonally adjusted) from 1996Q1–2017Q4. Sample is 27 advanced economies. ER Dummy is equal to 1 if country has a flexible exchange rate in column (4) or rigid exchange rate in column (5). The "Nonlinear PC term" is a dummy equal to 1 if domestic slack is positive and CPI inflation is less than 3 percent. A country is defined as having a flexible exchange rate if it is classified in regimes 10–13, or having a rigid exchange rate if it is classified in regimes 1–4, all according to the fine classifications in Ilzetzki, Reinhart, and Rogoff (2019). See text for other variable definitions. All estimates have robust standard errors in parentheses, with * p < 0.10, ** p < 0.05, *** p < 0.01.

Figure 16.3

Average CPI inflation in emerging-market and developing economies, by exchange rate regime

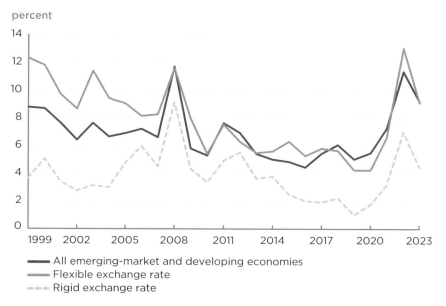

percent

All emerging-market and developing economies
Flexible exchange rate
Rigid exchange rate

Notes: A rigid exchange rate is defined as a conventional peg, currency board, or no separate legal tender. A flexible exchange rate is defined as any form of a float (independent float, free float, or managed float with no predetermined path). The sample is 130 emerging-market and developing economies (based on IMF definitions). Inflation is the annual consumer price index (CPI) inflation rate, averaged across countries in the group.

Sources: Exchange rate definitions are based on the IMF's *Annual Report on Exchange Arrangements and Exchange Restrictions* (IMF 2020). Inflation data are from the IMF's *World Economic Outlook* (October 2022), with forecasts starting in 2022.

Are the Findings Relevant for Emerging-Market and Developing Economies?

Many EMDEs have been less successful than advanced economies at keeping inflation around their targets and experienced greater price volatility. Simple comparisons of inflation rates in this group of economies suggest that the exchange rate regime may be more highly correlated with price stability than in advanced economies.

Figure 16.3 replicates the analysis in figure 16.1 with a sample of 130 EMDEs.[15] Countries with more rigid exchange rates consistently had lower

---

15. The sample includes all countries in the IMF's *World Economic Outlook* (October 2022) that are not classified as an advanced economy for which data on inflation and the exchange rate regime were available.

inflation, and inflation was closer to the 2–4 percent targeted in many EMDEs, than in economies with more flexible exchange rates. The average absolute deviation of inflation from 2 percent was about 6 percent for EMDEs with flexible exchange rates versus only 2 percent for EMDEs with rigid exchange rates. In contrast, in advanced economies there was no meaningful difference in inflation rates between economies with flexible and rigid exchange rates, and the deviation from 2 percent was smaller in economies with flexible rates (see figure 16.1).

Conclusion

Fifty years after the breakdown of the Bretton Woods system of exchange rates linked to gold, have economies found a way to stabilize prices without some type of anchor for the exchange rate? The analysis in this chapter yields a resounding yes, at least for advanced economies. The advanced economies in this analysis have established price stability in the absence of a golden anchor through a variety of exchange rate mechanisms.

All advanced economies abandoned exchange rate regimes anchored to gold. Some opted for new anchors (primarily through some type of link to the euro); others allowed their exchange rates to float freely. Economies that allowed their exchange rates to float did not experience more price instability than economies that maintained some type of anchor. Economies with floating exchange rates had the same average inflation rate since 1999 as economies with more rigid regimes, and they experienced smaller (rather than larger) deviations from 2 percent inflation targets. In addition, economies with floating exchange rates were no more sensitive to the shared global component in CPI inflation, and they were not significantly more sensitive to individual global shocks, such as from oil prices, nonoil commodity prices, world slack, and global value chains.

In fact, the analysis in this chapter suggests that economies with flexible exchange rates may have had slightly greater price stability—as measured by their deviation of inflation from 2 percent and their sensitivity to shared global movements in inflation and global value chains—although this result primarily reflects differences between economies that are currently in the euro area and non-European economies.

Advanced economies—whatever their exchange rate regime—appear to have found a new anchor: independent, inflation targeting central banks. Central banks in these economies provided price stability even in the face of large global shocks that have frequently driven inflation away from targets. Advanced economies seem to have successfully replaced the anchor of gold with that of the stone columns that frequently grace the facades of independent central banks—an impressive achievement given the increased role of global shocks in driving inflation.

Many EMDEs have also improved their ability to use monetary policy countercyclically, lowering interest rates to support incomes and employment in response to negative shocks without undermining price stability) (English, Forbes, and Ubide 2021; Ha, Kose, and Ohnsorge 2019). Progress in EMDEs has been less consistent than in advanced economies, however, and some economies in this group still have work to do to establish price stability.

On a more positive note, the experience of the advanced economies suggests that price stability is possible with inflation targeting central banks and a variety of exchange rate mechanisms—even in the absence of a golden anchor.

Appendix 16A

Table 16A.1
Classification of 35 advanced economies by exchange rate regime, 2019

Type of exchange rate regime	Economies
Floating	Australia, Canada, Czech Republic, Iceland, Israel, Japan, New Zealand, Norway, South Korea, Switzerland, Sweden, the United Kingdom, and the United States
Rigid	Austria, Belgium, Cyprus, Estonia, Denmark, Finland, France, Germany, Greece, Hong Kong, Ireland, Italy, Latvia, Lithuania, Luxembourg, Malta, the Netherlands, Portugal, the Slovak Republic, Slovenia, and Spain
Other	Singapore

Notes: A rigid exchange rate is a conventional peg, currency board, or no separate legal tender. A flexible exchange rate is any form of a float (independent float, free float, or managed float with no predetermined path). The sample is 35 advanced economies, based on IMF definitions, and excluding small island nations. Most of the economies defined as having a rigid exchange rate had adopted the euro by 2019. The two exceptions are Denmark (with the krone pegged to the euro) and Hong Kong (with a currency board to the US dollar). Many of the other countries in this group, however, did not have the euro as legal tender at the start of the sample, with different arrangements linking their national currencies to the euro over the sample period. The dates at which these countries adopted the euro are Cyprus in 2008, Estonia in 2011, Latvia in 2014, Lithuania in 2015, Malta in 2008, Slovak Republic in 2009, and Slovenia in 2007.

Source: Exchange rate definitions are based on the International Monetary Fund's *Annual Report on Exchange Arrangements and Exchange Restrictions* (IMF 2020).

References

Albuquerque, Bruno, and Ursel Baumann. 2017. *Will US Inflation Awake from the Dead? The Role of Slack and Non-Linearities in the Phillips Curve.* Working Paper 2001. Frankfurt: European Central Bank.

Edwards, Sebastian. 2001. *Exchange Rate Regimes, Capital Flows and Crisis Prevention.* NBER Working Paper 8529. Cambridge, MA: National Bureau of Economic Research.

English, Bill, Kristin Forbes, and Angel Ubide, eds. 2021. *Monetary Policy and Central Banking in the Covid Era.* Vox eBook. London: CEPR Press. Available at https://cepr.org/publications/books-and-reports/monetary-policy-and-central-banking-covid-era.

Forbes, Kristin. 2019. Inflation Dynamics: Dead, Dormant, or Determined Abroad? *Brookings Papers on Economic Activity* (Fall): 257–338. Washington: Brookings Institution.

Forbes, Kristin, Joseph Gagnon, and Christopher Collins. 2022. Low Inflation Bends the Phillips Curve around the World. *Economia* 45, no. 89: 52–72.

Gagnon, Joseph, and Christopher Collins. 2019. *Low Inflation Bends the Phillips Curve.* PIIE Working Paper 19-6. Washington: Peterson Institute for International Economics. Available at https://www.piie.com/publications/working-papers/low-inflation-bends-phillips-curve.

Galí, Jordi, and Mark Gertler. 1999. Inflation Dynamics: A Structural Econometric Analysis. *Journal of Monetary Economics* 44: 195–222.

Galí, Jordi, and David Lopez-Salido. 2005. Robustness of Estimates of the Hybrid New Keynesian Phillips Curve. *Journal of Monetary Economics* 52: 1107–18.

Garten, Jeffrey E. 2021. *Three Days at Camp David: How a Secret Meeting in 1971 Transformed the Global Economy.* New York: HarperCollins.

Ghosh, Atish, Anne-Marie Gulde, and Holger Wolf. 2003. *Exchange Rate Regimes: Choices and Consequences.* Cambridge, MA: MIT Press.

Giavazzi, Francesco, and Alberto Giovannini. 1989. *Limiting Exchange Rate Flexibility: The European Monetary System.* Cambridge, MA: MIT Press.

Ha, Jongrim, M. Ayhan Kose, and Franziska Ohnsorge. 2019. *Inflation in Emerging and Developing Economies: Evolution, Drivers and Policies.* Washington: World Bank. Available at https://www.worldbank.org/en/research/publication/inflation-in-emerging-and-developing-economies.

Hong, Gee Hee, Zsóka Kóczán, Weicheng Lian, and Malhar Nabar. 2018. *More Slack than Meets the Eye? Wage Dynamics in Advanced Economies.* IMF Working Paper WP/18/50. Washington: International Monetary Fund.

Ilzetzki, Ethan, Carmen Reinhart, and Kenneth Rogoff. 2019. Exchange Arrangements Entering the 21st Century: Which Anchor Will Hold? *Quarterly Journal of Economics* 134, no. 2: 599–646.

IMF (International Monetary Fund). 2020. *Annual Report on Exchange Arrangements and Exchange Restrictions.* Washington. Available at https://www.imf.org/en/Publications/Annual-Report-on-Exchange-Arrangements-and-Exchange-Restrictions/Issues/2021/08/25/Annual-Report-on-Exchange-Arrangements-and-Exchange-Restrictions-2020-49738.

IMF (International Monetary Fund). 2022. *World Economic Outlook.* Washington.

Li, Xin, Bo Meng, and Zhi Wang. 2019. Recent Patterns of Global Production and GFC Participation. In *Global Value Chain Production Report 2019*. Geneva: World Trade Organization.

Rogoff, Kenneth, Aasim Husain, Ashoka Mody, Robin Brooks, and Nienke Oomes. 2004. *Evolution and Performance of Exchange Rate Regimes*. IMF Occasional Paper 229. Washington: International Monetary Fund.

IV

FLOATING EXCHANGE RATES AND EMERGING MARKETS

17

How Much Insulation Do Flexible Exchange Rates Provide for Emerging Markets?

ANDRÉS VELASCO

In marking the 50th anniversary of the advent of floating exchange rates, I wish to ask whether flexible exchange rates have delivered monetary independence for emerging markets, as promised in 1973. I also want to ask why it is that many countries float their currencies but few countries float cleanly and even fewer explain clearly what they are doing. And I wish to echo as well some of the concerns about the patchy nature of the global financial safety net and the problems it creates for emerging markets.

We were all raised in the tradition of Mundell-Fleming and are therefore familiar with the Impossible Trinity, which posits that an economy cannot simultaneously maintain a fixed foreign exchange rate, free capital mobility, and an independent monetary policy. Nowadays, conventional monetary policymaking in open economies follows largely from this observation.

Things do not always work that way, however. Following the work of Hélène Rey and her colleagues, we have learned to worry about the dominant role of the dollar. One does not have to be the holder of a French passport to understand that whenever the value of the dollar moves, many things happen in the rest of the world that are very difficult for local authorities to counteract.

Asset prices and capital flows to emerging markets are highly correlated with measures of global risk appetite. And given the important share

Andrés Velasco is the Dean of the School of Public Policy at the London School of Economics and Political Science.

of the dollar in international funding, US monetary policy is the main driver of the risk cycle. Periods of loose monetary policy and active liquidity provision in the United States coincide with a weaker dollar, higher risk-taking, larger capital flows, rising asset prices, and increasing leverage in emerging markets. The opposite happens when the United States tightens its monetary policy: Investors run for the exits, and capital flows, asset prices, and leverage move in the opposite direction (Miranda-Agrippino and Rey 2020).

These findings are related to a point that Calvo, Reinhart, and Leiderman made in 1996: For emerging markets, the main driver of capital flows from abroad is whatever happens abroad. The size of capital flows into a country depends primarily on the global appetite for risk. This is very different, of course, from the standard narrative we teach undergraduates, in which domestic consumption and investment-smoothing pin down the current account and capital flows respond endogenously to fill whatever current account gap emerges.

If you have ever been close to a policymaking position in an emerging economy, you know that the exogeneity of capital flows seems very plausible. During the great financial crisis, José de Gregorio was president of the Central Bank of Chile and I was Chile's finance minister. I remember landing in Washington to attend the IMF–World Bank meetings and sitting down with José and our teams at the Dunkin' Donuts in National Airport, to review overnight developments. At the time, Chile had a massive fiscal surplus, very low public debt, well-regulated banks, and (of course) a floating exchange rate—but capital was flowing out and investors were leaving in droves! During times of stress, bad things can happen even to well-behaved countries.

The upshot is that the monetary policy independence promised by flexible exchange rates is a bit of a mirage. The domestic financial cycle in emerging markets remains highly correlated with the fortunes of the greenback. Floating the currency does not do away with this dominance of the dollar. As Hélène Rey puts it in a recent paper, "there is no *divine coincidence* which would guarantee that international financial conditions and domestic monetary authorities' objectives are aligned" (Rey 2023). Central banks in emerging markets can find themselves facing a boom in capital inflows at a time when they are trying to tighten to reduce inflation, and vice versa (Rey 2013).

So the reality of flexible exchange rates is less rosy than the Mundell-Fleming tradition, Milton Friedman, and others suggested. Does this mean flexible rates are useless when confronted with the mighty dollar? Not quite. A recent paper by Maurice Obstfeld and Hoanan Zhou (2022) makes the point persuasively. Obstfeld and Zhou argue that whatever happens to the dollar matters a great deal for outcomes in emerging markets, but that the degree to which changes in international conditions affects domestic financial markets in turn depends on a number of factors, the most important of which is the exchange rate regime. They find that in response to a 10 percent dollar appreciation, "GDP and investment fall more sharply for countries with exchange rate pegs" and so does the stock market (p. 386).

I conjecture that there are three plausible explanations for this finding. The first is that a peg requires greater tightening in response to the dollar appreciation. The second is that the shock is associated with lower risk appetite and a higher required excess return on emerging-market bonds. But as Şebnem Kalemli-Özcan (2019) shows, under flexible rates the required adjustment is achieved via a depreciation; under fixing, it is achieved via a damaging domestic interest rate spike. The third is that the old expenditure-switching story still matters: Under flexible exchange rates, it is easier to realign relative prices and export your way out of the problem.

A system of flexible rates is thus not a perfect system, but it does some of the required work. It does not allow emerging markets to survive episodes of dollar appreciation and lower risk appetite unscathed and unharmed. But it does provide partial, and welcome, insulation.

This conclusion has plenty of academic research behind it. But it also survives the gut feeling test. Anyone who has been a policymaker in an emerging market and has woken up at 3 a.m. in a panic (during a financial crisis, for example) knows what I am talking about. The first thing that comes to mind is that the floating regime leaves you very vulnerable, and you immediately draw up a mental list of all the things that could go wrong. But next you ask yourself whether there is any other exchange rate system that you would rather have in place. Do I wish the crisis had caught my country with a fixed exchange rate commitment? The answer is clearly no.

What about balance sheet effects? Most emerging markets borrow heavily abroad, for good reasons. By definition, an emerging market is a country that has too little capital, so it needs to invest. If the economy is growing, it will be richer tomorrow than it is today. It therefore makes sense to finance some of that investment by borrowing from the rest of the world. And to this day, 80 percent of external emerging market debt remains in US dollars (see Financial Stability Board 2022, 7).

After the Tequila Crisis of 1994 and the Asian crisis of the 1990s, a large body of academic literature on balance sheet effects emerged. Its main message was that whenever a shock hits and the nominal and real exchange rates depreciate sharply, the domestic currency value of debt service goes through the roof, and firms that earn income in domestic currency suffer. Therefore, depreciation can be contractionary, and flexible exchange rates do not necessarily have desirable insulation properties.

Back then, that line of argument seemed persuasive to many people. But it has not survived the test of time very well. In several recent episodes—including COVID and the most recent episode of dollar appreciation—emerging-market currencies tanked and no financial crisis followed.

What happened to balance sheet effects? One answer is that hedging markets have turned out to be deeper and more affordable than anyone anticipated, and many emerging-market corporates and banks are using them. Another is that the 80 percent dollar share is an average and therefore a bit misleading. In many countries—including Brazil, Colombia, Mexico, South Africa, and Turkey—external liabilities have largely moved toward domestic currency. Yet another factor is that domestic financial markets are now much deeper, so that both governments and corporates can satiate a growing share of their borrowing needs at home, where liabilities tend to be denominated in domestic currency.

But there are also more academic explanations for the apparent balance sheet effect puzzle. As a policymaker, I am surprised that large and persistent real depreciations have not done more damage to balance sheets; as an academic, I feel vindicated, because two decades ago coauthors and I wrote a paper that argued that even in the presence of balance sheet problems, depreciation need not be destabilizing. Two forces—the standard "good" effects of a depreciation under sticky prices and the "bad" balance sheet effects—push in different directions; which one prevails is an empirical matter. Under a peg, the same shock would cause a sharp increase in domestic rates, which, given the short maturity of many debt profiles, would do great damage to balance sheets (Céspedes, Chang, and Velasco 2004).

The impression that emerges, both from the academic literature and recent experience, is that the balance sheet problem is manageable. But the problem has not gone away, and a version of original sin is still with us. Borrowing in domestic currency, as Agustín Carstens and Hyun Song Shin (2019) of the Bank for International Settlements have argued, simply shifts currency risk to lenders, forcing international investors to bear duration, default, and currency risk. In the aftermath of a large depreciation, an international investor might say "nice little country, but not for me." Carstens and Shin (2019) report that dollar appreciation episodes amplify the sell-off in emerging-market local currency bonds but not dollar-denominated bonds—what they call "original sin redux."

In thinking about the isolation properties of flexible rates, credibility is key—not just the credibility of the anti-inflationary stance, which, of course, matters a great deal, but the credibility of the authorities' overall commitment to floating. This kind of credibility is important because the currency composition of debt is endogenous and depends on expectations about the policy regime.

Roberto Chang and I argued back in 2000 that two equilibria exist. If borrowers expect the central bank to float the currency, they will acquire a structure of liabilities such that ex post the central bank finds it optimal to float. Conversely, if people expect the central bank to fix the exchange rate, they borrow in dollars and do not hedge their positions, making it optimal for the central bank to fix. It is in this sense that a flexible exchange rate regime has to be credible (that is, that the authorities are perceived to be committed to floating no matter what the currency composition of liabilities) (Chang and Velasco 2000).

This need to come across as credible could be the reason why central banks tend to voice a commitment to floating that is not always confirmed by the facts. The conventional wisdom is that a well-behaved country should pursue inflation targeting (a regime in which the interest rate is targeted at internal balance and the exchange rate floats freely). Almost all central banks say they target inflation. But in South America, Southeast Asia, Southern Africa, and Eastern Europe, few central banks actually abstain from intervention.

Buried in the public statements on how they operate, some inflation targeting central banks admit that they will intervene if and only if the currency is perceived to be strongly misaligned (a clear definition of "misalignment" is seldom provided). But it is the commitment to floating that gets the headlines. In other words, their approach to exchange rate policy is to claim in public to stick to one pattern of behavior, but in private do something different.

The problem, of course, is that you can surprise some of the people some of the time but not all of the people all of the time. After a couple of episodes of intervention, market participants adjust their expectations. And given that they know that central banks will intervene when the nominal (and real) exchange rate moves too far in one direction or the other, borrowers have less of an incentive to avoid foreign currency–denominated debt. This dent to credibility is perhaps the reason why original sin (of the original kind) still afflicts many emerging economies.

Above and beyond the issue of communication, why would central banks pursue what looks like a target zone (with fuzzy intervention boundaries, to be sure)? I am not sure we have very good models that explain this kind of behavior. This area needs a great deal more research. The obvious conjecture is that concerns about balance sheet effects trigger intervention.

But that conjecture would seem to call for an asymmetric rule, intervening when the currency depreciates but not otherwise.

The only other hypothesis I can offer is that just as in models of speculative hyperinflations—think of the 1983 Obstfeld-Rogoff paper—where the price level is not uniquely determined, there is perhaps an equivalent result for nominal exchange rates: If agents expect that a currency will depreciate, they sell it and prompt the depreciation, a process that continues until the central bank steps in and puts an end to it (Obstfeld and Rogoff 1983).

The obvious theoretical question is what happens over time in the absence of central bank intervention. In closed economy models, expectations of inflation are self-fulfilling, because there is no terminal condition that rules them out. In an open economy, if prices are sticky, large nominal depreciations mean large real depreciations; if the process becomes persistent, it will likely violate some terminal condition. But if prices have been made flexible by a long inflationary history (think of countries like Argentina), the price level and the nominal exchange rate can move more or less in tandem, without necessarily causing the real exchange rate to explode without bound.

This hypothesis suggests that in this context sticky prices are a blessing. Put differently, the less inflationary a country's history, the less it requires the central bank to run an implicit or explicit exchange rate target zone. This observation seems to reflect experience; the approach of proclaiming one policy regime while in reality pursuing another is common among emerging markets that float, less so among advanced economies that float.

If flexible exchange rates are not a panacea, and some version of original sin is still with us, what else can the authorities in emerging markets do to raise the probability that their economies will remain financially stable?

One factor, which I mentioned already in passing, is key: Continue developing domestic capital markets, so that more borrowing can take place at home. Of course, doing so also requires a reasonably tight fiscal policy: Too large a fiscal deficit is likely to induce too large a current account deficit and hence excessive reliance on foreign savings.

Two other kinds of policies are available. One falls under the general label of macroprudential policies. Since the most dangerous consequence of "irrational exuberance" abroad is a lending boom at home, which sows the seeds of the next crisis, it makes sense to try to regulate leverage and risk-taking directly. For local banks, capital buffers, maximum loan-to-value and debt service-to-income ratios, limits on exposure to given sectors, and the requirement that assets and liabilities in the same currency be roughly matched all can play a useful role. A danger is that lending will migrate to the shadow banking sector, which is much tougher to regulate.

The other family of tools involves some kind of capital controls, including taxes on short-term inflows such as the one Chile used in the early 1990s, which have been much-studied since. Resorting to controls accords with Rey's view that it is not an impossible trinity or a trilemma but a dilemma: To ensure some monetary policy autonomy, authorities must jettison full mobility and manage capital flows (Rey 2013).

The application of capital controls remains contentious, in part because of ideological prejudices and in part because the empirical assessment of their effectiveness is plagued by all kinds of econometric issues, making it difficult to know how useful they are. Nonetheless, ex ante controls on inflows (as opposed, crucially, to ex post limits to outflows) should remain, it seems to me, in the toolkit of any prudent policymaker.

Allow me to make one last point. If the dollar cycle is here to stay, and the insulating properties of flexible exchange rates are limited, emerging markets will need access to dollars in at least three sets of circumstances. The first is during risk-off episodes, when dollar liquidity is king. The second is when they need to intervene in the exchange market, which requires reserves. The third is when banks go belly up, so that the central bank must act as a lender of last resort—not in local currency but in foreign currency, which requires access to dollar reserves.

Where do emerging markets get the dollars they need in times of stress? Today, they mostly self-insure and sit on a large pile of their own international reserves. But we economists know self-insurance is not efficient. The current approach may be individually rational, but it makes very little collective sense.

The handful of emerging markets that qualify for a swap arrangement with the Fed are able to engage in some risk-sharing. So can the handful of countries that have qualified for an IMF precautionary liquidity arrangement. For the remaining emerging markets, opportunities for risk-sharing are very limited, because the global financial safety net is geographically fragmented, full of holes, and simply not fit for purpose.

Take the COVID crisis. The IMF estimated that emerging markets would need access to $2 trillion, but it ended up lending (in additional terms) less than $200 billion (IMF 2023). The world can surely do better.

Having lived in the United Kingdom for a few years now, I will end on a British note. As Winston Churchill might have said, a system of flexible exchange rates is the worst system there is except for all the alternatives that have been tried from time to time.

References

Calvo, Guillermo A., Leonardo Leiderman, and Carmen M. Reinhart. 1996. Inflows of Capital to Developing Countries in the 1990s. *Journal of Economic Perspectives* 10, no. 2: 123–39.

Carstens, Agustín, and Hyun Song Shin. 2019. Emerging Markets Aren't Out of the Woods Yet. *Foreign Affairs*, March 15.

Céspedes, Luis Felipe, Roberto Chang, and Andrés Velasco. 2004. Balance Sheets and Exchange Rate Policy. *American Economic Review* 94, no 4: 1183–93.

Chang, Roberto, and Andrés Velasco. 2000. Currency Mismatches and Monetary Policy: A Tale of Two Equilibria. *Journal of International* Economics 69, no. 1: 150–75.

Financial Stability Board. 2022. *US Dollar Funding and Emerging Market Economy Vulnerabilities*. Working Paper. April. Available at https://www.fsb.org/wp-content/uploads/P260422.pdf.

IMF (International Monetary Fund). 2023. *The IMF's Emergency Response to the COVID-19 Pandemic*. Washington: Independent Evaluation Office.

Kalemli-Özcan, Şebnem. 2019. US Monetary Policy and International Risk Spillovers. Paper presented at the Federal Reserve Bank of Kansas City Economic Policy Symposium, Jackson Hole, WY.

Miranda-Agrippino, S., and Hélène Rey. 2020. US Monetary Policy and the Global Financial Cycle. *Review of Economic Studies* 87, no. 6: 2754–76.

Obstfeld, Maurice, and Kenneth Rogoff. 1983. Speculative Hyperinflations in Maximizing Models: Can We Rule Them Out? *Journal of Political Economy* 91, no. 4: 675–87.

Obstfeld, Maurice, and Haonan Zhou. 2023. 2022. The Global Dollar Cycle. *Brookings Papers on Economic Activity* (Fall): 361–427. Washington: Brookings Institution.

Rey, Hélène. 2013. Dilemma Not Trilemma: The Global Financial Cycle and Monetary Policy Independence. Paper presented at the Federal Reserve Bank of Kansas City Economic Policy Symposium, Jackson Hole, WY.

Rey, Hélène. 2023. Monetary and Financial Policies. Draft prepared for the London Consensus Conference, London School of Economics.

18

Emerging Markets and the Transition to Stability: Role of Flexibility of Exchange Rates

JOSÉ DE GREGORIO

Implementation of flexible exchange rate regimes in emerging-market economies (EMEs) occurred long after the dissolution of the Bretton Woods system, following numerous unsuccessful attempts to combat inflation through fixed exchange rates and severe fear of floating. Until the late 1990s, most crises in EMEs were linked to inflexible exchange rate regimes, as evident in the Latin America debt crisis in the 1980s, the Mexican crisis in 1994, the Asian financial crisis in 1997–98, and the Russian default with contagion to Brazil in 1998. These episodes were characterized by a combination of fragile financial systems and rigid exchange rate frameworks.

EMEs gradually transitioned toward greater exchange rate flexibility, leading to the emergence of new questions. In an environment where a significant portion of international trade is conducted and priced in US dollars (Gopinath et al. 2020), are exchange rates still effective in facilitating external adjustment? Do EMEs experience wealth losses when their currencies depreciate? How much does depreciation affect local borrowers, including the government?

This chapter examines the transition toward more flexible exchange rate regimes in EMEs, a phenomenon that coincided with a decline in global inflation and the adoption of inflation targeting frameworks. It analyzes the capacity of exchange rates to foster external adjustment, taking into account recent research in international pricing that casts doubt on their

José De Gregorio, nonresident senior fellow at the Peterson Institute for International Economics, is dean of the School of Economics and Business at the University of Chile. He was governor of the Central Bank of Chile from 2007 until 2011.

effectiveness. It also looks at currency mismatches and the implications for the net international investment position of EMEs and the effects of exchange rate fluctuations.

Inflation, Monetary Policy, and the Exchange Rate Regime

EMEs have been the prime example of fear of floating (Calvo and Reinhart 2002). Fear of floating arises for two reasons. The first is concerns about the inflationary effects of currency depreciation associated with the lack of credibility that leads to high exchange rate pass-through (ERPT). The second is the fear that currency depreciations may lead to financial disruptions, even to self-fulfilling equilibria. In this section I focus on inflation in EMEs and the monetary policy regime.

In the late 1990s, three main developments took place:

- Inflation declined. Even in Latin American economies characterized by high inflation, rates fell to single digits for the first time in decades (figure 18.1).

- Many countries adopted flexible inflation targeting regimes, characterized mainly by commitment to a specific value or range for the inflation rate, to be achieved in the medium term, with or without specifying a policy horizon (figure 18.2). Several countries announced that the target would be achieved within two years; others just mentioned the medium term.[1]

- Most EMEs abandoned pegged exchange rate regimes, moving to some type of intermediate regime, ranging from narrow bands to managed floating (figure 18.3).[2] It is difficult to find fully floating regimes, as most countries that adopt flexibility retain the possibility of intervention in some special circumstances; others follow some rules to provide some stability in the short run. Some countries that declare that they have narrow bands are just floating with frequent stabilizing interventions, without a specific numerical target for the exchange rate. Having a target for the value of the currency is

---

1. There are many lists of inflation targeting countries. The most comprehensive is http://www.centralbanknews.info/p/inflation-targets.html, which includes 74 countries. Several countries adopt a light version of inflation targeting; others, including Argentina, declare that they target inflation but actually do not.

2. The classification is conservative. Among countries following a narrow band, some (including Indonesia, Peru, and the Philippines) claim to have floating regimes and to conduct operations to stabilize short-run fluctuations.

Figure 18.1

Median inflation in Latin America, South America, and the world, 1980–2022

inflation rate, percent

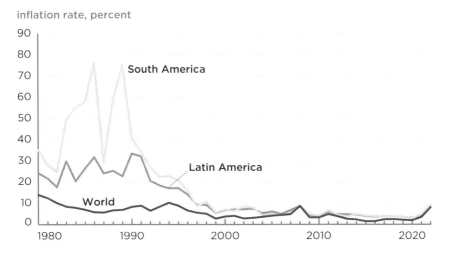

Note: Latin America comprises South American countries plus Costa Rica, El Salvador, Guatemala, Haiti, Honduras, Nicaragua, and Panama. Data for Argentina between 1980 and 1997 are from the *World Economic Outlook* Database, October 2014. In all subsequent editions of the *World Economic Outlook*, no inflation data are reported for Argentina between 1980 and 1997. For 1998 onward, data are from the *World Economic Outlook*, April 2023.
Source: IMF, *World Economic Outlook* Database, April 2023.

the central characteristic of rigid regimes and the loss of monetary autonomy, which becomes dominated by that numerical target, which could be an explicit narrow band.

There has been a clear policy trend toward flexibility in the exchange rate and inflation targets in the monetary policy regime. But these policy changes did not cause the decline in inflation. Indeed, inflation targeting is not a disinflation strategy but a regime for conducting monetary policy efficiently. Controlling inflation requires the elimination of its deep roots, mainly fiscal imbalances and central banks subject to political control, rendering lack of credibility to control inflation. In the 1990s, there was progress in both areas (Rogoff 2004). On the fiscal front, there was progress not only in high-income countries but also in places like Africa and Latin America. In addition, many countries granted independence to their central banks. There were also specific factors that contributed to the decline in inflation, such as increased competition through globalization and higher productivity as a result of advances in information technologies.

Figure 18.2

Number of countries operating under inflation targeting regimes, 1990–2017

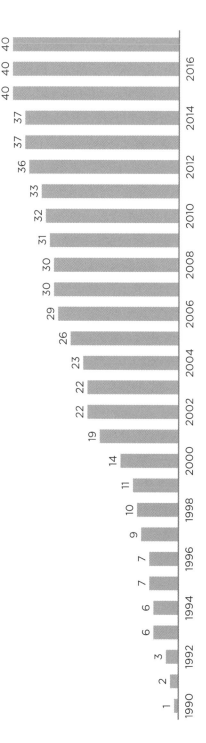

Note: Figure does not include euro area countries.

Sources: Roger (2010), Hammond (2011), and IMF's *Annual Report on Exchange Arrangements and Exchange Restrictions* (AREAER).

Figure 18.3

Exchange rate regimes in inflation targeting emerging-market economies, 1960–2019

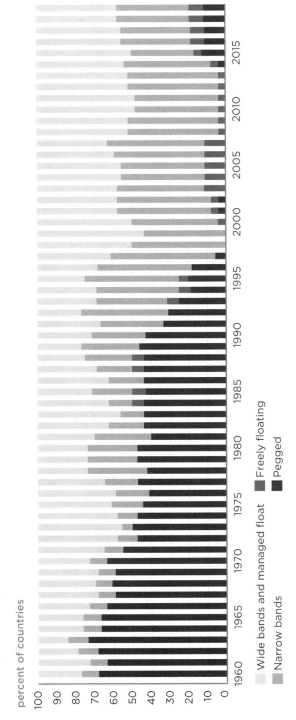

percent of countries

Wide bands and managed float

Narrow bands

Freely floating

Pegged

Note: Data exclude two regimes, "freely falling" and "dual market in which parallel market data is missing." Data are as of December of each year.

Source: Ilzetzki, Reinhart, and Rogoff (2022).

One big achievement in macroeconomic policies was allowing currencies to fluctuate. The last significant currency crisis in EMEs was the Asian crisis; no similar crises have occurred since then, despite very challenging world developments, including the global financial crisis of 2007–09 and the COVID-19 pandemic. Moreover, exchange rate fluctuations have not caused financial crises, as they often did in the past.

Apprehension surrounding the adoption of flexible exchange rates stemmed primarily from concerns about potential volatility in inflation caused by fluctuations in the exchange rate. Those fears did not materialize, particularly after inflation control was achieved. There is evidence of a significant decline in the ERPT in EMEs in the last 20 years, which fell to the levels of advanced economies. Although it is not easy to separate its causes, they reflect several factors, including the decline in inflation (Jasova, Moessner, and Takats 2019); the increased credibility of monetary policy (Cuitiño, Medina, and Zacheo 2022; Carrière-Swallow et al. 2021); and the adoption of inflation targets (Cabezas and Edwards 2022) or exchange rate flexibility (Borenzstein and Queijo von Heideken 2016). The enhancement in macroeconomic policies has mitigated the influence of exchange rate fluctuations on inflation dynamics, addressing one of the principal concerns associated with the fear of transitioning to flexible exchange rate regimes.

Exchange Rates and International Pricing

Exchange rates are relative prices that facilitate external adjustment. When there are exchange rate rigidities, because of fear of floating, external adjustment becomes limited. In such cases, changes in competitiveness occur through changes in the relative price of goods in their own currencies rather than through the relative price of currencies (the nominal exchange rate). Relying on relative price changes through movements of domestic prices is much more difficult, especially when a deflation is needed to regain competitiveness, than relying on changes in the value of the currency. Facilitating adjustment is one of the primary reasons for opting for a flexible exchange rate regime. However, doubts have emerged in recent years regarding the effectiveness of exchange rates in promoting adjustment.

The observation that ERPTs are small has led many researchers to argue that export prices are determined in the currency of the importer, a phenomenon known as local currency pricing (LCP). In this context, a depreciation of the bilateral exchange rate between the exporter and importer does not significantly affect the demand for exports, because relative prices remain unchanged. Extensive research has been conducted to investigate international pricing and its implications for external adjustment.

As a substantial portion of international invoicing is conducted in US dollars, Gopinath et al. (2020) have proposed the dominant currency paradigm (DCP), which suggests that international prices are set and fixed in US dollars. A depreciation of the bilateral exchange rate between the exporter and importer does not have a substantial impact on the demand for exports or imports, limiting external adjustment. When, however, the importer's currency depreciates against the US dollar, domestic relative prices rise and demand falls. Therefore, the exchange rate has more limited effects than those traditionally envisioned in the Mundell-Fleming model that assumes pricing in the producer's currency (PCP). In this case, for example, a depreciation of the currency reduces prices at destination and, hence, increases demand for exports.

The response of prices and quantities to exchange rate movements, both bilaterally and with respect to the US dollar, is an empirical matter. De Gregorio et al. (2023) explore this issue for Chilean exports of single exported products (at the 8-digit Harmonized System code) from 2010 to 2019. Their dataset includes exporting firms, destination countries, and the invoicing currency. The findings suggest that in the short run, prices are fixed in dollars, the currency used in around 90 percent of invoicing, resulting in an ERPT from the dollar exchange rate to local prices of 0.9 (figure 18.4). However, local importers' prices do not immediately react to bilateral depreciation, indicating that prices in the short run are fixed in dollars, the invoicing currency. Over time, the ERPT of the dollar declines to below 0.4 after eight quarters. In contrast, after a bilateral depreciation of the local currency against the exporter's currency, local importers' prices gradually increase, reaching an ERPT of 0.8 after eight quarters. In the short run, DCP prevails, as prices are fixed in dollars and respond only to changes in the dollar exchange rate of the importing country. This effect diminishes over time, and the traditional PCP mechanism comes into play. In the long run, exporters prefer to set prices in their own currency (home country bias).[3]

The impact of exchange rates on quantities is consistent with the findings for prices. In the short run, quantities are not affected. However, over time, as local prices begin to rise following a bilateral depreciation, export volumes decline as expected, thanks to a decrease in local demand.

The subdued reaction of export volumes to a depreciation of the local currency relative to the dollar—which exhibits an ERPT of approximately one in the short run—requires further analysis. It is likely the result of fric-

---

3. Gagnon and Sarsenbayev (2023, 5) find support for PCP: "Exports prices are more strongly influenced by domestic prices (PCP coefficient of 0.52) but importer prices also have an important effect (LCP coefficient of 0.321)."

Figure 18.4
Exchange rate pass-through to prices and quantities

a. Price

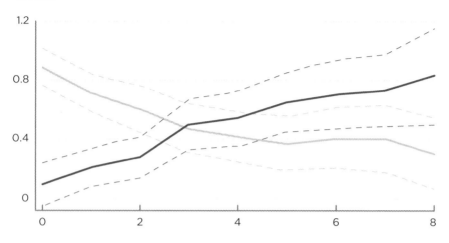

b. Quantity

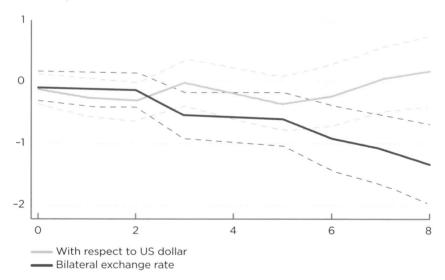

〰〰〰 With respect to US dollar
━━━ Bilateral exchange rate

Note: The dark gray (light gray) line represents the proportional effects of a depreciation of the local importers' currency against the Chilean peso (US dollar) on the local price and volume of Chilean exports. Dashed lines represent 95 percent confidence interval. The horizontal axes show quarters, and the vertical axes show proportion.
Source: De Gregorio et al. (2023).

tions in the transmission from increased prices at the dock to retail prices, as De Gregorio et al. (2023) argue. Distribution margins absorb these exchange rate fluctuations.

The evidence suggests that even in a world in which a dominant currency is used for most international transactions, exchange rates against the trading partner and the dollar still play a crucial role in facilitating external adjustment.

Exchange Rates and the Net International Investment Position

Fear of floating exchange rates is driven partly by the potential financial problems it may engender. EMEs have historically relied on borrowing in foreign currencies, particularly the US dollar, on international capital markets. The Latin American debt crisis in the early 1980s, characterized by inflexible exchange rates, significant currency mismatches, and weak financial systems, resulted in a lost decade for the region. The adoption of fixed exchange rates and the availability of international bank financing led to a substantial accumulation of external debt. When US interest rates sharply increased, a severe crisis unfolded. The Mexican crisis of 1994 and the Asian crisis in the late 1990s were also associated with exchange rate inflexibility and its subsequent impact on the financial system.

The pattern is simple: Countries experience a period of exchange rate stability, occasionally facing appreciation, and corporations and governments heavily borrow from highly liquid global financial markets. When an economic shock exerts pressure on the currency, fear of floating emerges, leading countries to adopt various measures, including raising interest rates, depleting reserves, and implementing capital controls, to safeguard their currencies.

These defensive measures often prove unsustainable, resulting in a sharp depreciation and a financial crisis stemming from currency mismatches at the corporate, financial, or governmental level.

A more nuanced scenario arises when the corporate sector borrows in foreign currency and regulations are lenient. Assuming the private sector will not incur currency risk ignores the moral hazard issues stemming from the chosen exchange rate regime. More recently, in contrast, and as a result of a costly crisis, many EMEs have built more resilient financial systems, enabling them to withstand crises such as the global financial crisis and the pandemic without major disruptions.

Another important discussion relating exchange rate and mismatches is "original sin" (Eichengreen, Hausmann, and Panizza 2007)—the inability of sovereigns to borrow in their own currencies, reducing the ability to share risk. Most sovereign borrowing is in US dollars. When EMEs' currencies depreciate, wealth transfers occur from them to foreign creditors, leading to serious fiscal problems. In contrast, the United States benefits from a depreciation of its currency thanks to its short position in dollars. Therefore, in the United States, a depreciation of the dollar contributes to external adjustment not only through trade effects but also via wealth effects. In contrast, in EMEs, these wealth effects could potentially hinder the effectiveness of a depreciation in fostering external adjustment.

Research by Gourinchas and Rey (2022) and Atkeson, Heathcote, and Perri (2022) sheds light on the role of the United States as a provider of insurance during the global financial crisis and the pandemic, which resulted in a transfer of wealth to the rest of the world. Hale and Juvenal (2023) find that EMEs did not experience significant losses in their net international investment positions during the pandemic.

Assessing empirically the extent to which EMEs are better protected against currency depreciations on their balance sheets requires examining their net international investment positions and the direction of valuation effects. Valuation effects can arise from exchange rate movements of different currency denominations on the asset and liability sides, as well as by price effects stemming from divergent performance of stock markets across countries.

De Gregorio and Peña (2023) provide evidence on this issue from Chile and a sample of 20 EMEs from 1999 to 2021. Figure 18.5 illustrates the evolution of Chile's net international investment position (NIIP) and the accumulated current account (also known as the hypothetical net international investment position—the net position a country would have in the absence of valuation effects). The difference between the two reflects movements in the real exchange rate and the relative stock market performance of Chile and the United States.

Chile began September 2019, just a month before serious social unrest, with an NIIP equivalent to approximately –20 percent of GDP. Between September 2019 and December 2021, its currency depreciated by 17 percent, the S&P index increased by 60 percent, and the Chilean stock market declined by 15 percent. Remarkably, during the same period, the NIIP improved from –20 percent to –5 percent of GDP, and the accumulated current account reached –6 percent of GDP. Consequently, Chile benefited from a favorable valuation effect of approximately 21 percent of GDP, signifying a substantial transfer of wealth from the rest of the world to Chile.[4]

---

4. In the first three quarters of 2022, the NIIP deteriorated by about 10 percent of GDP, a drop similar to that of the current account deficit, as there were no valuation effects.

Figure 18.5

Net international investment position, accumulated current account, and real exchange rate in Chile, December 2012–July 2022

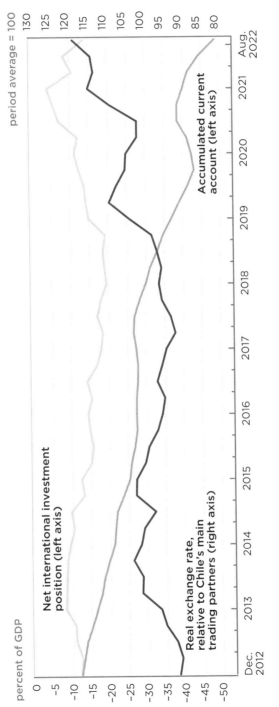

Source: Central Bank of Chile.

This analysis of risk-sharing is extended to a sample of 20 EMEs. It shows that currency depreciation and weaker domestic stock market performance relative to the United States have a positive impact on the NIIP. However, the influence of price effects depends on the degree of financial openness. The relevant explanatory variables encompass changes in prices (exchange rates and stock price) interacted with gross asset and liability positions. Although original sin is still a problem in some EMEs, particularly smaller ones (Eichengreen and Tsuda 2023), it diminishes substantially in the sample of De Gregorio and Peña (2023). These valuation effects have been statistically significant since 2008, when financial openness stabilized.

Over the past decades, advancements have been made in mitigating the pessimistic outlook regarding the impact of exchange rate depreciation on financial stability. Financial systems have become more resilient, and widespread mismatches do not appear to be prevalent. On average, EMEs exhibit short positions in their domestic currency and benefit from risk-sharing with the rest of the world. These developments signify progress in enhancing financial stability within EMEs, offering insights into their improved ability to cope with external shocks via exchange rate flexibility.

Concluding Remarks

The approach adopted by EMEs toward exchange rate flexibility has been characterized by pragmatism. Most EMEs intervene in the foreign exchange market; some do so on a permanent basis to ensure stability; others intervene only under specific circumstances. The traditional notion of setting numerical medium-term objectives for the exchange rate has gradually been discarded. The increased financial integration experienced by these economies highlights the limitations of tightly managing the exchange rate, which hampers the effectiveness of monetary policy. Attempts to resist exchange rate movements have often resulted in excessive volatility in capital flows. Actively combating depreciation, for example, often triggers significant capital outflows, undermining the efforts to prevent such a depreciation.

There have been only a few cases of large financial or macro collapses since the early 2000s. Indeed, no group of EMEs has undergone a crisis such as the debt crisis in Latin America or the Asian crisis. EMEs weathered both the global financial crisis and the COVID-19 pandemic. Even in the recent fight with inflation, monetary policy was tightened in EMEs before it was in advanced economies.

The evidence overwhelmingly establishes the positive outcomes associated with adoption of inflation targeting regimes and the establishment of policy credibility in EMEs. The greater flexibility embedded in their exchange rate regimes has proven to be a crucial factor in their overall success.

References

Atkeson, Andrew, Jonathan Heathcote, and Fabrizio Perri. 2022. *The End of Privilege: A Reexamination of the Net Foreign Asset Position of the United States*. NBER Working Paper 29771. Cambridge, MA: National Bureau of Economic Research.

Borenzstein, Eduardo, and Virginia Queijo von Heideken. 2016. *Exchange Rate Pass-Through in South America: An Overview*. IDB Working Paper IDB-WP-710. Washington: Inter-American Development Bank.

Cabezas, Luis, and Sebastian Edwards. 2022. Exchange Rate Pass-Through, Monetary Policy, and Real Exchange Rates: Iceland and the 2008 Crisis. *Open Economies Review* 33, no. 2: 197–230.

Calvo, Guillermo A., and Carmen M. Reinhart. 2002. Fear of Floating. *Quarterly Journal of Economics* 117, no. 2: 379–408.

Carrière-Swallow, Yan, Bertrand Gruss, Nicolas E. Magud, and Fabián Valencia. 2021. Monetary Policy Credibility and Exchange Rate Pass-Through. *International Journal of Central Banking* 17, no. 3: 61–94.

Cuitiño, María Fernanda, Juan Pablo Medina, and Laura Zacheo. 2022. Conditional Exchange Rate Pass-Through and Monetary Policy Credibility: Insights from Uruguay and Chile. *Economic Modelling* 114: 105926.

De Gregorio, José, Pablo García, Emiliano Luttini, and Marco Rojas. 2023. *From Dominant to Producer Currency Pricing: Dynamics of Chilean Exports*. Working Paper 970. Santiago: Central Bank of Chile.

De Gregorio, José, and Benjamín Peña. 2023. Valuation Effects, Exchange Rates, and Risk Sharing in Emerging Market Economies. Photocopy. Department of Economics, Universidad de Chile.

Eichengreen, Barry, Ricardo Hausmann, and Ugo Panizza. 2007. Currency Mismatches, Debt Intolerance and Original Sin: Why They Are Not the Same and Why It Matters. In *Capital Controls and Capital Flows in Emerging Economies: Policies, Practices, and Consequences*, ed. S. Edwards. Cambridge, MA: National Bureau of Economic Research.

Eichengreen, Barry, and Arslanalp Tsuda. 2023. Living with High Public Debt. Paper presented at the Jackson Hole Symposium at the meeting of the Federal Reserve Bank of Kansas City, Jackson Hole, WY.

Gagnon, Joseph E., and Madi Sarsenbayev. 2023. Dollar Not So Dominant: Dollar Invoicing Has Only a Small Effect on Trade Prices. *Journal of International Money and Finance* 137, article 102889.

Gopinath, Gita, Emine Boz, Camila Casas, Federico J. Díez, Pierre-Olivier Gourinchas, and Mikkel Plagborg-Møller. 2020. Dominant Currency Paradigm. *American Economic Review* 110, no. 3: 677–719.

Gourinchas, Pierre-Olivier, and Hélène Rey. 2022. *Exorbitant Privilege and Exorbitant Duty*. CEPR Discussion Paper 16944. Paris and London: CEPR Press.

Hale, Galina, and Luciana Juvenal. 2023. External Balance Sheets and the COVID-19 Crisis. *Journal of Banking & Finance* 147: 106570.

Hammond, Gill. 2011. State of the Art of Inflation Targetings. *Centre for Central Banking Studies Handbook* 29. London: Bank of England.

Ilzetzki, Ethan, Carmen M. Reinhart, and Kenneth S. Rogoff. 2022. Rethinking Exchange Rate Regimes. In *Handbook of International Economics 6*, ed. G. Gopinath, E. Helpman, and K. Rogoff, 91–145. Amsterdam: Elsevier.

Jasova, Martina, Richhild Moessner, and Elod Takats. 2019. Exchange Rate Pass-Through: What Has Changed Since the Crisis? *International Journal of Central Banking* 15, no. 3: 27–58.

Roger, Scott. 2010. Inflation Targeting Turns 20. *Finance & Development* 47, no. 1: 46–49.

Rogoff, Kenneth S. 2004. Globalization and Global Disinflation. *Monetary Policy and Uncertainty: Adapting to a Changing Economy*, 77–112. Federal Reserve Bank of Kansas City.

19

Why Do Oil Producers in the Middle East and North Africa Still Fix Their Currencies?

ADNAN MAZAREI

Exchange rate regimes are an important policy choice for emerging-market and developing economies (EMDEs), especially those that depend on oil exports. The choice of exchange rate regime can have significant implications for macroeconomic stability, competitiveness, and diversification.

The advanced economies turned to floating exchange rates 50 years ago, in March 1973. In contrast, many EMDEs were slow to move in that direction, with many countries in the Middle East and North Africa (MENA) continuing to embrace fixed exchange rates.

Much has been written about the advantages for oil-exporting EMDEs of flexible exchange rates, which can potentially help them adjust to external shocks such as oil price fluctuations and foster structural transformation.[1] Nevertheless, nearly all the oil-exporting countries in MENA—as well as many countries exporting other commodities—continue to peg their currencies, to either the US dollar or to a basket of currencies. Why do they do so? And are there any changes on the horizon?

---

1. See, for example, Frankel (2017), Obstfeld (2020), Rogoff et al. (2003), and Setser (2007). Researchers have argued that more flexible exchange rates could reduce vulnerability to external economic shocks, such as changes in US monetary policy or a decline in global demand for oil, and improve competitiveness in international trade.

Adnan Mazarei is nonresident senior fellow at the Peterson Institute for International Economics. He was deputy director of the Middle East and Central Asia Department of the International Monetary Fund. He is grateful to Ruchir Agarwal, Abdullah AlHassn, Rabah Arezki, Madona Devasahayam, Barbara Karni, and Egor Gornostay for their helpful comments and to Julieta Contreras and Asher Rose for their help with the data.

I first discuss the exchange rate policies of MENA oil exporters during the past five decades and the factors driving them. I then examine whether and how the current and prospective economic and political trends could bring about a change in the exchange rate policies of oil exporters.

What Determines the Exchange Rate Regimes of Oil Exporters?

In oil-exporting countries, the choice of the exchange rate regime is often based on economic considerations, including how best to insulate their economies from the vagaries of oil prices, institutional factors, and financial sector development. But other factors, including rent-seeking, corruption, and geopolitics, also influence these choices.

It is helpful to divide MENA oil producers into two groups: the Gulf Cooperation Council (GCC) (Bahrain, Kuwait, Oman, Qatar, Saudi Arabia, and the United Arab Emirates) and others (Algeria, Iran, Iraq, and Libya). The countries of the GCC are heavily dependent on oil and gas revenues and have had large financial assets. The region's other oil exports have experienced civil wars and conflicts or been subjected to international sanctions. Fixed exchange rates may have been suitable for the GCC countries, which have large foreign exchange reserves. Other MENA oil exporters, which are more vulnerable to oil price shocks and have less fiscal space and reserves than GCC members, could have benefited from more flexible exchange rates.

Global economic and political factors, such as the rise of China and its growing influence in international trade, could prompt oil exporters to reconsider their exchange rate policies. For example, the increased use of the renminbi in the pricing of traded goods and payments might incentivize oil exporters to adopt alternative currency pegs or more flexible systems. The likelihood of this transition has been overstated, however, as the depth of renminbi financial markets remains limited compared with the depth of US dollar markets. Any near-term impact of such changes on the global financial system is likely to be small.

For decades, all GCC countries other than Kuwait have pegged their currency to the US dollar (table 19.1).[2] The exchange rate regimes of the other oil exporters have evolved in a more complicated fashion. Algeria has followed a managed float aimed at keeping the real exchange rate stable, but it has been reluctant to allow enough flexibility to do so. Iran, Iraq, and Libya have historically had pegged exchange rates, but political upheaval

---

2. Kuwait pegs its currency to a basket of currencies. The composition of the basket is not disclosed but is believed to be heavily weighted toward the US dollar.

and conflict have made it difficult to maintain those pegs, forcing them to devalue—unwillingly—and then repeg or move to tightly managed rates. At times, these countries have adopted multiple exchange rates along with active free market rates that have differed widely from official rates.

Why Do the Gulf Cooperation Council Countries Fix Their Currencies?

GCC countries peg their currencies for several reasons:

- Oil prices are set in and trade is settled in dollars. Countries accumulate reserves when oil prices are high and draw on them when oil prices are low (Wills and van der Ploeg 2014). Oil receipts have also been recycled in dollars through the US financial system. The use of the dollar in petroleum-earning recycling partly reflects understandings between the United States and especially Saudi Arabia that the oil producers recycle their earnings in dollars in exchange for US security protection (El-Gamal and Jaffe 2010). Given the concentration of government financial assets in dollars, pegs to the dollar have helped eliminate much of the exchange rate risk to governments' foreign assets, although oil exporters have been diversifying their investments to outside the United States and dollar assets.

- Exchange rate pegs, backed by large reserves and sovereign wealth fund assets and access to global bond markets, have provided simple, visible, and (to date) credible nominal anchors that have helped—with considerable assistance from administered prices and subsidies—maintain a low rate of inflation (figure 19.1).

- Weak transmission to economic activity has reduced the effectiveness of monetary policy, partly because of the slow development of financial sectors, thereby limiting the value of monetary policy independence from the United States. The lack of significant economic diversification has also limited the effectiveness of monetary policy. The lack of flexible, uncompetitive exchange rates also helps explain the largely disappointing record of economic diversification.

- Fiscal policy has been the primary channel for distributing oil revenues to the population in order to maintain political control. Fiscal dominance is written into countries' institutional structures and policy patterns; national authorities have been unwilling to forgo the fiscal power and discretion that a flexible exchange rate regime, including fiscal rules, would have entailed. Chile adopted such a regime in 2001, allowing greater central bank autonomy.

Table 19.1

De jure and de facto exchange rate regimes in the oil-exporting countries of the Middle East and North Africa

Country	De jure	De facto	GCC member
Bahrain	Pegged to the US dollar	Pegged to the US dollar	Yes
Kuwait	Pegged to a basket of currencies		Yes
Oman	Pegged to the US dollar	Pegged to the US dollar	Yes
Qatar	Pegged to the US dollar	Pegged to the US dollar	Yes
Saudi Arabia	Pegged to the US dollar	Pegged to the US dollar	Yes
United Arab Emirates	Pegged to the US dollar	Pegged to the US dollar	Yes

Country			
Algeria	Managed float	Crawl-like arrangement	No
Iran	Managed float against a basket of currencies (multiple rates)	Stabilized arrangement (multiple rates)	No
Iraq	Pegged to the US dollar	Pegged to the US dollar	No
Libya	Pegged to Special Drawing Rights	Pegged to Special Drawing Rights	No

GCC = Gulf Cooperation Council
Source: IMF (2023a).

Figure 19.1

Inflation rates in the Gulf Cooperation Council countries, 1980–2022

annual percent change

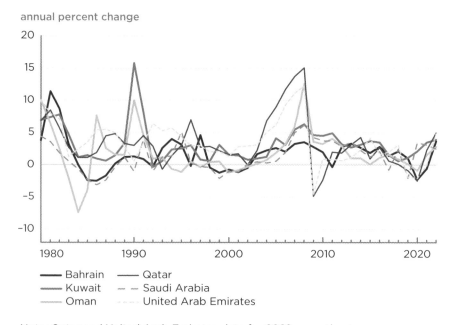

Note: Qatar and United Arab Emirates data for 2022 are estimates.
Source: IMF (2023b).

- Fiscal policy has served as the main tool for economic stabilization (by drawing down on the governments' sizable foreign assets when oil prices are low), relegating monetary and exchange policies to subordinate roles. In practice, however, at times of large drops in oil prices, such as in 1986, 2008, and 2014, government spending has been cut procyclically, causing sharp declines in nonoil economic activity.
- Flexible labor markets, provided by heavy reliance on expatriates with short-term contracts, serve as a partial alternative to exchange rate flexibility.
- The GCC countries have discussed forming a monetary union since the 1980s (Khan 2009). In 2003, they collectively fixed their exchange rates to the dollar. Doing so entailed fixing cross rates among the GCC countries, a step toward preparing for such a union. Although the GCC countries meet some of the criteria for a monetary union, plans to form a union have been abandoned because of political tensions among the GCC countries. The difficulties of putting in place fiscal and banking unions also preclude a GCC monetary union.

Given this background, the GCC countries have justifiably stuck with fixed exchange rates, though at times—such as during the oil price declines in 1986, 2008, 2014, and the recent pandemic—exchange rate flexibility could have eased the burden of adjustment on fiscal policy and helped protect external reserves. Figure 19.2 shows the strong comovement of government expenditures and oil revenues for the GCC countries. Overall, however, fixed exchange rates may have been the best exchange rate regime for the GCC countries.

Why Haven't Other Oil Exporters in the Region Floated?

The experiences of Algeria, Iran, Iraq, and Libya are more heterogenous and complex. All four had fixed exchange rates in 1973 but have had to make frequent changes in the face of political upheavals, conflicts, and sanctions; all of them have often allowed active parallel currency markets.[3]

Inflation has been high in these countries, and comovements in government revenues and expenditures have been significant (figures 19.3 and 19.4). Arguably, these countries—some of which do not have large foreign exchange reserves or sovereign wealth fund assets that could be easily accessed (because of sanctions)—should have adopted much more flexible exchange rate regimes to ease adjustment to shocks.

These countries have refrained from doing so for several reasons:

- Fear that floating in the face of frequent domestic and international political and economic shocks would induce exchange rate volatility and, therefore, inflation.
- Fiscal dominance and the role of fiscal policy in the distribution of oil revenues.
- Weak monetary policy frameworks and banking systems, which prevent the move to monetary policy frameworks needed to support more exchange rate flexibility.[4]

---

3. Algeria had a peg to the French franc from independence until 1974, when it switched to a basket of currencies. It shifted to a managed float in 1994, as part of a stabilization program with the International Monetary Fund. Recently, it has de facto followed a crawling peg regime (Chekouri, Chibi, and Benbouziane 2022). Iran has followed a fixed exchange rate regime, but since the 1979 revolution it has been unable to maintain a stable exchange rate, resorting to frequent adjustments and multiple exchange rates. At one point, it had 12 different exchange rates (Mazarei 1995). Iraq has had a dollar peg but has had to make frequent adjustments in the face of wars and security problems while tolerating multiple exchange rate systems. Libya had a dollar peg until 1986, when it shifted to peg to Special Drawing Rights (SDRs). It has occasionally devalued its currency and attempted to unify the multiple exchange rates.

4. Iran, for example, adopted an inflation targeting monetary regime in 2021, in part to serve as an anchor for forcing institutional and policy reforms to lower the high rates of

Figure 19.2

Government revenue and expenditure in the Gulf Cooperation Council, by country, 1990–2022

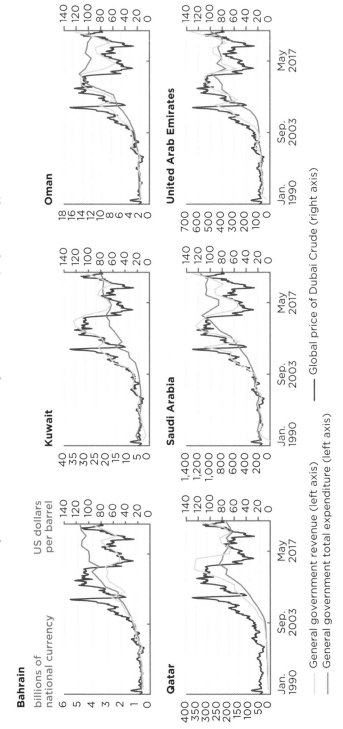

Notes: Oil price shown is the monthly average of Dubai Fateh. Revenues consist of taxes, social contributions, grants receivable, and other revenues. Total expenditures are total expenses and net acquisition of nonfinancial assets on an accrual basis. Revenue and expenditure data for 2022 are estimates for all countries except Oman.

Sources: IMF (2023b); primary commodity prices are from Federal Reserve Bank of St. Louis, Federal Reserve Economic Data, https://fred.stlouisfed.org/series/POILDUBUSDM.

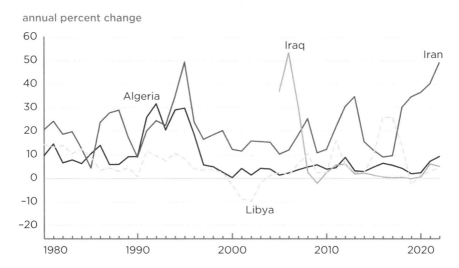

Figure 19.3

Inflation rates in Algeria, Iran, Iraq, and Libya, 1980–22

annual percent change

Notes: Data for Iraq and Libya for 2022 are estimates.
Source: IMF (2023b).

- The fact that multiple exchange rates serve as a system of taxes and subsidies favoring particular social and politically connected groups—a practice that has created systemic rent-seeking and corruption. In Iran and Iraq, the corruption associated with such practices has been a significant factor in the failure to unify the exchange rate system and allow more flexibility.
- Support for import substitution by maintaining overvalued exchange rates, in order to lower the cost of imported intermediate inputs.

Transitioning to more flexible exchange rate regimes is thus difficult, even when the benefits are clear.

Are Changes on the Horizon?

Several factors could encourage the MENA oil exporting countries to shift to exchange rate flexibility, albeit probably not soon. The healthy scenario would be one under which countries strengthen their policy frameworks,

---

inflation. The effort was abandoned because of continued fiscal dominance, sanctions that limited the central bank's access to its international reserves, and unwillingness to address banking sector problems (Mazarei 2020). An extreme example is Libya, which had two central banks during much of its civil war.

Figure 19.4

Government revenues and expenditures in Algeria, Iran, Iraq, and Libya and world oil prices, 1990–2022

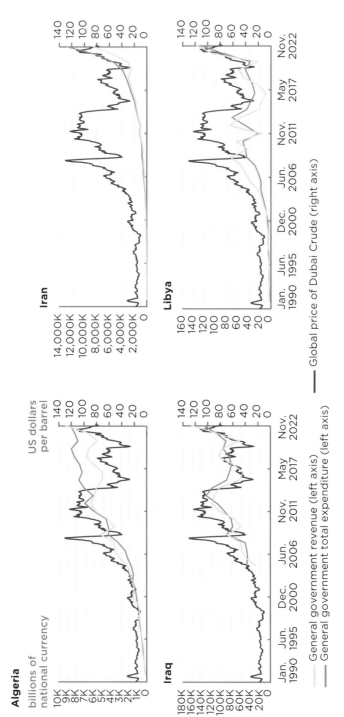

Notes: Oil price shown is the monthly average of Dubai Fateh. Revenues consist of taxes, social contributions, grants receivable, and other revenues. Total expenditures are total expenses and net acquisition of nonfinancial assets on an accrual basis. Revenue and expenditure data for 2022 are estimates for all countries except Libya.

Sources: IMF (2023b); primary commodity prices via Federal Reserve Bank of St. Louis, Federal Reserve Economic Data, https://fred.stlouisfed.org/series/POILDUBUSDM.

allowing a planned and measured transition to exchange rate flexibility to encourage economic diversification and adjust to changes, slowly and in a limited fashion, to a decline in the role of the dollar. The unhealthy scenario would be a disorderly transition effected by external factors such as disruptive geopolitical developments, including increased sanctions by the United States and Europe, and a speedy shakeup in the public finances of oil exporters from the rapid energy transition, leaving them with stranded oil and gas reserves.

Several factors will drive future exchange rate regime decisions in MENA oil exporters.

Desire for Greater Economic Diversification

There is widespread appreciation in the region of the need to accelerate economic diversification and exports. The GCC countries have focused on raising competitiveness through government subsidies, economic diversification, and regulatory reform. Down the road, the need to diversify may lead to greater emphasis on exchange rate changes to improve competitiveness.

The GCC countries have also made progress modernizing their banking systems, allowing them to handle exchange rate risks better. Quick changes in this area are hard to foresee, however, because policymakers are risk averse and further institutional preparations are needed before more active monetary and exchange rate policies can be pursued.

Geopolitical Changes

Changing geopolitical trends and deepening global divisions may induce greater diversification of the currency composition of financial assets (reserves and sovereign wealth funds) away from assets that could be subjected to US and European sanctions. China is becoming an increasingly important oil importer and trading partner. It is also becoming a place where oil exporters (mainly Saudi Arabia) seek to diversify their petroleum industry upstream. These trends may induce a shift toward the renminbi and other East Asian currencies and assets. This diversification in the currency composition of trade and finance may—though not necessarily—entail a shift, over time, away from dollar pegs toward more flexible exchange rates.

The currency of denomination of global oil trade and the settlement of payments for oil could also change, although there is little appetite among MENA oil exporters to consider denominating oil prices in renminbi and even less appetite for changing the currency of settlement of trade to that currency. By shifting the currency of oil pricing, petroleum exporters could subject themselves to currency manipulation by China, ceding to China some market power in determining the price of their exports.[5] A similar concern (together with limits in the size of renminbi-denominated financial assets) may dissuade oil exporters from moving a portion of their reserves and sovereign wealth fund assets into other currencies.

The pace of this shift away from the dollar will depend in good part on the sanctions policies of the United States rather than on what oil exporters do. If the currency of oil trade and settlement changes and oil exporters diversify their financial assets, there may be a very gradual move toward more flexible exchange rates in the GCC countries.[6]

Climate Change

Concerns about climate change could lead to accelerated efforts to shift away from fossil fuels, putting significant pressure on the export earnings and the fiscal sustainability of oil producers. Such a shift could rapidly reduce the ability of the GCC and other oil exporters to rely on foreign exchange earnings that allow pegging and defending exchange rates. Energy transition will heighten the need for accelerated economic diversification, which in turn requires more active macroeconomic management, particularly a more active use of exchange rate flexibility and monetary policy, including flexible approaches to inflation targeting (Arezki 2019).

Looking Ahead

The GCC countries need to prepare for flexible exchange rates down the road, especially to lower their heavy reliance on oil and gas revenues and adjust to the shift away from fossil fuels, but they don't feel much urgency.

The non-GCC countries should move quickly to greater exchange rate flexibility but are unlikely to do so. With greater exchange rate flexibility they could alleviate some of the macroeconomic pressures they face,

---

5. An issue that oil exporters need to consider in deciding whether to move toward with more exchange rate flexibility is the relationship between the movements between the dollar exchange rate and the price of oil. Historically, there has been a negative correlation between the two. With the Russian invasion of Ukraine, the direction of this relationship changed: There has been positive comovement between the dollar and the price of oil, making exchange rate movements less effective as a shock absorber. A new strand of thinking suggests that this shift from negative to positive comovements may reflect the fact that the United States is becoming a net exporter of oil, making the dollar behave as a commodity currency (Rees 2023). This change in the correlation between the dollar and oil prices is likely a temporary phenomenon.

6. This shift could be seen as a reversal of the currency invoicing and dominance issues raised by Gopinath et al. (2020), in which case exchange rate flexibility may help countries adjust better to adverse macroeconomic developments.

including those related to swings in oil prices, and protect their limited international reserves.[7] Their domestic governance problems—including corruption, fiscal dominance and inadequate central bank independence, and geopolitical constraints—are unlikely to be eased quickly, making policymakers unwilling to risk introducing flexible exchange rates.

References

Arezki, Rabah. 2019. *Monetary Policy in Fossil Fuel Exporters: The Curse of Horizons*. Policy Research Working Paper 8881. Washington: World Bank.

Chekouri, Sidi Mohammed, Abderrahim Chibi, and Mohamed Benbouziane. 2022. Identifying Algeria's de facto exchange rate regime: A wavelet-based approach. *Journal of Economic Structures* 11: 1–17. Available at https://ideas.repec.org/a/spr/jecstr/v11y2022i1d10.1186_s40008-022-00277-5.html.

El-Gamal, Mahmoud, and Amy Myers Jaffe. 2010. *Oil, Dollars, Debt and Crises*. Cambridge: Cambridge University Press.

Frankel, Jeffrey. 2017. *The Currency-Plus-Commodity Basket: A Proposal for Exchange Rates in Oil-Exporting Countries to Accommodate Trade Shocks Automatically*. CID Working Paper 333. Cambridge, MA: Center for International Development, Harvard University. Available at https://ideas.repec.org/p/cid/wpfacu/333.html.

Gopinath, Gita, Emine Boz, Camila Casas, Federico J. Díez, Pierre-Olivier Gourinchas, and Mikkel Plagborg-Møller. 2020. Dominant Currency Paradigm. *American Economic Review* 110, no. 3: 677–719.

IMF (International Monetary Fund). 2023a. *Annual Report on Exchange Arrangements and Exchange Restrictions 2022*. Washington. Available at https://www.elibrary.imf.org/display/book/9798400235269/9798400235269.xml?code=imf.org.

IMF (International Monetary Fund). 2023b. *World Economic Outlook*. Washington.

Khan, Mohsin S. 2009. *The GCC Monetary Union: Choice of Exchange Rate Regime*. PIIE Working Paper WP 09-1. Washington: Peterson Institute for International Economics. Available at https://www.piie.com/publications/working-papers/gcc-monetary-union-choice-exchange-rate-regime.

Mazarei, Adnan. 1995. *The Parallel Market for Foreign Exchange in an Oil Exporting Economy: The Case of Iran, 1978–1990*. IMF Working Paper 1995/069. Washington: International Monetary Fund.

Mazarei, Adnan. 2020. *Inflation Targeting in the Time of Sanctions and Pandemic*. November. Washington: Johns Hopkins School of Advanced International Studies, Iran under Sanctions Project.

Obstfeld, Maurice. 2020. *Harry Johnson's "Case for Flexible Exchange Rates"—50 Years Later*. PIIE Working Paper WP 20-12. Washington: Peterson Institute for International Economics. Available at https://www.piie.com/publications/working-papers/harry-johnsons-case-flexible-exchange-rates-50-years-later.

---

7. For the non-GCC countries, maintaining exchange rate stability has required considerable drawdown of reserves. For example, Algeria drew down its reserves by three-quarters, from $201 billion in 2012 to $56 billion. During the same period, Libya's reserves fell from $125 billion to $82 billion (https://data.worldbank.org).

Rees, Daniel. 2023. *Commodity Prices and the US Dollar*. BIS Working Paper 1083. Basel: Bank for International Settlements.

Rogoff, Kenneth, Aasim Husain, Ashoka Mody, Robin Brooks, and Nienke Oomes. 2003. *Evolution and Performance of Exchange Rate Regimes*. IMF Working Paper WP/03/243. Washington: International Monetary Fund.

Setser, Brad. 2007. *The Case for Exchange Rate Flexibility in Oil-Exporting Economies*. PIIE Policy Brief PB 07-8. Washington: Peterson Institute for International Economics. Available at https://www.piie.com/publications/working-papers/harry-johnsons-case-flexible-exchange-rates-50-years-later.

Wills, Samuel, and Rick van der Ploeg. 2014. Why Do So Many Oil Exporters Peg Their Currency? Foreign Reserves as a De Facto Sovereign Wealth Fund. Paper presented at the IMF Conference on Macroeconomic Challenges Facing Low-Income Countries, January 30–31, Washington.

20

Role of Flexible Exchange Rates in Three Financial Shocks in Indonesia

MUHAMAD CHATIB BASRI

After the Bretton Woods system of fixed exchange rates was abandoned in March 1973, many countries in the Organization for Economic Cooperation and Development (OECD) shifted to flexible exchange rates. Emerging markets began to implement flexible exchange rates only later, in the 1990s.

What have the experiences of these countries been? This chapter examines Indonesia because it experienced multiple financial shocks and crises under different exchange rate regimes. It is a fascinating laboratory for understanding, from both the theoretical and practical standpoints, the role of the exchange rate in adjusting to such shocks.

Before 1971, Indonesia had a complex system of multiple exchange rates, including a fixed exchange rate component and a free market component.[1] This framework fostered corruption and made smuggling a profitable business activity (Woo and Nasution 1978).

Indonesia terminated its multiple exchange rate system in 1971, adopting a fixed exchange rate until 1978. The high rate of inflation and Dutch Disease from an overvalued currency caused the Indonesian government to devalue in 1978 and to begin implementing a managed floating currency rate by depreciating by 5 percent every year, in order to increase exports.

From 1978 to 1997, a managed floating exchange rate regime was in place. During this period, Indonesia devalued the rupiah twice, in 1982

---

1. See Woo and Nasution (1978).

Muhamad Chatib Basri is senior lecturer in the Department of Economics at the University of Indonesia and former minister of finance of Indonesia.

and 1986, to help shore up the balance of payments. The managed floating exchange rate and devaluations in 1982 and 1986 succeeded in enhancing Indonesia's exports.

Because Indonesia experienced relatively high inflation (9–10 percent) from 1978 to 1997, interest rates were higher than in developed economies. High local interest rates and "guarantees" that the rupiah currency rate "would depreciate by only 5 percent" enticed Indonesian firms to borrow abroad (Basri 2018). As a result, the US dollar short-term debt skyrocketed. This short-term US loan was used to support domestic projects in the Indonesian rupiah. It was also used for long-term projects. The maturity and currency mismatch in this situation caused trouble during the Asian financial crisis. When Bank Indonesia floated the rupiah in 1997 as a result of the contagious effect of the Thai baht crisis in Thailand, many companies experienced problems with short-term US loans (because their debt in rupiah denomination increased), resulting in an increase in nonperforming loans and a banking crisis.

The Asian Financial Crisis, the Global Financial Crisis, and the Taper Tantrum

The Asian financial crisis of 1997–98, the global financial crisis of 2007–09, and the taper tantrum of 2013 had different effects on the Indonesian economy. Indonesia's GDP contracted 13.2 percent in 1998, exchange rates plummeted, and inflation skyrocketed. In contrast, during the global financial crisis and taper tantrum, Indonesia's economy grew—by 4.7 percent in 2009 (the second-highest among the G-20 countries) and by 5.6 percent in 2013. Currency depreciation and inflation also had a smaller impact than they did during the Asian financial crisis. During the taper tantrum, Indonesia and India were able to stabilize financial markets very quickly (seven months), allowing capital flows to resume. As a result India and Indonesia were able to leave the Fragile Five.[2]

These differences raises several questions:

- Why did Indonesia survive the 2007–09 global financial crisis and the 2013 taper tantrum but not the Asian financial crisis, even though the former were larger in magnitude than the latter?
- Why did tight fiscal and monetary policies help Indonesia overcome the taper tantrum but not the Asian financial crisis?
- What role did the exchange rate regime play in the first two questions?

---

2. One group of countries—Brazil, India, Indonesia, South Africa, and Turkey—experienced the worst effects. Morgan Stanley labeled them the Fragile Five.

- If a flexible exchange rate helped Indonesia survive the global financial crisis and the taper tantrum, could Indonesia fully adopt the Mundell-Fleming model (with its trilemma) and use the exchange rate as the only shock absorber?

When the Asian financial crisis hit Thailand in 1997, foreign investors began rebalancing their investments in Indonesia. The resulting capital outflow put downward pressure on the Indonesian rupiah. In response, Bank Indonesia widened its depreciation exchange rate band. Despite the move, pressure persisted. In July 1997, following Thailand's lead, Bank Indonesia abandoned its managed floating exchange rate regime in favor of a flexible exchange rate.

The shift from managed floating to flexible exchange rates happened quickly, without consideration of the fact that corporations had not hedged their exchange rates. The problem of short-term debts denominated in US dollars—which were relatively high and not hedged (as companies did not feel the need to hedge because depreciation was "guaranteed" at 5 percent per year)—worsened the balance sheet effect problem.

The poor condition of the banking system, as a result of weak governance, exacerbated this phenomenon, dubbed the "fear of floating" by Calvo and Reinhart (2002). Leverage was high, and credit was extended to parties related to firm owners without sufficient risk assessment. The share of nonperforming loans was estimated to be around 27 percent in September 1997 (Soesastro and Basri 1998; Hill 1999; Fane and MacLeod 2004).

To address Indonesia's weak banking system, the International Monetary Fund (IMF) recommended the closure of 16 banks. The decision to liquidate these banks without introducing a deposit guarantee program led to bank runs, which forced Bank Indonesia to provide liquidity support (Basri 2018). According to the IMF (2003), this liquidity support resulted in a loss of monetary control, further exacerbating the decline in the rupiah exchange rate. The collapse of the banking system caused by bank runs resulted in capital flight, causing the rupiah to plummet even further.

The situation was different in 2008 and 2013. In both years, the banking industry was significantly healthier than it had been in 1998, with the share of nonperforming loans below 4 percent and a capital adequacy ratio of about 17 percent (Basri 2018). These positive indicators were the result of reforms implemented in financial institutions, particularly banks, following the Asian financial crisis.

Another difference between the Asian financial crisis and the global financial crisis lies in the policy response (table 20.1). In 1998, the IMF asked Bank Indonesia to respond to the depreciation of the rupiah by raising interest rates. Given the relatively high level of nonperforming loans,

Table 20.1

Indonesia's policy response to the Asian financial crisis, the global financial crisis, and the taper tantrum

Type of response	Asian financial crisis	Global financial crisis	Taper tantrum
Monetary policy	Bank Indonesia (BI) pursued a very tight policy, increasing interest rates significantly. Deposit rates soared to 60 percent at the peak of the crisis, creating a liquidity squeeze.	BI lowered interest rates by 300 basis points, from 9.5 percent to 6.5 percent. Liquidity was sufficient.	BI increased interest rates by 175 basis points, from 6.0 percent to 7.75 percent.
Fiscal policy	The government initially targeted a budget surplus, then allowed a large budget deficit.	The government implemented a fiscal stimulus. The budget deficit grew, and income tax rates were reduced.	The government cut fuel subsidies.
Banking	Banking regulations were weak, with the share of nonperforming loans (NPLs) at 27 percent and the loan-to-deposit ratio (LDR) above 100 percent. Sixteen banks closed, resulting in a bank run.	Banking regulations were relatively tight. The share of NPLs was less than 4 percent, the LDR was 77 percent, and the capital adequacy ratio (CAR) was 17 percent. The government and the BI increased deposit insurance from Rp 100 million to Rp 2 billion per account.	Banking regulations were relatively tight. The share of NPLs was less than 4 percent, the LDR was 90 percent, and the CAR was 17 percent.

Trade	Liberalized the trade regime	The government maintained a relatively open trade regime.	The government maintained a relatively open trade regime.
Structural reform	The government liberalized the economy, busted monopolies, and licensing.	Import duty waivers	Removed quota imports on some food products to stabilize domestic products; import duty waivers
Exchange rate regime	The government maintained managed floating. Economic actors were unaccustomed to exchange rate risk and did not hedge.	BI maintained a flexible exchange rate.	BI maintained a flexible exchange rate.

Source: Basri (2018).

this policy increased the probability of default, leading to a banking crisis. The banking crisis hurt the economy and triggered further capital outflow (Stiglitz and Greenwald 2003).

In contrast, Bank Indonesia responded to the global financial crisis by lowering interest rates and ensuring sufficient liquidity in the banking system. As a result, the likelihood of default was significantly lower in 2008, and the impact on nonperforming loans was relatively modest.

Learning from the experiences of the Asian financial crisis, during the global financial crisis Indonesia strongly supported initiatives to restore confidence in the banking sector. The government and the central bank provided guarantees to maintain confidence in the banking sector, increasing the deposit guarantee ceiling from Rp 100 million to Rp 2 billion per account.[3] On the fiscal front, the government launched a countercyclical policy in 2008, mitigating the impact of the financial crisis on the most vulnerable groups by providing a social safety net.[4] The IMF-mandated reforms in 1997–98 had a positive effect on Indonesia in the medium term.

Banking reforms—in which Indonesia adopted Basel standards, higher capital adequacy ratios, strict banking supervision, and legal lending limitations—yielded substantial health benefits for the banking sector in 2008 and 2013. In addition, the IMF's recommendation that Indonesia apply a fiscal rule with a maximum budget deficit of 3 percent gave budgetary space for Indonesia to launch an economic stimulus in 2008. This fiscal discipline contributed to a reduction in Indonesia's debt-to-GDP ratio from 73 percent in 1998 to 25 percent in 2014. COVID-19 increased the debt-to-GDP ratio to 40 percent, but this ratio is still reasonable.

Indonesia's monetary system has also improved since the Asian financial crisis (Basri 2018). Bank Indonesia formally became independent in 1999, allowing it to control inflation. As a result, the average inflation rate fell and the exchange rate stabilized. In 2005, Bank Indonesia implemented a formal inflation targeting framework with a floating exchange rate; the government-set inflation objective is officially announced to the public, and monetary policy is aimed toward achieving the target. These measures have increased price stability, with inflation maintained near the target.

---

3. An evaluation by the IMF (2003) shows that in a crisis, the provision of a blanket guarantee is more effective than a limited deposit guarantee. There was disagreement within the Indonesian government regarding the blanket guarantee because of fear that it would repeat the case of Bank Indonesia liquidity support.

4. On fiscal policy, see Basri and Rahardja (2011).

Same Monetary and Fiscal Policy Tightening but Different Outcomes

The policies enacted during the taper tantrum were very similar to the ones adopted during the Asian financial crisis, albeit on a smaller scale. The government and Bank Indonesia implemented a policy of expenditure reduction and switching. To reduce spending, the government reduced gasoline subsidies by raising gasoline prices by approximately 40 percent in June 2013. Bank Indonesia gradually raised lending rates by 175 basis points. The government's strong support for a tight monetary policy was crucial because it allowed Bank Indonesia to act independently, strengthening the credibility of the policy.

Why were these policies successful in the taper tantrum but not in the Asian financial crisis? The main source of the crisis in the taper tantrum was the large current account deficit, not the weak banking sector. If banking conditions are generally sound, monetary and fiscal tightening will not cause a banking crisis, which could eventually lead to massive capital outflows. In addition, the Asian financial crisis was a financial crisis; the taper tantrum, despite its enormity, was more of a market panic, although it had the potential to cause a financial disaster if not properly controlled. Bank Indonesia's monetary tightening of 1.75 percent was tiny compared with the 60 percent increase in the Asian financial crisis. A combination of spending cuts and shifts in 2013–14 reduced the current account deficit and restored investor confidence. After seven months, capital inflows resumed. In contrast, during the Asian financial crisis, tight monetary and fiscal policies caused the banking system to fail, encouraging capital outflows.

Importance of the Exchange Rate Regime

The exchange rate regime is crucial in explaining the different impacts of the three financial crises on the Indonesian economy. The decision to apply a managed floating exchange rate with a 5 percent annual depreciation encouraged companies to borrow abroad without considering currency rate risk, encouraging carry trades[5] (Basri 2018). According to Nasution (2015), Bank Indonesia lacked sufficient data on short-term corporate foreign borrowings. As a result of allowing the rupiah to float, several businesses were unable to service their short-term external loans, resulting in nonperforming loans.

---

5. A carry trade is typically based on borrowing in a low-interest rate currency and converting the borrowed amount into another currency.

In contrast, during the global financial crisis and the taper tantrum, economic agents integrated exchange rate risk in their investment decisions, as a result of the use of a flexible exchange rate. Consequently, they diversified their portfolios and hedged their assets. As a result, if capital inflows were reversed, the impact would be more limited than it had been in 1998. Furthermore, when a flexible exchange rate is combined with inflation targeting, inflation decreases and interest rates fall. Lower interest rates, combined with an understanding of currency risks, create a disincentive for Indonesian enterprises to participate in carry trades. Consequently, when the value of the Indonesian rupiah dropped, the balance sheet effect was limited.

Basri (2016) argues that a combination of exchange rate depreciation and monetary and fiscal tightening has reduced the current account deficit, which calmed financial markets in both India and Indonesia in a relatively short period of time. One might argue that a flexible exchange rate helped Indonesia avoid the worst effect of its financial crisis.

Limits of the Trilemma Policy Choice

Basri and Sumartono (2023) identify three reasons why Indonesia finds it challenging to implement the trilemma-suggested policy and rely solely on exchange rates as a shock absorber to mitigate the volatility of capital flows. Despite the potential benefits of a flexible exchange rate, this policy choice is not straightforward because of several factors.

Multiple Goals of Monetary Policy

Monetary policies have multiple goals. The Federal Reserve's quantitative easing (QE) program, initiated in 2009, resulted in massive capital inflows into emerging economies, including Indonesia. This problem became more difficult because the commodity supercycle occurred at the same time.[6] The Mundell-Fleming model reminds us that monetary policy can remain independent in an open capital account regime if exchange rates are allowed to be flexible. The impact of capital movements can be reduced by using this prescription. However, exchange rate management has limits: Although a flexible exchange rate can help an economy insulate external shocks, it may not be enough to prevent financial instability (Rey 2013). Moreover, exchange rate management can be costly and challenging, especially in the presence of significant and volatile capital flows.

---

6. Frankel (2006) argues that expansive monetary policy in the United States contributed to increased commodity and energy prices. Saghaian and Reed (2015) and Kim (2022) show that QE affected commodity and energy prices.

Figure 20.1

GDP growth, current account/GDP, interest rate, and foreign exchange reserves in Indonesia, 2005–15

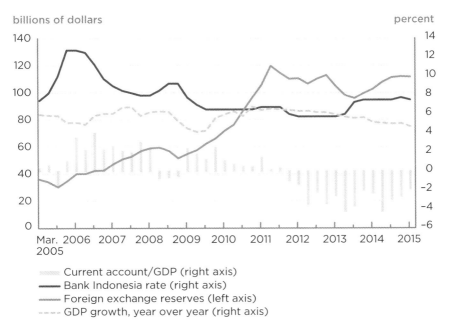

billions of dollars ⟶ percent

Legend:
- Current account/GDP (right axis)
- Bank Indonesia rate (right axis)
- Foreign exchange reserves (left axis)
- GDP growth, year over year (right axis)

Source: Basri (2017).

Rey's arguments align with Indonesia's experience. Bank Indonesia reduced interest rates in anticipation of capital inflows from the Fed's QE strategy. In the short term, the combination of lower interest rates, capital inflows, and increased terms of trade effects as a result of the commodity supercycle boosted Indonesian growth, which peaked in 2010Q4 (figure 20.1). However, the commodity supercycle also resulted in a surplus in Indonesia's trade and current account balances. Consequently, Indonesia faced a trade surplus and overemployment.

Bank Indonesia faced a dilemma. If it cut interest rates in anticipation of capital inflows, the already overheated economy would overheat further. If it attempted to address overemployment by raising interest rates, it would increase capital inflows, negatively affecting the trade balance. Bank Indonesia had the alternative of sterilization, but the cost was very high because of the substantial difference between the Fed Fund rate and the Bank Indonesia rate. Allowing the currency rate to appreciate would significantly affect Indonesia's exports. As a result, Bank Indonesia chose to lower interest rates and intervene in the foreign exchange market from 2009 to

2011, in order to mitigate the impact of capital inflows on the exchange rate. Basri and Sumartono (2023) show that two opposing impacts were at work. On the one hand, intervention in the foreign exchange market and lower interest rates curbed exchange rate appreciation, sustaining Indonesia's current account surplus. On the other hand, low interest rates boosted aggregate demand, reducing the current account surplus. In the medium term, the latter had a greater impact than the former.

The end of the commodity supercycle in 2012 exacerbated this issue, leading to a decline in economic growth and an increase in the current account deficit in 2013Q2. When tapering talks began, in 2013, widening current account deficits and decreasing foreign exchange reserves resulted in massive capital outflows. These capital flow dynamics weakened the central bank's independence in monetary policy, shifting its attention from managing inflation to controlling inflation and maintaining exchange rates (Juhro 2010; Goeltom and Juhro 2013).

Policymakers faced the conundrum of a current account deficit and declining economic growth—a situation that is consistent with Blanchard's (2017) argument that policymakers face a dilemma when choosing between multiple policy objectives. To close the current account deficit, the government and Bank Indonesia needed to implement a contractionary and expenditure-switching policy (reducing fuel subsidies, hiking interest rates, and allowing the currency to weaken)—all measures that would further slow economic development.

Volatility of the Exchange Rate

The volatile exchange rate plays a crucial role. Exchange rate overshooting significantly affects exchange rate expectations (Dornbusch 1976). In the case of the taper tantrum, if the Fed intended to raise interest rates, the rupiah had to depreciate substantially to maintain the smooth functioning of economic activity because net exports respond more slowly than exchange rates. This exchange rate overshooting causes market fear, which affects exchange rate expectations. The Asian financial crisis traumatized Indonesia; whenever a currency rate overshoots, financial investors become concerned and push for deeper depreciation (Basri 2018). Bank Indonesia therefore had to focus not only on managing inflation but also on maintaining currency rate stability. Excessive exchange rate shocks caused by sudden reversals in capital flows can lead to an overshoot in exchange rates, resulting in panic. In addition, continuous capital inflows may weaken the effectiveness of monetary policies.

Challenges of Balance Sheet Effects

Low interest rates in the United States have encouraged banks in Indonesia to increase lending through financial accelerators. In the case of original sin (Eichengreen, Hausmann, and Panizza 2007), appreciation caused by capital inflows has additional balance sheet consequences. According to Raghuram Rajan, strong currency and asset prices reduce agents' loan-to-value ratios, lowering the risk perception of leverage.[7] This oversupply of credit from cross-border lending leads to balance-of-payment issues.

During the taper tantrum, credit expansion dropped from 22 percent in 2013 to 11 percent in 2014, encouraging capital outflow from Indonesia. Unhedged foreign borrowings, exacerbated by the burden of US dollar-denominated debt, had a contractionary impact on companies in Indonesia.

Role of Fiscal Policies

In theory, the government should implement a tight fiscal policy to reduce the negative impact of capital inflows. The commodity supercycle made it difficult to implement a tight fiscal policy. Fiscal policies in resource-rich countries tend to be procyclical (Herrera, Kouame, and Mandon 2019; Kaminsky 2010). In Indonesia, the commodity supercycle increased government revenues but also increased the burden of energy subsidies, as a result of rising energy prices, leading to a procyclical fiscal policy. Cutting fuel subsidies is also unpopular and politically challenging, even when direct cash transfers are made to assist the poor.

Indeed, when capital inflows occur, no emerging market countries adopt stringent fiscal policies (Ghosh, Ostry, and Qureshi 2018). One reason they do not is that they adhere to the budget cycle. In addition, commodity supercycles have undesirable redistributive consequences that these countries try to avoid (Basri and Sumartono 2023). Monetary policies alone are insufficient to address this issue.

The combination of commodity supercycles and fiscal procyclicality makes implementing the trilemma particularly challenging. These characteristics of the Indonesian economy influence policymakers' decisions and policy choices. In such circumstances, a mix of monetary, macroprudential, and fiscal policies becomes essential.

Indonesia and India managed the taper tantrum reasonably well. But they did so at the expense of economic growth. I believe that additional tools for managing macroeconomic stability and capital flows, such as

---

7. Raghuram Rajan, "A Step in the Dark: Unconventional Monetary Policy after the Crisis," Andrew Crockett Memorial Lecture, Bank for International Settlements, Basel, June 23, 2013.

capital flow management, will assist them and other developing economies in responding to capital flow volatility.

Conclusion

Reforms implemented to improve the soundness of the banking sector and the independence of Bank Indonesia, adoption of fiscal rules and flexible exchange rates, and appropriate monetary and fiscal policy responses helped Indonesia deal relatively well with the global financial crisis and taper tantrum. Flexible exchange rates forced economic agents to consider exchange rate risk in their investment decisions, leading to diversified portfolios and hedged assets. As a result, when capital inflows suddenly reversed, the impact was smaller than it was during the 1998 Asian financial crisis. When a flexible exchange rate is combined with inflation targeting, the domestic interest rate falls, discouraging carry trades. Consequently, when the Indonesian rupiah plummeted, the balance sheet effect was limited.

Indonesia cannot fully rely on the exchange rate as its sole shock absorber, however—contrary to what the Mundell-Fleming model suggests. The case of Indonesia reveals the difficulty of implementing a trilemma policy choice and the significant costs to the economy of doing so. Combining monetary policy, macroprudential policy, and fiscal policy is critical. To make policy choices more successful, it is vital that policymakers consider the role of capital flow management.

References

Basri, M.C. 2016. *The Fed's Tapering Talk: A Short Statement's Long Impact on Indonesia.* Ash Centre Occasional Paper. Cambridge, MA: Harvard Kennedy School. Available at https://ash.harvard.edu/files/ash/files/taper_tantrum.pdf?m=1466604066.

Basri, M.C. 2017. India and Indonesia: Lessons Learned from the 2013 Taper Tantrum. *Bulletin of Indonesian Economic Studies* 53, no. 2: 13760.

Basri, M.C. 2018. Twenty Years after the Financial Crisis. In *Realizing Indonesia's Economic Potential*, ed. L.E. Bruer, J. Guajardo, and T. Kinda. Washington: International Monetary Fund. Available at https://www.elibrary.imf.org/view/IMF071/24870-9781484337141/24870-9781484337141/ch2.xml.

Basri, M.C., and S. Rahardja. 2011. Mild Crisis, Half Hearted Fiscal Stimulus: Indonesia During the GFC. In *Assessment on the Impact of Stimulus, Fiscal Transparency and Fiscal Risk*, ed. T. Ito and F. Parulian. Economic Research Institute for ASEAN and East Asia, Jakarta RIA.

Basri, M.C., and Luqman Sumartono. 2023. The Impossibility of the Impossible Trinity? The Case of Indonesia. *Oxford Review of Economic Policy* 39: 341–55.

Blanchard, O. 2017. Currency Wars, Coordination, and Capital Controls. *International Journal of Central Banking*, 13, no. 2 (June): 283.

Calvo, G., and C. Reinhart. 2002. Fear of Floating. *Quarterly Journal of Economics* 117, no. 2: 379–408.

Dornbusch, R. 1976. *Open Economy Macroeconomics*. New York: Basic Books.

Eichengreen, B., R. Hausmann, and U. Panizza. 2007. Currency Mismatches, Debt Intolerance and Original Sin: Why They Are Not the Same and Why it Matters. In *Capital Controls and Capital Flows in Emerging Economies: Policies, Practices and Consequences*. University of Chicago Press, 121–70.

Fane, George, and Ross McLeod. 2004. *Banking Collapse and Restructuring in Indonesia, 1997–2001*. Departmental Working Paper 2001-10. Canberra: Australian National University, Arndt-Corden Department of Economics.

Frankel, J. 2006. *The Effect of Monetary Policy on Real Commodity Prices*. NBER Working Paper 12713. Cambridge, MA: National Bureau of Economic Research.

Ghosh, A.R., J.D. Ostry, and M.S. Qureshi. 2018. *Managing the Tide: How Do Emerging Markets Respond to Capital Flows?* Cambridge, MA: MIT Press.

Goeltom, M., and S. Juhro. 2013. *The Monetary Policy Regime in Indonesia*. Working Paper WP/17/2013. Jakarta: Bank Indonesia.

Herrera, S., W.A. Kouame, and P. Mandon. 2019. *Why Some Countries Can Escape the Fiscal Pro-Cyclicality Trap and Others Cannot?* Policy Research Working Paper 8963. Washington: World Bank.

Hill, Hal. 1999. *The Indonesian Economy in Crisis: Causes, Consequences and Lessons*. New York: Palgrave/Macmillan.

IMF (International Monetary Fund). 2003. *Evaluation Report: The IMF and Recent Capital Account Crises: Indonesia, Korea and Brazil*. Washington: Independent Evaluation Office.

Juhro, S. 2010. *The Vicious Circle of Rising Capital Inflows and Effectiveness of Monetary Control in Indonesia*. Research Note. Jakarta: Bank Indonesia.

Kaminsky, G. 2010. *Terms of Trade Shock and Fiscal Cycles*. NBER Working Paper 15780. Cambridge, MA: National Bureau of Economic Research.

Kim, M. 2022. Transmission of US Monetary Policy to Commodity Exporters and Importers. *Review of Economic Dynamics* 43: 152–67.

Nasution, Anwar. 2015. *How Indonesia Reformed Its Risky Financial Sector*. East Asia Forum, April 24. Available at http://www.eastasiaforum.org/2015/04/24/how-indonesia-reformed-its-risky-financial-sector/.

Rey, H. 2013. *Dilemma not Trilemma: The Global Cycle and Monetary Policy Independence*. Proceedings of the Economic Policy Symposium, Jackson Hole, WY, August 1–2. Kansas City: Federal Reserve Bank of Kansas City.

Saghaian, S., and M. Reed. 2015. Spillover Effect of the US Federal Reserve's Recent Quantitative Easing on Canadian Commodity Prices. *International Journal of Food and Agriculture Economics* 3, no. 1: 33–43.

Soesastro, H., and M.C. Basri. 1998. Survey of Recent Developments. *Bulletin of Indonesian Economic Studies* 34, no. 1: 3–54.

Stiglitz, J., and B. Greenwald. 2003. *Towards a New Paradigm in Monetary Economics*. Cambridge: Cambridge University Press.

Woo, Wing Thye, and Anwar Nasution. 1978. Exchange Rate Policy. In *Developing Country Debt and Economic Performance*, vol. 3 of *Country Studies: Indonesia, Korea, Philippines, Turkey*, ed. Jeffrey Sachs and Susan Collins. Chicago: University of Chicago Press.

THE DOLLAR AND INTERNATIONAL FINANCIAL MARKETS

The Fed's International Dollar Liquidity Facilities and the COVID-19 Period

LINDA S. GOLDBERG

This chapter provides perspective on the Federal Reserve's creation, expansion, and deployment of its international dollar liquidity backstop facilities, all of which affect the stability of the broader international monetary environment, with the dollar as a central currency. The starting points are events that occurred in 2020 and the strains that developed in global dollar funding markets. The analysis informs the types of facilities the Federal Reserve has in place to address pressures in offshore dollar funding and US Treasury dislocation.[1] I also review evidence on what those facilities seem to have been achieving.

Global Dollar Funding Markets in March 2020

Several forces contributed to strains in global dollar funding markets at the onset of the pandemic shutdowns. First, the supply of dollars to funding markets fell, as lenders held dollars as a precaution amid the significant economic and financial disruption and uncertainty.

---

1. This chapter draws on Cetorelli, Goldberg, and Ravazzolo (2020); Choi et al. (2022); and Goldberg and Ravazzolo (2023).

Linda S. Goldberg is a financial research advisor at the Federal Reserve Bank of New York, following previous roles at the Fed, including senior vice president, head of Global Economic Analysis, and head of the International Research function. Views are those of the author and do not necessarily reflect the views of the Federal Reserve Bank of New York or the Federal Reserve System. The author thanks Maurice Obstfeld for helpful comments.

Second, funding and hedging demand for dollars increased. Some foreign banks in the United States faced new funding needs from corporate drawdowns of committed credit lines and reduced access to other funding sources, along with higher funding costs. Regulatory data collected in the United States show that the US branches of foreign banks sourced net liquidity from their parents during this episode (Cetorelli, Goldberg, and Ravazzolo 2020). The status of US branches as net recipients of liquidity from their parent organizations was a reversal of the pattern exhibited during the global financial crisis, when some US branches of foreign banks were initially tapped to provide dollar liquidity to parent banks that faced new funding needs as a result of the asset-backed commercial paper losses brought onto their balance sheets.[2]

Figure 21.1 illustrates this dynamic. The sourcing by US branches of more net liquidity from their parents, reflected in the net due balances, is consistent with a supervisory and regulatory regime in which parent banks play a key role. Parent banks had to come up with more dollars. As dollar funding costs increased, borrowers who went to financial markets were faced with prices that reflected these stress conditions.

How Dollar Backstop Facilities Help Mitigate Market Stresses

The network of US dollar liquidity swap lines serves as a liquidity backstop to ease strains in global funding markets, mitigating the effects of such strains on the supply of credit to households and businesses. The central bank's dollar facilities allow commercial banks outside the United States to access US dollar liquidity, obviating the need for them to bid up market rates excessively. If banks do not have to sell less-liquid assets to obtain dollar liquidity, fire sales of dollar-denominated assets abroad or in the United States and the associated price externalities for other firms are reduced. Having this dollar liquidity access means that banks can continue to provide credit in their local economies as well as in the United States. When these banks have access to central bank–supplied dollars, they can also continue to intermediate funds to other financial and nonfinancial institutions, such as corporations.

The dollar liquidity swap lines eliminate the need for some central banks to intervene in the foreign exchange market to meet dollar needs of their own domestic entities. Some central banks have their own network of

---

2. For a discussion of internal capital market flows in global banks during the global financial crisis in relation to dollar liquidity provision in central banks, see Goldberg and Skeie (2011) and Cetorelli and Goldberg (2011, 2012).

Figure 21.1

Funding needs of US branches of foreign banking organizations during the COVID-19 crisis, January–May 2020

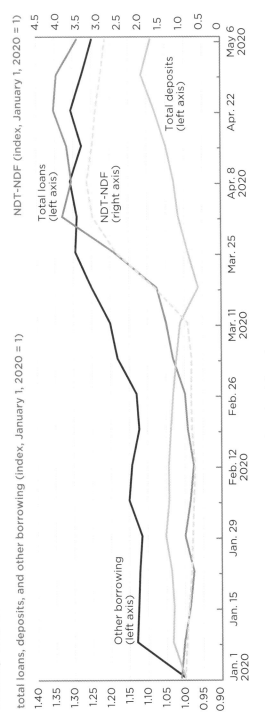

total loans, deposits, and other borrowing (index, January 1, 2020 = 1)

NDT-NDF (index, January 1, 2020 = 1)

NDT-NDF = Net due to less net due from, measured on the right axis

Note: Sample contains 65 foreign banking organizations (FBOs), defined as institutions that submit both FR 2644 and FFIEC 002 forms.

Sources: Federal Reserve, FR 2644; Federal Financial Institutions Examination Council, FFIEC 002.

swap line arrangements with other central banks. Serving financial center roles, these central banks more broadly distribute dollars. These swap lines are priced as a backstop facility; they are minimally and sporadically used during normal market conditions to encourage private transactions.

Actions by the Federal Open Market Committee in March 2020 to Address Global Dollar Funding Strains

With central bank dollar swap lines in place, parent banks with direct access to US dollar operations of foreign central banks could draw on those operations for sourcing dollar funding instead of trying to borrow dollars from private funding markets.[3] In March 2020, the Federal Open Market Committee (FOMC), in collaboration with its standing swap central bank (SSCB) counterparties (the European Central Bank, the Bank of Japan, the Bank of England, the Swiss National Bank, and the Bank of Canada) took a series of steps to ease access to the swap lines. First, the network lowered the price, from a spread of 50 basis points to a spread of 25 basis points over the overnight indexed swaps rate, and added an operation for 84-day term lending to its existing weekly operation for 7-day funds. Then, it increased the frequency of the operations for 7-day funds from weekly to daily. In addition, the FOMC extended temporary lines through December 2021 with nine other central banks (temporary swap central banks [TSCBs]), the same group that provided these temporary swap lines in the global financial crisis.[4]

Draws on these facilities generated a total of $449 billion outstanding by May 2020, far lower than the $598 billion peak in the global financial crisis. The concentration of dollar funding activity shifted somewhat from Europe to Asia after the global financial crisis. This shift is also reflected in the regional peak outstanding positions relative to the COVID-19 period (figure 21.2). As Fleming et al. (2022) show, March 2020 was also characterized by extensive strains on US Treasury markets and dash-for-dollar dynamics (Barone et al. 2022). Specifically related for international counterparties with accounts managed at the Federal Reserve Bank of New York, on March 30, 2020, a new facility for Foreign and International Monetary Authorities (FIMA) was deployed (Choi et al. 2022). The new FIMA repo facility allows a broader range of foreign official entities to temporarily exchange their US Treasury securities held with the System Open Market Account of the Federal Reserve for US dollars. This dollar liquidity can

---

3. For a discussion of actions by the Federal Open Market Committee (FOMC) to address global dollar funding strains, see Choi et al. (2022).

4. See Goldberg, Kennedy, and Miu (2011).

Figure 21.2

Peak US dollar swap balances outstanding during the global financial crisis and the COVID-19 pandemic

a. Standing swap line central banks

billions of US dollars

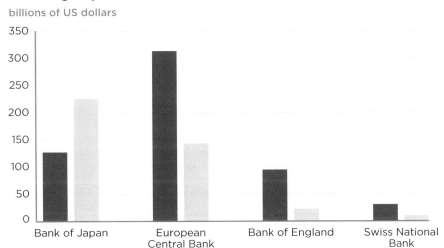

b. Temporary swap line central banks

billions of US dollars

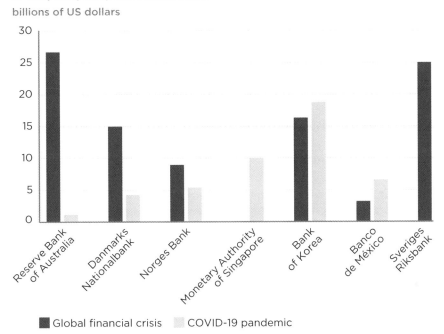

■ Global financial crisis　□ COVID-19 pandemic

Note: The Bank of Canada, Central Bank of Brazil, and Reserve Bank of New Zealand never used the facility.

Source: Federal Reserve Bank of New York, desk computations.

then be made available to institutions in their jurisdictions. The facility was used with different levels of intensity from its inception through early 2023 (figure 21.3). Initially a temporary facility, it was formalized as a standing facility on July 28, 2021. With the dollar still the leading component of countries' official foreign exchange reserves, this innovation represented an important addition to the global financial safety net.

Effects of the Fed's International Dollar Liquidity Facilities

Goldberg and Ravazzolo (2021) examine whether the data support the conjectures about what these facilities do. One conjecture pertains to reducing strains in dollar funding markets. The other is a broader issue, related to the observation that global liquidity flows are highly responsive to risk sentiment and risk events (Goldberg 2023). As the general goal is to systemically reduce the risk sensitivity of international flows, if the facilities actually can play a reassuring role, extra demand for dollar liquidity in a stress period should decline and cross-border flow volatility should fall. Of course, declaring as definitive any evidence from the period from February 2020 through the months that followed is impossible, given the pandemic and the policy responses to it around the world. Goldberg and Ravazzolo (2021) note that challenges in identification make their results, described below, indicative rather than conclusive.

Countries with central bank access to standing or temporary swap lines saw reduced the costs of borrowing dollars in the foreign exchange swap market. Following the establishment of the FIMA repo facility, other countries enjoyed declines in local dollar funding costs, despite minimal aggregate usage. Both facilities were associated with reduced risk sensitivity of funding costs, with risk measured using the Chicago Board Options Exchange's CBOE Volatility Index (the VIX). Strains in offshore dollar funding markets and in cross-border bank and international capital flows normalized at a slower pace and to a lesser extent in countries without access. Cross-border bank flows did not collapse following the pandemic shock. However, banking systems with access to Fed facilities maintained stronger cross-border lending relative to banking systems without such access. Capital flows to countries in which central banks had swap lines were more robust than they were in other countries. Equity flows were not differentiated by facility access. Overall, the evidence suggests that the dollar facilities were associated with reduced dollar funding strains, continuing provision of credit by banks, and lower risk sensitivity of international flows.

Figure 21.3

Outstanding Foreign and International Monetary Authorities (FIMA) repo: Daily average within week, January 1, 2020 to March 1, 2023

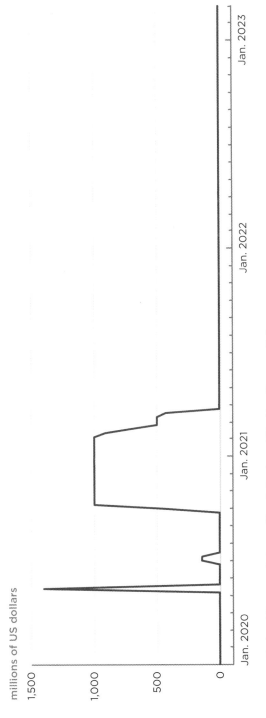

Source: Federal Reserve Balance Sheet: Factors Affecting Reserve Balances.

Can the Dollar-Based System Be Improved?

The international roles of the dollar are central to understanding the determination of flexible exchange rates, flows of liquidity across borders, and frictions in intermediating dollar liquidity. The backstop functions of dollar facilities support credit provision to the real economy and aim to mitigate the effects of prolonged credit contractions to households and businesses.

Future analytics can deepen understanding and possibly lead to refinements in official liquidity provision. They can consider the speed, magnitude, and pass-through of backstop dollar liquidity. Researchers can also continue to investigate how the functioning and scale of facilities best match the evolving structure and characteristics of financial intermediaries, the dollar-related financial system, international capital flow pressures (Goldberg and Krogstrup 2023), and broader dollar use internationally. For example, nonbank financial institutions can access credit only after it is intermediated by banks. Additional questions relate to how different facilities implement their own restrictions, pricing, and incentives for use. Discussion of the need for and operation of dollar liquidity facilities can focus not only on the structures and reach of the supply of dollar liquidity but also on reducing the risk sensitivity of dollar liquidity flows when stress events occur (Goldberg 2023).

References

Barone, Jordan, Alain Chaboud, Adam Copeland, Cullen Kavoussi, Frank M. Keane, and Seth Searls. 2022. *The Global Dash for Cash: Why Sovereign Bond Market Functioning Varied across Jurisdictions in March 2020.* Federal Reserve Bank of New York Staff Report 1010.

Cetorelli, Nicola, and Linda S. Goldberg. 2011. Global Banks and Their Internal Capital Markets during the Crisis. *Liberty Street Economics*, July. Federal Reserve Bank of New York.

Cetorelli, Nicola, and Linda S. Goldberg. 2012. Liquidity Management of US Global Banks: Internal Capital Markets in the Great Recession. *Journal of International Economics* 88, no. 2: 299–311.

Cetorelli, Nicola, Linda S. Goldberg, and Fabiola Ravazzolo. 2020. How Fed Swap Lines Supported the US Corporate Credit Market amid COVID-19 Strains. *Liberty Street Economics*, June. Federal Reserve Bank of New York.

Choi, Mark, Linda S. Goldberg, Robert Lerman, and Fabiola Ravazzolo. 2022. The Fed's Central Bank Swap Lines and FIMA Repo Facility. *Economic Policy Review* 28, no. 1. Federal Reserve Bank of New York.

Fleming, Michael J., Haoyang Liu, Rich Podjasek, and Jake Schurmeier. 2022. The Federal Reserve's Market Functioning Purchases. *Economic Policy Review* 28, no. 1. Federal Reserve Bank of New York.

Goldberg, Linda S. 2023. *Global Liquidity: Drivers, Volatility and Toolkits*. Federal Reserve Bank of New York Staff Report 1064, June.

Goldberg, Linda S., and Signe Krogstrup. 2023. International Capital Flow Pressures and Global Factors. *Journal of International Economics* 146 (December).

Goldberg, Linda S., and Fabiola Ravazzolo. 2021. *The Fed's International Dollar Liquidity Facilities: New Evidence on Effects*. Federal Reserve Bank of New York Staff Report 997, December.

Goldberg, Linda S., and David Skeie. 2011. Why Did US Branches of Foreign Banks Borrow at the Discount Window during the Crisis? *Liberty Street Economics*, April. Federal Reserve Bank of New York.

Goldberg, Linda S., Craig Kennedy, and Jason Miu. 2011. Central Bank Dollar Swap Lines and Overseas Dollar Funding Costs. *Economic Policy Review* 17, no. 1: 3–20. Federal Reserve Bank of New York.

22

The Dollar-Based Financial System through the Window of the Foreign Exchange Swap Market

HYUN SONG SHIN

The international role of the dollar is often discussed in the context of the current accounts of both advanced and emerging-market economies and their accumulation of reserve assets. Several chapters in this volume reflect this focus on the current account. I believe it is better to view the dollar's outsize importance in global affairs as deriving more from its preeminent role as the funding currency of choice in global capital markets for banks and nonbank financial intermediaries (NBFIs) and the pivotal role of central bank dollar swap lines as a liquidity backstop in keeping the global financial system on an even keel (Avdjiev, McCauley, and Shin 2016).

When the Bretton Woods system of fixed exchange rates collapsed, in early 1973, many doubted that the dollar would retain its preeminence in the world monetary system. In the event, the massive expansion of domestic and international financial markets in the last five decades of floating rates helped make the dollar's global role more pivotal than ever before.

The markets for foreign exchange (FX) swaps and forwards provide a window on this global role of the dollar as the main funding currency for both banks and nonbanks. FX swap and forward positions are very large in gross terms, but they do not always map neatly to current account balances. Most of the time, FX swaps are out of sight and out of mind. They are

Hyun Song Shin is economic adviser and head of research at the Bank for International Settlements (BIS). The views expressed here are his and do not necessarily reflect those of the BIS. He is grateful to Patrick McGuire for allowing him to draw on joint research and to Marjorie Santos for excellent research assistance. He also thanks the conference attendees for helpful comments.

thrust into the limelight during periods of dollar funding stresses, most recently in the early phase of the COVID shock, in March 2020, and most dramatically during the 2007–09 global financial crisis. Piecing together the size and structure of FX swaps and the resulting ongoing dollar repayment obligations reveals that the vulnerabilities to dollar funding stresses are larger in advanced economies than in emerging market economies, in a sense to be made clear in this chapter.

Dollar Dominance in Foreign Exchange Swaps and Forwards

At its most basic, an FX swap is an arrangement in which two parties exchange currencies at the spot rate today (the spot leg) and agree to unwind that transaction at a pre-agreed upon exchange rate at some pre-agreed upon time (the forward leg). Once the spot leg transaction is complete, only the forward leg remains. Unlike most other derivatives, FX swaps require payment of the full principal amount at maturity; they thus have debt-like attributes. Unlike other forms of collateralized borrowing (such as repos), the prevailing accounting convention does not record the obligations from FX swaps as debt on the balance sheet.

The textbook case for FX swaps/forwards is for hedging currency exposures. Exporters and importers often use forwards to hedge their international trade–related accounts payables/receivables. An exporter with expected dollar receipts may sell dollars forward to lock in the local currency value of the export proceeds. Doing so allows the exporter to hedge the costs associated with the domestic wage bill or other investment costs locally.

Much more important than these real economy uses is hedging by NBFIs. Consider the case of a life insurer or pension fund that has obligations to policy holders or beneficiaries in euros, yen, sterling, or Swiss francs. Although these obligations are in domestic currency, the life insurer or pension fund typically holds a globally diversified portfolio, much of it comprising dollar assets. To hedge the currency risk, the life insurer or pension fund can enter into an FX swap with a global bank, in effect borrowing dollars while pledging domestic currency as collateral.

The amounts involved in such hedging transactions are very large (see, for instance, Borio, McCauley, and McGuire 2022): The outstanding obligations to pay US dollars in FX swaps/forwards, mostly very short term, amounted to more than $80 trillion in 2022 (BIS 2022b). This sum exceeds the stocks of dollar Treasury securities, repos, and commercial paper combined. In terms of flows, the latest Bank for International Settlements (BIS) Triennial Central Bank Survey finds that the churn of deals approached $5 trillion a day in 2022, accounting for two-thirds of daily global FX turnover in all currencies.

Figure 22.1 draws on the BIS Triennial Central Bank Survey to illustrate the average daily global turnover in foreign exchange.[1] For stocks, BIS OTC derivatives statistics track global outstanding amounts for FX swaps/ forwards semiannually, with detail by currency and sector.[2]

For roughly two decades, average daily FX turnover scaled by world GDP trended upward (figure 22.1). In 2022, an amount equivalent to total world GDP turned over every 14 days or so, significantly more rapidly than every 25 days in 2001. This growth can be attributed to greater use of FX swaps by nonbank financial firms, as argued below.

Dollar dominance is clearly evident in figure 22.1. FX contracts with the US dollar on one side (the light gray line) grew in tandem with the global total. By contrast, turnover with the euro, yen, sterling, or Swiss franc barely kept pace with underlying economic activity, as measured by global GDP.

Turning to outstanding stocks, it is useful to focus squarely on FX swaps/forwards. Markets for these instruments are periodically subject to funding squeezes. Swaps and forwards are typically short term and have debt-like attributes, as explained below. They are key to understanding the financial factors that determine the fluctuations in risk premiums (see Avdjiev, McCauley, and Shin 2016; Shin 2016; Obstfeld and Zhou 2022; and chapter 4 by Robert Aliber, chapter 23 by Şebnem Kalemli-Özcan, and chapter 17 by Andres Velasco in this volume). As panel a of figure 22.2 shows, FX swaps/forwards with the US dollar on one side (the light gray line) grew to more than 80 percent of world GDP. By contrast, and in line with the flows in figure 22.1, FX swaps/forwards with the euro, yen, Swiss franc, or sterling have been stable.

The scale of the US dollar (light gray lines) relative to other currencies in figures 22.1 and panel a of figure 22.2 reflects its status as the global

---

1. The BIS Triennial Central Bank Survey is the most comprehensive source of information on the size and structure of global over-the-counter FX markets. It is coordinated by the BIS, in cooperation with central banks and other reporting authorities in more than 50 jurisdictions. The survey has been conducted in April every three years since 1986. The most recent survey was conducted in April 2022 (with results published in November 2022). It covered average daily turnover at more than 1,200 banks and other dealers.

2. FX swaps and outright forwards cannot be distinguished in BIS stocks data. Currency swaps are FX swaps with a maturity of more than one year in which coupons are also exchanged. Ideally, one would exclude from analysis nondeliverable forwards (NDFs), which entail just a fractional payment, but they are not identified individually in the stocks data. NDFs account for less than 10 percent of the average daily turnover of FX swaps, forwards, and currency swaps.

Figure 22.1

Turnover of foreign exchange spot, swaps, and forwards as percent of GDP, 1989–2022

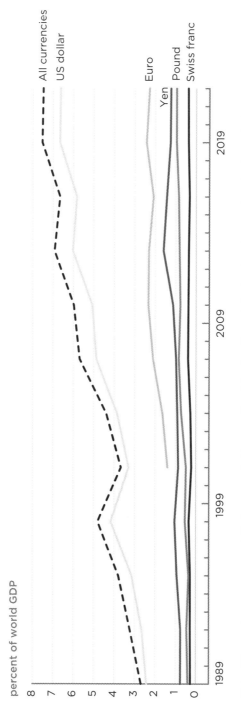

percent of world GDP

Note: Figure shows average daily turnover in the month of April, adjusted for local and cross-border inter-dealer double-counting (i.e., on a "net-net" basis).

Sources: IMF, *World Economic Outlook*, October 2022, for world GDP and BIS Triennial Survey, April 2022, for turnover.

funding currency of choice. But what is the reason for the increase in its slope? The answer is revealing and highlights the network effects that arise from the mutually reinforcing choices of financial and nonfinancial firms in their funding and hedging choices (see chapter 25 by Jeffrey Frankel, and chapter 27 by Philippe Martin, in this volume).

Consider first the choices faced by importers and exporters on the real side of the economy. In both advanced economies and emerging markets, corporate borrowers that borrow internationally tend to borrow in US dollars (Maggiori, Neiman, and Schreger 2020). Firms that purchase inputs denominated in dollars need working capital in dollars and thus borrow dollars short term from banks. Dollar-denominated trade creates dollar-denominated debt. An exporter of oil or other commodities invoiced in dollars who wants to make a long-term capital investment may find it prudent to borrow long term in dollars in order to eliminate currency risk. Trade invoicing begets dollar-denominated debt.

From a capital markets viewpoint, trade invoicing in dollars produces a preponderance of dollar-denominated debt that investors are invited to finance. The size and depth of dollar capital markets create thick market externalities that attract both investors and issuers. The more investors enter the market, the more issuers they attract, and vice versa. Long-term investors such as pension funds and life insurance companies have long-term obligations to their policyholders and thus demand long-term assets to match duration for asset-liability management.

For investors operating outside the United States, there are often not enough securities, or not enough diversity of securities, in their home markets to fill their very large balance sheets. Such investors typically have globally diversified asset portfolios that include large shares of dollar-denominated securities. As these long-term investors' obligations to policyholders and beneficiaries are generally in their local currency, many of them hedge the currency risk using FX swaps.[3] This is where global banks enter the story, as they are the counterparties to investors who wish to hedge by borrowing dollars. These banks (mostly non–US banks) will source dollars in wholesale dollar funding markets. For this reason, the global banking system itself runs on dollars.

---

3. The degree to which currency risk is hedged depends on the type of asset and the type of investor. Equity portfolios are generally more volatile and have less predictable cash flows than fixed-income portfolios and are thus hedged to a lesser extent. Investors that are more tightly regulated, such as insurance companies, tend to have more conservative exposures than other types of investors, such as pension funds and asset managers. See McGuire et al. (2021) for a discussion.

Figure 22.2

Foreign exchange swaps, foreign exchange forwards, and currency swaps outstanding as percent of world GDP, 2001–22

a. By currency

percent of world GDP

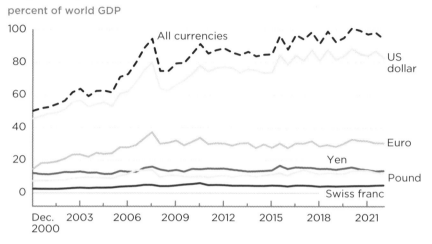

b. By maturity

percent of world GDP

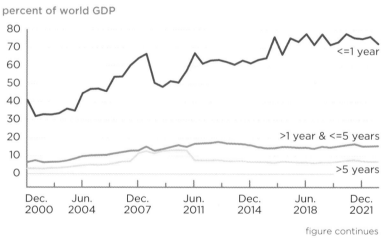

figure continues

Panel c of figure 22.2 gives a sense of the relative importance of the real and financial sector pieces of the FX swap market. On the real side, world trade grew very rapidly until roughly the global financial crisis but has since flatlined. The use of FX swaps/forwards by nonfinancial users, mainly importers and exporters to hedge accounts receivables/payables, has kept pace (see the light gray shaded area in the figure). The amounts involved are small relative to the use of these instruments by the financial

Figure 22.2 continued

Foreign exchange swaps, foreign exchange forwards, and currency swaps outstanding as percent of world GDP, 2001–22

c. By counterparty sector

percent of world GDP

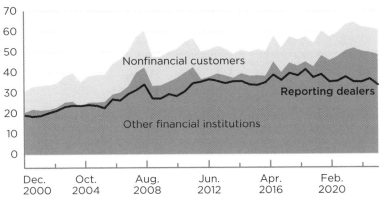

Sources: IMF, *World Economic Outlook*, October 2022, for world GDP and BIS over-the-counter (OTC) derivatives statistics, November 2022, for the derivatives data.

sector. "Other financial institutions" (the dark gray-shaded area, our proxy for NBFIs) have emerged as the dominant players.[4,5] Their dominance partly reflects the growth in outward portfolio investment by pension funds, insurance companies, and asset managers in countries with aging populations. McGuire et al. (2021), for example, document a sharp rise in such investment and demand for FX hedging services by NBFIs in six Asian economies.

Economic Asymmetry in Foreign Exchange Swap Markets

FX swaps have attributes of collateralized borrowing in which a currency instead of securities is used as collateral. Unlike repos and other forms of collateralized borrowing, the payment obligations are not recorded on the balance sheet as debt.

---

4. In the BIS derivatives statistics, the counterparty group "other financial institutions" comprises mainly NBFIs, but it also includes nonreporting banks.

5. In panel c of figure 22.2, the reporting dealers' portion is included for completeness; it captures activity associated with the banking sector that actually makes markets in these instruments.

Contractually, an FX swap is symmetric: Two parties exchange two currencies and reverse the transaction at a later agreed upon date. During the life of the contract, each party has a symmetric debt obligation to the other. At the macro level, however, the dominance of the dollar in the FX swap market gives rise to an economic asymmetry in the following sense. When there is a dollar shortage, borrowers of dollars in the FX swap market must join the scramble for dollar funding, even if they receive euros, yen, sterling, or Swiss francs in return. Their payment obligation is in dollars, so they must source dollars somehow. Typically, a long-term investor who has borrowed in dollars in the swap market has bought long-term dollar assets, such as long-dated Treasuries, agency securities, or dollar-denominated corporate bonds. Not all of these assets can be sold immediately to repay dollars in maturing swaps. In this respect, the dollar borrowers in the swap market face a maturity mismatch between short-term dollar payment obligations, which are due immediately, and long-term dollar assets, which are illiquid. The maturity mismatch is a natural consequence of banks' business model of intermediating short-term funds, given their overall funding model.

The asymmetry between the dollar and other currencies is most evident during periods of market stress. FX swaps and forwards require the payment of the full principal amount at maturity. As they are typically short term, they need to be rolled over frequently.[6] These attributes make FX swap markets vulnerable to funding squeezes, as was evident during the global financial crisis and again in March 2020, when the COVID-19 pandemic wrecked havoc. During these episodes, market participants scrambled to roll over dollar hedges just as dealer banks pulled back.

To the extent that financial firms in advanced economies account for the lion's share of FX swap activity, the vulnerability to dollar funding stresses is greater for advanced economies than emerging economies. It is only the accounting convention of disregarding swap repayment obligations as debt that obscures this vulnerability in normal times.

The economic asymmetry in FX swap markets shows up in the pricing of FX swaps. The interest rate on dollar borrowing implied by the forward exchange rate tends to diverge systematically from the interest rate in dollar money markets, in violation of covered interest parity. For much of the period after the global financial crisis, market participants paid more

6. Almost four-fifths of outstanding amounts at the end of June 2022 in panel b of figure 22.2 matured in less than a year. Data from the April 2022 BIS Triennial Survey show not only that instruments maturing within a week accounted for some 70 percent of FX swaps turnover but also that instruments maturing overnight accounted for more than 30 percent.

to borrow dollars in the FX swap market than in the dollar money market. This premium on dollar funding in FX swaps has fluctuated substantially, depending on financial conditions. It is one more example of the fluctuations in risk premiums highlighted by several contributors to this volume.

The dollar payment obligations associated with FX swaps/forwards are not measured well, presenting challenges for monitoring and mitigation. BIS statistics capture overall outstanding amounts; they do not provide information on how the dollar payment obligations are distributed across countries and sectors. Estimates based on assumptions detailed in Borio, McCauley, and McGuire (2017, 2022) put the dollar debt from FX swaps/forwards of nonbanks outside the United States at around $25 trillion in mid-2022, double their $13 trillion in on-balance sheet dollar debt. The estimate for non–US banks is about $35 trillion, more than double the estimated $15 trillion in on-balance sheet dollar debt.

Lack of information about the geography of dollar-denominated debt from FX swaps/forwards poses challenges to the implementation of policies to cushion shocks. To restore market functioning during the global financial crisis, and again in March 2020, central bank swap lines between the Federal Reserve and major central banks channeled dollars to central banks around the world, which on-lent to private financial institutions in jurisdictions that were scrambling for dollars. (See chapter 21 by Linda Goldberg in this volume.)

To the extent that the dollar shortages result from funding transactions of the largest non–US financial firms, the debt-like obligations are an advanced economy story. Central bank swap lines take on great significance for maintaining the orderly functioning of global capital markets. Through central bank swap lines, central banks can obtain dollar liquidity from the Federal Reserve to meet underlying demand from banks and nonbanks in their jurisdictions, which pledge domestic currency as collateral.

In March 2020, the Federal Reserve used its network of swap lines with 14 central banks to channel dollar liquidity globally, significantly easing global dollar funding conditions. Tapping the swap lines generated a sharp increase in global cross-border banking flows, particularly in cross-border claims on banks located in the United States (panels a and b in figure 22.3). This rise was less a reflection of the increased external funding needs of banks located in the United States and more the result of a sudden increase in global demand for dollar liquidity—a symptom of a system under stress. In effect, the Fed provided a grand dollar overdraft to backstop the global dollar financial system (Aldasoro et al. 2020).

These exceptional movements reflect the ways in which banks manage liquidity across borders through their global network of branches and

Figure 22.3

Cross-border banking flows and central bank swap lines, 2017–20

a. Cross-border claims on the United States, by sector

quarterly changes, billions of dollars

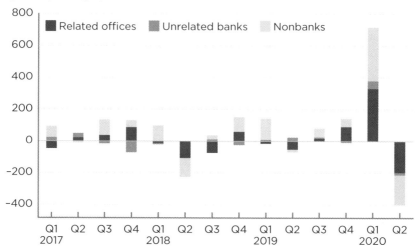

b. Non-US banks' US dollar intragroup claims

quarterly changes, billions of dollars

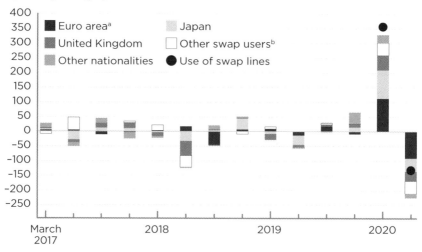

a. Banks headquartered in any of the 13 BIS reporting euro area countries.
b. Comprises Australia, Switzerland, Denmark, South Korea, Mexico, Norway, and Singapore (South Korea and Mexico started to use their swap lines in 2020Q2).

figure continues

Figure 22.3 continued

Cross-border banking flows and central bank swap lines, 2017–20

c. Local positions of foreign affiliates in the United States, 2020

billions of dollars

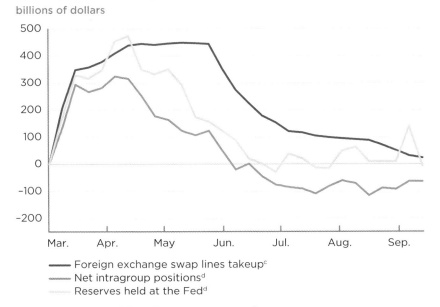

— Foreign exchange swap lines takeup[c]
— Net intragroup positions[d]
····· Reserves held at the Fed[d]

c. Central bank liquidity swaps outstanding.
d. Cumulative weekly changes since March 18, 2020, at foreign branches and agencies in the United States.

Source: Aldasoro et al. (2020).

subsidiaries. By end-March 2020, a total of $358 billion had been drawn, most prominently by banks in the euro area, Japan, and the United Kingdom. The overall rise in these banks' dollar-denominated intragroup claims correlates with the uptake at their central banks' dollar auctions. The use of swap lines illustrates the mechanics of cross-border capital flows as well as the "elastic" nature of the global banking system, which comprises both central and commercial banks (panel c of figure 22.3).

Three main lessons emerge from an examination of the FX swap market:

1. Although attention has often focused on the current account, the bigger issue for global financial conditions stems from the large gross flows associated with the role of the dollar as the funding currency of choice in capital markets.

2. Although dollar shortages often focus on emerging-market economies, the protagonists in dollar funding scrambles are financial firms in advanced economies.
3. Central bank dollar swap lines are the essential backstop that keeps the global financial system on an even keel.

References

Aldasoro, I., C. Cabanilla, P. Disyatat, T. Ehlers, P. McGuire, and G. Von Peter. 2020. Central Bank Swap Lines and Cross-Border Bank Flows. *BIS Bulletin* 34, December.

Avdjiev, S., R. McCauley, and H.S. Shin. 2016. Breaking Free of the Triple Coincidence in International Finance. *Economic Policy* 31, no. 87.

BIS (Bank for International Settlements). 2022a. BIS Triennial Central Bank Survey. Basel.

BIS (Bank for International Settlements). 2022b. Over-the-Counter (OTC) Derivatives Statistics (November). Basel.

Borio, C., R. McCauley, and P. McGuire. 2017. FX Swaps and Forwards: Missing Global Debt? *BIS Quarterly Review* (September).

Borio, C., R. McCauley, and P. McGuire. 2022. Dollar Debt in FX Swaps and Forwards: Huge, Missing and Growing. *BIS Quarterly Review* (December).

Maggiori, M., B. Neiman, and J. Schreger. 2020. International Currencies and Capital Allocation. *Journal of Political Economy* 128, no. 6.

McGuire, P., I. Shim, H.S. Shin, and V. Sushko. 2021. Outward Portfolio Investment and Dollar Funding in Emerging Asia. *BIS Quarterly Review* (December).

Obstfeld, M., and H. Zhou. 2022. The Global Dollar Cycle. *Brookings Papers on Economic Activity* (Fall): 361–427. Washington: Brookings Institution.

Shin, H.S. 2016. Global Liquidity and Procyclicality. Speech at the World Bank Conference "The State of Economics, The State of the World," June 8. Washington: World Bank.

23

Dollar Dominance in Global Finance and Exchange Rate Policies

ŞEBNEM KALEMLI-ÖZCAN

Fifty years after many predicted it would lose its primacy with the end of the Bretton Woods system, the US dollar remains the dominant currency in the international system. The dollar's unique role gained special salience recently because of its weaponization amid the financial sanctions Russia faced after invading Ukraine. The current consensus is that there is no alternative hegemonic currency—but this need not remain the case forever. To inform the debate over the dollar's present and prospective role, we need to understand how the dollar retains its dominant place, why other currencies cannot (for now) replace it, and what the dollar's dominance implies for the world economy and exchange rate policies.

A dominant currency plays a central role in world trade, world finance, and central banks' reserves. It serves as a medium of exchange, a unit of account, and a store of value throughout the global economy. The dollar satisfies all these three requirements for a dominant currency. The euro and the renminbi do not.

Although the role of the dollar in world trade is singular, I focus here on its dominant role in world finance and central bank reserves. The reason for this focus is the theme of this conference: how well the floating exchange rate system is doing 50 years after its birth. Nurkse (1944) describes the potentially destabilizing effects of floating exchange rates; Friedman (1953)

Şebnem Kalemli-Özcan is the Neil Moskowitz Endowed Professor of Economics at the University of Maryland-College Park, coeditor of the *American Economic Journal: Macro*, and an NBER and CEPR research associate. She serves on the editorial board of the *American Economic Review*.

focuses on the shock-absorbing properties of flexible rates. Floating rates absorb a large fraction of risk premia shocks (Kalemli-Özcan 2019), which are frequent in the global financial system (Rey 2013). Floating exchange rate countries enjoy higher output and lower output volatility than fixed exchange rate countries in the face of these risk premia (or "sentiment" shocks.) The dominant role of the dollar in world finance makes the case for countries to have flexible exchange rates vis-à-vis the dollar, protecting them from risk sentiment shocks that are global in nature and also linked to fluctuations in US monetary policy.

One striking development of the past 50 years has been the growth of emerging economies, their progressive integration into global markets for goods and assets, and in many cases their embrace of greater exchange rate flexibility. Since the 1990s, emerging-market economies have suffered when the dollar strengthened. Obstfeld and Zhou (2022) show that, even if the dollar initially appreciates only against advanced-economy currencies, emerging markets suffer negative effects, including depreciations of their own currencies. Bruno and Shin (2015) show that the dollar is unique among advanced currencies in this way and that its impacts work largely through the bilateral dollar exchange rates of the emerging markets. As a result, emerging markets are very reluctant to let their exchange rates float vis-à-vis the dollar—"fear of floating" (Calvo and Reinhart 2002)—and therefore usually operate managed floats. They accumulate dollar reserves, which help them put their savings in a safe asset and gives them the power to manage their currencies with foreign exchange interventions in response to financial shocks.

A large body of literature on the global financial cycle that began with the work of Rey (2013) and was extended by Miranda-Agrippino and Rey (2020) shows the important role of risk sentiment shocks for financial and real outcomes across the world. This line of work argues that the expenditure-switching property of a flexible exchange rate may not be enough to insulate countries from global financial shocks: Countries may face a dilemma between financial openness and monetary autonomy rather than a trilemma in which exchange rate flexibility allows monetary policy freedom despite openness to international capital flows. That is, even with flexible exchange rates, countries are exposed to financial risk/sentiment shocks. This is because even a favorable shift in net exports will not entirely protect a country's financial markets if global investors take a risk-off position and run for the safety of the dollar. However, in such a scenario, flexible exchange rates can still help via asset markets instead of limited help via goods market, as Kalemli-Özcan (2019) shows. In this risk-off environment, flexible exchange rates help because of their risk premia-absorbing properties, as argued by Friedman (1953), leading to a smaller rise in risk premia and lower capital outflows, resulting in a soft landing for their domestic economies.

This risk shock–absorbing property of flexible rates is important for emerging markets because the main reason they suffer more than advanced economies from a US dollar appreciation is the greater risk sensitivity of their capital flows (Kalemli-Özcan 2019, Di Giovanni et al. 2022). Any risk-off episode will be priced in as higher borrowing costs for emerging markets, for their firms and sovereigns, captured by higher sovereign spreads on dollar borrowing (Longstaff et al. 2011) and higher uncovered interest parity (UIP) risk premia on local currency borrowing of private agents (Kalemli-Özcan 2019). Thus, UIP, a key international wedge, passes thorough domestic lending rates for households and firms (Di Giovanni et al. 2022). These effects do not occur in advanced economies as capital flows to those countries are less sensitive to risk.

How is US Monetary Policy Transmitted to the Rest of the World?

The literature on the global financial cycle also connects risk sentiment shocks to US monetary policy, as US policy transmits strongly through US financial markets, a critical component of global financial markets. As a result, it is hard to separate the impact on emerging markets of US dollar shocks, risk-off shocks, per se, from that of US monetary policy, as US monetary policy affects both the dollar and the relative pricing of risky and risk-free assets in financial markets, where emerging markets account for a large share of risky assets.

To see how transmission occurs, consider the effect of US monetary policy on Mexico. A tighter US policy will lead to dollar appreciation and peso depreciation, which, if trade elasticities are high enough, leads to higher export values and lower import values for Mexico via expenditure switching. In theory, this trade channel should have an expansionary effect in Mexico. But the data show that depreciations in emerging markets are generally contractionary.

Some models were developed to explain why, focusing on balance sheets (Krugman 1999; Cespedes, Chang, and Velasco 2004). A higher domestic value of dollar-denominated debts, as a result of dollar appreciation, weakens Mexican balance sheets, thereby hampering borrowing and investment, counteracting the expansionary force of higher net exports. The need to import intermediate inputs can amplify the contraction (Mendoza and Yue 2012), leading to recessions.

Another explanation is that higher US interest rates raise borrowing costs. And because emerging markets are a risky asset class, tighter monetary policy in the United States also means higher risk premia in such countries.

Mexico's own monetary policy response is also endogenous and has an impact. Tight monetary policy in Mexico could be attractive if exchange rate pass-through leads to inflation; however, if the financial channel is very strong, leading to higher risk premia and capital outflows, resulting in a contraction in Mexico and a tighter monetary policy will make everything worse. During sudden stop events, related to tight US monetary policy, emerging markets cannot borrow to smooth shocks; even if they tighten monetary policy, due to higher risk premia, capital will flow in only one direction (out of Mexico, into the United States). Higher policy rates combined with higher risk premia slow the economy, limiting the availability of external finance even more. Any policy that aims for a bigger external deficit after a sudden stop would thus just force risk premia up until the desired current account deficit falls to a level consistent with the limited amount foreign lenders are willing to provide. If balance sheet effects are of no concern—that is, the volume of dollar debt in Mexico is low—a more accommodative monetary policy by Mexico's central bank is preferable, as peso depreciation would absorb the higher risk premia, lowering the cost of external finance for Mexico and stabilizing output.

Figure 23.1 (from Kalemli-Özcan 2019) shows how risk premia act differently in emerging markets and advanced economies in response to an exogenous tightening of US monetary policy. When US monetary policy tightens, the difference between the yield on 12-month domestic government bond and 12-month US Treasuries rises more in countries like Mexico than in countries like Canada. In fact, the spread falls in advanced economies, which let their exchange rates depreciate vis-à-vis the dollar and do not tighten their monetary policies in response to the US tightening. In emerging markets, spreads rise even if they do not tighten their monetary policy in response to US tightening, because of higher risk premia, as global investors switch to a risk-off mindset (De Leo, Gopinath, and Kalemli-Özcan 2023).

De Leo, Gopinath, and Kalemli-Özcan (2023) also show the contractionary effects of US tightening on emerging markets even if they loosen their monetary policy. Output falls; capital flows out; and inflation rises initially, as a result of the peso depreciation, before falling, as a result of a slowing economy.

A looser monetary policy may not be the optimal policy. Kalemli-Özcan (2019) shows that looser policy and depreciated exchange rates serve

Figure 23.1
Responses of sovereign spreads to US monetary policy tightening (US 3-month Treasury rate shock)

a. Emerging-market economies

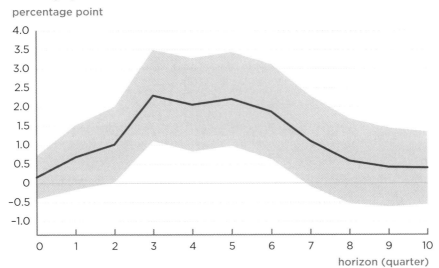

b. Advanced economies

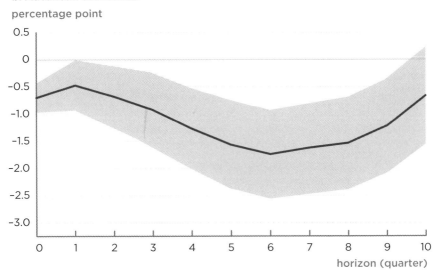

Source: Kalemli-Özcan (2019).

Figure 23.2

Responses in emerging markets to a risk-off (VIX) shock in the United States

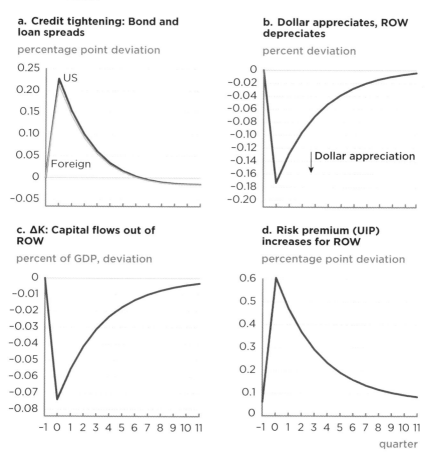

a. Credit tightening: Bond and
loan spreads

percentage point deviation

b. Dollar appreciates, ROW
depreciates

percent deviation

c. ΔK: Capital flows out of
ROW

percent of GDP, deviation

d. Risk premium (UIP)
increases for ROW

percentage point deviation

quarter

ROW = rest of world
Source: Akinci, Kalemli-Özcan, and Queralto (2022).

emerging markets much better in the face of tighter US policy that induces a risk-off sentiment. Gourinchas (2018) shows that an easier policy would be optimal to stimulate the domestic economy; the fact that the peso is depreciating is irrelevant and should not be counteracted with tighter policy to fight the depreciation and attract capital. Kalemli-Özcan (2019) shows that this is the case because a tighter policy increases risk premia and makes the contraction even deeper but does not solve the depreciation problem.

Figure 23.2 digs deeper into the reasons for the contractionary effects of a US tightening in emerging-market economies. Such tightening creates a risk-off environment globally. Using the calibrated open-economy model, Akinci, Kalemli-Özcan, and Queralto (2022) plot the simulated results of a positive uncertainty/risk-off shock, measured by the VIX (the Volatility Index of the Chicago Board Options Exchange [CBOE]). Although it is a US market variable, the VIX captures global uncertainty shocks, because volatility in US financial markets is a prime driver of volatility in global financial markets. Higher uncertainty in the United States leads to higher borrowing costs, wider credit spreads, an appreciation of the dollar, and capital outflows from emerging markets. Risk premia—measured as excess returns on emerging-market currencies compared with an uncovered interest parity benchmark—also rise.

Benefits of Floating Exchange Rates

The evidence strongly shows the benefits of floating exchange rates, especially given the central role of the dollar in world finance and the global financial cycle. Floating rates absorb risk premia shocks rooted mainly in US financial markets, which can result from changes in US monetary policy that spread to the world given the dominant role of the dollar in global financial transactions.

One original intention of the move to floating exchange rates 50 years ago was to reduce systemic asymmetry associated with the dollar's special status. That goal was not achieved; dollar dominance is a by-product of the current system.

Another was for flexible exchange rates to absorb macroeconomic shocks. Given the interconnected nature of the global financial system, today's macroeconomic shocks are increasingly macro-financial shocks rather than more conventional productivity or demand shocks. Despite concerns that floating exchange rates provide little insulation from the global financial cycle (because switching demand for goods via net exports cannot fully offset financial shocks), the evidence shows that floating exchange rates have indeed been absorbing global risk shocks. Policymakers in emerging-market countries should take note and reevaluate exchange rate management policies that may lead to greater exposure to global financial shocks.

References

Akinci, O., Ş. Kalemli-Özcan, and A. Queralto. 2022. *Uncertainty Shocks, Capital Flows, and International Risk Spillovers*. NBER Working Paper w30026. Cambridge, MA: National Bureau of Economic Research.

Bruno, V., and H.S. Shin. 2015. Cross-Border Banking and Global Liquidity. *Review of Economic Studies* 82, no. 2: 535–64.

Calvo, G.A., and C.M. Reinhart. 2002. Fear of Floating. *Quarterly Journal of Economics* 117, no. 2: 379–408.

Cespedes, L., R. Chang, and A. Velasco. 2004. Balance Sheets and Exchange Rate Policy. *American Economic Review* 94, no. 4: 1183–93.

De Leo, P., G. Gopinath, and Ş. Kalemli-Özcan. 2023 (revised). *Monetary Policy Cyclicality in Emerging Economies*. NBER Working Paper w30458. Cambridge, MA: National Bureau of Economic Research.

Di Giovanni, J., Ş. Kalemli-Özcan, M.F. Ulu, and Y.S. Baskaya. 2022. International Spillovers and Local Credit Cycles. *Review of Economic Studies* 89, no. 2: 733–73.

Friedman, Milton. 1953. *Essays in Positive Economics*. Chicago: University of Chicago Press.

Gourinchas, Pierre-Olivier. 2018. Monetary Policy Transmission in Emerging Markets: An Application to Chile. In *Monetary Policy and Global Spillovers: Mechanisms, Effects and Policy Measures*, ed. Enrique G. Mendoza, Ernesto Pastén, and Diego Saravia. Santiago: Central Bank of Chile.

Kalemli-Özcan, Şebnem. 2019. US Monetary Policy and International Spillovers. In *Challenges for Monetary Policy*. Jackson Hole Symposium Proceedings. Kansas City, MO: Federal Reserve Bank of Kansas City.

Krugman, Paul R. 1999. Balance Sheets, the Transfer Problem, and Financial Crises. *International Tax and Public Finance* 6 (November): 459–72.

Longstaff, F.A., J. Pan, L.H. Pedersen, and K.J. Singleton. 2011. How Sovereign Is Sovereign Credit Risk? *American Economic Journal: Macroeconomics* 3, no. 2: 75–103.

Mendoza, Enrique, and Vivian Z. Yue. 2012. A General Equilibrium Model of Sovereign Default and Business Cycles. *Quarterly Journal of Economics* 127, no. 2: 889–946.

Miranda-Agrippino, S., and H. Rey. 2020. US Monetary Policy and the Global Financial Cycle. *Review of Economic Studies* 87, no. 6: 2754–76.

Nurkse, Ragnar. 1944. *International Currency Experience: Lessons of the Inter-War Period*. Geneva: Economic and Financial Office, League of Nations.

Obstfeld, M., and H. Zhou. 2022. The Global Dollar Cycle. *Brookings Papers on Economic Activity* (Fall): 361–427. Washington: Brookings Institution.

Rey, Hélène. 2013. Dilemma Not Trilemma: The Global Financial Cycle and Monetary Policy Independence. In *Global Dimensions of Unconventional Monetary Policy*. Jackson Hole Symposium Proceedings. Kansas City, MO: Federal Reserve Bank of Kansas City.

24

Strengths and Flaws of the Dollar-Based System

HÉLÈNE REY

Global public goods are goods accessible to all countries, though countries do not necessarily have an individual interest in producing these goods (Kindleberger 1986). The global public goods most often cited are the maintenance of peace or the preservation of the planet. From an economic perspective, the Great Depression of the 1930s brought to the fore global public goods such as an open and regulated international trading system or economic institutions and policies that ensure monetary and financial stability. An attempt to build such institutions was consciously made in 1944 with the Bretton Woods regime.

Since the collapse of the fixed exchange rate system and the convertibility of the dollar into gold 50 years ago, the international monetary system has become more ill-defined. Is the new dollar-based system providing the global public goods the world needs? What are its strengths and weaknesses?

Hegemony and the Stability of the International Financial System

According to Kindleberger (1973), it is essential that a hegemon stabilize the international financial system. Periods of transition between great powers—such as the 1930s, when the economic influence of the United

Hélène Rey is the Lord Bagri Professor of Economics at London Business School. This chapter does not represent the views of the Haut Conseil de Stabilité Financière (the French macroprudential authority), of which the author is a member.

Kingdom waned and that of the United States was not yet fully established—are considered particularly dangerous for financial stability.

A hegemon provides various global public goods. It provides open markets in times of gluts, supplies in times of acute shortages, steady flows of capital to developing economies, international money, the coordination of macroeconomic policy, and last resort lending (Kindleberger 1986).

The hegemon's economic leadership is often contested. In the 1960s, for example, France became increasingly frustrated with the asymmetries inherent to Bretton Woods. On February 16, 1965, Valéry Giscard d'Estaing, President Charles de Gaulle's minister of finance, echoing the General's words at a press conference on February 4, famously summarized them by saying that the country issuing the reserve currency enjoys an "exorbitant privilege." He was referring to the fact that in the event of a deficit, the United States does not have to take restrictive measures because it has the possibility of issuing securities that are always in high demand by the rest of the world, thanks to the international role of the dollar—an advantage he considered unfair.

One of the key facts underlying the architecture of the international monetary and financial system is that the hegemon provides safe assets to the rest of the world. For this to be the case, the hegemon must have strong fiscal governance and institutions, a broad and liquid market, and a robust and transparent financial ecosystem. The United States is a global banker, with long positions in risky foreign assets and risk-free liquid liabilities in dollars (Bénétrix, Lane, and Shambaugh 2015), thus meeting the strong demand from the foreign public and private sectors, as Gourinchas and Rey (2007a), Krishnamurthy and Vissing-Jorgensen (2012) and Gourinchas, Rey, and Sauzet (2019) show.

The dollar exchange rate is a key relative price in the global economy and in international commodity and financial markets. Gopinath et al. (2020) show the importance of dollar invoicing for international trade. Chahrour and Valchev (2022) analyze the links between international trade finance and the dominant currency. Ilzetski, Reinhart, and Rogoff (2019) show that a large part of the world economy is a dollar zone because of the de facto exchange rate regimes stabilizing numerous currencies vis-à-vis the dollar. Obstfeld and Zhou (2022) document that dollar appreciation shocks predict declines in output, consumption, investment, and government spending in for emerging-market and developing economies. These shocks can be caused by several factors, such as US monetary policy or pressures in international or domestic markets for dollar funds, which themselves may be correlated with global risk appetite. Hikes in the federal funds rate lower the risk tolerance of investors—the risk-taking channel of monetary policy (Borio and Zhu 2012)—with strong effects on capital flows; credit spreads; and, for emerging markets, sovereign risk premia (Kalemli-Özcan 2019; Miranda-Agrippino and Rey 2020; Degasperi, Hong, and Ricco 2021; Cesa-Bianchi and Sokol 2022; Bauer, Bernanke, and Milstein 2023). Obstfeld (2022) discusses the strong links between dollar and commodity markets. Gourinchas and Rey (2007b) note that the issuance of international currency confers on the hegemon excess returns on its net foreign asset position, facilitating the process of international adjustment and reinforcing the robustness of the position of the center country (the exorbitant privilege).

In normal times, these excess returns come from the global banking activity of the hegemon; in times of global crisis, when the value of safe US assets in dollars held by the rest of the world appreciates while the prices of risky assets the United States holds abroad fall (these assets tend to be in foreign currencies), they are associated with large net transfers of wealth to the rest of the world. These wealth transfers reflect the hegemon's provision of insurance to the rest of the world in times of global turmoil—the "exorbitant duty" (Gourinchas and Rey 2022, Kekre and Lenel 2021).

In recent years, the net positions in equity and foreign direct investment of the United States have turned negative, because of the high returns on US external equity liabilities since 2008 (Atkeson, Heathcote, and Perri 2022), and the United States' net debt position has moved farther into negative territory (Lane and Milesi-Ferretti 2018).[1] Exchange rate effects now dominate the wealth transfer to the rest of world: The dollar appreciates in bad times and increases the value of safe dollar assets held by foreign residents, while the value of US equity investment abroad (in foreign currencies and mostly unhedged for exchange rate risk) decreases. As the net foreign asset position of the United States deteriorates over time, the value of the "exorbitant privilege" seems to have declined (Gourinchas 2023), although it remained positive over the postwar period as a whole.

For the hegemon, this external balance sheet structure with most liabilities in dollars and most assets in foreign currencies contributes to international financial stability by transferring resources form the United States to the rest of the world during a global crisis, such as the financial crisis of 2007–09. Between the fourth quarter of 2007 and the first quarter of 2009, the wealth transfer from the United States to the rest of the world represented about 13 percent of US GDP (Gourinchas and Rey 2022). This transfer is the other side of the coin of its exorbitant privilege in normal

---

1. As returns are highly volatile, it may be too early to determine whether this trend is cyclical or secular. Similarly, the "exorbitant privilege" has to be computed on long time series in order to not be dominated by cyclical fluctuations.

times; it can be considered a kind of insurance fee. During times of global stress, the real resource transfer may also be associated with international liquidity support via swap lines: The hegemon central bank is the issuer of the international currency and acts as a lender of last resort. At the peak of the financial panic of 2008, swap lines between the Federal Reserve and the European Central Bank were instrumental in stabilizing the European banking sector, which was exposed to a dollar shortage as a result of duration mismatch between assets and liabilities. As C. Fred Bergsten noted during the conference, the provision of public goods such as insurance during periods of stress or being the "importer of last resort" should not be taken for granted; future US administrations may take very different attitudes from those of the post–World War II period in this respect. Kindleberger (1986, 8) ventures that a hegemon may be "willing to bear an undue part of the short-run costs of these goods, either because it regards itself as gaining in the long run, because it is paid in a different coin, such as prestige, glory, immortality, or some combination of the two." These rewards are bound to have very different appeals for different administrations.

Absence of Qualified Competitors

The roles of a dominant international currency are multiple and involve the three classic functions of money: medium of exchange, store of value, and unit of account. There are many synergies between the international use of a currency in its various roles. These complementarities, on top of the network externalities associated with the medium of exchange function, reinforce the domination of the hegemonic currency and perpetuate it. For this reason, existing international currencies are difficult to replace. If a currency does not belong to an ecosystem with large and liquid financial markets, with good fiscal governance, transparency in property rights, and open markets, it has little chance of being embraced by many actors in the world economy.

The renminbi lacks many of these characteristics. Because of the efforts by the Chinese leadership to broaden its role in invoicing, trade credit, and commodity markets, use of the renminbi will likely increase in goods and possibly in commodity trade. It may become more of an anchor currency for a number of countries, especially countries along the Belt and Road. It will not gain much more international status, however, until Chinese financial markets open up and become resilient, liquid, and broad.

The euro has more potential in the short run, but the resilience of safe assets denominated in euros remains questionable unless the fiscal framework of the euro area improves. In times of global stress, the euro area experiences capital flight from the periphery to the core and widening spreads, as there are no generic euro area safe assets (there are only small issuances of joint EU liabilities via a limited number of programs). Instead, one observes market segmentation of national bond markets.

Cryptocurrencies are also disqualified as international currencies. In many cases, they lack the most basic properties of good money, and in all cases they lack proper governance, fiscal backing, and a financial ecosystem.

The Vanishing Hegemon and the New Triffin Dilemma

The asymmetry inherent in a hegemonic system can create financial fragilities that eventually lead to its disappearance. In the early 1960s, Yale economics professor Robert Triffin noted that the United States would not be able to simultaneously provide the international liquidity needed for the global economy and maintain the parity of the dollar with gold, as required by the Bretton Woods system. The world would face a growing shortage of international liquidity or confidence in the value of the dollar would plummet—the famous Triffin Dilemma (1961).

Triffin's analysis turned out to be prescient. As dollar liabilities exceeded the United States' stock of gold, capital flight took place, forcing policymakers to abandon the peg between the dollar and gold in the early 1970s.

Triffin's analysis was incomplete, however, because despite the abandonment of the dollar-gold peg, the dominance of the dollar has increased since the collapse of the Bretton Woods exchange rate system in 1973. In a world in which the United States can issue the international currency at will and invest it in illiquid assets (the role of world banker), it is vital that it maintain the confidence of the rest of the world. Doing so is bound to become increasingly difficult as the relative size of the US economy shrinks: The demand for dollar-denominated assets backed by the US Treasury tends to grow in tandem with the world economy, but in the process, the United States' fiscal capacity to provide that backing is likely to shrink in relative terms. Moreover, the interest rates investors demand may jump upward if risk aversion is on the rise.

This "vanishing hegemon" problem (Gourinchas and Rey 2022) is one of the factors that may contribute to the downward trend in the real rate, as demand for safe assets increases more rapidly than their supply. A flight of capital could occur not because investors fear a drop in the parity with gold, as in the 1960s, but because they fear a fall in the dollar exchange rate if the fiscal capacity of the United States to honor its debts is called into question. External liabilities could also depreciate because of geopolitical motivations, such as seizures or freezes of official foreign exchange reserves, as Obstfeld (2023) notes. The international monetary and financial system may thus be facing a New Triffin Dilemma (Gourinchas and Rey 2007a; Farhi, Gourinchas, and Rey 2011; Obstfeld 2013; Farhi and Maggiori 2018).

A Multipolar World?

In principle, the emergence of a multipolar world could solve the New Triffin Dilemma. By increasing the supply of reserve assets, a multipolar world naturally solves the Triffin Dilemma, provided confidence in the issuers of all the safe assets can be maintained. A multipolar world expands the fiscal capacity underlying the provision of safe assets. This fiscal capacity would be determined by the collective ability of the countries issuing the reserve currencies, so it can adapt and grow with the needs of the global economy. In a multipolar world, countries that issue reserve assets would be able to benefit from the "exorbitant privilege" as long as their fiscal capacity and credibility allow them to maintain their status as issuers of reserve assets.

Finally, through an increase in the degree of substitution between different reserve assets, a multipolar world would limit movements in the interest rate (the price of reserve assets) and potentially alter the downward trend in real rates (though many other factors are at play), as the supply of safe assets would increase. For all of these reasons, it could be desirable to accelerate the transition to a multipolar world.[2]

There is, however, the possibility that a multipolar world would exacerbate economic and financial shocks, as Farhi, Gourinchas, and Rey (2011) note. The emergence of a multipolar world implies the coexistence of safe assets denominated in different currencies, which must be seen as largely interchangeable. A corollary of this substitutability is that small changes in fundamentals—or the perception of these fundamentals—can cause massive capital flows. Loss of trust in one of the reserve currencies could trigger capital flight, for example, as comparable investment opportunities.

Imagine a world in which the United States, China, and the eurozone each issue a reserve currency. Their assets are regarded as highly substitutable in terms of liquidity, safety, and performance. Now suppose that one of these regions—say, China—experiences a financial crisis that tests the country's fiscal capacity. Investors would immediately attempt to switch their holdings of renminbi-denominated assets into euro- or dollar-denominated assets, which would be perceived as less risky. This phenomenon would be reinforced by strategic complementarities among investors,

---

2. Such a transition would also have large geopolitical implications, which are not discussed here.

which may make the system prone to self-fulfilling portfolio shifts. The value of a currency to an investor depends crucially on the perception of other investors; a currency could suddenly lose its reserve currency status following a collective loss of confidence in its value. Such a shift would be accompanied by violent capital flows as well as potentially large fluctuations in exchange rates and interest rates. The impact of this sudden stop on the integrated world economy could be severe.

An episode of this type would also endogenously reduce the supply of safe assets in the global economy, reinforcing the Triffin Dilemma. In the absence of fundamental shocks, such crises may find their origin in self-fulfilling phenomena. These crises could well create run dynamics among investors, whose individual interest lies in anticipating the runs by converting their reserves before the others do. A multipolar world is thus likely to experience periods of stability alternating with periods of crisis.

Some of these mechanisms were at work within the eurozone during the European sovereign debt crisis, albeit on a smaller scale. From 1999 until the summer of 2009, the debt securities of European states were regarded as relatively interchangeable, with very low spreads. The Greek crisis shattered this perception, and massive portfolio flights out of the periphery in favor of core countries (such as Germany) occurred.

The shift toward a multipolar world may be unavoidable, given the changes in the relative size of the economic blocs and the geopolitical fragmentation, and it may be desirable from the point of view of the New Triffin Dilemma. But it may also be a very risky transformation for the world economy. And from the point of view of the provision of global public goods, it remains unclear whether such a system can deliver financial stability and perform an operational lender of last resort function, which would likely require some cooperation among reserve currency issuers. A plausible outcome may be increased regionalization of currencies and the provision of regional public goods to the detriment of global integration. Such an outcome would create tensions and make the job of multilateral institutions such as the International Monetary Fund even more challenging.

A Dollar-Based System in Need of Reform

Within the current dollar-based system, it is desirable to encourage governments of emerging countries to set up effective lender of last resort systems in their economies. Having such a system is part of good market infrastructure, alongside avoiding foreign currency liabilities, developing local currency markets, and increasing fiscal capacity and equity-based finance. Public authorities have a comparative advantage in providing liquidity during times of macroeconomic crisis, thanks to the sovereign power of taxation, which gives them considerable resources and a long-term perspective. In times of crisis, it is natural for public authorities to provide liquidity in the form of recapitalizations, debt guarantees, loans against collateral with central banks, asset purchases, and so forth.

The natural counterpart to this function of lender of last resort is the requirement to regulate beneficiary financial institutions in order to reduce moral hazard (Farhi and Tirole 2012). The current dollar system, characterized by large, procyclical capital flows and excessive risk taking, is prone to financial crisis (see Calvo, Leiderman, and Reinhart 1996; Reinhart and Rogoff 2009).

A sophisticated macroprudential framework, possibly including capital flow management tools, should be a key piece of the financial architecture to manage systemic risk and deal with the global financial cycle (Rey 2013). Flexible exchange rates can help buffer shocks (Obstfeld, Ostry, and Qureshi 2019), but they can do so more effectively if they are supported by a credible central bank and a credible macroprudential authority. Tools other than monetary policy are in general needed to set the stance of monetary and financial conditions according to domestic goals. More discussion on global liquidity management would also help (Eichengreen et al. 2011).

The macroprudential arsenal contains multiple weapons. Basel III introduces a countercyclical capital buffer to absorb losses and avoid credit crunches in bad times. For real estate, which has historically been associated with the worst financial crises, limits on debt service to income ratios for borrowers or additional sectoral capital buffers for banks may be used. At the heart of the excessive risk-taking mechanism is often the ability of financial intermediaries to quickly take on debt at high levels when financing conditions are favorable. Credit seems overly sensitive to funding costs. Regulation should aim to prevent risk-taking from being excessively procyclical, in borrowing and in lending countries. By imposing stricter limits on leverage, limiting the extent of exposures, dollarizing of liabilities, and requiring liquidity buffers financial regulators and supervisors can reduce the ability of the financial system to engage in destabilizing spirals. A complementary option is to perform frequent stress tests of the balance sheet of the financial sector (banks and nonbanks).

Conclusions and Further Thoughts

The New Triffin Dilemma could be alleviated by switching to a more multipolar system, if several credible reserve currency ecosystems emerge. The transition to a more multipolar international monetary system is fraught with risks, however, as it is not clear how the global public goods linked to the hegemonic position of the dollar in the international system since Bretton Woods would be provided in a world with competing reserve currencies, let alone in a world with disruptive geopolitical fragmentation. The development of macroprudential tools would make the current imperfect dollar-based system, in which the Federal Reserve has major influence on international financial market conditions, more manageable. More adequately taking into account the risk-taking channel of monetary policy in economic models would be highly desirable (Bruno and Shin 2015a, 2015b; Coimbra and Rey 2023; Coimbra, Kim, and Rey 2022).

In the current dollar-based financial system, cross-border financial flows reflect two global factors: the global financial cycle and the global commodity and trade cycle (Davis, Van Wincoop, and Valente 2021; Miranda-Agrippino and Rey 2022; Aldasoro et al. 2023). The current financial architecture appears unable to channel capital to places where it would have high marginal social value (for example, to help deal with climate and biodiversity loss mitigation and adaptation). It created massive volumes of dollar-denominated asset-backed mortgage securities, collateralized debt obligations, and other instruments that distorted real estate prices and contributed to the havoc that ensued in 2008. The world's incomprehensible and highly detrimental lack of action to clamp down on offshore centers has created a world in which capital flows are shaped partly by tax evasion and money laundering schemes (Lane and Milesi-Ferretti 2011, Coppola et al. 2021). This tendency could be exacerbated by the expanding use of cryptocurrencies, making it more urgent than ever to change the incentives of investors and create an infrastructure that transforms and complements the Bretton Woods institutions (the World Trade Organization, the International Monetary Fund, and the World Bank) so that they can deal with climate change and biodiversity loss. The pricing of greenhouse gases, the massive scaling up of blended finance to invest in energy transition mitigation and adaptation, and properly regulated carbon offset markets have to take center stage. By design these changes should profoundly alter the patterns of international capital flows.

References

Aldasoro, Iñaki, Stefan Avdjiev, Claudio Borio, and Piti Disyatat. 2023. Global and Domestic Financial Cycles: Variations on a Theme. *International Journal of Central Banking* 19, no. 5 (December).

Atkeson, Andrew, Jonathan Heathcote, and Fabrizio Perri. 2022. *The End of Privilege: A Reexamination of the Net Foreign Asset Position of the United States*. NBER Working Paper 29771. Cambridge, MA: National Bureau of Economic Research.

Bauer, Michael D., Ben S. Bernanke, and Eric Milstein. 2023. Risk Appetite and the Risk-Taking Channel of Monetary Policy. *Journal of Economic Perspective* 37, no. 1: 77–100.

Bénétrix, Agustin S., Philip R. Lane, and Jay C. Shambaugh. 2015. International currency exposures, valuation effects and the global financial crisis. *Journal of International Economics* 96, no. 1: 98–109.

Borio, Claudio, and Haibin Zhu. 2012. Capital Regulation, Risk-Taking and Monetary Policy: A Missing Link in the Transmission Mechanism? *Journal of Financial Stability* 8: 236–51.

Bruno, Valentina, and Hyun Song Shin. 2015a. Capital Flows and the Risk-Taking Channel of Monetary Policy. *Journal of Monetary Economics* 71: 119–32.

Bruno, Valentina, and Hyun Song Shin. 2015b. Cross-Border Banking and Global Liquidity. *Review of Economic Studies* 82, no. 2: 535–64.

Calvo, Guillermo A., Leonardo Leiderman, and Carmen M. Reinhart. 1996. Inflows of Capital to Developing Countries in the 1990s. *Journal of Economic Perspectives* 10, no. 2: 123–39.

Cesa-Bianchi, Ambrogio, and Andrej Sokol. 2022. Financial Shocks, Credit Spreads, and the International Credit Channel. *Journal of International Economics* 135, Article 103543.

Chahrour, Ryan, and Rosen Valchev. 2022. Trade Finance and the Durability of the Dollar. *Review of Economic Studies* 89, no. 4: 1873–910.

Coimbra, Nuno, Daisoon Kim, and Hélène Rey. 2022. Central Bank Policy and the Concentration of Risk: Empirical Estimates. *Journal of Monetary Economics* 125: 182–98.

Coimbra, Nuno, and Hélène Rey. 2023. Financial Cycles with Heterogeneous Intermediaries. *Review of Economic Studies* (April).

Coppola, Antonio, Matteo Maggiori, Brent Neiman, and Jesse Schreger. 2021. The Map of Global Capital Flows: The Role of Cross-Border Financing and Tax Havens. *Quarterly Journal of Economics* 136, no. 3: 1499–56.

Davis, J. Scott, Eric Van Wincoop, and Giorgio Valente. 2021. Global Drivers of Gross and Net Capital Flows. *Journal of International Economics* 128 (January).

Degasperi, Riccardo, Seokki Simon Hong, and Giovanni Ricco. 2021. The Global Transmission of US Monetary Policy. Unpublished manuscript. University of Warwick, UK.

Eichengreen Barry, Mohamed El-Erian, Arminio Fraga, Takatoshi Ito, Jean Pisani-Ferry, Eswar Prasad, Raghuram Rajan, Maria Ramos, Carmen Reinhart, Hélène Rey, Dani Rodrik, Kenneth Rogoff, Hyun Song Shin, Andres Velasco, Beatrice Weder Di Mauro, and Yongding Yu. 2011. *Rethinking Central Banking*. Brookings Institution and Alfred P. Sloan Foundation e-book. Committee on International Economic Policy and Reform.

Farhi, Emmanuel, Pierre-Olivier Gourinchas, and Hélène Rey. 2011. *Reforming the International Monetary System*. CEPR eReport. Paris and London: CEPR Press.

Farhi, Emmanuel, and Matteo Maggiori. 2018. A Model of the International Monetary System. *Quarterly Journal of Economics* 133, no. 1: 295–355.

Farhi, Emmanuel, and Jean Tirole. 2012. Collective Moral Hazard, Maturity Mismatch, and Systemic Bailouts. *American Economic Review* 102, no. 1: 60–93.

Gopinath, Gita, Emine Boz, Camila Casas, Federico Diez, Pierre-Olivier Gourinchas, and Mikkel Plagborg-Moller. 2020. Dominant Currency Paradigm. *American Economic Review* 110: 677–719.

Gourinchas, Pierre-Olivier. 2023. International Macroeconomics: from the Great Financial Crisis to COVID-19, and Beyond *IMF Economic Review* 71: 1–34.

Gourinchas, Pierre-Olivier, and Hélène Rey. 2007a. From World Banker to World Venture Capitalist: US External Adjustment and the Exorbitant Privilege. In *G7 Current Account Imbalances: Sustainability and Adjustment*, ed. Richard Clarida, 11–66. Chicago: University of Chicago Press.

Gourinchas, Pierre-Olivier, and Hélène Rey. 2007b. International Financial Adjustment. *Journal of Political Economy* 115, no. 4: 665–703.

Gourinchas, Pierre-Olivier, and Hélène Rey. 2022. *Exorbitant Privilege and Exorbitant Duty*. CEPR Discussion Paper 16944. Paris and London: CEPR Press.

Gourinchas, Pierre-Olivier, Hélène Rey, and Maxime Sauzet. 2019. The International Monetary and Financial System. *Annual Review of Economics* 11, no. 1: 859–93.

Ilzetzki, Ethan, Carmen M. Reinhart, and Kenneth S. Rogoff. 2019. Exchange Arrangements Entering the Twenty-First Century: Which Anchor Will Hold? *Quarterly Journal of Economics* 134, no. 2: 599–646.

Kalemli-Özcan, Şebnem. 2019. US Monetary Policy and International Risk Spill-Overs. In *Economic Policy Symposium Proceedings: Challenges for Monetary Policy*. Jackson Hole, WY: Federal Reserve Bank of Kansas City.

Kekre, Rohan, and Moritz Lenel. 2021. *The Flight to Safety and International Risk Sharing*. NBER Working Paper 29238. Cambridge, MA: National Bureau of Economic Research.

Kindleberger, Charles P. 1973. *The World in Depression: 1929–1939*. Berkeley: University of California Press.

Kindleberger, Charles P. 1986. International Public Goods Without International Government. *American Economic Review* 76, no. 1: 1–13.

Krishnamurthy, A., and A. Vissing-Jorgensen. 2012. The Aggregate Demand for Treasury Debt. *Journal of Political Economy* 120, no. 2: 233–67.

Lane, Philip R., and Gian Maria Milesi-Ferretti. 2011. Cross-Border Investment in Small International Financial Centers. *International Finance* 14, no. 2: 301–30.

Lane, Philip R., and Gian Maria Milesi-Ferretti. 2018. The External Wealth of Nations Revisited: International Financial Integration in the Aftermath of the Global Financial Crisis. *IMF Economic Review* 66, no. 1: 189–222.

Miranda-Agrippino, Silvia, and Hélène Rey. 2020. US Monetary Policy and the Global Financial Cycle. *Review of Economic Studies* 87, no. 6: 2754–76.

Miranda-Agrippino, Silvia, and Hélène Rey. 2022. The Global Financial Cycle. In *Handbook of International Economics*, vol. 6, ed. Gita Gopinath, Elhanan Helpman, and Kenneth Rogoff, 1–43. Amsterdam: North Holland.

Obstfeld, Maurice. 2013. The International Monetary System: Living with Asymmetry. In *Globalization in an Age of Crisis: Multilateral Economic Cooperation in the Twenty-First Century*, 301–36. Cambridge, MA: National Bureau of Economic Research.

Obstfeld, Maurice. 2022. The International Financial System After Covid-19. In *Prospects of the Global Economy after Covid-19*, ed. Thorsten Beck and Yung Chul Park, 39–72. Paris and London: CEPR Press.

Obstfeld, Maurice. 2023. Calvo, Currencies, and Commitment. Paper presented at the Credibility of Government Policies: Conference in Honor of Guillermo Calvo, Columbia University, New York, February 23–24.

Obstfeld, Maurice, Jonathan D. Ostry, and Mahvash S. Qureshi. 2019. A Tie That Binds: Revisiting the Trilemma in Emerging Market Economies. *Review of Economics and Statistics* 101, no. 2: 279–293.

Obstfeld, Maurice, and Haonan Zhou. 2022. The Global Dollar Cycle. *Brookings Papers on Economic Activity* (Fall): 361–427. Washington: Brookings Institution.

Reinhart, Carmen, and Kenneth Rogoff. 2009. *This Time Is Different: Eight Centuries of Financial Folly*. Princeton, NJ: Princeton University Press.

Rey, Hélène. 2013. Dilemma Not Trilemma: The Global Financial Cycle and Monetary Policy Independence. In *Global Dimensions of Unconventional Monetary Policy*. Jackson Hole Symposium Proceedings. Kansas City, MO: Federal Reserve Bank of Kansas City.

Triffin, Robert. 1961. *Gold and the Dollar Crisis: The Future of Convertibility*. New Haven, CT: Yale University Press.

VI

THE FUTURES OF THE DOLLAR, THE EURO, AND THE RENMINBI

25

"Dollar Rivals": Can the Dollar-Based System Be Improved or Replaced?

JEFFREY A. FRANKEL

The question of the international currency status of the dollar versus its potential rivals is not new, but it has been accorded an unusual amount of attention in the past few years, among scholars and non-scholars alike. With more data available than ever before, it is a good time to take stock. This chapter examines possible alternatives to a unipolar dollar-based system. It examines measures of international currency use, potential challengers to the dollar, whether a multipolar currency system is consistent with the existence of network externalities, and gold and digital currencies as alternatives to national currencies.

Measures of International Currency Use

An international currency like the dollar serves many functions (table 25.1). It is a currency in which central banks and sovereign wealth funds hold international reserves, an anchor currency to which smaller countries' currencies can peg, a currency to use in denominating or invoicing trade, and a vehicle currency for foreign exchange trading.[1]

---

1. A standard analogy illustrates its role (Kindleberger 1967). If Brazilians want to communicate with Filipinos, they are likely to find it more convenient to do so via some third language, such as English or Spanish, because the chances that either group speaks the other's language is slim. Similarly, if someone in the Philippines wishes to conduct business with someone from Brazil, they will find it more convenient to transact via some

Jeffrey A. Frankel is James W. Harpel Professor of Capital Formation and Growth at Harvard University's Kennedy School.

Table 25.1

Roles of an international currency

Function of money	Governments	Private actors
Store of value	International reserves held by central banks	Currency substitution (private dollarization)
Medium of exchange	Vehicle currency for foreign exchange intervention	Vehicle currency for private foreign exchange trades
Unit of account	Anchor for pegging smaller currencies	Invoicing trade and financial transactions

Sources: Cohen (1971), as revised by Kenen (1983) and Frankel (1992).

Data are most complete for the first criterion, from central banks' reported reserve holdings. The dollar's share of foreign exchange reserves has been declining gradually since the turn of the century. In 1999, when the newborn euro took the place of the French franc and German mark, the dollar constituted 71 percent of allocated holdings (that is, reserve holdings of which the currency composition is known).[2] By mid-2023, its share had declined to 59 percent, a rate of decline of about half a percentage point a year, according to the Currency Composition of Official Foreign Exchange Reserves (COFER) site of the International Monetary Fund (IMF).[3]

The dollar still remains far ahead of the next-most important international currency, the euro, which represents 20 percent of allocated holdings, a share that is not growing. If the dollar's share were to continue to decline by half a percentage point per year, it would take another 70 years for it to fall to the euro's share.[4]

---

third currency, such as dollars or euros, than to try to find someone who wants to take the other side of a *peso-real* trade.

2. Eichengreen and Mathieson (2001) characterize the currency composition of reserves as stable in the 1980s and 1990s. In fact, the dollar share declined after 1977, in tandem with the value of the dollar, recovering only in the late 1990s.

3. Prasad (2019) notes that the unallocated proportion of global reserves has become less of a limitation of the COFER statistics since China began to share the currency breakdown of its reserves with the IMF, a policy that it phased in over the period 2014–18.

4. This calculation assumes that the euro's share remains unchanged. If central banks switched out of dollars into euros, the catch-up date would be sooner.

The euro is well ahead of the yen, which ranks third. The yen is followed by the pound sterling in fourth place. The much-ballyhooed renminbi moved into fifth place only relatively recently, having passed the Canadian dollar and the Australian dollar.

Use of a currency internationally for one purpose is highly correlated with its use for others, both causally and statistically (Aiyar et al. 2023). Causally, Gopinath and Stein (2018, 2021) show that the international use of a currency with which to invoice trade (unit of account) is bidirectionally related to the use of the currency financially (store of value, particularly in the case of a currency with safe-haven properties, like the dollar and yen).

The correlation is also evident statistically. The dollar remains number one not only by the criterion of reserve holdings but also by the criteria of denominating and invoicing trade (Engel 2006; Goldberg and Tille 2008; Gopinath 2015; Boz et al. 2020), denominating international debt and loans, foreign exchange turnover (BIS 2022), and global payments.[5] According to an overall measure of international currency use computed at the Federal Reserve, the dollar remains three times as important as the euro and far more important than the yen, pound, or renminbi (Bertaut, von Beschwitz, and Curcuru 2021).

Only in the case of global SWIFT payments does the euro come close to the dollar's share (SWIFT 2023). In 2023, 32.6 percent of payments were in euros, and 41.7 percent were in US dollars. The renminbi was in fifth place, at 2.3 percent.[6]

The Challengers

When the Bretton Woods system came undone 50 years ago, the dollar seemed to lose its special status. Initially, some expected that the IMF's Special Drawing Rights (SDRs) could fill the gap (Grubel 1963; Solomon 1976; Kenen 1987; Williamson 2009). The SDR had been proposed and created as a means of repairing the Bretton Woods system by offering an alternative to dollar reserves. But the synthetic unit never caught on as an international currency (Eichengreen and Frankel 1996; Obstfeld 2011). By 1979, 12 countries (16 percent of all peggers), many of them in Africa or

---

5. As of April 2022, the dollar was used in almost three times as many foreign exchange transactions as the euro, its nearest competitor, whether by simple spot trades or derivatives. Following the dollar and euro in the ranking come the yen, pound, renminbi, Australian dollar, Canadian dollar, and Swiss franc, in that order.

6. Recent growth in the renminbi would show up more strongly if data on the Cross-Border Interbank Payment System, which China launched in 2015, or other non-SWIFT alternative payments systems, could be included.

the Middle East, had pegged their currencies to the SDR. That figure rose to 16 (23 percent) by 1982, but it was all downhill from there. By 1995, the number had declined to just three (Libya, Myanmar, and Seychelles). The SDR largely fell out of use, except as an international reserve asset for central banks.[7]

The SDR lacks the advantage of a base where it is the indigenous national currency. In the linguistic analogy, if the dollar is akin to the English language as the world's lingua franca, then the SDR is akin to Esperanto. Both the SDR and Esperanto were deliberately designed for maximum practicality but remain little used in practice, precisely because they were created artificially rather than growing organically out of a substantial home base.

Excitement over rival currencies tends to come in waves of pessimism regarding the role of the dollar.[8] In the last 40 years, a procession of other currencies has been characterized as potentially challenging the dollar as premier international currency. The Deutsch mark in 1973-90 (Tavlas 1993); the yen in 1984-91 (Frankel 1984; Tavlas and Ozeki 1992; Hale 1995; and Takagi 2011); and the euro in the 2000s (Alogoskoufis and Portes 1992; Bergsten 1997; Portes and Rey 1998; Frieden 2000; Chinn and Frankel 2007; Posen 2008; Goldberg 2010) each had its turn. Since around 2009, it has been the turn of the renminbi (Dobson and Masson 2009; Ito 2010; Park and Song 2010; Eichengreen 2011b; Subramanian 2011a, 2011b; Prasad and Ye 2012; Frankel 2012; and Zhang 2023).

Predictions that the renminbi might challenge the dollar for the number one spot by 2020 were obviously premature. China's currency has two of the three necessary conditions to be a leading international currency—economic size and the ability to keep its value. It lacks the third—deep, liquid, open financial markets—however. Much as the Chinese government craves the global stature of a major international currency, it has not been willing to give up capital controls and allow free convertibility. It halted its efforts to internationalize Chinese financial markets after 2014, when 10 years of net capital inflows gave way to 10 years of net capital outflows. China also lacks a democratic form of government, a free media, and an independent central bank, which most international currencies have.

---

7. The IMF occasionally still issues new batches of SDRs, as it did in August 2009 in response to the global financial crisis (Truman 2022).

8. One wave of declarations that the dollar was on its way out came in 1995, at the nadir of a 10-year decline in its foreign exchange value against the mark and yen (not that there need be any connection between international use of a currency and its exchange rate). See, for example, Kindleberger (1995), Kunz (1995), and Frankel (1995).

In 2023, the BRICS (Brazil, Russia, India, China, and South Africa) began talking about establishing a new currency as an alternative to the dollar.[9] Details are scarce. Because of its size, China would dominate a BRICS currency, however, and it is hard to imagine that five such disparate countries could live with a common currency, whether or not it would be China's. Russia has proposed that the BRICS currency might be a new basket of the five national currencies. If such a new synthetic currency is envisioned alongside the five existing currencies, it would fail for lack of a home base, like the SDR but more so.

The gradual move of global central bank reserve holdings out of dollars is not primarily into any of the aforementioned challengers but rather into new, relatively small reserve currencies, such as the Canadian dollar, Australian dollar, South Korean won, Swedish krona, and Norwegian krone (Arslanalp, Eichengreen, and Simpson-Bell 2022). Some other relatively small currencies, such as the Singapore dollar, the South African rand, and the New Zealand dollar, are held as reserves or considered as anchor currencies by a few countries that are still smaller, located in their respective regions. One might add these small units to the list of international currencies, though obviously not as candidates for the number one slot.

Is a Multicurrency System Consistent with Network Externalities?

The traditional view of international currencies accords a very strong role to network externalities (Kindleberger 1981; Krugman 1984; Matsuyama, Kiyotaki, and Matsui 1993; Rey 2001; and Gopinath and Stein 2018, 2021). Like the English language, people find the dollar convenient to use, given that everyone else is using it. Like a language, there are good reasons to have a single currency dominate at any given time. It is more efficient to use one currency internationally for the same reasons that it is more efficient to have a single currency *within* a country.

One implication of network externalities is inertia in the world's "choice" of the top international currency ("choice" is in scare quotes because these models tend to have multiple equilibria and thus path dependence). There may be long lags between the time that one currency's fundamental advantages, especially the size of the home economy, surpass those of another currency, and the time that the system reaches the tipping point, when the challenger currency overtakes the incumbent in international use.

---

9. Paul McNamara, "Why a BRICs Currency Is a Flawed Idea," *Financial Times*, February 10, 2023.

Statistical studies of reserve holdings find a lot of inertia (Lindert 1969; Krugman 1984; Chinn and Frankel 2007; Iancu et al. 2022; and others). The traditional view is that inertia explains why the dollar did not fully supplant the pound as the premier international currency until 1950 or so. The fundamental determinants had come to favor the dollar over the pound by around 1920. The United States passed the United Kingdom in economic size in 1872 and had acquired a central bank in 1913; Britain had lost the strength that goes with being a large international creditor as a result of borrowing during World War I. But inertia delayed the overturning of the old order (Schenk 2010).

A new view posits that network externalities are not as large as previously believed and that multiple leading international currencies can exist simultaneously (Eichengreen 2010, 2011a, 2011b). Eichengreen and Flandreau (2009, 2012) and Chiṭu, Eichengreen, and Mehl (2014) argue that the dollar had surpassed the pound by 1925. A reasonable verdict is that international use of the dollar attained approximately the same level as the pound in the 1920s and 1930s; the dollar pulled decisively ahead of the pound only after World War II.

The global monetary system can be usefully viewed as a tradeoff between the advantage of a single currency (network externalities) and the disadvantage (the fact that the issuing country may abuse its exorbitant privilege, provoking countries to look for alternatives) (Farhi and Maggiori 2018). Abusing the exorbitant privilege used to mean excessive budget deficits, money growth, current account deficits, inflation, and depreciation.[10] Econometric estimation of the determination of international currency shares included the ability of a country's currency to hold its value. (Two other standard determinants are country size and the openness and liquidity of the country's financial markets. See Dooley, Lizondo, and Mathieson 1989; Eichengreen and Mathieson 2001; Chinn and Frankel 2007; Ito and McCauley 2020; Aizenman, Cheung, and Qian 2020; Arslanalp, Eichengreen, and Simpson-Bell 2022; and Chinn, Ito, and McCauley 2022.)

Lately, overuse of exorbitant privilege has taken on an additional meaning. It has been increasingly evident that frequent use of sanctions by the United States can provoke some countries to move away from reliance on dollars.

10. The 1973 collapse of the monetary system was not simply the culmination of the Triffin Dilemma (Triffin 1960); it was accelerated by the fiscal and monetary expansion of the Vietnam War era, under Presidents Lyndon B. Johnson and Richard M. Nixon. Since 1973, the United States has accumulated another $31 trillion in national debt, in 2020 attaining the highest ratio of debt to GDP since World War II.

Most international sanctions are thought to have accomplished relatively little, historically, when applied without multilateral support (Bapat and Morgan, 2009). Most experts view them as a way for a country to register a clear protest, one of the few options between armed intervention and doing nothing. But sanctions have been used more often in recent years, particularly financial sanctions.

The US government's exploitation of the dollar's global dominance in order to extend the extraterritorial reach of US law and policy has been called "weaponization of the dollar."[11] An attempt to shut Iran out of the international banking system was among the economic sanctions applied in response to its threatened development of nuclear weapons. Initially, in 2005, the United States had multilateral support. Europeans occasionally grumbled about US extraterritoriality, suspecting that the United States might be quicker to impose large penalties on European banks than on their American peers for violating sanctions, but they went along. Sanctions were lifted when Iran agreed to halt its nuclear weapons program under the 2015 Iran nuclear deal (the Joint Comprehensive Plan of Action).

The sanctions garnered little multilateral support when President Donald J. Trump reinstated them in September 2020. In 2018, he had pulled the United States out of the 2015 agreement. In the eyes of the international community, Iran's compliance with the terms of that agreement made it difficult to justify sanctions in the name of a global public good and easier to characterize them as an abuse of the United States' exorbitant privilege.[12] Not just China but Europe as well looked for channels to pay for purchases of Iranian oil outside the US-controlled banking system. The episode added to concerns that the dollar might lose its long-standing primacy.

When Russia seized Crimea and invaded the eastern provinces of Ukraine, in 2014, the US, EU, and other allies applied financial and other sanctions. Their effects turned out to be limited. Worse, they motivated the Russian government to spend the next seven years building up its financial defenses. With the aid of substantial current account surpluses, its central bank by early 2022 had accumulated $643 billion worth of international reserves, equal to an impressive 40 percent of GDP. Further, the Bank of

---

11. Jeffrey Frankel, "How a Weaponized Dollar Could Backfire," *The Guardian*, October 23, 2019. Available at https://www.project-syndicate.org/commentary/donald-trump-weaponized-dollar-could-backfire-by-jeffrey-frankel-2019-10.

12. Quint Forgey, "Trump Administration Unveils New Sanctions on Iran Despite Foreign Resistance," *Politico*, September 21, 2020. Available at https://www.politico.com/news/2020/09/21/trump-administration-sanctions-iran-419408.

Russia, almost alone among the world's central banks, deliberately shifted most of the composition of its international reserves out of dollars and into renminbi, other nondollar currencies, and gold.

Before the 2022 invasion of Ukraine, cutting off Russian banks from the global financial system, via the SWIFT system or otherwise, seemed an ambitious goal. In the event, the United States and its allies were able to achieve it and much more. The US Treasury, together with the European Union, Japan, other G-7 countries, Switzerland, South Korea, and Singapore, jointly took almost unprecedentedly strong action on February 28, 2022. They denied the Russian authorities (the central bank and the sovereign wealth fund) access to their foreign exchange reserves and other assets held overseas, thereby disarming Russia's carefully prepared financial defenses. As a result, the ruble plummeted 30 percent, on top of earlier declines, bringing it below $0.01 in value. The ruble soon recovered its value. But it fell sharply once again in 2023, standing in November at 20 percent below the preinvasion level.

By late 2023, the results of the sanctions seem to have been less than expected. The expansion of alternative payment mechanisms, in renminbi and other nondollar currencies, has facilitated evasion of sanctions.

A few recent studies examine whether the countries that are geopolitically the least aligned with the United States—and thus the most exposed to the threat of sanctions—are generally the ones that have been shifting their reserve holdings out of dollars. Eichengreen, Mehl, and Chiţu (2017) use a dummy variable reflecting whether a country has a defense pact with the United States. Mosler and Potrafke (2020) and Perez-Saiz, Zhang, and Iyer (2023) use the frequency with which the country votes in agreement with the United States in United Nations General Assembly resolutions. Arslanalp, Eichengreen, and Simpson-Bell (2022), use both variables. The case of Russia notwithstanding, the general finding in these studies is little significant positive effect of these measures of geopolitical proximity on dollar holdings.[13]

Alternatives to National Currencies

National currencies are not necessarily the only sort of international reserves or international unit of account or means of payment. Other options include gold—until recently considered by most economists a relic of the barbarous past—and cryptocurrency (a sign of a barbarous future?).

---

13. Eichengreen, Mehl, and Chiţu (2019), do find effects of bilateral military alliances on currency composition of reserves in the period before World War I.

Economists long believed that central bank holdings of gold were an anachronism. Monetary authorities in many countries still held some gold, but they did not treat it as an active part of their international reserves; that is, they did not buy or sell it. In recent years, central banks, especially in Asia, have been actively buying (and selling) gold (Arslanalp, Eichengreen, and Simpson-Bell 2023). Ferranti (2023) finds that from 2016 to 2021, countries that faced a higher risk of US sanctions increased the share of gold in their international reserves more than countries facing a lower risk of US sanctions.

Ferranti (2023) explores whether it is sensible for a country that faces a modest risk of sanctions to diversify some of its central bank's portfolio out of US Treasuries and into cryptocurrency, specifically bitcoin (see also Smales 2019 and Aysan et al. 2019).[14] Somewhat surprisingly, he concludes that the answer is yes. Given that bitcoin is the asset that is hardest for US authorities to block, the threat of sanctions gives bitcoin a place in some portfolios and a fundamental long-run value.

Conclusion

The US currency has withstood repeated blows over the last five decades, most of them self-inflicted. An alarming example is the danger that repeated standoffs over the debt ceiling between the two political parties will eventually force the US Treasury to default at least partially on its obligations, which are a main component of dollar foreign exchange reserves.

So far, there is still little sign of the dollar losing its position as the leading international currency. Various measures show that it is still comfortably in the number one position. For example, the latest IMF data on the composition of foreign exchange reserves, covering 2023, show the dollar's share in allocated global reserves rising slightly. Tellingly, when a global shock raises perceptions of risk on the part of financial markets, investors still rush to the US dollar as the safe haven currency—even when the shock originates in the United States, as was the case with the 2007–09 global financial crisis.

---

14. The cryptocurrency question is distinct from the question of whether countries will issue central bank digital currencies (CBDCs) that are used internationally. If successful, CBDCs would be merely another technological step akin to—but probably less important than—the laying of the first successful trans-Atlantic cable in 1865, which allowed the real-time trading of dollars for pounds (giving this bilateral trade the name "cable"). CBDCs would not eliminate the need for an international vehicle currency, a role now played by the dollar (Eichengreen 2021).

The dollar retains its primacy because of the lack of a good alternative. The euro remains wounded from the 2010 crisis among its periphery members, and too few highly rated government bonds are issued in euros. The economies of Japan, the United Kingdom, and Switzerland are not big enough to sustain the number one role. China is big enough, but it lacks financial markets that are sufficiently deep, open, and liquid. With respect to the store-of-value function of an international reserve asset, the recent resuscitation of gold could make it more important. Even bitcoin could conceivably join the roster. But neither asset can fulfill the functions of a unit of account or a means of payment, at least not as well as the dollar.

It is normal for an important economy like the eurozone or China to conduct some of its trade in its own currency rather than entirely in dollars. It is even normal for such a currency to be used in some transactions between other pairs of countries in its region. This kind of use does not make a currency a plausible candidate to supplant the dollar as the number one international currency, however.

Perhaps the need to balance network externalities against the danger of abuse of the exorbitant privilege can give rise to an equilibrium in which multiple currencies of equal size would serve as the top international currencies. There may be an a priori logic supporting three global currencies (the dollar, the euro, and the renminbi). If there is only one premier international currency in the system, its government has a strong incentive to run deficits and profit from the resulting international seigniorage; it can finance its deficits more easily than other currencies, because there is an extra demand for its debt. Having three international currencies would put a check on the single currency's seigniorage. Every time that two of them are tempted to collusively abuse the exorbitant privilege, the third government could keep them honest by exercising greater monetary and fiscal discipline, thereby offering a higher rate of return on its currency and attracting holders away from the first two.

A better equilibrium would be one in which the dollar has a substantially greater role than the euro, the euro has a substantially greater role than the third-place currency, and so on, as in Zipf's Law (Chau, Ilzetzki, and Rogoff 2022). If the dollar was able to withstand the inflation of the Vietnam War era and its aftermath, the Nixon shocks of 1971–73, the 2007–08 subprime mortgage crisis, the 2017–20 American loss of interest in global leadership, and the blowback from the 2022 sanctions imposed on Russia, perhaps it can also withstand the partisan politics that threaten a downgrading of US government debt.

References

Aiyar, Shekhar, Jiaqian Chen, Christian H. Ebeke, Roberto Garcia-Saltos, Tryggvi Gudmundsson, Anna Ilyina, Alvar Kangur, Tansaya Kunaratskul, Sergio L. Rodriguez, Michele Ruta, Tatjana Schulze, Gabriel Soderber, and Juan P. Trevino. 2023. *Geoeconomic Fragmentation and the Future of Multilateralism.* Staff Discussion Note 001. Washington: International Monetary Fund. Available at https://www. elibrary.imf.org/view/journals/006/2023/001/article-A001-en.xml.

Aizenman, Joshua, Yin-Wong Cheung, and Xingwang Qian. 2020. The Currency Composition of International Reserves, Demand for International Reserves, and Global Safe Assets. *Journal of International Money and Finance* 102, article 102120.

Alogoskoufis, George, and Richard Portes. 1992. European Monetary Union and International Currencies in a Tripolar World. In *Establishing a Central Bank: Issues in Europe and Lessons from the US*, ed. Matthew Canzoneri, Vittorio Grilli, and Paul Masson, 273–302. Cambridge: Cambridge University Press.

Arslanalp, Serkan, Barry Eichengreen, and Chima Simpson-Bell. 2022. The Stealth Erosion of Dollar Dominance and the Rise of Nontraditional Reserve Currencies. *Journal of International Economics* 138. Available at https://www.sciencedirect.com/ science/article/abs/pii/S0022199622000885.

Arslanalp, Serkan, Barry Eichengreen, and Chima Simpson-Bell. 2023. *Gold as International Reserves: A Barbarous Relic No More?* Working Paper WP/23/14. Washington: International Monetary Fund.

Aysan, Ahmet Faruk, Ender Demir, Giray Gozgor, and Chi Keung Marco Lau. 2019. Effects of the Geopolitical Risks on Bitcoin Returns and Volatility. *Research in International Business and Finance* 47: 511–18.

Bapat, Navin A., and T. Clifton Morgan. 2009. Multilateral Versus Unilateral Sanctions Reconsidered: A Test Using New Data. *International Studies Quarterly* 53, no.4: 1075–94.

Bergsten, C. Fred. 1997. The Dollar and the Euro. *Foreign Affairs* (July/August): 83–95.

Bertaut, Carol, Bastian von Beschwitz, and Stephanie Curcuru. 2021. *The International Role of the US Dollar.* Fednotes, October 6. Washington: Federal Reserve System. Available at https://www.federalreserve.gov/econres/notes/feds-notes/the-inter-national-role-of-the-u-s-dollar-20211006.html.

BIS (Bank for International Settlements). 2022. *Triennial Central Bank Survey of Foreign Exchange* (December). Basel. Available at http://www.bis.org/statistics/rpfx22.htm.

Boz, Emine, Camila Casas, Georgios Georgiadis, Gita Gopinath, Helena Le Mezo, Arnaud Mehl, and Tra Nguyen. 2020. *Patterns in Invoicing Currency in Global Trade.* Washington: International Monetary Fund.

Chau, Vu, Ethan Ilzetzki, and Kenneth Rogoff. 2022. *Zipf's Law for International Currencies* (March). Cambridge, MA: Harvard University.

Chinn, Menzie, and Jeffrey Frankel. 2007. Will the Euro Eventually Surpass the Dollar as Leading International Reserve Currency? In *G7 Current Account Imbalances: Sustainability and Adjustment*, ed. Richard Clarida, 339–76. Chicago: University of Chicago Press. Available at https://www.nber.org/books-and-chapters/g7-current-account-imbalances-sustainability-and-adjustment/will-euro-eventually-surpass-dollar-leading-international-reserve-currency.

Chinn, Menzie D., Hiro Ito, and Robert N. McCauley. 2022. Do Central Banks Rebalance Their Currency Shares? *Journal of International Money and Finance* 122.

Chiţu, Livia, Barry Eichengreen, and Arnaud Mehl. 2014. *When Did the Dollar Overtake Sterling as the Leading International Currency? Evidence from the Bond Markets.* Working Paper 1433. Frankfurt: European Central Bank. Available at https://www.ecb. europa.eu/pub/pdf/scpwps/ecbwp1433.pdf.

Cohen, Benjamin J. 1971. *The Future of Sterling as an International Currency.* London: Macmillan.

Dobson, Wendy, and Paul Masson. 2009. Will the Renminbi Become a World Currency? *China Economic Review* 20, no. 1: 124–35.

Dooley, Michael, J. Saul Lizondo, and Donald Mathieson. 1989. *The Currency Composition of Foreign Exchange Reserves.* IMF Staff Paper 36: 385–434. Washington: International Monetary Fund.

Eichengreen, Barry. 2010. Managing a Multiple Reserve Currency World. In *The Future Global Reserve System: An Asian Perspective*, ed. Jeffrey Sachs, Masahiro Kawai, Jong-Wha Lee, and Wing Thye Woo: Manila: Asian Development Bank. Available at https://aric.adb.org/grs/about.php.

Eichengreen, Barry. 2011a. *Exorbitant Privilege: The Rise and Fall of the Dollar and the Future of the International Monetary System.* Oxford: Oxford University Press.

Eichengreen, Barry. 2011b. The Renminbi as an International Currency. *Journal of Policy Modeling* 33, no. 5: 723–30.

Eichengreen, Barry. 2021. Will Central Bank Digital Currencies Doom Dollar Dominance? *Project Syndicate*, August 9.

Eichengreen, Barry, and Marc Flandreau. 2009. The Rise and Fall of the Dollar (or When Did the Dollar Replace Sterling as the Leading Reserve Currency)? *European Review of Economic History* 13, no. 3: 377–411.

Eichengreen, Barry, and Marc Flandreau. 2012. The Federal Reserve, the Bank of England and the Rise of the Dollar as an International Currency, 1914–39. *Open Economies Review* 23, no. 1: 57–87.

Eichengreen, Barry, and Jeffrey Frankel. 1996. The SDR, Reserve Currencies, and the Future of the International Monetary System. In *The Future of the SDR in Light of Changes in the International Financial System*, ed. Michael Mussa, James Boughton, and Peter Isard, 337–78. Washington: International Monetary Fund.

Eichengreen, Barry, and Donald Mathieson. 2001. The Currency Composition of Foreign Exchange Reserves: Retrospect and Prospect. In *The Impact of EMU on Europe and the Developing Countries*, ed. Charles Wyplosz, 269–93. Oxford: Oxford University Press.

Eichengreen, Barry, Arnaud Mehl, and Livia Chiţu. 2017. *How Global Currencies Work.* Princeton, NJ: Princeton University Press.

Eichengreen, Barry, Arnaud Mehl, and Livia Chiţu. 2019. Mars or Mercury? The geopolitics of international currency choice. *Economic Policy* 34, no. 98: 315–63.

Engel, Charles. 2006. Equivalence results for optimal pass-through, optimal indexing to exchange rates, and optimal choice of currency for export pricing. *Journal of the European Economic Association* 4, no. 6 (December): 1249–60.

Farhi, Emmanuel, and Matteo Maggiori. 2018. A Model of the International Monetary System. *Quarterly Journal of Economics* 133, no. 1: 295–355.

Ferranti, Matthew. 2023. Hedging Sanctions Risk: Cryptocurrency in Central Bank Reserves. Chapter 2 of PhD thesis, Department of Economics, Harvard University, Cambridge, MA.

Frankel, Jeffrey. 1984. *The Yen/Dollar Agreement: Liberalizing Japanese Capital Markets*. Policy Analyses in International Economics 9. Washington: Institute for International Economics.

Frankel, Jeffrey. 1992. On the Dollar. In *The New Palgrave Dictionary of Money and Finance*. London: Macmillan Press Reference Books.

Frankel, Jeffrey. 1995. Still the Lingua Franca: The Exaggerated Death of the Dollar. *Foreign Affairs* 74, no. 4: 9–16.

Frankel, Jeffrey. 2012. Internationalization of the RMB and Historical Precedents. *Journal of Economic Integration* 27, no. 3: 329–65.

Frieden, Jeffry. 2000. The Political Economy of the Euro as an International Currency. In *The Euro as a Stabilizer in the International Economic System*, ed. Robert Mundell and Armand Clesse, 203–13. Boston: Kluwer Academic Publishers.

Goldberg, Linda. 2010. Is the International Role of the Dollar Changing? *Current Issues in Economics and Finance* 16, no. 1.

Goldberg, Linda S., and Cédric Tille. 2008. Vehicle Currency Use in International Trade. *Journal of International Economics* 76, no. 2: 177–92.

Gopinath, Gita. 2015. *The International Price System*. Jackson Hole Symposium, vol. 27. Federal Reserve Bank of Kansas City.

Gopinath, Gita, and Jeremy C. Stein. 2018. Trade Invoicing, Bank Funding, and Central Bank Reserve Holdings. *American Economic Review Papers and Proceedings* 108: 542–46.

Gopinath, Gita, and Jeremy C. Stein. 2021. Banking, Trade, and the Making of a Dominant Currency. *Quarterly Journal of Economics* 136, no. 2: 783–830.

Grubel, Herbert G. 1963. *World Monetary Reform: Plans and Issues*. Stanford, CA: Stanford University Press.

Hale, David. 1995. A Yen for Change: Why the Yen as a Reserve Currency Is Not Far-Fetched. *The International Economy*, May/June.

Iancu, Alina, Lucine Lusinyan, Yiqun Wu, Andrea Gamba, Sakai Ando, Gareth Anderson, Neil Meads, Ethan Boswell, and Shushanik Hakobyan. 2022. Reserve Currencies in an Evolving International Monetary System. *Open Economies Review* 33, no. 5: 879–915.

Ito, Takatoshi. 2010. China as Number One: How about the Renminbi? *Asian Economic Policy Review* 5, no. 2: 249–76.

Ito, Hiro, and Robert N. McCauley. 2020. Currency Composition of Foreign Exchange Reserves. *Journal of International Money and Finance* 102, article 102104.

Kenen, Peter. 1983. *The Role of the Dollar as an International Currency*. Occasional Paper No. 13. New York: Group of Thirty.

Kenen, Peter. 1987. Changing Views about the Role of the SDR and Implications for Its Attributes. In *The International Monetary System and Its Reform, Part II*, ed. Sidney Dell, 373–85. Amsterdam: North Holland.

Kindleberger, Charles. 1967. *The Politics of International Money and World Language*. Princeton Essays in International Finance 61. Princeton, NJ: International Finance Section, Princeton University.

Kindleberger, Charles. 1981. *International Money*. London: George Allen & Unwin.

Kindleberger, Charles. 1995. Is the Dollar Going the Way of Sterling, the Guilder, the Ducat, and the Bezant? *The International Economy*, no. 3: 609–11. Reprinted in Kindleberger. 1999. *Essays in History: Financial, Economic, Personal*. Ann Arbor: University of Michigan Press.

Krugman, Paul. 1984. The International Role of the Dollar: Theory and Prospect. In *Exchange Rate Theory and Practice*, ed. John Bilson and Richard Marston, 261–78. Chicago: University of Chicago Press.

Kunz, Diane. 1995. The Fall of the Dollar Order. *Foreign Affairs* 74: 22–27.

Lindert, Peter. 1969. Key Currencies and Gold: 1900-1913. *Princeton Studies in International Finance* 24: 16–22.

Matsuyama, Kiminori, Nobuhiro Kiyotaki, and Akihiko Matsui. 1993. Toward a Theory of International Currency. *Review of Economic Studies* 60 (April): 283–07.

Mosler, Martin, and Niklas Potrafke. 2020. International Political Alignment During the Trump Presidency: Voting at the UN General Assembly. *International Interactions* 46, no. 3: 481–97.

Obstfeld, Maurice. 2011. *The SDR as an International Reserve Asset: What Future?* International Growth Centre Working Paper, March. London: London School of Economics.

Obstfeld, Maurice, and Haonan Zhou. 2022. The Global Dollar Cycle. *Brookings Papers on Economic Activity* (Fall): 361–427. Washington: Brookings Institution.

Park, Yung Chul, and Chi-Young Song. 2010. RMB Internationalization: Prospects and Implications for Economic Integration in East Asia. *Asian Economic Papers* 10, no. 3.

Perez-Saiz, Hector, Longmei Zhang, and Roshan Iyer. 2023. *Currency Usage for Cross Border Payments*. IMF Working Paper No. 2023/072. Washington: International Monetary Fund.

Portes, Richard, and Hélène Rey. 1998. The Emergence of the Euro as an International Currency. *Economic Policy* 13, no. 26: 306–43.

Posen, Adam S. 2008. Why the Euro Will Not Rival the Dollar. *International Finance* 11, no. 1: 75–100.

Prasad, Eswar. 2019. *Has the Dollar Lost Ground as the Dominant International Currency?* Washington: Brookings Institution. Available at https://www.brookings.edu/wp-content/uploads/2019/09/DollarInGlobalFinance.final_.9.20.pdf.

Prasad, Eswar, and Lei (Sandy) Ye. 2012. *The Renminbi's Role in the Global Monetary System*. Washington: Brookings Institution. Available at https://www.brookings.edu/wp-content/uploads/2016/06/02_renminbi_monetary_system_prasad.pdf.

Rey, Hélène. 2001. International Trade and Currency Exchange. *Review of Economic Studies* 68, no. 2: 443–64.

Schenk, Catherine. 2010. *The Decline of Sterling: Managing the Retreat of an International Currency*. Cambridge: Cambridge University Press.

Smales, L. A. 2019. Bitcoin as a Safe Haven: Is It Even Worth Considering? *Finance Research Letters* 30: 385–93.

Solomon, Robert. 1976. The *International Monetary System. 1945–1976: An Insider's View*. New York: Harper and Row.

Subramanian, Arvind. 2011a. *Eclipse: Living in the Shadow of China's Economic Dominance* Washington: Peterson Institute for International Economics. Available at https://www.piie.com/bookstore/eclipse-living-shadow-chinas-economic-dominance.

Subramanian, Arvind. 2011b. *Renminbi Rules: The Conditional Imminence of the Reserve Currency Transition*. Working Paper Series 11-14. Washington: Peterson Institute for International Economics. Available at https://www.piie.com/publications/working-papers/renminbi-rules-conditional-imminence-reserve-currency-transition.

SWIFT. 2023. *RMB Tracker: Monthly Reporting and Statistics on Renminbi (RMB) Progress towards Becoming an International Currency*. Available at http://www.swift.com/our-solutions/compliance-and-shared-services/business-intelligence/renminbi/rmb-tracker/rmb-tracker-document-centre (accessed April 2023).

Takagi, Shinji. 2011, Internationalizing the Yen, 1984–2003: Unfinished Agenda or Mission Impossible? In *Asia and China in the Global Economy*, ed. Y.W. Cheung and G. Ma, 219–244. Singapore: World Scientific Publishing.

Tavlas, George. 1993. The Deutsche Mark as an International Currency. In *International Finance: Contemporary Issues*, ed. Dilip Das, 566–79. London: Routledge.

Tavlas, George, and Yuzuru Ozeki. 1992. *The Internationalization of Currencies: An Appraisal of the Japanese Yen*. IMF Occasional Paper 90. Washington: International Monetary Fund.

Triffin, Robert. 1960. *Gold and the Dollar Crisis*. New Haven, CT: Yale University Press.

Truman, Edwin M. 2022. *The IMF Should Enhance the Role of SDR to Strengthen the International Monetary System*. PIIE Working Paper 22-20. Washington: Peterson Institute for International Economics. Available at https://www.piie.com/publications/working-papers/imf-should-enhance-role-sdrs-strengthen-international-monetary-system.

Williamson, John. 2009. *Why SDRs Could Rival the Dollar*. PIIE Policy Brief 09-20. Washington: Peterson Institute for International Economics. Available at https://www.piie.com/publications/policy-briefs/why-sdrs-could-rival-dollar.

Zhang, Longmei. 2023. *Capital Account Liberalization and China's Financial Integration*. M-RCBG Associate Working Paper Series no. 196. Cambridge, MA: Harvard University.

26

The Dollar Might Slip but Will Still Rule

ESWAR PRASAD

In the 50 years since the end of Bretton Woods, the fundamentals underpinning the US dollar have weakened in many respects. The US economy now accounts for about 25 percent of global GDP (at market exchange rates), down from 30 percent in 1973. Indeed, the locus of economic power, as measured by the share of global output and trade, has been shifting toward the emerging market economies, led by China, for over two decades. US gross federal debt now amounts to over 120 percent of GDP, a ratio even higher than the previous post–World War II high. The United States is a net debtor to the rest of the world to the tune of over $16 trillion.

Despite all these ostensible setbacks to the position of the United States in the world economy, the dollar's dominance still pervades every aspect of global finance. Nearly 60 percent of the foreign exchange reserves of the world's central banks' are invested in dollar-denominated assets. Almost all commodity contracts, including those for oil, are priced and settled in dollars. The dollar is used to denominate and settle a majority of international financial transactions.

The dollar has maintained its dominance amidst a tumultuous couple of decades in the world economy. But economic and geopolitical changes have been under way that could undermine this dominance.

Eswar Prasad is a professor in the Dyson School at Cornell University, senior fellow at the Brookings Institution, and author of *The Future of Money: How the Digital Revolution is Transforming Currencies and Finance*. An earlier version of this chapter appeared in *Finance & Development*.

Meanwhile, the emergence of digital currencies, both private and official, is shaking up domestic and international finance. International payments are inherently complicated, because they involve multiple currencies, payment systems operating on diverse protocols, and institutions governed by varying regulations. As a result, cross-border payments tend to be slow, expensive, and difficult to track in real time.

New technologies spawned by the cryptocurrency revolution are making cheaper and practically instantaneous payment and settlement of transactions feasible. Even central banks are getting into the game, using the new technologies to increase the efficiency of payment and settlement mechanisms for cross-border transactions conducted by their domestic financial institutions. Various central bank consortia are engaged in similar exercises.

These developments will alleviate payment-related frictions in international trade—quicker settlement reduces risks from exchange rate volatility. Economic migrants sending remittances back home—a key source of revenue for many developing economies—will also benefit. Exporters and importers will benefit from quicker settlement of their transactions, reducing the need for hedging against the risks of exchange rate volatility stemming from long delays in processing and finalizing payments.

Changes are under way in foreign exchange markets as well. For instance, transactions between pairs of emerging-market currencies are becoming easier as these countries' financial markets and payment systems mature. China and India, for instance, will soon no longer need to exchange their currencies for dollars to conduct trade cheaply, as exchanging renminbi for rupees directly will become cheaper. As a result, reliance on "vehicle currencies," particularly the dollar, will decline.

The Renminbi Rises but Is Unlikely to Rule

Digital technologies are also affecting other aspects of money. With the rapid decline in the usage of physical currency (cash), many central banks are moving forward with or at least experimenting with central bank digital currencies (CBDCs). China is among the major economies that is well into advanced trials of its CBDC.

The prospect of a digital renminbi being available worldwide has intensified speculation that China's currency could gain in prominence, perhaps even rivaling the dollar. By itself, the digital renminbi will not shift the balance of power among major currencies; most international payments are already digital. It is China's Cross-Border Interbank Payment System (CIPS), which can communicate directly with other countries' payment systems, that will enhance the renminbi's role as an international payment currency. The CIPS' messaging capabilities could even sideline SWIFT, the international consortium of banks that now monopolizes messaging for all transactions between banks in different countries. The payment systems of other emerging-market economies are also gaining in sophistication and maturity.

These changes have important geopolitical implications. The dollar-dominated global financial system and US influence over SWIFT have long been the main sources of traction for US financial sanctions. Such sanctions have rankled not just US rivals such as Russia but even allies exposed to secondary sanctions that affect their firms' and financial institutions' access to global finance. The efficacy of such sanctions will erode.

But digitization by itself will not elevate the status of the renminbi or other emerging-market currencies as reserve currencies, which are regarded as international stores of value. China has made progress on removing restrictions on cross-border capital flows and leaving its currency's value to market forces, and it has broadened foreign investors' access to its bond markets. But the government has abjured institutional changes, including an independent central bank and the rule of law, that are essential to garner the trust of foreign investors.

The renminbi has made progress: By some measures, it is used for about 3 percent of international payment transactions, and roughly 3 percent of global foreign exchange reserves are now held in renminbi. Such measures of the prominence of the renminbi will almost certainly increase in the coming years as the Chinese economy and its financial markets grow and foreign investors, including central banks, start allocating a larger share of their portfolios to renminbi-denominated assets for diversification purposes at least. But it is unlikely that the renminbi will pose a serious threat to the dollar's dominance.

A Mixed Blessing

Emerging-market and developing economies will benefit from new financial technologies that are improving their households' and firms' access to global financial markets. Reduced frictions in international payments will enable firms in these economies, even small and medium-sized ones, to gain access to global pools of capital. Households in these economies will have easier access to opportunities for international portfolio diversification, achieving better returns on their savings while managing risk.

At the same time, the proliferation of conduits for money to flow across national borders will intensify developing economies' vulnerability to the vagaries of major central banks' policies and the whims of both domestic and international investors. It is also likely to render capital controls less effective. Even cryptocurrencies such as bitcoin have been used as conduits for capital flight when a country's currency is collapsing and domestic investors lose trust in their country's banking system. In short, greater capital flow and exchange rate volatility will complicate domestic policy management, with deleterious consequences for economic and financial stability in these economies.

Exposure to such volatility creates a conundrum for emerging-market policymakers eager to protect their economies against such outcomes by further expanding their stocks of hard currency foreign exchange reserves. They now recognize that there are circumstances in which even those war chests might become unavailable to them at a time of dire need.

Russia lost access to its stock of foreign exchange reserves as a result of Western sanctions imposed in response to its invasion of Ukraine. The loss generated speculation about whether emerging-market economies will look to alternative assets, rather than just the government bonds issued by advanced economies, for their reserve holdings.

The reality, though, is that assets such as gold are not viable alternatives because their markets are not as liquid; it would be difficult to sell a large stock of gold within a short period without precipitating a plunge in gold prices. Cryptocurrencies such as bitcoin have the additional problem of being highly unstable in value. Even renminbi reserves might be of limited help, given that that currency is not yet fully convertible.

The supply of "safe assets" that are liquid, available in large quantities, and backed up by countries with trusted financial systems is limited, and demand for them is strong and perhaps even rising. The US dollar—which represents a powerful combination of the world's largest economy and financial system, backed up by a strong institutional framework—remains by far the dominant supplier of such assets.

Innocent Bystanders

Changes coming to the international monetary system pose additional threats to the currencies of smaller and less developed economies. Some of them, especially those with central banks or currencies that lack credibility, could be overrun by nonnative digital currencies. The easy availability of digital versions of the major currencies or even stablecoins issued by multinational corporations or global banks would pose an existential threat to many national currencies.

National currencies issued by central banks, particularly currencies seen as less convenient to use or volatile in value, could be displaced by private stablecoins and perhaps also CBDCs issued by the major economies. Such displacement would imply a loss of monetary sovereignty, as these countries' central banks would lose control over the circulation of money in their economies.

Even a volatile cryptocurrency such as bitcoin might, in addition to enabling capital flight, be preferred to the local currency in times of economic turmoil. But it is more likely that the result of such turmoil will be further dollarization of economies, particularly if digital versions of such well-known currencies as the dollar become easily available worldwide.

The Dollar Endures

Digital technologies are enabling new forms of money that could challenge fiat currencies, setting off a new era of domestic and international currency competition. It is equally likely, however, that these new forces end up creating even more centralization, with some currencies accreting even more power and influence. Paradoxically, many of these changes could reinforce rather than weaken the dollar's dominance.

The upshot is that the dollar's role as the dominant reserve currency will likely persevere, even if its status as a payment currency erodes. Private stablecoins—private cryptocurrencies backed by US dollars, in order to maintain stable value—might well gain more acceptance worldwide than those backed by other currencies, implicitly bolstering the dollar's prominence. A likelier prospect is a reshuffling of the relative importance of other currencies while the dollar retains its primacy.

In short, rather than knocking the dollar off its pedestal, new technologies and geopolitical developments might entrench its position.

27

US and Dollar Dominance in the International Monetary System: Weakening but Not Disappearing

PHILIPPE MARTIN

France has two concerns that some may see as obsessions. One is its long-standing concern about the "exorbitant privilege" of the dollar. The second concerns the US Inflation Reduction Act (IRA). A French policymaker recently connected the two by arguing that the transatlantic divergence of instruments used in the climate transition (subsidies in the United States and taxes in Europe) reflects the near absence of a US government budget constraint provided by dollar dominance, which allows the US government to borrow at discounted interest rates. This connection may not be backed by evidence, but the anecdote suggests that US and dollar dominance can have repercussions far beyond trade and financial areas, including even climate strategies.

The economic world order based on multilateral rules, international economic relations interpreted as a positive-sum game, and tacit acceptance of American political and economic dominance is under attack in an unprecedented manner. Imminent de-dollarization has been announced for decades, but it has never happened. Is this time different?

A unique set of economic and political forces may lead to a weakening of dollar dominance. The erosion of economic mechanisms behind currency dominance and the geopolitical tensions that will perturb the

Philippe Martin, who attended the March 2023 PIIE conference and wrote this chapter, tragically passed away at the age of 57 on December 17, 2023. He was professor of economics in the department of economics at Sciences Po and its first chair from 2009 to 2013; dean of Sciences Po's School of Public Affairs; CEPR research fellow; and codirector of the Macroeconomics Program at CEPREMAP.

current equilibrium will probably not be enough to eliminate global dollar dominance, but they may enable more regionally dominant currencies to emerge.

Economists have accumulated a good theoretical understanding of the self-reinforcing mechanisms that give rise to currency dominance in trade and finance (see Gopinath and Itskhoki 2021). On the financial side, the positive feedback cycle is based on the liquidity and safety of assets: More issuance in the more liquid US dollar–denominated market raises the liquidity of that market, increasing the incentive to issue in dollars. This complementarity of the issuance incentives of private actors strengthens currency dominance (see Coppola, Krishnamurthy, and Xu [2023] for a recent theoretical model), and the strong path dependency (or hysteresis) enhances the dollar's status.

This complementarity also exists in international trade, where the dollar's share in invoicing (40 percent) is larger than the US economy's share of goods trade (10 percent). Here, too, self-reinforcing mechanisms are at work, because invoicing trade in dollars provides incentives for other firms (especially firms that are part of global value chains) to invoice in the same currency, in order to reduce currency risks (Mukhin 2022). The mechanisms in trade and finance are also interrelated (Chahrour and Valchev 2023), because of the need for collateral guarantees in international trade and the appeal of issuing dollar-denominated debt in a large and liquid dollar money market, which facilitates dollar settlement. The role of trade finance (which was crucial during the global financial crisis) also reinforces the stability of the equilibrium with dollar dominance.

The two channels (trade and finance) that lead to currency dominance reinforce each other, but researchers have analyzed either a sequence beginning with increased invoicing of world trade (Gopinath and Stein 2021) or a sequence beginning with a country that offers a large stock of safe and liquid assets denominated in its own currency that can be traded by the rest of the world (Chahrour and Valchev 2023). Given the strength and stability of the dollar dominance equilibrium, a shift in currency dominance would not originate solely from a shift in trade flows or financial flows but would likely require both.

The fragmentation of international economic relations is likely to continue, but it is difficult to predict its extent. On both the financial and the trade sides, the "hyperglobalization" era before the global financial crisis of 2008–10 is over, with trade and financial flow growth not exceeding GDP growth and some flows (such as manufacturing trade) increasing even more slowly. The rise of geopolitical tensions and economic sanctions will also affect trade and financial flows. Political tensions and, particularly, military conflicts reduce trade, and the impact can be long-lasting. Even low levels of military conflict reduce bilateral trade flows in a persistent (more than 15 years) and sizable (around 35 percent) manner (Martin, Mayer, and Thoenig 2008). Another source of reduction in trade flows is the rise in protectionism, which has both political and macroeconomic origins (Delpeuch, Fize, and Martin 2023) that are here to stay.

All of these trends suggest that the trade and financial forces behind the self-reinforcing mechanisms giving rise to currency dominance will weaken in the coming years. Except in a scenario of large military conflicts and the disintegration of trade and financial flows, however, they will not disappear. The unwinding of global value chains—a standard explanation for the drop in the ratio of trade in manufactures to GDP (Baldwin 2022)—may also weaken the strategic complementarities in global supply chains that favor dollar dominance. Countries' integration into global value chains is robustly associated with dollar invoicing because it allows firms to hedge against variations in imported input costs arising from exchange rate fluctuations. Re-regionalization of trade should favor the use of regional currencies, even if it does not eliminate dollar dominance.

A shift in the dollar's global dominance would require the rise of a competing global currency. The fact that at least two currencies, the renminbi and the euro, are potential competitors has contributed to the stability of the dollar dominance equilibrium up to now. The rise of China as a global trade giant starting in the 2000s may also have strengthened the dominant status of the dollar at the expense of the euro (Georgiadis et al. 2021).

Several developments in international economic relations favor a larger role for the Chinese renminbi. First, it is likely that China will move farther away from a fixed exchange rate with the dollar, as it has already partly done, reducing the gains of anchoring to the dollar. At the same time, the costs of fixing the exchange rate (in terms of monetary sovereignty in the context of the Mundell trilemma) may rise, especially if China moves farther toward opening its financial markets. If it does, volatility of the Chinese exchange rate against the dollar may increase and more firms may want to invoice in renminbi (rather than dollars), as the isomorphism between the two currencies is broken (Mukhin 2022).

On the financial side, because China still has important capital controls and seems unlikely to give them up soon, the renminbi can be ruled out as a substitute for the dollar. With active policy support—through loans and currency swaps by the People's Bank of China (Eichengreen et al. 2022)—however, even in the absence of capital account convertibility, it can still develop into a consequential regional reserve currency. American financial sanctions on assets held in the United States or the European Union may put into doubt the legal safety of assets held in those jurisdictions, but the comparison of their legal infrastructure with the rule of law in China is nonetheless not to the latter's advantage.

On the trade side, the "China shock" is behind, not ahead of, us. China's extremely rapid rise in world trade and its current dominance (with a larger global trade share than the United States) was not accompanied by a parallel and proportionate increase in renminbi use. But that ascension in world trade occurred in a period when the United States did not resist China's integration and China did not actively contest the role of the dollar.

The situation has completely changed today. Geopolitical tensions between China and the United States are greater than at any time since the restoration of bilateral diplomatic relation in the 1970s, and there is bipartisan agreement in the United States on the objective of economic decoupling with respect to China. Market-driven mechanisms were sufficient to create dollar dominance over the past 50 years. The extent to which political pressure can be a substitute for these economic mechanisms is not clear.

The economic mechanisms that have supported dollar dominance are consistent with international economic relations viewed as positive-sum games (because, for example, of the efficiency gains from economies of scale). They are much less consistent with a world based on a zero-sum approach, protectionism, and political and economic segmentation between China and the United States. It is possible that politically driven "friendshoring" could cause dollar dominance to be replaced by friend "currencing," with multiple regional currencies; it would not cause the renminbi to replace the dollar, however. Chinese authorities could go farther in restricting the use of the US dollar, for both trade and financial transactions. Such a political decision would impose efficiency costs on various economic actors, including Chinese exporters. In both China and the United States, these potential economic efficiency costs will have less weight in political decisions in a world with strong geopolitical tensions.

Three factors work against the euro gaining market share:

- Europe's share of world trade is likely to decline.
- The euro crisis has cast some doubt on the safety of some euro members' sovereign debt, and it will take time to regain confidence. A large, liquid, unified public debt market is not likely to replace the present segmented ones in the near future.
- Europe is still too closely aligned with the United States to be a credible alternative for the diversification of political risk.

The regionalization of production supply chains may have a modest positive impact on the use of the renminbi, the euro, and other currencies in invoicing trade flows, reducing dollar dominance. At the same time, regionalization will prevent any of these currencies from emerging as a global currency like the dollar. A more likely scenario is the spread of more regionally dominant currencies.

A low-probability but very negative scenario could lead to a dramatic decline in the US dollar as a dominant currency. The New Triffin Dilemma (Fahri and Maggiori 2018) puts the implicit promise of stability and safety of the dollar into question, in particular because of the large size of US external and public debt. The fragility of the United States' leveraged external position—the fact that it borrows short term and invests long term—could end abruptly because of a loss of confidence in the fiscal capacity of the United States. This scenario is not impossible, but if anything, the behavior of the dollar during the global financial and COVID crises showed that global confidence in the dollar is still very strong and that the dollar performs well its role of providing the world with insurance during global crises (Gourinchas, Rey, and Gavillot 2017).

I would like to end with the exorbitant privilege issue and the gains and losses of dollar dominance for the United States and the rest of the world. This evaluation is not an easy one, particularly because the extent and sign of the US exorbitant privilege is not stable over time. One indirect and partial way to quantify it is to look at the difference between the United States' net international investment position and its cumulative net borrowing. During the "global imbalances" period of 1998–2008, the United States ran very large current account deficits and engaged in massive net borrowing from overseas, but its net debtor position barely moved. By 2020, this situation had reversed, with a sharp deterioration in the United States' net international investment position, mostly as a result of changes in the market value of US-owned assets abroad and foreign-owned assets in the United States, according to Milesi-Ferretti (2021) and Atkeson, Heathcote, and Perri (2022).

One can conjecture the impact of a scenario of financial deglobalization in which financial flows grow more slowly than global GDP and gross external assets and liabilities as a fraction of GDP are reduced. In this scenario, two related but different mechanisms would lead to a reduction in the gains for the United States of being the dominant currency: first, a narrowing of the gap between the returns on US assets and liabilities and second, a reduction in the leverage effect that comes from the size of gross positions. Financial (and trade) deglobalization would weaken (but not eliminate) some of the channels behind dollar dominance, possibly reducing the attractiveness of US assets for foreign investors and therefore the excess return of US gross external assets over its gross external liabilities, which Gourinchas, Rey, and Gavillot (2017) estimate to have been worth about 2–3 percent a year between 1952 and 2016. The gap in returns may also apply to smaller gross positions (assets and liabilities) if financial deglobalization reduces gross flows. Financial deglobalization with reduced gross positions may thus weaken (but not eliminate) global dollar dominance and reduce the gains associated with it.

References

Atkeson, Andrew, Jonathan Heathcote, and Fabrizio Perri. 2022. *The End of Privilege: A Reexamination of the Net Foreign Asset Position of the United States.* NBER Working Paper 29771. Cambridge, MA: National Bureau of Economic Research.

Baldwin, Richard. 2022. The Peak Globalisation Myth: Part 3—How Global Supply Chains Are Unwinding. VoxEU Column, September 2.

Chahrour, Ryan, and Rosen Valchev. 2022. Trade Finance and the Durability of the Dollar. *Review of Economic Studies* 89, no. 4: 1873–910.

Coppola, Antonio, Arvind Krishnamurthy, and Chenzi Xu. 2023. *Liquidity, Debt Denomination, and Currency Dominance.* NBER Working Paper 30984. Cambridge, MA: National Bureau of Economic Research.

Delpeuch, Samuel, Etienne Fize, and Philippe Martin. 2023. *Trade Imbalances, Fiscal Imbalances and the Rise of Protectionism: Evidence from G20 Countries.* Working paper on file with author.

Eichengreen, Barry, Camille Macaire, Arnaud Mehl, Eric Monnet, and Alain Naef. 2022. *Is Capital Account Convertibility Required for the Renminbi to Acquire Reserve Currency Status?* Working Paper 892. Paris: Banque de France. Available at https://publications.banque-france.fr/en/capital-account-convertibility-required-renminbi-acquire-reserve-currency-status.

Farhi, Emmanuel, and Matteo Maggiori. 2018. A Model of the International Monetary System. *Quarterly Journal of Economics* 133, no. 1: 295–355.

Georgiadis, Georgios, Helena Le Mezo, Arnaud Mehl, and Cédric Tille. 2021. *Fundamentals vs. Policies: Can the US Dollar's Dominance in Global Trade Be Dented?* Working Paper 2574. Frankfurt: European Central Bank. Available at https://www.ecb.europa.eu/pub/pdf/scpwps/ecb.wp2574˜664b8e9249.en.pdf.

Gopinath, Gita, and Oleg Itskhoki. 2021. *Dominant Currency Paradigm: A Review.* NBER Working Paper 29556. Cambridge, MA: National Bureau of Economic Research.

Gopinath, Gita, and Jeremy C. Stein. 2021. Banking, Trade, and the Making of a Dominant Currency. *Quarterly Journal of Economics* 136, no. 2: 783–830.

Gourinchas, Pierre-Olivier, Hélène Rey, and Nicolas Govillot. 2017. *Exorbitant Privilege and Exorbitant Duty.* Working Paper. Available at http://helenerey.eu/Content/_Documents/duty_23_10_2017.pdf.

Martin, Philippe, Thierry Mayer, and Mathias Thoenig. 2008. Make Trade Not War? *Review of Economic Studies* 75, no. 3: 865–900.

Milesi-Ferretti, Gian Maria. 2021. The US Is Increasingly a Net Debtor Nation. Should We Worry? Brookings Commentary, April 14. Available at https://www.brookings.edu/articles/the-us-is-increasingly-a-net-debtor-nation-should-we-worry.

Mukhin, Dmitry. 2022. An Equilibrium Model of the International Price System. *American Economic Review* 112, no. 2: 650–88.

28

Fifty Years since the End of Bretton Woods, 25 Years since the Launch of the Euro

PHILIP R. LANE

The year 2023 marks not only 50 years since the end of Bretton Woods but also the 25th year of the euro. In this chapter, I interpret the end of the Bretton Woods system as launching a search process for a sustainable and durable set of monetary arrangements for Europe, with a focus on the European Union.

Through this lens, although the end of the Bretton Woods System in 1973 is certainly a milestone, a retrospective assessment of Europe in the 1973-2015 period should classify the period as a multistep experimental phase. From 1973 to 1978, repeated attempts were made to regulate intra-European exchange rate movements. These efforts eventually led to the creation of the European Monetary System (EMS) in 1979.[1] The EMS period saw various exchange rate realignments and a wave of currency crises in 1992-93. At the end of 1995, the final decision was made to establish the monetary union, with a launch date of 1999.

Creation of the euro did not mark the culmination of the search for a stable monetary system. Although the euro area operated reasonably well during its first decade according to many metrics, clear vulnerabilities were embedded in the design of the euro area (Lane 2006). During 2007-12, the euro area was tested by the global financial crisis and the euro area sovereign debt crisis, which raised many questions about the euro's resilience

---

1. See Corsetti, Hale, and Weder di Mauro (2023) for an assessment of the EMS.

Philip R. Lane is a member of the European Central Bank's Executive Board. He was governor of the Central Bank of Ireland (2015-2019).

(Lane 2012, 2019, 2021). The years 2013–15 saw challenges associated with the resolution of the financial crises in Cyprus and Greece, including through the imposition of restrictions on cross-border financial flows in these countries. The summer of 2015 can be viewed as the final stage in this euro-specific learning episode, following the decision by the Greek government to work within the prevailing European policy framework (including the terms of the official funding program of the European Union [EU] and the International Monetary Fund [IMF]), despite the result of the July 5 referendum, which had strongly rejected that program's terms. The euro area has been much stabler as a monetary system since 2015.

Analytically, the search for a stable monetary regime can be viewed as driven by the need to reconcile the three policy trilemmas: the international monetary policy, the financial, and the political economy trilemmas. The international monetary policy trilemma is the impossibility of simultaneously maintaining fixed exchange rates, international capital mobility, and independent monetary policies (Obstfeld, Shambaugh, and Taylor 2005). The single currency navigates this trilemma by eliminating national currencies within the euro area but adopting a common monetary policy while maintaining international capital mobility. The single currency set-up should be understood to be intricately connected to the unique institutional framework provided by the European Union, which pools sovereignty in many policy spheres (Lane 2021). As the single currency required complete pooling of monetary sovereignty, it was also recognized that curbs on national fiscal policies would be necessary. The initial design of the euro did not impose extensive conditions on participating countries in other policy areas, especially relative to EU member countries that did not adopt the euro.

The financial trilemma is the impossibility of combining internationally integrated financial system, international capital mobility, and independent national financial stability policies (Schoenmaker 2011). National banking systems remained under domestic supervision, and financial stability policies were determined largely at the national level in the first decade of the euro. The 2008–12 crises triggered major reforms, including the strengthening of EU-wide financial regulations, the consolidation of banking supervision under the European Central Bank (ECB)–led Single Supervisory Mechanism, the area-wide facilitation of bank resolution through the creation of the Single Resolution Fund, the rollout of national macroprudential policy frameworks to limit the risk and impact of credit boom-bust cycles, and the creation of the European Stability Mechanism as the official funding backstop facility.

The international political economy trilemma is the incompatibility of international economic and financial integration, transnational governance, and autonomous national democratic systems (Rodrik 2000). The

European Union is a unique response to this trilemma, with member states sharing sovereignty (to varying degrees) in many policy areas. Transnational governance arrangements have evolved, with power shared via a "trilogue" policy decision making process in which the European Commission formulates policy proposals that have to be agreed to by the European Parliament and the European Council, which brings together the national governments of all member countries.

In relation to the single currency, monetary sovereignty is pooled by member countries through the Eurosystem, which consists of the ECB and the national central banks of member countries. Monetary policy is determined by the ECB Governing Council, consisting of six Executive Board members (appointed by the European Council) and the governors of the 20 national central banks of countries using the euro. The ECB is accountable to the European Parliament, including through quarterly hearings in which the President of the ECB appears before its Committee on Economic and Monetary Affairs.

In the unique institutional context of the European Union, then, a common currency and a shared monetary policy are a singular response relative to the long-running debate (especially since the collapse of the Bretton Woods system) about the relative merits of floating versus fixed exchange rate regimes. The common currency has provided a new type of monetary regime that corresponds to neither floating nor pegging at the national level.

In assessing the properties of the European Monetary Union (EMU), it is necessary to follow a two-level approach. First, the creation of a large monetary bloc also affects the operations of the global monetary system, especially linkages between the euro area, the broader European region, and the rest of the world. Second (and more importantly), a common currency shapes economic and financial outcomes inside the euro area, in terms of both area-wide aggregates and the performance of individual national economies.

Although the dollar remains the most important global currency, the euro is the dominant currency for euro area trade, in relation to both intra-area trade and trade with the rest of the world (figures 28.1 and 28.2). Financial transactions within the euro area are also overwhelmingly denominated in euro, and the euro is a significant global and regional financial currency (figure 28.3). For firms, households, and governments in the euro area, the euro is the dominant currency. At the level of the broader European regional economy, the centrality of the euro area in trade means that network effects among trading partners have made the euro the dominant currency for the pan-European economy (Mehl, Mlikota, and Van Robays 2023). At the global level, many international financial transac-

Figure 28.1

Share of exports and imports invoiced in euros, by area in 2019

percent

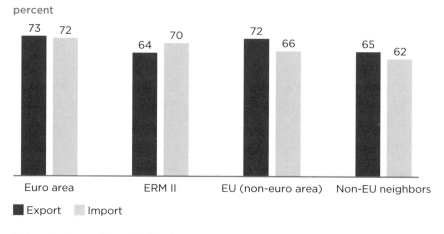

Notes: Exchange Rate Mechanism II (ERM II) includes Bulgaria; EU (non-euro area) is the average of the Czech Republic, Hungary, Poland, Romania, and Sweden; Non-EU neighbors is the average of Albania, Bosnia and Herzegovina, Iceland, Serbia, Tunisia, and the United Kingdom. The shares for Italy, Spain, Denmark, and Croatia are missing.
Sources: IMF and ECB staff calculations.

tions are denominated in euro, partly because European counterparts can stipulate its usage (figure 28.3).

A monetary union faces fewer challenges if economic and financial shocks are mostly common; it faces more challenges if shocks are country-specific. A key question is the incidence and scale of common relative to country-specific shocks in the EMU.

It is also important to differentiate between asymmetric exogenous shocks and asymmetric national policy errors. A common monetary policy is more effective if such policy errors at the national level are minimized through coherent policy frameworks on fiscal policy, macroprudential policy, and supervision of the financial system (Martin and Philippon 2017, Lane 2021).

The initial design of the euro area lacked sufficient crisis management capabilities to ensure monetary stability for member countries. This feature may have been an intentional design choice, intended to avoid the moral hazard risks associated with the establishment of transnational crisis management instruments (James 2014). Even at the time, the lack of crisis management capabilities could have been foreseen as a high-risk strategy. The risk of adverse dynamic loops between fixed exchange rates and boom-bust cycles in international financial flows was demonstrated in the 1990s

Figure 28.2

Total trade invoiced in euros, by European country in 2019

percent

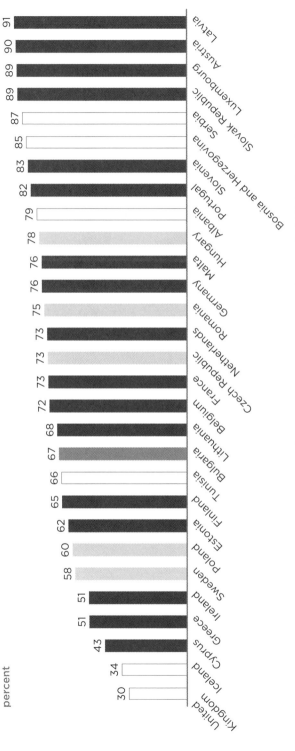

Notes: The bars show the average of the shares of exports and imports invoiced in euro in 2019. Dark gray shows euro area countries, medium gray shows Exchange Rate Mechanism II (ERM II) countries, light gray shows EU (non-euro area) countries and white shows non-EU neighbor countries. The shares for Italy, Spain, Denmark, and Croatia are not available.

Sources: IMF and ECB staff calculations.

Figure 28.3

Use of major currencies in the international monetary system, by purpose

percent

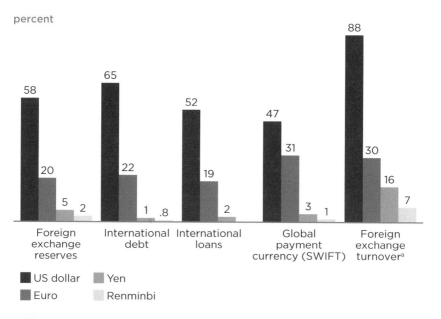

a. Since transactions in foreign exchange markets always involve two currencies, shares add up to 200 percent. Turnover adjusted for local and cross-border inter-dealer double-counting ("net-net" basis).

Notes: The latest data for foreign exchange reserves, international debt and international loans are for the fourth quarter of 2022. SWIFT data as of December 2022. Foreign exchange turnover in April 2022.

Sources: Bank for International Settlements, International Monetary Fund, Society for Worldwide Interbank Financial Telecommunication (SWIFT), and European Central Bank calculations.

crisis episodes (the EMS, Scandinavian banking, Mexico, Asian financial, and Russian crises). In particular, the integration of EMU member countries with very different initial positions in terms of interest rate levels and growth prospects, together with the predictable increase in international financial mobility with the elimination of currency risk inside the euro area, posed adjustment challenges at the very launch of the euro.

Several lessons emerged from the twin crises of 2008–12. The EMU provided insulation from the global financial crisis shock. The area-wide provision of central bank liquidity eased external funding pressure on member countries experiencing liquidity runs (Lane 2019). As a result, acute crises did not occur in 2008–09. The slower pace of macroeconomic adjustment without an independent currency contributed to the persistent financial strains experienced by the euro area periphery, however, resulting in a series of crisis events in 2010–12.

In the absence of sufficient official funding support, the euro area faced the prospect of significant default events in 2010–12. Although Greece engaged in substantial restructuring of its sovereign debt, it also relied heavily on official funding programs of the European Union and the IMF. Ireland, Portugal, and Cyprus also depended on such support, and Spain received funding to underpin the restructuring of its banking system. The scale of the official funding requirements resulted in the establishment of the European Financial Stability Facility (EFSF) and, subsequently, the permanent European Stability Mechanism (ESM). With fiscal positions and banking sectors underpinned by an ESM backstop (subject to policy conditionality) and a commitment by European leaders to establish a banking union, the ECB could provide more comprehensive liquidity support with the announcement of the Outright Monetary Transactions (OMT) program in 2012. This period proved that a stable monetary union requires a sufficiently comprehensive crisis management capability that is underpinned by an area-wide fiscal backstop.

Reassurance that an official funding backstop is in place can enable the central bank to deter liquidity attacks. In particular, the array of crisis management systems and official funding tools allowed the ECB to develop its OMT program in 2012 and its new Transmission Protection Instrument (TPI) in 2022. The TPI provides the ECB with the capability to counter unwarranted, disorderly market dynamics that pose a serious threat to the transmission of monetary policy across the euro area. In particular, subject to the fulfillment of established criteria, the Eurosystem will be able to intervene in bond markets if a deterioration in financing conditions is not warranted by country-specific fundamentals. As such, the TPI represents further progress in containing speculative attack pressures within a monetary union.

The high costs of the 2010–12 crisis also clarified the necessity of taking greater preventive measures to reduce crisis risks. Most importantly, the crisis triggered a sea change in the regulation and supervision of the banking system, with a fundamental shift from national oversight to pan-European supervision. The reforms also included higher capital requirements on banks and more extensive deployment of macroprudential measures to lean against financial sector imbalances. Although the reforms also included more extensive limitations on national fiscal policies and greater ex ante monitoring of macro-financial imbalances, the economic governance framework remains highly contested in terms of striking the right balance between observable numerical fiscal benchmarks and judgment-based assessments of national fiscal policies.

In recent years, most of the challenges Europe has faced have been common ones. The common challenge facing monetary policy during 2015–19, for example, was the need to combat below-target inflation by adopting unconventional policy measures (including negative policy interest rates quantitative easing). During this period, the fiscal priority in many member countries was to reduce the budget deficits and public debt levels, which had surged during the crisis period.

The pandemic shock of 2020–21 triggered large-scale monetary and fiscal responses. The pandemic posed a severe challenge for both the monetary union and countries running independent currencies. Three interlocking policy decisions were essential in ensuring that it did not cause a severe financial crisis in Europe:

- In March 2020, the ECB forcefully countered incipient fragmentation pressure (with investors exiting weaker member countries and turning to safe havens) by launching the Pandemic Emergency Purchase Programme (*PEPP*), which was designed to be flexible in its country-by-country purchasing allocations. This flexibility option calmed the nerves of investors.

- The NextGenerationEU recovery plan with its associated joint debt program was very powerful in reassuring markets that the European Union stood together in responding to the pandemic common shock.

- With favorable financing conditions, governments could support pandemic-affected households and firms, protecting the health of these key sectoral balance sheets.

The pandemic highlighted once again that a flexible exchange rate regime does not protect a country from international financial shocks. European countries outside the euro area must self-insure by holding considerable foreign exchange reserves; a number of countries arranged swap lines or repo lines with the ECB to enhance liquidity management capabilities, as Lane (2023) shows.

Another common external shock was the 2022 energy shock caused by Russia's war against Ukraine. The common inflation surge triggered by high energy prices and pandemic-related sectoral mismatches of demand and supply required a considerable turnaround in monetary policy, with the ECB moving its monetary stance from highly accommodative to restrictive.[2] It is difficult to envisage that the required policy responses to these shocks would have been more effective under a system of national currencies rather than a common currency.

---

2. Other European central banks also tightened monetary policy, with the scale of rate

Figure 28.4
Popular support for the euro in the euro area, 2010–23

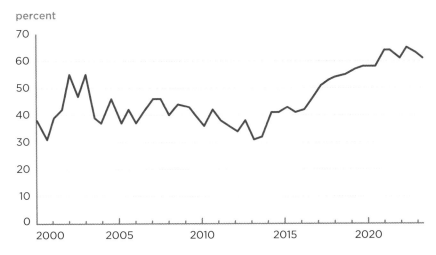

percent

Note: Net support is the percentage of people supporting the euro minus the percent of people opposing the euro. Figure shows population-weighted average net support in the euro area.
Source: Eurobarometer poll.

Going forward, major structural forces, such as climate change and geopolitical shifts, represent common challenges for the euro area.

The enhanced collective capability of a common currency to respond to common shocks has increased the popularity of the euro (figure 28.4; see chapter 11 by Linda Tesar in this volume). It would be a mistake, however, to be complacent about the resilience of the euro area. Further progress is needed in terms of crisis management capabilities, banking union, capital markets union, and central fiscal capacity. The incompleteness of the crisis management framework, the partial nature of the banking union (still lacking a European deposit insurance scheme), and limited progress on capital markets union remain crisis risk factors, in view of the embedded lack of cross-border risk sharing (Cimadomo et al. 2022).

Only incremental steps toward further integration look politically feasible in the near term, but recent events have reinforced the logic of further integration as a compelling long-term vision (Draghi 2023). Rising external geo-political risks increase the desirability of further integration, which would improve the resilience of the euro area to common external

---

hiking generally much sharper in the Central and Eastern European countries that remained outside the euro area (including the Czech Republic, Hungary, and Poland).

shocks. And Brexit has underlined the potential costs of exit and increased the incentives for individual member countries to embrace more completely the unique institutional setting of the European Union, which offers the potential to deliver effectiveness through shared sovereignty where it is necessary while maintaining considerable national autonomy along many policy dimensions.

References

Cimadomo, Jacopo, Esther Gordo Mora, and Alessandra Anna Palazzo. 2022. *Enhancing Private and Public Risk Sharing*. ECB Occasional Paper 306. Frankfurt: European Central Bank.

Corsetti, Giancarlo, Galina Hale, and Beatrice Weder Di Mauro, eds. 2023. *The Making of the European Monetary Union: 30 years since the ERM crisis*. Paris and London: CEPR Press.

Draghi, Mario. 2023. *The Next Flight of the Bumblebee: The Path to Common Fiscal Policy in the Eurozone*. Martin Feldstein Lecture, NBER Summer Institute. Cambridge, MA: National Bureau of Economic Research.

James, Harold. 2014. *Making the European Monetary Union*. Cambridge, MA: Harvard University Press.

Lane, Philip R. 2006. The Real Effects of European Monetary Union. *Journal of Economic Perspectives* 20, no. 4: 47–66.

Lane, Philip R. 2012. The European Sovereign Debt Crisis. *Journal of Economic Perspectives* 26, no. 3: 49–68.

Lane, Philip R. 2019. Macrofinancial Stability and the Euro. *IMF Economic Review* 67, no. 3: 424–42.

Lane, Philip R. 2021. The Resilience of the Euro. *Journal of Economic Perspectives* 35, no. 2: 3–22.

Lane, Philip R. 2023. Lessons from the European Monetary System (EMS) Crisis for European Monetary Union. In *The Making of the European Monetary Union: 30 Years Since the ERM Crisis*, ed. Giancarlo Corsetti, Galina Hale, and Beatrice Weder Di Mauro, 99–106. Paris and London: CEPR Press.

Martin, Philippe, and Thomas Philippon. 2017. Leverage and the Great Recession in the Eurozone. *American Economic Review* 107, no. 7: 1904–37.

Mehl, Arnaud, Marko Mlikota, and Ine Van Robays. 2023. *How Does a Dominant Currency Replace Another? Evidence from European Trade*. CEPR Discussion Paper 18264. Paris and London: CEPR Press.

Obstfeld, Maurice, Jay C. Shambaugh, and Alan M. Taylor. 2005. The Trilemma in History: Tradeoffs among Exchange Rates, Monetary Policies, and Capital Mobility. *Review of Economics and Statistics* 87, no. 3: 423–38.

Rodrik, Dani. 2000. How Far Will International Economic Integration Go? *Journal of Economic Perspectives* 14, no. 1: 177–86.

Schoenmaker, Dirk. 2011. The Financial Trilemma. *Economics Letters* 111, no. 1. 57–59.

29

The Renminbi in the Post–Bretton Woods Era

SHANG-JIN WEI

To call the post–Bretton Woods period an era of floating exchange rate regimes would be a gross simplification. Many countries continue to manage the external values of their currencies tightly against an anchor currency, in most cases the US dollar. The Chinese currency, the renminbi ("people's money" in Chinese), is one such currency.

The renminbi often receives outsized attention, in both media and policy circles, for two reasons. First, while many currencies that are pegged to the dollar suffer from overvaluation, the Chinese currency is often said to be undervalued. The supposed undervaluation of the renminbi is in turn said to have contributed to China's very large current account surplus, which is an important component of so-called global imbalances.

Second, as China progressively surpassed more countries in terms of both GDP and trade volume—and is now within striking distance of the United States—one starts to wonder whether China's currency can also catch up with the US dollar sometime soon as a leading international trade settlement currency and a major reserve currency. Indeed, since 2016, when the renminbi became part of the International Monetary Fund's Special Drawing Rights (SDRs) basket, there has been more chatter about such a prospect in the media and among think tanks.

In this chapter I review the behavior of the renminbi exchange rate and the arguments that link it to China's current account behavior. I also

Shang-Jin Wei is N.T. Wang Professor of Chinese Business and Economy and Professor of Finance and Economics at Columbia University's Graduate School of Business and School of International and Public Affairs.

examine the prospects for and challenges facing the Chinese currency becoming a leading currency in international trade and finance.

Several studies point to the role of structural factors in the Chinese economy in shaping its trade and current account balance. Although a more flexible nominal exchange rate regime may be beneficial to China, its role in moderating China's trade or current account surplus may be more modest than often assumed. Separately, although the international profile of the renminbi has risen in recent years, it is still a long way from becoming an international currency as important as the US dollar, or even the euro, in either trade settlement or foreign exchange reserves. Two important hindrances for the renminbi are capital controls and a lack of a deep and liquid domestic bond market. Some of China's experiments in "controlled liberalization" may be interesting to watch.

The Chinese Exchange Rate and Trade Balance

The Chinese exchange rate system—characterized by a relatively stable bilateral exchange rate with respect to the US dollar in recent years—has often been said to be substantially undervalued and the cause of the country's large current account surplus. Indeed, China's large trade (and current account) surplus is often taken as prima facie evidence of the undervaluation of its currency. The argument is noteworthy because many, perhaps most, other countries with pegged or heavily managed exchange rates are said to overvalue their currencies. A country's ability to defend an overvalued currency is limited, as there is a finite amount of foreign currency one can sell in exchange for the home currency. Therefore, when one worries about possible problems with a fixed exchange rate, one worries about an abrupt devaluation and associated foreign currency crisis. Defending an undervalued currency is easier, as one can always choose to buy up more foreign currency using the home currency. For this reason, it is unsurprising that the Chinese are able to maintain an undervalued currency for a long period.

Over the last two decades, China only rarely had the highest trade surplus as a share of GDP. Singapore almost always had a larger ratio. However, given China's economic size, China's surplus is considered a major component of the "global current account imbalance," which has been blamed for contributing to the global financial crisis of 2007–09 and to a rise in trade protectionism in the United States and other countries (Obstfeld and Rogoff 2005, 2007, 2010).[1]

---

1. See also Ben Bernanke, Global Imbalances: Links to Economic and Financial Stability, speech given at the Banque de France Financial Stability Review launch event, February 2011, Paris.

Figure 29.1
Nominal renminbi-dollar exchange rate, 1980–2023

renminbi per dollar

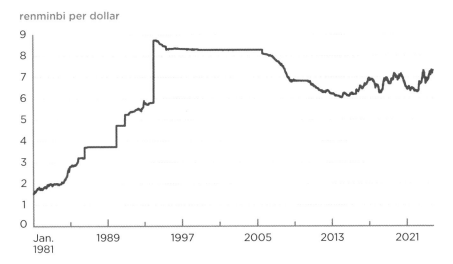

Source: Macrotrends, Dollar-Yuan Exchange Rate-35 Year Historical Chart, https://www.macrotrends.net/2575/us-dollar-yuan-exchange-rate-historical-chart.

These characteristics of China's exchange rate and trade balance are recent. At the time of the collapse of the Bretton Woods system in 1973, China was not at all integrated into the international trading system, and it was not a member of the IMF. The Chinese government set the official exchange rate at approximately RMB2 per US dollar, which very likely represented a gross overvaluation of the renminbi (figure 29.1). The extent of the overvaluation was not clearly visible, as currency black markets were strictly forbidden. Moreover, both exports and imports were tightly controlled and undertaken by only a small number of state-owned trading companies. In the 1980s, when Deng Xiaoping's economic reforms were under way, a black market for foreign currencies emerged. While the official exchange rate was about RMB3.7 per US dollar, the black market rate was at least RMB8, a clear sign that the Chinese currency was vastly overvalued at the official rate.

An important exchange rate reform took place on January 1, 1994, when the official exchange rate was reset at the prevailing black market rate of RMB8.7 per dollar. The renminbi rose in value soon afterward, before the Chinese authorities fixed it at RMB8.3 per dollar in July 1995. Very little international attention was paid to the Chinese exchange rate, mostly because China was not a big trading country at the time.

The renminbi bilateral exchange rate was kept broadly at this level for about a decade, until the next major reform, in July 2005, when the renminbi was allowed to appreciate in nominal value. Formally, the daily exchange rate movement against the dollar was limited to within 2 percent. Still, pressure for renminbi appreciation was released over time, and the (nominal) value of the renminbi peaked in October 2013 at RMB6.1 per dollar.

One important background variable that runs parallel to the renminbi exchange rate is China's evolving trade (and current account) surplus. A persistent trade surplus started to emerge in the mid-1990s, widening further following China's accession to the World Trade Organization (WTO) near the end of 2001 (figure 29.2). By 2006, China's trade surplus had reached 7 percent of its GDP, one of the largest in the world.

On the surface, the rise in the current account surplus during this period seems puzzling, as many of the Chinese trade reforms are unilateral liberalization (i.e., China having to reduce its trade barriers unilaterally based on its WTO accession protocol without getting partner countries to reciprocate with their reforms). If China increased its imports, should its trade deficit not have increased (or its trade surplus declined)?

If the trade surplus is not explained by the trade reform, it is then taken to be *prima facie* evidence of Chinese exchange rate manipulation. However, a country's trade balance also reflects its saving and investment imbalance.

Research on this topic has produced some interesting insights. In particular, it has shown that China's high corporate saving rate is partly driven by imperfections in its financial system (Song, Storesletten, and Zilibotti 2011). Because non-state-owned firms were able to take advantage of the opportunities made available by the economic reform but were not able to secure enough funding from either the domestic banks or the capital market, they accumulated huge internal savings.

The research also suggests that China's high household saving is partly driven by a gender ratio imbalance (Wei and Zhang 2011). A shortage of brides—the cumulative consequence of years of gender-selective abortions—has motivated households with unmarried sons to raise their saving rate in order to be more competitive in the marriage market. Because greater wealth by women also raises their chances of being matched with men with greater wealth, there is no corresponding decline in savings by households with daughters (Du and Wei 2013). The rising gender ratio in the last two decades is estimated to have contributed to about one-third to one-half of the observed increase in the household saving rate. With the rise in the saving rate surpassing that of investment, China exhibits an increasingly large trade and current account surplus.

Figure 29.2

China's exports, imports, and trade balance as shares of GDP, 1952–2022

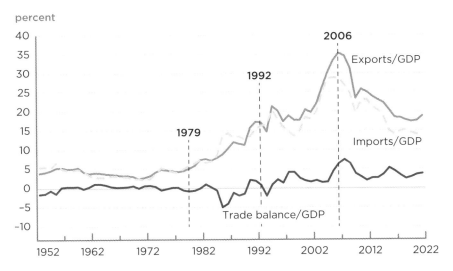

Source: Wei and Yu (2023).

Another contributing factor may have been unilateral trade liberalization, which in a labor-abundant country such as China should be expected to result in a larger trade surplus, as Ju, Shi, and Wei (2021) suggest. Before 2001, China's average tariff rate was as high as 14 percent; it declined to a more modest 5 percent by 2004 and stayed that low afterward (figure 29.3). At the same time, China's current account surplus was not significant the year before China joined the WTO but started to rise afterward until 2007, when it began to fall.

As this finding is counterintuitive, let us reflect on the explanation. The analysis of Ju, Shi, and Wei (2021) goes beyond the traditional partial equilibrium framework to show how a general equilibrium analysis could overturn the partial equilibrium intuition. Under the traditional partial equilibrium analysis, a reduction in a country's trade barriers (such as tariffs) leads to an increase in its imports, reducing the current account surplus of the importing country and improving the current account deficit of the exporting country.

Thinking from a general equilibrium perspective leads to a completely different conclusion: For labor-abundant countries, a reduction in import barriers can actually increase their current account surplus, and capital-abundant countries may experience a current account deficit. The economic

Figure 29.3

Tariff rates and current account in China, 1998–2010

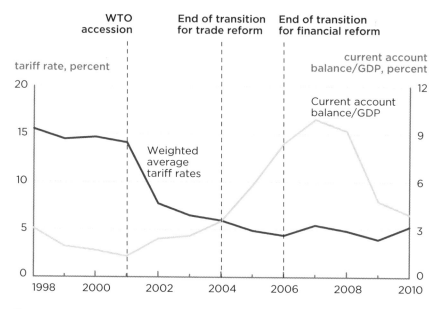

Source: Ju, Shi, and Wei (2021, figure 1).

logic behind this is as follows: Suppose the importing country is labor abundant. With trade liberalization, i.e., a reduction in import barriers, the country imports more capital-intensive products. The reduction in tariffs leads to a decrease in the price of imported products. According to the Stolper-Samuelson theorem in the Heckscher-Ohlin model, the decrease in the price of imported products leads to a decrease in the return to capital, the factor used intensively in the production of imported products, namely, the interest rate. The decrease in domestic interest rates means that the domestic return on capital is lower than the foreign return, which leads to an increase in the country's foreign capital holdings, resulting in a capital outflow and a current account surplus for the country.

These studies do not exclude exchange rate undervaluation as a possible contributing factor to China's trade (and current account) surplus. But they caution against the tendency to exaggerate the role of the exchange rate regime in understanding a country's trade or current account balance. Indeed, the evidence on the role of a more flexible nominal exchange in facilitating current account adjustments is weaker than commonly assumed (Chinn and Wei 2013).

The Renminbi as an International Currency: Progress, Prospects, and Policy Experiments

After years of speculation and false starts, the internationalization of the renminbi seems finally to be well under way. In March 2023, China and Brazil announced plans to trade using their own currencies rather than the US dollar. The same month, the Chinese National Offshore Oil Company and France's TotalEnergies completed their first-ever renminbi-denominated liquefied natural gas trade.[2] Russian president Vladimir Putin said that he wants to use the Chinese currency not just for trading with China but also as a form of payment in trade with other countries in Asia, Africa, and Latin America.[3] Saudi Arabia has been in talks with China since 2022 about accepting payments for some oil exports in renminbi,[4] creating quite a stir in the media and some think tanks.[5]

It is no secret that China would like to transform the renminbi into an international currency and reduce the global dominance of the US dollar. This desire is often interpreted as a geopolitical move, a way to insulate China from possible US–led economic sanctions in the future. Transforming the renminbi into one of the world's leading settlement currencies could also bring real benefits to the Chinese economy, including lower costs of borrowing in the international capital market by its firms and the government. Elevating the renminbi to an international currency could also help protect China from a future exchange rate crisis, if its currency is used to denominate bonds and loans or is otherwise used as an accepted means of payment in cross-border financial transactions. For some of the same reasons, other countries, including India and the ASEAN countries, are trying to internationalize their currencies, too.[6]

2. RFI, "'Petrodollar' at Risk as TotalEnergies Sells LNG to China in Yuan," March 31, 2023, https://www.rfi.fr/en/business/20230331-petrodollar-under-threat-as-france-s-totalenergies-sells-lng-to-china-in-yuan.

3. Tass, "Russia Supports Yuan Payments in Trade with Other Countries—Putin," March 21, 2023, https://tass.com/economy/1592277?utm_source=google.com&utm_medium=organic&utm_campaign=google.com&utm_referrer=google.com.

4. Maha El Dahan and Aziz El Yaakoubi, "China's Xi Calls for Oil Trade in Yuan at Gulf Summit in Riyadh," Reuters, December 10, 2022, https://www.reuters.com/world/saudi-arabia-gathers-chinas-xi-with-arab-leaders-new-era-ties-2022-12-09.

5. See Zongyuan Zoe Liu, "China Is Quietly Trying to Dethrone the Dollar," *Foreign Policy*, September 21, 2022, https://foreignpolicy.com/2022/09/21/china-yuan-us-dollar-sco-currency.

6. Pallavi Singhal, "India Expanding Rupee Trade with Several Countries, Talks in Advance Stages—Piyush Goyal," *Money Control*, March 14, 2023.

Panel a of figure 29.4 illustrates the progress China has made in internationalizing the renminbi. The dark gray line traces South Korean firms' renminbi-denominated exports as a share of their total exports to China between 2006 and 2020. It shows that the renminbi share rose from 0 percent before 2008 to nearly 7.4 percent in 2020.

These are impressive milestones, but one should not exaggerate the degree to which the renminbi is encroaching on the greenback's position. As the dashed line in figure 29.4, panel a, shows, the US dollar's share of South Korean exports to China declined from nearly 98 percent in 2006 to roughly 87 percent in 2020. In other words, the dollar has gone from being overwhelmingly dominant to being slightly less dominant. Even in bilateral trade between China and South Korea (for which China is the largest trading partner), the renminbi is not even close to displacing the dollar.

Moreover, evidence from Jiao et al. (2023) shows that 99 percent of South Korean exports to the United States during the same period were denominated in dollars; none was denominated in renminbi. By contrast, the dollar's share of South Korean exports to Japan was roughly 45 percent in 2020, about equal to that of the yen, with the won and the euro accounting for the rest (figure 29.4, panel b). The US dollar thus continues to dominate global trade, including in bilateral trade that does not involve the United States; the renminbi is essentially used only in transactions involving China. Part of the reason for the greenback's continued preeminence is that, in addition to its status as a large trading power, the United States has a very large and liquid capital market, in which foreign investors can park and withdraw their dollar-denominated funds at ease. Capital can flow in and out of the United States subject to no capital controls (except for national security or sanctions reasons). In comparison, China imposes capital controls and its domestic financial market is far less liquid, making the renminbi unattractive to international investors.

Theoretically, China could raise the renminbi's global profile by loosening capital controls. But doing so could come at significant cost, exposing the Chinese economy to the (often negative) consequences of US interest rate movements and global financial cycles (see chapter 24 by Hélène Rey). Moreover, premature liberalization of the capital account could exacerbate distortions within China's financial system, where domestic savings are not always channeled to the most productive firms. The Chinese authorities are keenly aware of these risks, which is why they have been prioritizing financial stability over renminbi internationalization.

There are, however, other ways to promote the renminbi. A series of currency swap agreements between the People's Bank of China and its counterparts in other countries, for example, could help make the renminbi less risky for international firms and investors (Jiao et al. 2023).

Figure 29.4

Shares of invoicing of South Korean exports to China and Japan, by currency, 2006–20

a. Exports to China

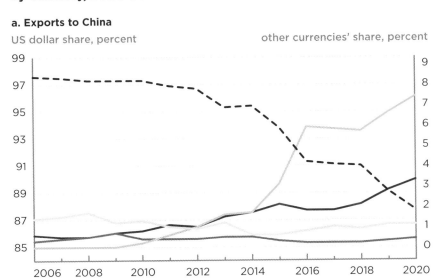

US dollar share, percent

other currencies' share, percent

- - - - US dollar (left axis)　——— South Korean won　——— Euro
——— Chinese yuan (renminbi)　　Japanese yen

b. Exports to Japan

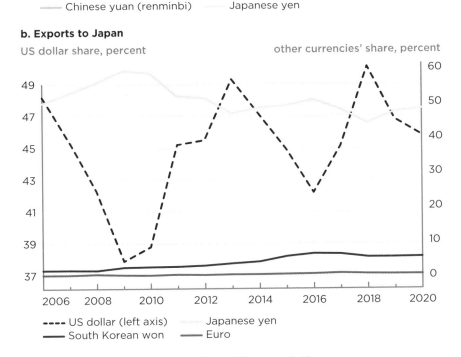

US dollar share, percent

other currencies' share, percent

- - - - US dollar (left axis)　　Japanese yen
——— South Korean won　——— Euro

Source: Bank of Korea: Trade Settlement Currency in Korea.

China also has a number of "controlled capital account liberalization" experiments that are interesting to watch. For example, foreign central banks, mutual funds, hedge funds, and sovereign wealth funds may apply for "qualified foreign institutional investor" (QFII) status, which allows them to invest in Chinese securities, including stocks and bonds, and convert the investment principals and returns back to US dollars, bypassing Chinese capital controls. In July 2023, the IMF itself applied for and received QFII status.

In the future, a digital renminbi could be used to facilitate partial capital account liberalization without formally removing capital controls. By removing the anonymity of foreign investors, a digital renminbi would allow the Chinese central bank to limit cross-border financial transactions to less volatile types and more conveniently turn on a circuit break when needing it. Being able to separate inflows of "hot money" from more stable types of foreign investment could convince the central bank to relax some capital controls and allow financial capital to flow more freely.

Conclusion

China is one of many developing economies that continues to heavily manage its nominal exchange rate against some anchor currencies. It stands out for the size of its foreign exchange accumulation. Although its nominal exchange rate is often asserted to be responsible for its trade and current account surpluses, various structural factors may have played bigger roles.

China has achieved some progress toward making the renminbi an invoicing currency for some trade and a reserve currency for central banks, but it is still far from reaching its goal. It could use a digital currency in the future to deliver de facto partial capital account liberalization, but China will not undermine the dollar's hegemony without going much farther in loosening capital controls and building a large and liquid domestic bond market.

References

Amiti, M., and B.S. Javorcik. 2008. Trade Costs and Location of Foreign Firms in China. *Journal of Development Economics* 85, no. 1–2: 129–49.

Bahaj, Saleem, and Ricardo Reis. 2022. *Jumpstarting an International Currency*. Working paper. London: London School of Economics.

Chinn, Menzie, and Shang-Jin Wei. 2013. A Faith-Based Initiative Meets the Evidence: Does a Flexible Exchange Rate Regime Really Facilitate Current Account Adjustment? *Review of Economics and Statistics* 95, no. 1: 168–84.

Du, Q., and S.J. Wei. 2013. A Theory of The Competitive Saving Motive. *Journal of International Economics* 91, no. 2: 275–89.

Jiao, Yang, Ohyun Kwon, Saiah Lee, and Shang-Jin Wei. 2023. Currency Swaps and Currency Invoicing in Trade. Draft working paper.

Ju, J., K. Shi, and S.J. Wei. 2021. Trade Reforms and Current Account Imbalances. *Journal of International Economics* 131, article 103451.

Obstfeld, Maurice, and Kenneth Rogoff. 2005. Global Current Account Imbalances and Exchange Rate Adjustments. *Brookings Papers on Economic Activity* 1, 67–146. Washington: Brookings Institution.

Obstfeld, Maurice, and Kenneth Rogoff. 2007. The Unsustainable US Current Account Position Revisited. In *G7 Current Account Imbalances: Sustainability and Adjustment*, ed. Richard H. Clarida. Chicago: University of Chicago Press.

Obstfeld, Maurice, and Kenneth Rogoff. 2010. Global Imbalances and the Financial Crisis: Products of Common Causes? *Asia and Global Financial Crisis*. In Asia and the Global Financial Crisis, ed. Reuven Glick and Mark M. Spiegel. Asia Economic Policy Conference. San Francisco, CA: Federal Reserve Bank of San Francisco.

Song, Z., K. Storesletten, and F. Zilibotti. 2011. Growing Like China. *American Economic Review* 101, no. 1: 196–233.

Wang, Z., and S.J. Wei. 2010. *What Accounts for the Rising Sophistication of China's Exports?* NBER Working Paper w16500. Cambridge, MA: National Bureau of Economic Research.

Wei, Shang-Jin, and Xinding Yu. 2023. China's Journey in Embracing Economic Openness. *Arc of the Chinese Economy*, March.

Wei, S.J., and X. Zhang. 2011. The Competitive Saving Motive: Evidence from Rising Sex Ratios and Savings Rates in China. *Journal of Political Economy* 119, no. 3: 511–64.

Index

advanced economies
allowing exchange rates to float, 192
capital flows less sensitive to risk, 291
currencies floating freely, 42
equity investments in the United
States, 144
excess stock and bond holdings of
selected (2001–21), 136–39*f*
exchange rate regimes (2019), 209*t*
with flexible exchange rates, 193
holdings of US equities after 2018, 131
import surcharges in the 1950s and
1960s, 176
inflation for, 196
responses to US monetary policy
tightening, 293*f*
shift from fixed to floating exchange
rates, 74
shifting investments, 128–29, 144
stabilizing prices without an anchor,
207
vulnerability to dollar funding stresses,
284

Abe, Shinzo, 42
Abenomics, 121
advanced economies
allowing exchange rates to float, 192
capital flows less sensitive to risk, 291
currencies floating freely, 42
equity investments in the United
States, 144
excess stock and bond holdings of
selected (2001–21), 136–39*f*
exchange rate regimes (2019), 209*t*
with flexible exchange rates, 193
holdings of US equities after 2018, 131
import surcharges in the 1950s and
1960s, 176
inflation for, 196
responses to US monetary policy
tightening, 293*f*
shift from fixed to floating exchange
rates, 74
shifting investments, 128–29, 144
stabilizing prices without an anchor,
207
vulnerability to dollar funding stresses,
284
Algeria, 238, 243, 243*n*3, 245*f*, 246*f*
"America First" hostility, 28
anchor, 196, 207
anchor country, 88, 90
anchor currency, 88, 93

Argentina, 74, 224*n*1
ASEAN countries, internationalizing
currencies, 357
Asian financial crisis of the 1990s, 217,
252, 253, 257, 260
asset prices, 60, 61, 66
asset returns, in the US, China, and
Europe (2009–2023), 145*f*

backstop dollar liquidity, 274
backstop facilities, 268–70
"bad" balance sheet effects, 218
"bad yen depreciation," in Japan, 123
Baker, James, 177
balance of payments
adjusting, 55, 59, 61, 67, 87, 91, 92–93
crisis, 71
issues, 261
balance sheet, concerns about, 219–20
balance sheet effects, 217, 218, 261, 281
Balladur, Edouard, 99, 107, 108
bank credit, supply of, 65
Bank Indonesia, 256, 259
banking crises, associated with currency
crises, 54
banking problems, from fluctuating
exchange rates, 24
banking reforms, yielding benefits, 256
banking systems, 243, 247, 253, 272
bank loans, surges in, 60

Bank of Japan, 114, 121
banks
    dollar as funding currency of choice
        for, 277
    failures of since 1980, 59
    managing liquidity across borders,
        285, 287
Basel Committee on Banking
    Supervision, 24
basket currency, 99
beggar-thy-neighbor policies, 63
beneficiary financial institutions,
    regulating, 304
benign neglect, as a US Policy, 54, 55,
    62–65
bigrams (word pairs), 149, 150–51, 150f,
    151t
bilateral currency misalignment,
    intensified China shock, 178
bilateral depreciation, local prices and,
    229
bilateral dollar exchange rates, of
    emerging markets, 290
bilateral geopolitical proximity,
    measuring, 135
bilateral trade, 143, 335
biodiversity loss, 305
BIS Triennial Central Bank Survey, 279,
    279n1
bitcoin, 319
Black Monday, China's risk-off event,
    162
blanket guarantee, 256n3
blocs, world sliding back into, 28
"Blue Wall," fall of in November 2016,
    164
Blumenthal, Michael, 104, 106
bond holdings
    in advanced economies, 138–39f
    in emerging market economies, 131,
        140–41f, 218
bond markets, Eurosystem intervening
    in, 347
bond returns, in US, China, and
    Germany (2009–2023), 145f
Bretton Woods system
    abiding by obligations, 72
    as also a nonsystem, 41
    balance of payments crises during, 71
    breakdown of followed by crises, 80
    built on currencies' par values, 36

centered on the International
    Monetary Fund (IMF), 10–11
collapsed because of US domestic
    politics, 94
developments in the last years of, 2
ending of, 1–2, 35, 92, 341
features of, 116–17t
fixed but adjustable exchange rates,
    74, 174
member states treating dollars as
    "good as gold," 88–89
never fully functioning as intended,
    41–42
pegged exchange rates expired in 1973,
    9
response to the breakup of, 97
served Japan well, 120
transforming institutions, 305
trilemma solution of, 20
US resisted the breakdown of, 77
Brexit, 28, 350
BRICS (Brazil, Russia, India, China,
    and South Africa), establishing a new
    currency and, 315
brides, shortage of in China, 354
British foreign exchange crisis,
    negotiating on, 72
broad real dollar index (1971–2022), 37f
bubble economy, in Japan, 121n9
budget cycle, adhering to, 261
Bundesbank, 102, 107

capital, channeling, 305
capital account, liberalization of, 358
capital controls
    of China, 8, 314, 335
    remaining contentious, 221
    on short-term inflows, 220–21
capital flows
    assessing sustainability of, 73
    complicating domestic policy
        management, 330
    contributed to the collapse of Bretton
        Woods, 44
    depending on the global appetite for
        risk, 216
    effects on exchange rates and trade
        balances, 170
    exchange rate movements dominated
        by, 43–44

narrowing excessive trade imbalances, 171

in and out of the United States, 358

rise in information transmission and, 80

risk sensitivity of for emerging markets, 291

tax evasion and money laundering and, 305

capital inflows, 220–21, 261

capital markets, 24, 358

capital outflows, 47, 260, 261

carry-trade investors, differing from momentum traders, 58

carry trades, 257, 257n5, 262

Carter, President, 99, 105

cash, 135, 281n3, 328

CBOE. See Chicago Board Options Exchange [CBOE]

CBOE Volatility Index (VIX), 272

central banks
absence of intervention by, 220
digital currencies (CBDCs), 328, 330
dollar swap lines, 78, 271f, 277, 285, 288
inflation targeting by, 207
intervening if the currency is misaligned, 219
landscape radically different by the 2020s, 20
as a lender of last resort, 221
as marginal buyers, 65
monetary independence of, 56, 58
political control of, 225
portfolios to renminbi-denominated assets, 329
purchases of US dollar-denominated securities, 55, 66–67
replacing gold with inflation targeting, 5
statutory independence for, 19
supporting global liquidity, 81
tending to floating, 219
using new technologies, 328
varying exchange rates, 183

Chicago Board Options Exchange [CBOE], 272, 295

Chile, 216, 232, 233f, 239

China
BRICS currency and, 315
buying US dollar-denominated securities, 61

currency manipulation by, 159, 248

current account balances and financial flows (1980–2020), 23f

devaluation of the renminbi, 179

developing its financial markets, 78

economic growth (1980–2022), 27f

exchange rate management, 360

exchange rate system said to be undervalued, 352

exports, imports, and trade balance as shares of GDP (1952–2022), 355f

fixed exchange rate with the dollar and, 335

imposing capital controls, 358

institutional changes and, 329

internationalizing the renminbi, 358

lacking financial markets, 320

as largely autonomous, 12

with large surpluses, 92

as a major official lender, 75

managing exchange rate, 7

as oil importer and trading partner, 247

opening its bond market, 131

preventing appreciation of renminbi against the dollar, 178

providing diversification for foreigners, 144

reintegration into the world economy, 127

reluctant to lose control over financial markets, 79

rise of, 26–27, 238

shaping trade and current account balance, 352

surpassing the US in trade intensities, 130

tariff rates and current account in (1998–2010), 356f

transforming renminbi into an international currency, 357

US excess foreign direct investment in (2009–21), 142f

China shock, 159, 160, 161f, 163, 178, 336

Chinese National Offshore Oil Company, 357

climate change, 28–29, 248, 305

commercial openness, flexible exchange rates and, 178

Committee of Twenty (C20), 21, 39, 40, 41, 48

Great Depression of the 1930s, 173–74, 297
Great Inflation, in Japan, 120, 121n9
Great Moderation, 49, 189
"Great Moderation before the Great Moderation," in Japan, 120
Great Recession of 2009, exchange rate movements and, 178
Great Society, fiscal demands of, 13
Greece, 152, 342, 347
Greenspan, Alan, 110
Gulf Cooperation Council (GCC) (Bahrain, Kuwait, Oman, Qatar, Saudi Arabia, and United Arab Emirates)
 comovement of government expenditures and oil revenues, 243
 fixed exchange rates to the dollar, 242
 focused on raising competitiveness, 247
 government revenue and expenditure in (1990–2017), 244f
 inflation rates in (1980–2022), 242f
 pegging currencies, 238, 239–43, 248

Heavily Indebted Poor Countries (HIPC) initiative, 75
Heckscher-Ohlin model, 356
Heckscher-Ohlin-Mundell trade framework, 128
hedging markets, 218
hegemon, 79, 297–98, 301
hegemon central bank, as a lender of last resort, 300
hegemonic stability, as desirable, 79
"hegemonic stability theory," 77
hegemonic system, coping with shared challenges, 6–7
higher core inflation, countries having, 201
home-currency devaluation, export prices and, 185
households
 effects of large swings in exchange rates, 163
 in the second half of the 1980s, 61
 with unmarried sons in China, 354
  Houthakker-Magee study, impact on policy, 13n7
hyperglobalization, 193, 334
hypothetical net international investment position, 232

Iceland, 60–61
importers, 229, 281
import prices, dollar-driven pound depreciation and, 185
import substitution, by maintaining overvalued exchange rates, 245
Impossible Trinity, 215
indebted borrowers, as distress sellers, 60
independent monetary policy, of United States, 12
India, 178–79, 357
Indonesia, 251–62, 254–55t
industrial organization approach, focusing on microeconomics of firm behavior, 185
inertia, in the world's "choice" of the top international currency, 315–16
inflation
 accelerating, 72
 controlling, 225
 declined in the late 1990s, 224
 defining as low, 199n10
 in double digits in the 1970s, 19
 expectations of as self-fulfilling, 220
 global reemergence of in 2021, 20
 as high for oil exporters, 243
 indications of higher, 200
 in Latin America, South America and the world, 225f
 in major industrial economies (1960–2020), 14f
 objective of a central banker, 181
 sensitivity to global factors, 192, 195–206
 stabilizing aggregate at a lower trend rate, 187
 tight monetary policy bringing down, 78, 188
 as a variable, 199
inflation rate, 74, 193, 195, 256
inflation targeting
 adoption of, 228
 combining with a flexible exchange rate, 258
 features of, 116–17t
 framework Bank Indonesia implemented in 2005, 256
 lists of countries, 224n1
 as a nominal anchor, 114
 as not a disinflation strategy, 225
 policy framework of, 19–20

provided a much needed nominal
anchor, 115
pursuing a credible target, 186–87
well-behaved country should pursue,
219
inflation targeting regimes
countries adopting in the late 1990s,
224
countries operating under (1990–
2017), 226f
establishing a full-fledged in Japan,
121
in Japan, 114–15
positive outcomes associated with
adoption of, 234
inflow of foreign funds, leading to
consumption booms, 63
inflows, ex ante controls on, 221
insurance companies, conservative
exposures, 281n3
intellectual trends, reflecting political
developments, 4
interdependence, of world economies, 29
interest rates
changes in linked to capital account
balance, 59
differentials between the US and the
United Kingdom, 188
in Indonesia (2005–15), 259f
lower creating a disincentive, 258
low held down the burden of the net
debt, 170
multicentury global downward trend
in real, 80
on US dollar-denominated securities
and securities denominated in other
currencies, 66
zero lower bound on, 169
international capital flow restrictions, US
motivations for rejecting, 21–22
international commitments, requiring
domestic political support, 94
international currency
as difficult to replace, 300

limited progress toward establishing,
50
measures of use, 311–13
multiple existing simultaneously, 316
renminbi as, 357–60
roles of, 312t

international debt, use of major
currencies, 346f
international dollar liquidity facilities,
COVID-19 period and, 267–74
international dollar politics, 17
international economic order, replacing,
48
international economic relations,
fragmentation of, 334
international finance, 1973 compared to
2023, 77–81
international financial spillovers, 6
international financial stability, 92,
297–300
international financial transactions,
growth of, 22–24
international gold standard, key virtues
once claimed for, 4
internationalization, of the renminbi,
357
international liquidity, as adequate, 49
international loans, use of major
currencies, 346f
international monetary arrangements,
political economy of, 87–95
international monetary evolution,
politics, institutions, and ideas in, 3–4
International Monetary Fund (IMF), 143
Articles of Agreement, 36, 56
artificial currency (Special Drawing
Right), 99, 314n7
Bretton Woods system centered on,
10–11
commenced operations in 1947, 11
enabling normal financing of trade
operations to resume, 75
large trade imbalances and, 167
management of floating exchange
rates, 40
precautionary liquidity arrangement,
countries qualifying for, 221
recommended bank closures in
Indonesia, 253
international monetary order, remaking
of, 97
international monetary policy trilemma,
342
international monetary reforms, 47–51
international monetary regimes, 113
international monetary stability, 88–90

two central banks during much of its civil war, 245*n*4

local currency pricing (LCP), 228

London gold market, manipulating, 12

long-term investors, buying long-term dollar assets, 281, 284

"lost decades," starting point of Japan's, 121

low-inflation bend model, 198

macroeconomic policies, US affecting the world, 90

macroeconomic responsibilities, shunting onto others, 93

macroeconomics, 80, 149

macroeconomic shocks, 152, 295

macroeconomies policies, 228

macroprudential framework, 304

macroprudential policies, 81, 220

macroprudential tools, development of, 305

manufacturing
US dollar exchange rate and (1973–2019), 159*f*
US driven by secular trends, 159

manufacturing employment, location of in the US, 4

manufacturing industries, floating dollar and, 157–64

March 1973 decision, historical perspective on, 2–3

market crises, few during the 2000s, 5–6

market failure, in Iceland, 61

market fear, exchange rate overshooting causing, 260

market forces, US dollar and, 65

market sentiment, about the dollar shifting suddenly, 170

market stress, asymmetry between the dollar and other currencies, 284

Marshall-Lerner condition, holding, 182–83

Marshall Plan, 71

maturity mismatch, dollar borrowers in the swap market facing, 284

Mexico, effect of US monetary policy on, 291–92

Middle East and North Africa (MENA), EMDEs embracing fixed exchange rates, 237–49

military conflicts, reducing trade, 335

momentum traders, carry-trade investors differing from, 58

monetary cooperation, international monetary system and, 44

monetary instability (1980–2020), source of, 53–67

monetary policy
credibility of, 228
ensuring some autonomy, 221
exchange rates pass through and, 186
expansionary by countries that abandoned the gold standard, 175
expansive in the United States, 258*n*6
of Germany, 89
goals of, 258–60
responses of sovereign spreads to tightening US, 293*f*
tightening, 257, 292
tighter effect on inflation, 186
US as the main driver of the risk cycle, 216
US transmitted to the rest of the world, 291–95
weakness of frameworks, 243

monetary regime, search for a stable, 342

monetary sovereignty, 330

monetary stability, among member states, 87

monetary system, of Indonesia, 256

monetary union, 99, 102, 109, 242, 344

monetary upheavals, of 1971–73, 48

money, 103, 300

money market shocks, responses to, 58

money market traders, 55, 58, 66

multicurrency system, network externalities and, 315–18

multilateral institutions, serving global goals, 76

multiple exchange rate system, Indonesia terminated in 1971, 251

multipolar international monetary system, transition to, 304–305

multipolar world, 302, 303

Mundell-Fleming model, 229, 258

Mundell trilemma, 335

narrow bands, countries following, 224, 224*n*2

national banking systems, remaining under domestic supervision, 342

national currencies, 318–19, 330

national fiscal policies, curbs on, 342

national governments, monetary arrangements among, 87, 90

national monetary authority, anchor currency and, 88

national policymakers, answerable to domestic constituencies, 88

NBFIs. *See* nonbank financial intermediaries (NBFIs)

neoliberalism, supply-side economics and, 25–26

net debt, of the US, 168, 169–70, 299

net foreign asset position, of the United States, 299

net international investment, in Chile, 233*f*

net international investment position (NIIP)
of Chile, 232
of the US, 168

net investment income flows, in the US, 170

network externalities, 7, 315, 320

New Keynesian model, 200

New Keynesian Phillips curve, 198

New Triffin Dilemma, 79, 302, 304–305, 337. *See also* Triffin dilemma

New Zealand, 114

NextGenerationEU recovery plan, 348

Nixon, Richard M., 10–28, 36, 89, 127

Nixon administration, 2, 92

Nixon Shock of 1971, 15, 176

"Nixon shocks," reforms forced by, 48

nominal exchange rate, 228, 360

nonbank financial institutions, accessing credit, 274

nonbank financial intermediaries (NBFIs), 277, 278, 283

nondeliverable forwards (NDFs), 279*n*2

nonfuel commodity prices, quarterly annualized change in world, 199

non-GCC countries, 248–49

non-state-owned firms, internal savings in China, 354

non-US banks, 281, 285, 286*f*

Norway, asset accumulation, 169

official exchange rate, China's reset at the black market rate, 353

oil, movements between the dollar exchange rate and the price of, 248*n*5

oil-exporting countries, 61, 73, 238

oil-exporting EMDEs, 23*f*, 237

oil pricing, shifting the currency of, 247–48

oil producers, 237–49

Organization of the Petroleum Exporting Countries (OPEC), 17–19, 92

original sin, 231–32, 234, 261

"original sin redux," 218

other oil exporters, reasons for not floating, 243–45

Outright Monetary Transactions (OMT) program, in 2012, 347

overvaluation, of the renminbi, 353

Pandemic Emergency Purchase Programme (*PEPP*), launch of, 348

pandemic shock of 2020–2021, 348. *See also* COVID-19 crisis

pan-European economy, euro as the dominant currency, 344

Paris agreements, results of, 40–42

Paris meetings, of 1973, 38–40

parities, 11, 63, 64

partner countries, 90, 135

par-value regime, 36

par-value system, Volcker on the abandonment of, 41

pass-through, for banks, 186–87

payment deficits, US, 56, 64, 93

payment imbalances, 91

pegged exchange rates, 167, 192

peso depreciation, absorbing higher risk premia in Mexico, 292

peso devaluation, in Mexico, 163

Peterson, Peter G., 51

petrodollar recycling, eurodollar market and, 24

physical currency (cash), rapid decline in using, 328

Plaza Accord of September 1985, 17, 120, 163

Plaza Agreement, correction of imbalances after, 49

Plaza Meeting, aftermath of, 107–110

Pöhl, Karl Otto, 104–105, 108, 109

policy decisions, in Europe during the pandemic, 348

policy objectives, policymakers choosing between, 260

policy trilemmas, reconciling, 342

Pompidou, Georges, 103

Other Publications from the
PETERSON INSTITUTE FOR INTERNATIONAL ECONOMICS

BOOKS

Banking on Basel: The Future of International Financial Regulation   Daniel K. Tarullo
September 2008   ISBN 978-0-88132-423-5

US Pension Reform: Lessons from Other Countries   Martin Neil Baily and Jacob Funk Kirkegaard
February 2009   ISBN 978-0-88132-425-9

How Ukraine Became a Market Economy and Democracy   Anders Åslund
March 2009   ISBN 978-0-88132-427-3

Global Warming and the World Trading System
Gary Clyde Hufbauer, Steve Charnovitz, and Jisun Kim
March 2009   ISBN 978-0-88132-428-0

The Russia Balance Sheet   Anders Åslund and Andrew Kuchins
March 2009   ISBN 978-0-88132-424-2

The Euro at Ten: The Next Global Currency?
Jean Pisani-Ferry and Adam S. Posen, eds.
July 2009   ISBN 978-0-88132-430-3

Economic Sanctions Reconsidered, 3d ed.
Gary Clyde Hufbauer, Jeffrey J. Schott, Kimberly Ann Elliott, and Barbara Oegg
REPRINTED 2009
ISBN paper 978-0-88132-412-9
ISBN paper/CD-ROM 978-0-88132-431-0

Financial Globalization, Economic Growth, and the Crisis of 2007–09   William R. Cline
May 2010   ISBN 978-0-88132-499-0

Russia after the Global Economic Crisis
Anders Åslund, Sergei Guriev, and Andrew Kuchins, eds.
June 2010   ISBN 978-0-88132-497-6

Sovereign Wealth Funds: Threat or Salvation?
Edwin M. Truman
September 2010   ISBN 978-0-88132-498-3

The Last Shall Be the First: The East European Financial Crisis, 2008–10   Anders Åslund
October 2010   ISBN 978-0-88132-521-8

Witness to Transformation: Refugee Insights into North Korea   Stephan Haggard and Marcus Noland
January 2011   ISBN 978-0-88132-438-9

Foreign Direct Investment and Development: Launching a Second Generation of Policy Research, Avoiding the Mistakes of the First, Reevaluating Policies for Developed and Developing Countries   Theodore H. Moran
April 2011   ISBN 978-0-88132-600-0

How Latvia Came through the Financial Crisis
Anders Åslund and Valdis Dombrovskis
May 2011   ISBN 978-0-88132-602-4

Global Trade in Services: Fear, Facts, and Offshoring   J. Bradford Jensen
August 2011   ISBN 978-0-88132-601-7

NAFTA and Climate Change   Meera Fickling and Jeffrey J. Schott
September 2011   ISBN 978-0-88132-436-5

Eclipse: Living in the Shadow of China's Economic Dominance   Arvind Subramanian
September 2011   ISBN 978-0-88132-606-2

Flexible Exchange Rates for a Stable World Economy   Joseph E. Gagnon with Marc Hinterschweiger
September 2011   ISBN 978-0-88132-627-7

The Arab Economies in a Changing World, 2d ed.   Marcus Noland and Howard Pack
November 2011   ISBN 978-0-88132-628-4

Sustaining China's Economic Growth After the Global Financial Crisis   Nicholas R. Lardy
January 2012   ISBN 978-0-88132-626-0

Who Needs to Open the Capital Account?
Olivier Jeanne, Arvind Subramanian, and John Williamson
April 2012   ISBN 978-0-88132-511-9

Devaluing to Prosperity: Misaligned Currencies and Their Growth Consequences   Surjit S. Bhalla
August 2012   ISBN 978-0-88132-623-9

Private Rights and Public Problems: The Global Economics of Intellectual Property in the 21st Century   Keith E. Maskus
September 2012   ISBN 978-0-88132-507-2

Global Economics in Extraordinary Times: Essays in Honor of John Williamson
C. Fred Bergsten and C. Randall Henning, eds.
November 2012   ISBN 978-0-88132-662-8

Rising Tide: Is Growth in Emerging Economies Good for the United States?   Lawrence Edwards and Robert Z. Lawrence
February 2013   ISBN 978-0-88132-500-3

Responding to Financial Crisis: Lessons from Asia Then, the United States and Europe Now
Changyong Rhee and Adam S. Posen, eds.
October 2013   ISBN 978-0-88132-674-1

Fueling Up: The Economic Implications of America's Oil and Gas Boom   Trevor Houser and Shashank Mohan
January 2014   ISBN 978-0-88132-656-7

How Latin America Weathered the Global Financial Crisis   José De Gregorio
January 2014   ISBN 978-0-88132-678-9

Confronting the Curse: The Economics and Geopolitics of Natural Resource Governance
Cullen S. Hendrix and Marcus Noland
May 2014   ISBN 978-0-88132-676-5

Inside the Euro Crisis: An Eyewitness Account
Simeon Djankov
June 2014   ISBN 978-0-88132-685-7

Managing the Euro Area Debt Crisis
William R. Cline
June 2014   ISBN 978-0-88132-687-1

Markets over Mao: The Rise of Private Business in China   Nicholas R. Lardy
September 2014   ISBN 978-0-88132-693-2

Bridging the Pacific: Toward Free Trade and Investment between China and the United States
C. Fred Bergsten, Gary Clyde Hufbauer, and Sean Miner. Assisted by Tyler Moran
October 2014   ISBN 978-0-88132-691-8

The Great Rebirth: Lessons from the Victory of Capitalism over Communism
Anders Åslund and Simeon Djankov, eds.
November 2014   ISBN 978-0-88132-697-0

Ukraine: What Went Wrong and How to Fix It
Anders Åslund
April 2015   ISBN 978-0-88132-701-4

From Stress to Growth: Strengthening Asia's Financial Systems in a Post-Crisis World
Marcus Noland and Donghyun Park, eds.
October 2015   ISBN 978-0-88132-699-4

BOOKS IN PROGRESS